Deleuze, A Stoic

Plateaus – New Directions in Deleuze Studies

'It's not a matter of bringing all sorts of things together under a single concept but rather of relating each concept to variables that explain its mutations.'
Gilles Deleuze, *Negotiations*

Series Editors
Ian Buchanan, University of Wollongong
Claire Colebrook, Penn State University

Editorial Advisory Board
Keith Ansell Pearson, Ronald Bogue, Constantin V. Boundas, Rosi Braidotti, Eugene Holland, Gregg Lambert, Dorothea Olkowski, Paul Patton, Daniel Smith, James Williams

Titles available in the series
Christian Kerslake, *Immanence and the Vertigo of Philosophy: From Kant to Deleuze*
Jean-Clet Martin, *Variations: The Philosophy of Gilles Deleuze*, translated by Constantin V. Boundas and Susan Dyrkton
Simone Bignall, *Postcolonial Agency: Critique and Constructivism*
Miguel de Beistegui, *Immanence – Deleuze and Philosophy*
Jean-Jacques Lecercle, *Badiou and Deleuze Read Literature*
Ronald Bogue, *Deleuzian Fabulation and the Scars of History*
Sean Bowden, *The Priority of Events: Deleuze's Logic of Sense*
Craig Lundy, *History and Becoming: Deleuze's Philosophy of Creativity*
Aidan Tynan, *Deleuze's Literary Clinic: Criticism and the Politics of Symptoms*
Thomas Nail, *Returning to Revolution: Deleuze, Guattari and Zapatismo*
François Zourabichvili, *Deleuze: A Philosophy of the Event* with *The Vocabulary of Deleuze* edited by Gregg Lambert and Daniel W. Smith, translated by Kieran Aarons
Frida Beckman, *Between Desire and Pleasure: A Deleuzian Theory of Sexuality*
Nadine Boljkovac, *Untimely Affects: Gilles Deleuze and an Ethics of Cinema*
Daniela Voss, *Conditions of Thought: Deleuze and Transcendental Ideas*
Daniel Barber, *Deleuze and the Naming of God: Post-Secularism and the Future of Immanence*
F. LeRon Shults, *Iconoclastic Theology: Gilles Deleuze and the Secretion of Atheism*
Janae Sholtz, *The Invention of a People: Heidegger and Deleuze on Art and the Political*
Marco Altamirano, *Time, Technology and Environment: An Essay on the Philosophy of Nature*
Sean McQueen, *Deleuze and Baudrillard: From Cyberpunk to Biopunk*
Ridvan Askin, *Narrative and Becoming*
Marc Rölli, *Gilles Deleuze's Transcendental Empiricism: From Tradition to Difference*, translated by Peter Hertz-Ohmes
Guillaume Collett, *The Psychoanalysis of Sense: Deleuze and the Lacanian School*
Ryan J. Johnson, *The Deleuze-Lucretius Encounter*
Allan James Thomas, *Deleuze, Cinema and the Thought of the World*
Cheri Lynne Carr, *Deleuze's Kantian Ethos: Critique as a Way of Life*
Alex Tissandier, *Affirming Divergence: Deleuze's Reading of Leibniz*
Barbara Glowczewski, *Indigenising Anthropology with Guattari and Deleuze*
Koichiro Kokubun, *The Principles of Deleuzian Philosophy*, translated by Wren Nishina
Felice Cimatti, *Unbecoming Human: Philosophy of Animality After Deleuze*, translated by Fabio Gironi
Ryan J. Johnson, *Deleuze, A Stoic*

Forthcoming volumes
Justin Litaker, *Deleuze and Guattari's Political Economy*
Nir Kedem, *A Deleuzian Critique of Queer Thought: Overcoming Sexuality*
Jane Newland, *Deleuze in Children's Literature*
Sean Bowden, *Expression, Action and Agency in Deleuze: Willing Events*
Andrew Jampol-Petzinger, *Deleuze, Kierkegaard and the Ethics of Selfhood*

Visit the Plateaus website at edinburghuniversitypress.com/series/plat

DELEUZE, A STOIC

Ryan J. Johnson

EDINBURGH
University Press

Edinburgh University Press is one of the leading university presses in the UK. We publish academic books and journals in our selected subject areas across the humanities and social sciences, combining cutting-edge scholarship with high editorial and production values to produce academic works of lasting importance. For more information visit our website: edinburghuniversitypress.com

© Ryan J. Johnson, 2020, 2022

Edinburgh University Press Ltd
The Tun – Holyrood Road,
12(2f) Jackson's Entry,
Edinburgh EH8 8PJ

First published in hardback by Edinburgh University Press 2020

Typeset in 11/13 Sabon LT Std by
Servis Filmsetting Ltd, Stockport, Cheshire

A CIP record for this book is available from the British Library

ISBN 978 1 4744 6215 0 (hardback)
ISBN 978 1 4744 6216 7 (paperback)
ISBN 978 1 4744 6218 1 (webready PDF)
ISBN 978 1 4744 6217 4 (epub)

The right of Ryan J. Johnson to be identified as the author of this work has been asserted in accordance with the Copyright, Designs and Patents Act 1988, and the Copyright and Related Rights Regulations 2003 (SI No. 2498).

Contents

Acknowledgements · vii
List of Abbreviations · ix

Introduction: The Egg · 1

Part I: Physics
1 The Yolk A: Stoic Metaphysics · 25
2 The Yolk B: Incorporeals · 48
3 The Yolk C: Space · 79

Part II: Logic
4 The Shell A: Λεκτα · 107
5 The Shell B: Paradoxes · 143
6 The Shell C: Living Logic · 175

Part III: Ethics
7 The Albumen A: Time · 203
8 The Albumen B: The Act · 227
9 The Albumen C: Eternal Return · 255

Conclusion: Cracking the Egg · 278

Bibliography · 289
Index · 303

Acknowledgements

The writing of this book happened partially because of the support from Elon University's Summer Fellowship (especially Tim Peeples) and an Elon College of Arts and Sciences Teaching Sabbatical. Another Elon person I want to thank is former Senior President Robert Minton for his helpful work as a copyeditor, as well as Nathan Ravenel, who did months of copyediting and compiled the index. I also thank several readers of drafts of chapters: Elizabeth Grosz, Filippo Screpanti, Thomas Nail, Chris Davidson, Jacob Greenstine, Dave Mesing and Matthew Coate. Each of them, in different ways, inspired me to be a better thinker, writer, philosopher and person, and I am grateful to have walked and talked with them. Out of all my friends and colleagues, Abraham Jacob Greenstine, my fellow Hegelian from the Bluff, has been one of my truest philosophical friends. I also thank Carol MacDonald and the fabulous staff at Edinburgh University Press for their gracious help and guidance. Madison Aycock was essential to the final stages of this book, especially her extensive work on the index. Yet the most important person in my life, the one who puts up with all my madness, is my wonderful, beautiful wife, Erin Rutherford. My cosmos turns around her.

List of Abbreviations

AO Gilles Deleuze and Félix Guattari, *Anti-Oedipus*, trans. Robert Hurley, Mark Seem and Helen R. Lane (New York: Viking, 1977).
ATP Gilles Deleuze and Félix Guattari, *A Thousand Plateaus: Capitalism and Schizophrenia I* (1980), trans. Brian Massumi (Minneapolis: University of Minnesota Press, 1987).
DL Diogenes Laërtius, *Lives of Eminent Philosophers, Volumes I and II*, trans. R. D. Hicks (Cambridge, MA: Harvard University Press, 1925).
CAS Émile Bréhier, *Chrysippe and l'ancien stoïcisme* (Paris: Contemporary Publishing, 2005).
DR Gilles Deleuze, *Difference and Repetition* (1968), trans. Paul Patton (New York: Columbia University Press, 1994).
HP A. A. Long and D. N. Sedley, *The Hellenistic Philosophers Volume I and II* (Cambridge: Cambridge University Press, 1987).
LS Gilles Deleuze, *The Logic of Sense* (1969), trans. Mark Lester with Charles Stivale, ed. Constantin Boundas (New York: Columbia University Press, 1990).
LSJ *The Online Liddell-Scott-Jones Greek–English Lexicon*, available at http://stephanus.tlg.uci.edu/lsj/#eid=1&context=lsj (last accessed 8 February 2019).
SS Victor Goldschmidt, *Le Système stoïcien et l'idée de temps* (Paris: J. Vrin, 1969).
SVF *Stoicorum Veterum Fragmenta, Volumen I–IV*, Joannes Ab Arnim (col.) (Stuttgart: Bibliotheca Scriptorum Graecorum et Romanorum Teubneriana, 1903–1905).
TI Émile Bréhier, *La Théorie des incorporels dans l'ancien stoïcism* (Paris: J. Vrin, 1928; 9th edn 1997).
WP Gilles Deleuze and Félix Guattari, *What is Philosophy?*, trans. Hugh Tomlinson and Graham Burchell (New York: Columbia University Press, 1994).

This book is dedicated to the man who taught me the meaning of poetry: Maj Raigan, my poetry teacher at Kent State University. Maj died while I was writing the last lines of this book. I will never forget his Nietzschean lesson: 'catching in the act the beauty proper to everything'. He is my model of what a person should be.

Introduction: The Egg

What Comes before the Study of Deleuze

Imagine we are students in a school of philosophy in late antiquity. We are learning about ancient Stoic philosophy and it is the beginning of the course. The first thing that the master would teach us is a now-forgotten genre of philosophical writing called 'What Comes before the Study of . . .' (Πρὸ τῆς ἀναγνώσεως . . .).[1] Before studying their materialist metaphysics, before analysing their propositional logic, before dissecting their ethical doctrines, students first learned about the way of life of a classic Stoic philosopher – her βίος – which detailed when and where she lived, with whom she studied, tales of important travels, with whom she spent time, the historical context in which she worked, her *catalogue raisonné*, among other biographical details. While most examples of this ancient genre are lost, Diogenes Laërtius' *Lives of Eminent Philosophers* collected anecdotes from them. Details of the philosophers' in Diogenes' *Lives* are amusing, contradictory, sometimes preposterous, although they still convey something essential about philosophers that cannot be found in their theoretical treatises and manuscripts. Nietzsche too appreciates this: 'I for one prefer reading Diogenes Laërtius to Zeller, because the former at least breathes the *spirit of the philosophers* of antiquity.'[2] Before all else, students learned the kind of life a philosopher lived, and only afterwards, if this way of life was still desired, did students learn about their corresponding logical system or criterion of truth. Since scholars in the ancient schools organised courses according to a fixed sequence, this bio-philosophical genre acted as the first part of a *schema isagogicum*, or introductory scheme.[3]

In our book, we develop a systematic account of ancient Greek and Roman Stoicism through its encounter with Gilles Deleuze and related twentieth-century French philosophers, beginning with a *schema isagogicum* of Deleuze himself.

A few months after he died, one of Deleuze's students – André Bernold – published a biography of his old teacher, which we might consider a new contribution to that forgotten genre of writing: 'What Comes before the Study of Deleuze'.[4] Bernold wrote:

> Deleuze, philosopher, son of Diogenes and Hypatia, sojourned at Lyon. Nothing is known of his life. He lived to be very old, even though he was often very ill. This illustrated what he himself had said: there are lives in which the difficulties verge on the prodigious. He defined as active any force that goes to the end of its power. This, he said, is the opposite of a law. Thus he lived, always going further than he had believed he could. Even though he had explicated Chrysippus, *it is above all his steadfastness that earned him the name of Stoic.*[5]

Let us repeat that last line: 'it is above all his steadfastness that earned him the name of *Stoic*'. According to some of his students, Deleuze deserved to be called a Stoic. Hence the title of our book: *Deleuze, A Stoic*.

Diogenes' *Lives* usually include a philosopher's reported *catalogue raisonné*. Since most of what is listed there are now lost, we cannot be certain as to whether these works were real or imaginary. In that vein, Bernold's biography ends with an imaginary or unwritten *catalogue raisonné* of Deleuze. Let us highlight twelve titles:

> *Of the Event*, in 34 books ... *Of the Impassability of Incorporeals. Of Paradox and Fate. On the Wounds that are Received While Sleeping ... Of the Egg ... Of Nobody. On Universal Collapse. In Praise of Lucretius. Of the Viscera ... Of the Singularities that Unsettle Us ... The Cloak ... Of Absolute Depth. Of Unknown Joy.*

As fate would have it, these titles are the main themes of the story of Deleuzian Stoicism. While imaginary, we argue that these themes were expressed in Deleuze's life, especially in his study of Stoic theory. In a way, our book is an attempt to write these imagined stories and discover Deleuze's unwritten treatises. To do this, we must locate Stoicism in the context of ancient Greece. For Deleuze, antiquity was a spirited competition among rival philosophical schools, differentiated by their various theoretical orientations for thinking and living. Let us consider the competitors.

Four Ancient Philosophical Orientations

A *strange surface* structures Stoicism. It is strange because it borders on the paradoxical; it is a surface because it acts like a border, boundary, frontier, or limit of bodies. This surface is central to our understanding of Stoicism, and so will wind through the entire text.

Introduction: The Egg

In order to grasp the edges of this strange Stoic surface and pull it within view, let us contrast it with three ancient philosophical orientations: the pre-Socratic, the Platonic and the Aristotelian. In the Conclusion, we will return to these by characterising them as forms of ancient philosophical comedy. According to Deleuze's playful depiction, pre-Socratics are thinkers of depth, Platonists thinkers of height, Aristotelians thinkers of inwardness, and Stoics thinkers of surface.[6]

To see how the pre-Socratics are thinkers of depths, Deleuze recalls Diogenes Laërtius' recounting of the legendary death of Empedocles.[7] As the story goes, Empedocles 'set out on his way to Etna; then, when he had reached it, he plunged into the fiery craters and disappeared, his intention being to confirm the report that he had become a god' (DL 8.69). Putting his metaphysics into practice, Empedocles dives deep into the volcano, aiming to sink his body back into the primordial elements of nature from which it was birthed. Deleuze characterises other pre-Socratics, especially the Milesians, as thinkers of depths. The main difference among them is the element each selects as the deepest of the depths: Thales' water, Anaximenes' air, Heraclitus' fire and so forth. Whatever is selected as the most basic element, each posits it as the deepest, darkest, most originary ontological category. This metaphysical orientation enacts a 'turning below', a *pre-Socratic subversion*.[8]

The Platonic axis of thought points the opposite direction. Rather than down towards the depths, Platonic philosophy looks up towards the heights. In the imagery of Plato's *Republic*, the 'philosopher is a being of ascents', of escaping the cave and climbing up into the light (*LS* 127).[9] Even once one has escaped the cave and recognised the shadows for what they really are, the Platonic imperative is to ascend even higher, up the divided line, straining for the height of heights, the light of lights. Hence the Platonic image of the philosopher as the one who strives for the intelligible realm up on high, the uppermost realm of transcendent ideas. 'Height', Deleuze writes, 'is the properly Platonic Orient' (*LS* 127). Up there among the clouds, where Aristophanes focuses Socrates' attention in *The Clouds*, Plato locates truly true beings. Even among the immaterial forms, there remain even higher rungs to climb. In the *Republic*, the form of the Good is perched at the top of it all; other dialogues give a certain priority to the forms of the One and Being.[10] Like the sun, situated at the apex of the world, emitting the *numen lumen* illuminating the bodies strewn about the surface of the earth, the form of the Good causes the vertical ontological order and upright intelligibility, letting us glimpse true knowledge. Socratic dialectic is an education in how to ascend to the heights, to follow the 'flight of ideas'. It is a *Platonic conversion* (*LS* 128).[11]

Though Deleuze skips Aristotle in his classification of ancient philosophical orientations, we should consider the Stagirite before considering the Stoics.[12] Aristotle constructs a detailed metaphysical and scientific hierarchy that shifts Platonism, while still echoing its general direction. As with Plato, Aristotelian philosophy is, with two important caveats, generally oriented upward along a vertical chain of being, in so far as he continues to prioritise formal causes. The first caveat is that, for Aristotle, formal principles are never independent of matter; together, form and matter are individuated as compounds.[13] The second caveat is that while formal causes are 'etiologically prior' to material causes, Aristotle goes 'up' the chain of being to god through *efficient*, not formal, causes (perhaps because formal causes do not lead to god). The point is that *both* material and teleological explanations are fundamental to his work, especially in the biological writings. Thus 'being' is always individuated in material composites, and is separable only in thought not in fact.[14] In short, every thing and every way of being depends on οὐσία as the primary 'thing' and 'being'. This prioritisation of οὐσία orients Aristotle towards the 'insides' of things (for example, 'nature' as an *inner principle of motion and rest*, the priority of activity to potentiality, οὐσία as the primary subject of which other categories are accidents). Aristotle thus 'takes down' what was, for Plato, above, placing it within the world's particulars, and 'brings up' the depths of the pre-Socratics. Many scholars call this inwardisation of the heights and depths hylomorphism.[15] The result: interiority or height-within. We call this philosophical operation *Aristotelian inwardness*.[16]

In contrast to pre-Socratic depth, Platonic height and Aristotle interiority, the Stoics are thinkers of surface. The Stoics do not simply return to the depths of primordial matter, nor do they erect a hierarchy reaching up into the heights of the intellect, either above or within. Instead, they develop a new kind of ontological orientation. 'Stoicism', according to Alain Beaulieu, 'constitutes a paradigmatic model of experimentation of reality independently of reference to primordial elements [of the pre-Socratics], the Idea-forms [of the Platonists], and the prime Mover [of Aristotle].'[17] Although Deleuze suggests that Plato himself provokes the overturning of Platonism, 'the Stoics', Deleuze states, 'are the first to reverse Platonism' (*DR* 68,

Introduction: The Egg

244; *LS* 7). But even this is not quite right. The Stoics do not simply *reverse* Platonism; they *pervert* it, along with their other philosophical predecessors. Stoicism thus initiates a philosophical perversion.[18] Before detailing this, a table:

Ancient school	Orientation	Movement	Operation
Pre-Socratics	Depth	Descent	Subversion
Plato/Socrates	Height	Ascent	Conversion
Aristotle	Interiority	Inward	Inversion
Stoics	Surface	Per-scent[19]	Perversion

Stoic Perversion

The pervert is a recurring character in Deleuze's writings.[20] Consider a few examples from different texts. Deleuze calls Lewis Carroll, one of the driving voices in *Logic of Sense*, 'a little pervert', echoing Artaud's own characterisation (*LS* 84). In *Anti-Oedipus*, the pervert is the one who 'resisted oedipalization'; the 'village pervert' is given a prominent role there too (*AO* 75, 163). In interviews, Deleuze sometimes mentions the 'polymorphic pervert'.[21] Perhaps most interesting of all is the centrality of perversion in the twelfth issue of Guattari's journal *Revue Recherches*, *Three Billion Perverts: The Grand Encyclopedia of Homosexuality*, to which Deleuze anonymously contributed.[22] Its publication caused a scandal in 1973. Immediately upon publication, it was

> seized, and Félix Guattari, as the director of publications, was fined 600 francs for affronting public decency ... [It] was judged to constitute a 'detailed display of depravities and sexual deviations,' and the 'libidinous exhibition of a perverted minority.' All copies of the issue were ordered to be destroyed.[23]

David Lapoujade, Deleuze's student, appreciates the importance of philosophical perversity in Deleuze. 'Perversion', writes Lapoujade, 'is an essential operation in Deleuze and the pervert a central figure of his philosophy, like the famous "schizo" of *Anti-Oedipus*.'[24] Following *Anti-Oedipus'* imagery of a 'schizophrenic out for a walk', we can think of the Deleuze's Stoicism as akin to 'a pervert out for a walk' through the Stoa, a different model than that of the neurotic lying on Agathon's couch in Plato's *Symposium*. If we seek a 'breath of fresh air, a relationship with the outside world', we find it in

Deleuze's image of the Stoic as philosophical pervert (*AO* 2). In Deleuze's imagery, the perversity specific to Stoicism appears in the 'new philosophical operation' that 'opposes at once Platonic conversion and pre-Socratic subversion' and we add Aristotelian inversion (*LS* 133).

Deleuze calls this operation 'perversion' in so far as Stoicism 'befit[s] the system of provocations of this new type of philosopher' (*LS* 133). While Platonic ascension and pre-Socratic descension are mere inversions of each other, and Aristotelian inversion a turning of both within, the Stoics do not simply go up or down a vertical axis, nor do they just place them both inside; they instead pervert these vertical philosophical orientations by 'turning things inside-out'. As Jacques Brunschwig notices, Plato's *Sophist* 'provide[s] the Stoics [with] an argument that they could *turn inside-out*'.[25] A combination of *per* ('through, thoroughly, exceedingly') + *vertere* ('to turn'), etymologically 'perversion' is a turning-through such that what was inside is now outside and outside now inside. More than inverting the vertical plane, so that what was formerly above is placed below or vice-versa, the Stoics thoroughly turn the axis of philosophy on its side, creating a flat, smooth surface. 'One could say', Deleuze suggests, 'that the old depth having spread out became width' (*LS* 9). Width, rather than height, depth or interiority, is new in Stoicism. The Stoics 'no longer expect salvation from the depths of the

> point of departure of an operation that consists neither in negating nor even destroying, but rather in radically contesting the validity of that which is: it suspends belief in and neutralizes the given in such a way that a new horizon opens up beyond the given and in place of it.[26]

This process of neutralisation is key to perversion and reveals one of its four main logical characteristics: *inclusive disjunction*.

In order not to abuse the metaphorics of height, depth, inward and surface, we should be precise about what these terms mean. 'Height' and 'inward' refer to an order of prioritisation, where what is 'above' or 'within' is prior in relevant ways – ontologically, epistemologically, ethically and so on. Consider the top-heavy vertical hierarchies of Platonic (where first causes perch on the highest rung), the heavy-weighted brute materialism of Empedocles and others (which place what is below, rather than above, first), or the turning-inwards of Aristotelian metaphysics (which locates an essential interiority of things along a vertical chain of being). For all three, it is a question of causation. Prioritising height means prioritising formal and final

Introduction: The Egg

causes, prioritising depth means prioritising material and efficient causes, and prioritising interiority means prioritising formal causes individuated as material compounds.[27] The Stoic 'surface', however, eliminates these orders of prioritisation in order to collapse the overall organisation of formality and materiality and turn it inside-out. 'Perversion', Lapoujade writes, 'is a critique of all ground [as heights, depths, or interiority] carried out as part of the most zealous search for a ground', that is, an ungrounding.[28] The surface is the perverse figure of the groundless ground, and the 'Deleuzian hero is *the pervert*'.[29] The 'pervert', for Lapoujade, 'is the "structural" hero who escapes the undifferentiated depths of psychosis' of the pre-Socratics 'as well as the manic-depressive circles of neurosis' of Socrates and Plato.[30]

The Three Parts of Philosophy

To understand the precise significance of Stoic philosophical perversion, let us pose that famous question of philosophy. What, for the Stoics, should be *first philosophy*? They offer three possibilities: physics, logic and ethics. According to Diogenes Laërtius, Apollodorus calls these 'Heads of Commonplace', Chrysippus and Eudromus refer to them as 'specific divisions' and others see them as 'generic divisions' (DL 7.40). Contemporary French scholar of ancient philosophy Frédérique Ildefonse sees this division as 'less a question of parts than of place, of species, or of kinds'.[31] The different 'parts' of philosophy are thus best thought of as different places or locations in an integrated system. They are integrated Stoic spaces, if we can use topological language. As Ildefonse stresses, this sense of 'integration' or 'integral' will be essential for the whole Stoic system.

Different Stoics prioritize different topics, and thus start in different places. 'Diogenes of Ptolemais ... begins with ethics, and Apollodorus puts ethics second; Panaetius and Posidonius start with physics', while 'Chrysippus thought that young men should study logic first, ethics second, and afterward physics' (DL 7.41).[32] While the order of philosophical topics remained a problem to which different Stoics offered different responses, they almost all agree that the three parts are integrated. For the Stoics, 'no part [of philosophy] is separated from another, but the parts are mixed' (DL 7.40). In order to explain the exact nature of this mixture, the Stoics compare the tripartite integration of philosophy to various things. They compare it to an '*animal*: Logic corresponding to the bones and sinews, Ethics to the flesh parts, Physics to the soul'; to a '*productive field*: Logic being the encircling fence, Ethics the crop, Physics the Soil or the trees'; or to 'a *city*', presumably with the infrastructure as the physics, the walls as the logic, and the citizens and laws as the ethics (DL 7.40). For the purposes of this story of the Deleuze–Stoicism encounter that we are telling, we insist on the comparison of philosophy to an *egg*, as Diogenes writes: 'Another simile they use is that of an egg: the shell is Logic, next comes the albumen, Ethics, and the yolk is Physics' (DL 7.40). Let us put all these characterisations of the philosophical topics in a table:

Divisions	Animal	Fertile field	City	Egg
Physics	Soul	Soil or trees	[Infrastructure]	Yolk
Logic	Bones and sinews	Fence	[Walls and laws]	Shell
Ethics	Fleshy parts	Crop	[Citizens]	Albumen

The figure of the egg also plays an essential role in Deleuze's own writings. To cite only a few examples of this: the egg is the prime example of an intensive field,[33] the 'Dogon egg' is the instance of 'the distribution of intensities',[34] 'the body without organs is an egg', and much more (*DR* 250–1; *ATP* 149; *AO* 19). Most clearly of all, Deleuze repeats claim that 'The entire world is an egg' (*DR* 216, 251).[35] The concept and image of the egg appears in nearly every one of Deleuze's texts.[36] It is one of the most common conceptual figures in his œuvre.

The Sage and the Egg

The 'Twentieth Series' of *Logic of Sense* is dedicated to Stoicism. It begins with the passage of Diogenes Laërtius mentioned above, where it emphasises sense of philosophy as an egg. 'We must imagine', he writes, 'a situation in which a student [*disciple*] is posing a question of signification: O master, what is ethics? The Stoic sage then takes out a hard-boiled egg from his reversible cloak [*manteau doublé*] and designates the egg with his staff' (*LS* 142). This seems confusing, for if only of my students asked me 'What is ethics?' and my response was to whip out an egg and point to that, my dean might have a few questions. So, what is going on? Two things.

First, the sage is responding to a question specifically about ethics by pointing to an object – an egg – that is intensively organised.

Introduction: The Egg

The point of the imagery of the egg, as with the imagery of the others – animal, fertile field and so forth – is that the parts cannot be completely separated. Without being homogeneous, they are both distinct yet interdependent and interconnected. When we crack an egg, a little of the albumen remains attached to the yolk and a little still sticks to the shell. Similarly, trying to talk about only the albumen, without referring to the yolk or shell, fails, just as trying to talk about only ethics, in isolation from physics and logic, is impossible, or at least misses the complicated yet necessary interrelations among all three. Deleuze knows this: 'the place of ethics is clearly displayed between the two poles of the superficial, logical shell and the deep physical yolk'[37] (*LS* 142). Unlike Modern Philosophy's clean divisions between the domain of truth, beauty and goodness, or epistemology, aesthetics and morality, the Stoics considered the parts of philosophy as necessarily integrated. Ethical theory has a direct, albeit oblique, connection to physics and logic, and the same goes among all parts. Just as the parts of an egg are distinct yet inseparable from each other, so are the parts of Stoic philosophy. Deleuze appreciates that there is, in Stoicism, 'an ethics of . . . physics', and we can fill out the rest of the relations: an ethics of logic; a physics of ethics and a physics of logic; a logic of ethics and a logic of physics.

The second reason, which resonates with the first, for pointing to an egg in response to the student's ontological question about ethics – *What is* ethics? – is that the Stoic sage answers with a body. Rather than just responding with words and theory, the sage trains the student to consider matter first. As we will see, this rhythm of moving from words to bodies and back again is the adventure of becoming a Stoic. Deleuze likens this to Alice's adventures in Lewis Carroll's Wonderland, which 'consists of climbing back from the depth of bodies to the surface of words and back to bodies' (*LS* 142). Moreover, not only are the Stoics thoroughgoing materialists, they are the ancient thinkers who pushed philosophical commitments to matter further than anyone else, and it is this excessive push that makes Stoicism perverse. Hence we call Stoic theory a perverse materialism, or what Claude Imbert calls 'empiricism unhinged'.[38] The Stoic sage points to an egg in order to orient the student of Stoicism to the bodies composing the cosmos and, we will see, to the incorporeals required by a thoroughgoing materialism. If Alice is the Stoic apprentice, Deleuze asks perversely, '[i]s not Humpty Dumpty himself the Stoic master?' (*LS* 142).

The Yolk, the Shell and the Albumen

Like that ovoid riddler from Lewis Carroll's *Alice Through the Looking-Glass* and like the Stoics' reported characterisation of their own philosophical system, our text is structured like an *egg*. 'The Yolk' is Part I: Physics, 'The Shell' Part II: Logic, and 'The Albumen' Part III: Ethics. Each part divides into three subparts. Part I: Physics divides into 'The Yolk A: Stoic Metaphysics', 'The Yolk B: Incorporeals' and 'The Yolk C: Space'. Part II: Logic divides into 'The Shell A: Λεκτα', 'The Shell B: The Paradoxes' and 'The Shell C: Living Logic'. Part III: Ethics divides into 'The Albumen A: Time', 'The Albumen B: The Act' and 'The Albumen C: Eternal Recurrence'. This three-part intensive ovoid structure resonates with Deleuze's writings in so far as his *Logic of Sense*, the text on which we will focus most, is full of such structures. To list a few, there are the three dimensions of the proposition (denotation, manifestation, signification), three stages of the genesis of language (primary order, secondary organisation, tertiary ordinance), three phases of dynamic genesis (connective, conjunctive, disjunctive), three languages (real language, ideal language, esoteric language), and so on.

Yet the most important reason why our text is divided into these three parts of the egg is in order to make a heterodoxical claim concerning what Deleuze deems the most perverse concepts in Stoics: *the incorporeal* [ασώματα]. While we will fully explain what an incorporeal is in Part I: 'The Yolk B', we can now say that in Stoic metaphysics there are two basic types of *something*: corporeals [σώματα] and incorporeals. *Something* is the broadest metaphysical category in Stoic theory. Corporeals and incorporeals are differentiated by metaphysical modalities: corporeals *exist*, incorporeals *subsist*. Corporeals are bodies in depth and incorporeals subsist as that strange surface that runs through all Stoicism. It is this dual insistence on corporeality and incorporeality that makes Stoic theory not just a materialism but a *perverted materialism*.

According to the orthodox scholarly interpretation, there were four types of incorporeals in Stoicism: void, place, λεκτα (roughly: meaning or sense) and time. Contrary to everyone, however, we make a heterodoxical claim: *there are three, not four, incorporeals*. While it will take the entire book to sufficiently support this claim, we will show that Deleuze's Stoicism articulates the following as the three incorporeals: space, λεκτα and time. Each of these three incorporeals is studied by each of the three parts in our book: *Physics*

Introduction: The Egg

studies space, *Logic* studies λεκτα and *Ethics* studies time. Here is a table so that we can picture our path through our book:

Divisions	Egg parts	Incorporeals
Physics	Yolk	Space
Logic	Shell	Λεκτα
Ethics	Albumen	Time

Part I is about Stoic physics and metaphysics, especially in so far as it is considered *perverse*. 'The Yolk A' situates Stoic metaphysics by articulating 'something', τι, as the broadest metaphysical category for the Stoics. As we will see, 'something' divides into two basic types: corporeals and incorporeals. This distinction is a perverse response to a distinction from Plato's *Sophist*, which is intended to distinguish the two sides of the Stoic incorporeal surface. We then consider the nuanced meaning of the incorporeals' metaphysical modality – subsistence – before situating all of Stoic metaphysics as the first self-consciously articulated *system*, σύστημα. Deleuze's main contribution here is to articulate the difference between the two sides of the strange Stoic surface as composed of an extensive face and an intensive face, and integration and differentiation are their respective operations. 'The Yolk B' focuses directly on the Stoics' concept of incorporeality, with a special emphasis on distinguishing corporeals as bodily causes from incorporeals as both effects and yet quasi-causes. Since this concept of a 'quasi-cause' is so confusing and elusive, we will trace it back to its first appearance it the writings of Clement of Alexandria. We then consider how quasi-cause operates as what Deleuze calls 'static genesis', which contrasts with corporeal dynamic genesis, thus revealing a kind of double causality in Stoic metaphysics. To understand this double causality we uncover in Deleuze a hidden twist of Immanuel Kant's Table of Judgements, which allows us to develop two metaphysical logics: a formal logic of bodies that corresponds to one side of the incorporeal surface, and a transcendental logic of incorporeals that corresponds to the other side. This latter logic follows four classes: (1) infinite, (2) singular, (3) disjunctive and (4) problematic. 'The Yolk C' concludes Part I by making our argument for our heterodoxical claim: there are three, not four, incorporeals. In Stoic physics, this claim is made by collapsing the canonical incorporeals – place and void – into just one – space. We will offer three reasons and three advantages for this heterodoxy. To articulate space in Stoicism, we consider the technical meanings of several related terms (such as 'whole', 'all', 'infinite divisibility') before turning directly to Stoic place and void, which we contrast with Aristotelian place and atomic void. We argue that the Stoics were the first to isolate a single notion of space, and space is the single incorporeal in so far as it is composed of place and void. Place and void are different ways of considering space: place is the extensive side facing bodies and void the intensive side facing away from bodies. We finish 'The Yolk C' by showing that the same double-sided structure of the incorporeal surface, which appears as space when considered from the perspective of physics, repeats when that surface is considered by logic and by ethics. From a logical point of view, the surface is λεκτα, and is composed of two faces: the extensive side consists of conjugated verbs and the intensive side consists of infinitive verbs. Isomorphically, considering the surface from an ethical point of view the surface is time, and it too is composed of two sides: the extensive side consists of a kind of time called chronos and the intensive side consists of a kind of time called aion.

Part II turns to Stoic logic and philosophy of language. 'The Shell A' begins by considering the history and etymology of the ancient concept: λεκτα. With λεκτα, the Stoics create a theory of attributes that contrasts with Platonic predicates. Λεκτα is how the Stoics explain the genesis of linguistic meaning or sense out of meaningless matter, which Deleuze calls 'a final task' in so far as it applies to all materialist philosophies. Deleuze here helps us take up this final task through several Deleuzian concepts from his philosophy of language: primary order, secondary organisation and tertiary ordinance, as well as the three dimensions of the circle of the proposition (denotation, manifestation and signification). Linguistic meaning, we will see, is generated out of meaningless matter through two geneses: dynamic and static. After comparing Epicurean and Stoic philosophies of language, we conclude 'The Shell A' by claiming that λεκτα is the Stoic incorporeal considered from the perspective of logic, and it is composed to two opposed sides: the extensive side facing bodes corresponds to conjugated verbs (such as 'I cut', 'he cut', 'she has cut' and so on) and the intensive side facing away corresponds to infinitive verbs (such as 'to cut' or 'to walk'). 'The Shell B' considers the importance of paradoxes in Stoic logic, specifically in so far as they pervert good and common sense. We then see how the Stoics brilliantly developed a new logic in antiquity: a propositional system that is a logical alternative to Aristotelian categorical logic. Given

Introduction: The Egg

these innovations, the Stoics were especially interested in the force of paradoxes. Paradoxes are, we will see, absurd, and there are three dimensions of absurdity, corresponding to the three dimensions of the circle of the proposition. Paradoxes are important for materialists like the Stoics and Deleuze because they are the means for accounting for genesis of language and logic. To see this precisely, we articulate four classic Stoic paradoxes: The Heap, The Liar, The Master and The Nobody. Each of these express the structure of ambiguity: a double-sided structure that turns on what Deleuze calls the 'aleatory point'. We close our story of Stoic paradoxes by considering two forms of inference: *ergo* is cognitive deduction involved in propositional logic and *igitur* is the production of cognition through the Stoic art of paradoxes. 'The Shell C' uses the results from the previous chapters in order to construct a *Handbook of Paradoxes*. Logical handbooks have a long tradition in Stoicism, the goal of which was not simply to improve at formal logic but to train students to create concepts for living. In this tradition, we write a *Handbook of Paradoxes*, which consists of four acts: Infinite Act, Singular Act, Disjunctive Act and Problematic Act. These four correspond to the four paradoxes from the four classes from the Transcendental Logic of Incorporeals we sketched out in 'The Yolk B': (1) infinite, (2) singular, (3) disjunctive and (4) problematic. Deleuze notices a profound link between Stoic logic and ethics, and constructing our *Handbook* expresses this profound link and thus prepares for Part III: Ethics.

Part III closes our book with an account of Stoic ethics. To avoid as much disappointment as possible, let us clarify what we mean by 'ethics'. Ethics, for Deleuze's Stoicism, does not refer to the traditions of normative theory or applied morality, which mostly focus on issues of right and wrong, virtue and vice, good and evil. We, instead, begin from the perspective of time, ontology and action in order to read, later on, the more traditional moral question. This is why 'Albumen A' considers time the third and final incorporeal. We first contrast Stoic time with Platonic time and Aristotelian time. While some scholars are confused by the presence of two seemingly incompatible theories of time in Stoic writings, which Victor Goldschmidt calls aion and chronos, the Deleuze's Stoicism sees aion and chronos as two sides of a single incorporeal surface: time. We distinguish these sides through their different senses of the present: the chronological now and the aionic instant. We then consider the twisted genealogy of chronos and aion, before articulating how time also has that same strange double-sided structure: chronos is the extensive side of facing limited and determinate bodies, and aion is the intensive side facing away from bodies. 'Albumen B' considers the status of an *ethical act* given time's double-sided surface structure. To do this, we consider the event of dying, specifically the suicides of Seneca and Deleuze. We then take up Deleuze's consideration that chronos and aion correspond to two methods of interpretation (divination and usage of representations), two moral attitudes (cosmic perspective and singular perspective) and two ethical tasks (counter-actualisation and actualisation). We concretise all of this in the figure of the Stoic sage, Deleuze's select example of which is the Surrealist poet Joe Bousquet. Through the 'Bousquet proposition', which concerns the fated nature of the poet's wound, we find that the act and the event are the same paradoxical object, viewed either from one side (the act) or the other (the event), and counter-actualisation is the ethical task that corresponds to the act. Here we will see what is involved in 'how to make oneself a Stoic' in so far as it entails a principle of *amor fati*. In 'Albumen C' we take up Deleuze's suggestion that there are two eternal returns, corresponding to the two methods of interpretation, two moral attitudes and two ethical tasks we detailed in 'Albumen B'. After giving a short history of the Stoic doctrine of the cosmic conflagration, we take inspiration from Nietzsche's seemingly disingenuous authorship of eternal recurrence through two short stories by Jorge Luis Borges, 'Pierre Menard, Author of the *Quixote*' and 'Death and the Compass'. These stories articulate the difference between the two eternal returns: the cyclical return of chronos and the return as the straight line of aion. These two forms of the eternal return express the paradox of action, which combines the ethical imperative to act and the impossibility of acting because of the Stoic insistence on fate. Following Deleuze's lead, we close the book by considering the 'crack-up' of the American writer F. Scott Fitzgerald and what he calls 'laughing Stoicism'.

In the 'Conclusion' we return to the four ancient philosophical orientations given above in order to articulate corresponding forms of philosophical comedy. *Slapstick* is the comedic form of pre-Socratic depths, *irony* of Socratic/Platonic heights, *sarcasm* of Cynic rawness, *wit* of Aristotelian inwardness and *humour* of Stoicism. Stoic humour, we will see, seems perverse in comparison to the other ancient comedic forms (except Cynicism). After viewing Stoic humour through the American comedian Steve Martin's stand-up routines from the 1970s, we end this tale of the Deleuze–Stoic encounter by showing that Stoic humour is the proper philosophical

Introduction: The Egg

response to the paradox of action and the course of fate. As we turn that final page and close the book, we should hear the echoes of what Deleuze considers a species of laughter that comes from one who speaks of freedom and power: the laughter of Spinoza.

French Stoicism

To tell the story of Deleuze, a Stoic, we consider the ideas and writings of Deleuze's teachers and students, or the prior and the subsequent generations of French philosophers of Stoicism.

The person who shaped Deleuze's encounter with Stoicism most significantly was Émile Bréhier (1876–1952), the influential French scholar of the history of philosophy.[39] Who is Bréhier? Early in life, Bréhier fought in the First World War, where he lost his left arm in battle, and became a Commander in the French Legion of Honour.[40] Later, he studied under Henri Bergson, was a classmate of the great poet Charles Péguy, and in 1944 succeeded Bergson as the Chair of Philosophy at the Academy of Moral and Political Sciences, serving until Gabriel Marcel took over in 1952.[41] Before then, he taught around France (Laval, Beauvais, Rennes, Bordeaux), as well as in Egypt and Brazil. In addition to Stoicism, Bréhier's scholarship engaged with Philo of Alexandria, Plotinus, F. W. J. Schelling, and he produced a massive four-volume *Histoire de la philosophie*. Evidence of his influence on French philosophy is clear. For example, he directed Maurice Merleau-Ponty's thesis, and his *Histoire de la philosophie allemande* had an impact on the work of Georges Bataille.[42] In our text we will focus on his work on Stoicism, with a special emphasis on his 1907 doctoral thesis: *La Théorie des incorporels dans l'ancien stoicism* (The Theory of Incorporeals in Ancient Stoicism). We seek to extract the fuller story of Deleuze's Stoic lessons from Bréhier.

The other older philosopher working in early twentieth-century France who greatly shaped Deleuze's understanding of Stoicism was Victor Goldschmidt (1914–71), who was about a decade older than Deleuze. Born in Berlin, Goldschmidt moved to France in 1933, although he never lived in Paris. Instead, he worked at the Centre national de la recherche scientifique and later taught at the universities at Rennes, Clermont-Ferrand and, finally, at what he liked to call 'the smallest university in France, Amiens'.[43] Goldschmidt was inclined towards philology and the classic forms of the history of philosophy. His first book, *Essai sur le Cratyle*, was the first to

15

prove the Pythagorean influence on Plato.[44] He studied with George Dumezil and wrote his doctoral thesis on Plato's Dialogues under the direction of Bréhier (1945). He wrote important works on Descartes, Rousseau, Epicurus, Aristotle and others, although we are most interested in his 1953 book *Le Système stoïcien et l'idée de temps* (The Stoic System and the Idea of Time) because it clearly inspired Deleuze's encounter with Stoicism, especially the two senses of time: chronos and aion. Goldschmidt's own encounter with Stoicism and ancient philosophy was shaped by his teacher Martial Gueroult, who conveyed the 'structural method'.[45]

Deleuze's Stoicism does not end with Deleuze's relationship with the ancient Stoics, or with those the older generation of French philosophers who taught Deleuze his Stoicism, but spills into the next generation of French thinkers, post-Deleuze, who are now premiere French scholars of Stoicism. In Part I: Physics we engage with Goldschmidt's student Jacques Brunschwig. Throughout our book we engage the works of Frédérique Ildefonse, Jean-Baptiste Gourinat and Thomas Benatouïl. While they all consider Deleuze in one form or another, Benatouïl was actually part of 'a small group of young philosophers at ENS [École normale supérieure] . . . [who] had discovered Deleuze and Guattari and found their work entirely out of sync with their period'.[46] While the older Brunschwig has been recognised by many English-speaking scholars of antiquity and had several essays translated, these younger French philosophers are still relatively unknown in British and American scholarship. We hope that this book might be part of an introduction to their work. The complete story of the *Deleuze, A Stoic* thus spreads out to a time before and after Deleuze, and we aim to tell that story as fully as possible.

Double-Sided Surface

Since this strange, double-sided surface structures the perspective from which this story unfolds, our focus will be equally strange and double. At various points, our focus will slip back and forth, from one side to the other. The effect will be a telling of one story from two perspectives: (1) the perspective of Stoic philosophy to which is added a Deleuzian reading, and (2) a Deleuzian reading of Stoic philosophy that is heterodoxical to other readers of Stoicism. In short, we offer heterodoxical readings of Stoicism by means of, yet not reducible to, Deleuze's own reading of the Stoics. The goal of

Introduction: The Egg

telling a single story told from two simultaneous perspectives for both Stoic and Deleuzean scholarship is to contribute to the uncovering of a relatively ignored tradition in philosophical materialism so as to generate momentum for future materialisms. While the Stoics and Deleuze individually contribute to this momentum, combining them in this strange way generates something new, something that could only result from placing both stories together so as to form a single, double-sided surface.

We might thus call this a 'materially focused history of philosophy' in order to place it among recent continental readings of ancient philosophy, such as my co-edited volume *Continental Encounters with Ancient Metaphysics* and my monograph *The Deleuze–Lucretius Encounter*, as well as other Edinburgh University Press authors, such as Thomas Nail's ongoing trilogy on Lucretius. Such continental philosophies, especially those inspired by Deleuze, offer new ways of engaging antiquity that differ from at least three more standard readings of the history of philosophy. First are the 'returns' to antiquity, which assume an account of history as a decline that needs saving by returning to its origins. We consider such histories too nostalgic for our and messianic for our tastes. Second are the 'historicist' readings, which restrict themselves to a historical context so greatly that they ignore the efficacy of texts to generate ideas beyond that specific context. We consider historicity readings too static or stuck because they overlook the dynamism of a text to generate new concepts today. Finally there is 'reception studies'. Similar to historicism, reception studies treats new figures like past figures, rather than seeing all figures as alive and as potential contributors to the philosophical exigencies of the present and future. Our disagreement here is that they focus too much about clarifying rather than producing new concepts and ways of living.

Contrary to these three, a materially focused history of philosophy takes up a major continental philosopher who engages with an ancient figure, such as Deleuze on Lucretius or Malabo on Plato, in order to unearth a conceptual dynamism that is already there but remains unexploited. These dynamisms generate effects that are indeterminable in advance, and only appear through encounters with them. We thus place this book in a materialist tradition that is based on productivity because it is attuned to the ways in which the canon of philosophy shapes the contemporary scene by prioritising questions and problems over answers and puzzles. In our eyes, the canon is not a set and fixed linear story, but a distinct provocative geography structured by sites of contestations. The geography of this story is the double-sided surface. The focus of *Deleuze, A Stoic* is a materially focused history of philosophy from a continental angle, as admittedly strange at it is.

Notes

1. 'The biography of a philosopher or literary figure was often placed at the beginning of an edition of his works, but it could also circulated independently, or as part of a collection of biographies of individual figures.' Jaap Mansfeld, *Prolegomena: Questions to Be Settled Before the Study of an Author, or a Text* (Leiden: Brill, 1994), 6.
2. Friedrich Nietzsche, *Untimely Meditations* (1876), trans. R. J. Hollingdale, ed. Daniel Breazeale (Cambridge: Cambridge University Press, 1997), 186–7; emphasis added.
3. Mansfeld, *Prolegomena*, 7.
4. Bernold was also a student of Jacques Derrida, and a one of the few intimate friends of Samuel Beckett. https://www.theguardian.com/books/2015/dec/29/becketts-friendship-andre-bernold-nicholas-lezard (last accessed 8 February 2018).
5. André Bernold, 'Suidas', *Philosophie* 47 (1995), 8–9, trans. Timothy S. Murphy; https://www.webdeleuze.com/textes/189 (last accessed 8 February 2018); emphasis added.
6. Deleuze does not include Aristotle in this depiction, but we will introduce a Deleuzian account of Aristotelianism in order to put this picture into conversation with another of the traditions of ancient philosophy: the Peripatetics.
7. While Deleuze references the story of Empedocles' death in the volcano at Etna, recent scholarship on Empedocles is quite different from what Deleuze might have known, partially due to archeological discoveries (such as the discovery of the Strasbourg papyrus in 1997) and technological developments that provide more access to writings previously unknown. See N. van der Ben, 'The Strasbourg Papyrus of Empedocles: Some Preliminary Remarks', *Mnemosyne*, Fourth Series, 52, Fasc. 5 (October 1999), 525–54; Peter Kingsley, *Ancient Philosophy, Mystery, and Magic: Empedocles and Pythagorean Tradition* (Oxford: Clarendon Press, 1997); and *The Empedoclean Κόσμος: Structure, Process, and the Question of Cyclicity Papers*, ed. Apostolos Pierris (Patras: Institute for Philosophical Research, 2005).
8. In the hopes of putting this text into conversation with other contemporary continental philosophy, we can align these ancient philosophical orientation with the division that Graham Harman provides in the first chapter of *The Quadruple Object*. What we are calling Pre-Socratic sub-

Introduction: The Egg

version would be akin to Harman's 'overmining' of objects, as Harman too identifies this strategy with Thales, Anaximenes, Democritus, and others. For Harman, subversion *'undermine[s]* objects as the root of philosophy' because 'objects are too specific to deserve the name of ultimate reality'; put differently, 'objects are a sort of derivative product' because they are 'too shallow to be the fundamental reality in the universe.' Graham Harman, *The Quadruple Object* (Zero Books, 2011), 10.

9. It is not surprising that Plato's thinking of Being as unified and transcendent depends greatly on a prior thinker of heights – Parmenides – who was carried by the daughters of Helios, the sun god, into the high home of the goddess. That being said, some scholars argue that the goddess in Parmenides' poem is actually Night. For example, see John Palmer, *Parmenides and Presocratic Philosophy* (Oxford: Oxford University Press, 2013), 51–62.
10. This theory appears in Plato, e.g., *Phaedrus* 247c, *Sophist* 246b, 247b–c, *Statesman* 286a, *Republic* 5.476a.
11. Continuing with Harman's analysis from *The Quadruple Object*, Platonic conversion is a philosophical strategy of *overmining*. Harman writes that a 'different way of dismissing objects is . . . to reduce them upward rather than downward. Instead of saying that objects are too shallow to be real, it is said that they are too deep. Although he associates overmining with empiricists, he also sees it in 'post-Kantian anti-realists', the 'idealism of Berkeley' or sceptical agnosticism (11). These three, taken together, resonate strongly with Platonic conversion in so far as 'these positions overmine the object, treating it as a useless substratum easily replaced by direct manifestations', such as grasping of ideal Forms (12).
12. Michael James Bennett, *Deleuze and Ancient Greek Physics* (London: Bloomsbury Academic, 2017), 117–64.
13. We here ignore Aristotle's god, which is not a form.
14. This is why it is inaccurate to call formal causes 'immaterial'.
15. Gideon Manning, 'The History of Hylomorphism', *Journal of the History of Ideas* 74.2 (April 2013): 173–87.
16. Continuing to align our Deleuzian organization with Harman's, Aristotelian inwardness or interiority is akin to Harman's own version of object-oriented project, as Harman himself notices: 'Only with Aristotle do individual objects first become the central player in philosophy.' Harman, *The Quadruple Object*, 17. The 'theories of Aristotle', Harman continues, 'can all be called theories of substance. The object-oriented philosophy proposed in this book is the latest theory in the same lineage', although he admits that 'the theory proposed here is significantly weirder'. Harman, *The Quadruple Object*, 18.
17. Alain Beaulieu, 'Deleuze et les Stoïciens', in Alain Beaulieu and Manola

Antonioli (eds), *Gilles Deleuze: héritage philosophique* (Paris: Presses universitaires de France, 2005), 49.

18. While Harman's undermining aligns with pre-Socratic subversion, his overmining with Platonic conversation, and his object-oriented philosophy with Aristotelian inwardness, he does not have a place for Stoic perversion. Before considering himself a sort of contemporary 'weird' Aristotelian, Harman does address (and dismiss) 'materialism', which is a combination of overmining and undermining, he does not engage with the perverted materialism of the Stoics. Since the Stoics are not brute materialists, they sidestep his critiques of materialism in so far as they are not simply combining overmining and undermining but instead making what we might call a lateral or horizontal move; this move addresses the problems that Harman sees in pre-Socratic undermining not with overmining but with their strange surface. In my research, I have only seen Harman mention the Stoics once, when he contrasted '[Ian] Bogost's ethics of play' with Stoic ethics. Graham Harman, *Object-Oriented Ontology: A New Theory of Everything* (London: Pelican Books, 2018), 223–4. But he never mentions Stoic physics, logic or the perverse parts of their ethics. While Harman appreciates *weirdness*, he does not seem to have a time for *perversion*. We should wonder what he would say about the Stoics' perverse materialism.

19. 'Perscend' is a neologism combined of *per* ('through, along' or 'thoroughly, exceedingly') plus *scandere* ('to climb, mount, clamber'), thus meaning something like 'to climb along exceedingly' or 'to move thoroughly through'.

20. Lapoujade claims that 'the figure of the pervert appears everywhere in Deleuze's writings' while he was working on *Logique du sens*. David Lapoujade, *Aberrant Movements: The Philosophy of Gilles Deleuze* (2014), trans. Joshua David Jordan (South Pasadena: Semiotext(e), 2017), 143–4.

21. Gilles Deleuze, *Two Regimes of Madness: Texts and Interviews 1975–1995*, ed. David Lapoujade, trans. Ames Hodges and Mike Taormina (New York: Semiotexte, 2006), 80 and Gilles Deleuze and Claire Parnet, *Dialogues* (1977), trans. Hugh Tomlinson and Barbara Habberjam (New York: Columbia University Press, 1977), 77.

22. *Trois milliards de pervers: Le Grande Encyclopédie des homosexualités*, March 1973.

23. Félix Guattari, *The Guattari* Reader, ed. Gary Genesko (Oxford: Blackwell, 1996), 192n.

24. Lapoujade, *Aberrant Movements*, 25. In this vein, we are trying to do with 'pervert' what Deleuze and Guattari did with 'schizo'.

25. Jacques Brunschwig, *Papers in Hellenistic Philosophy* (Cambridge: Cambridge University Press, 1994), 121; emphasis added.

Introduction: The Egg

26. Gilles Deleuze, *Masochism: Coldness and Cruelty* (1971), trans. Jean McNeil (New York: Zone Books, 1989), 31.
27. As is the case with many of Deleuze's concepts, this is not the final word on 'depth'. In different contexts, 'depth' comes to mean something very different from what it does here. For an engaging account of other meanings of 'depth' in Deleuze, one that connects Deleuze to Merleau-Ponty, see Henry Somers-Hall, *Deleuze's Difference and Repetition* (Edinburgh: Edinburgh University Press, 2013), 170–4.
28. Lapoujade, *Aberrant Movements*, 144.
29. Michel Surya, *Georges Bataille: An Intellectual Biography*, trans. Krzysztof Fijalkowski and Michael Richardson (London: Verso, 2010), 189.
30. Lapoujade, *Aberrant Movements*, 143.
31. Frédérique Ildefonse, *Les Stoïciens I: Zénon, Cléanthe, Chrysippe* (Paris: Les Belles Lettres, 2000), 23.
32. Plutarch, *On Stoic Self-Contradictions*, 1035a.
33. We can hear echoes of Stoics' fertile field in Deleuze's sense of intensive field: 'The vital egg is nevertheless already a field of individuation, and the embryo is a pure individual, and the one in the other testifies to the primacy of individuation over actualisation' (*DR* 250).
34. An image of the Dogon egg marks the beginning of Chapter 6, 'November 28, 1947: How Do You Make Yourself a Body without Organs?'
35. See also Jeffrey A. Bell, 'The World is an Egg: Realism, Mathematics, and the Thresholds of Difference', *Speculations* IV (2013): 65–70.
36. In addition to *Anti-Oedipus*, *A Thousand Plateaus*, *Difference and Repetition* and *Logic of Sense*, it appears in the 'interview' and collections (*Desert Islands*, *Two Regimes of Madness*, *Negotiations*, *Dialogues*, *Essays Critical and Clinical*), as well as *The Fold*, *Cinema I and II*, *What is Philosophy?*, *Francis Bacon*, *Kafka* and *Masochism*.
37. I translated the three instances of the French *jaune* (167) as 'yolk' rather than 'yoke' (142, 143), which is Mark Lester's English translation of *Logique du sens*. Unless this is a sophisticated point that goes over my head, I assume it is just an unfortunate translation mistake. The French for 'yoke' would be something like *joug*, which' is not the word Deleuze uses.
38. Jean Khalfa (ed.), *Introduction to the Philosophy of Gilles Deleuze* (London: Bloomsbury Academic, 2003), 133–48.
39. Christophe Charle, 'Bréhier (Émile, François, Désiré)', *Bibliothèque de l'Éducation* (1986), 40–1.
40. Ibid. 41.
41. Édouard Salin, 'Notice sur la vie et les travaux de M. Louis Bréhier, member de l'Académie', *Comptes rendus des séances de l'Académie des inscriptions et belles-lettres* 98.2 (1954): 172–85, at 171.

42. Alan D. Schrift, *Twentieth-Century French Philosophy: Key Themes and Thinkers* (Malden, MA: Wiley-Blackwell, 2005), 166. Surya, *Georges Bataille*, 189.
43. Pierre Vidal-Naquet, 'La mort du professeur Victor Goldschmidt de Platon à Rousseau: l'analyste opiniâtre de dystèmes', *Le Monde* (10 December 1981).
44. Ibid.
45. Victor Goldschmidt, 'Remarques sur la méthode structurale en histoire de la philosophie', in *Metaphysique et histoire de le philosophie. Recueil d'études offert à Fernand Brunner* (Neuchâtel: Éditions de la Baconnière, 1981).
46. François Dosse, *Gilles Deleuze and Félix Guattari: Intersecting Lives*, trans. Deborah Glassman (New York: Columbia University Press, 2011), 504.

PART I
Physics

1
The Yolk A: Stoic Metaphysics

> Oh, those Greeks! They knew about *living*: for this, it is necessary to stop courageously at the surface . . . Those Greeks were superficial – *out of profundity*!
>
> Friedrich Nietzsche, *The Gay Science*[1]

Introduction

With their strange surface, Stoic physics and metaphysics enact a philosophical *perversion* that begins with an articulation of *something*, an original ontological concept that the Stoics constructed in response to their philosophical predecessors. Tracing Stoic metaphysics to a debate from Plato's *Sophist*, this chapter will show that there are two modalities of reality in Stoicism: existent corporeality and subsistent incorporeality. To understand the complexities involved in Stoic theory, we introduce a Deleuzian distinction that continues through the entire text: the intensive and the extensive. We conclude by connecting the intensive and extensive to, respectively, two mathematical operations: integration and differentiation. These integrating extensities and differentiating intensities structure the strange surface. With this surface the Stoics push materialism further than anyone before and few after, leading them to develop some of the most fascinating concepts in the ancient world. Let us now begin to construct a Deleuzian system of Stoicism, starting with physics.

Something

To understand Stoic perversity and the philosophical 'surface' orientation, we begin with their broadest metaphysical category: 'something', τι. Contrary to other ancient schools, writes Seneca, rather than making being ('what is', *quod est*) the highest category, the 'Stoics want to place beyond [*superpowered*] this yet another, more primary [*magis principale*] genus'.[2] Stoics think that the primary genus is 'something [*quid*]'.[3]

Something provoked a long history of hostile receptions to Stoic metaphysics – from the ancient critiques in Plutarch's *On Common Conceptions against the Stoics* and *On Stoic Contradictions* through Alexander's charges of 'impropriety' up to contemporary scholarship, which deems Stoic ontology embarrassing.[4] Responding to these critiques, Jacques Brunschwig argues that the Stoics did not always consider 'something' the broadest category. He suggests:

> if there were good reasons to believe that the Stoics initially professed a theory that attributed to the *existent* the rank of supreme genus, and only at a more or less later date came to replace the *existent* by *something* in the position of supreme genus, we should have good reasons to regard that substitution as a defensive strategy, rendered necessary by the difficulties raised by the original doctrine in conjunction with the other dogmas to which the Stoic School was attached.[5]

If Brunschwig is correct, we should read this possibly defensive shift in the organisation of Stoic ontology as an expression of their full commitment to *philosophical materialism*.[6]

The Stoics divide the 'supreme genus' *something*, although the division is slightly convoluted. Seneca writes, 'I divide "what is [*quod est*]" into three species: things are corporeal or incorporeal; there is no third possibility.'[7] Seneca says there are three species, but lists only two because the third is polemical: it mockingly designates things that do not exist, merely fictional entities such as Centaurs, Giants and Plato's transcendent Forms. Strictly speaking, it is not even a third category, more of a catch-all trash bin for fantastical creatures, or any 'bit of Plato's personal baggage', Seneca chides.[8] The Stoics are concerned only with the other two species: corporeals and incorporeals.

The division between corporeals and incorporeals is modal. Corporeals and incorporeals are both modes of *something*. Both are real. Then comes the twist: only corporeals *exist*. Stoicism is clear here: *to be is to be a body*. Existence and corporeality are coextensive. All existence is material; only bodies exist. 'Something is an *existent* if and only if it is a body', Brunschwig writes.[9] There is no immaterial existence in Stoicism. From beginning to end, Stoicism is a thoroughgoing materialism, albeit a perverse one. In fact, it is their unrelenting commitment to materiality that produces the following perversity: Stoic materialism leads to an original account of immateriality.

This perversity is why Brunschwig is right to claim that Stoicism advocates an 'expansive' rather than a 'deflationist ontology', just as he is right to see 'good reason for putting inverted commas around the word "materialism"'.[10] As Bréhier suggests, the formulation of the ontological category of 'the incorporeal' follows from pushing materialism to its logical conclusion.[11] Much of *Deleuze, A Stoic* follows the perverse implications of pushing materialism as far as it can go.[12]

The Giants

In their thoroughgoing materialism, Stoics redeploy a suggestion in Plato's *Sophist* to their own perverse ends. Brunschwig notices Stoics' perversity in his description of the Stoics' relationship to Plato's metaphysics 'not in terms of a direct influence, but rather in terms of a challenge to be taken up'.[13]

In a long passage in Plato's *Sophist* (245e–249d), the Eleatic Stranger launches a critique of the sort of metaphysics that will eventually frame the Stoics' ontological materialism. Plato describes an allegorical battle between two sets of characters: (1) the Gods, defenders of Forms and heights, and (2) the Giants or Sons of the Earth, proponents of matter and depth. In their interminable battle, the Gods argue that true existence belongs to transcendent incorporeals located up on high. They 'defend their position', writes Plato, 'from somewhere up out of sight. They insist violently that true being is certain non-bodily forms that can be thought about'.[14] One of the problems of this position is that it places existence so high up, so far from our world, that such non-physical forms lack causal power. Forms are rendered fixed, impotent, merely rational objects.

A Giant, by contrast, 'drags everything down to earth from the heavenly region of the invisible, actually clutching rocks and trees with their hands. Taking hold of all these things, they insist that only what offers tangible contact *is*, since they define being as the same as body.'[15] Plato argues that the Giants' position is indefensible and must be revised, and so suggests an amended principle: since soul exists, it must be a body. Hence the revision: soul is corporeal but imperceptible.[16] The uncomfortable result is that the Giants now include imperceptible corporeality in their metaphysics. Things become more uncomfortable when they consider 'ways in which the soul can be qualified or disposed', that is, vices and virtues.[17] Since a soul can be just at one time or unjust at another, virtues like justice seem to be even less corporeal, and thus even less real, than soul.[18]

Conceding this, while still wanting to claim that virtues are real, the Giants nervously accept a new ontological principle, which Plato provides: 'a thing really is if it has any capacity at all, either by nature to do something to something else or to have even the smallest thing done to it by even the most trivial thing, even if it only happens once. I'll take as a definition that *those which are* amount to nothing other than *capacity*.'[19] Put differently, being (τὸ ὄν) is that which has the power to act or be acted upon. However strong or weak, however rare or common, an existent is that which affects or is affected. David Hahm twists a Lucretian syllogism to connect physicalism to this provisional principle: 'Whatever exists either acts or is acted upon. Nothing can act or be acted upon without body. Therefore, only bodies exist.'[20]

While the Giants were reluctant to deem the soul an invisible body, and even more reluctant to include virtues and vices into such a strange metaphysical category, the Stoics embrace the paradoxical implications that follow from rendering soul, virtues and vices existent, bodily and perceptible. The 'Stoics', Brunschwig writes, 'take over Plato's formula according to which an existent is capable of acting and being acted upon, and turn it round, to work against his intentions.'[21] The Stoics accept the ontological audacity of calling corporeal what others will not. Rather than arguing (like the Gods) that forms are the most existent beings, the Stoics argue (like the Giants) that only bodies exist. For the Stoics, to exist means to be able to engage in causal relations, to bring about effects in, and to suffer effects from, other bodies. As Spinoza or Deleuze might put it, 'to be' means to have the capacity to affect or be affected, activity or passivity.[22] Being is power. Hence Frédérique Ildefonse sees the Stoics developing 'a physics of effectivity or of actuality: they are thinkers of power, theorists of an acting or effective power'.[23]

While Brunschwig and Ildefonse argue, in essence, that the Stoics pervert the *Sophist*, Bréhier claims that the active–passive distinction displaces an Aristotelian duality.[24] The Stoics' 'agent–patient duality', he writes, 'corresponds to the form and matter peripatetic duality' (CAS 115). By activating materiality, the Stoics make matter more than the passive recipient of form. Siding more with the Giants, as well as revealing their Heraclitean inclinations, early Stoic formulations, especially Zeno's, identified the active principle with a kind of body: fire, πῦρ. Later versions, especially Chrysippus', construe activity as a slightly different kind of body: breath, πνεῦμα. In ancient biology, fire and breath were closely related. Fire was considered the

The Yolk A: Stoic Metaphysics

principle of organismic life. Cicero explains, life continues 'as long as this [fire] remains in us, so long as sensation and life remain, but when the heat has been chilled and extinguished, we ourselves die and are extinguished'.[25] All organisms are alive and active, emitting fiery heat, and become cold and rigid after death, after they lose the vital blaze. Stoicism, Ildefonse notes, is thus grounded in 'a physics of bodies, and it defines as bodies that which is susceptible of acting or being acted upon [*susceptible d'agir ou de pâtir*]. The division between acting and being acted upon is essential for Stoic physics and underlies the Stoic theory of causality.'[26] There is one type of thing – corporeality – that is either active or passive.

The Stoics pervert the active–passive criterion for another reason: to argue for the non-existent reality of incorporeals. As Cicero says, 'neither what acts nor what it acts on could be incorporeal'.[27] Since the power to act and be acted upon cannot pertain to non-bodily things, incorporeals cannot possess causal efficacy. While Plato and Aristotle reject the inefficacy of their incorporeals – be they transcendent ideas or embodied forms – the Stoics embrace it. Now for the twist: *incorporeals are not less real because they are causally impotent*. Affectivity is not the sole criterion of reality. Incorporeals are real *in so far as* they are neither active nor passive; the reality of incorporeality is *due* to their inactivity and impassivity. While *existence* means 'being able to act and be acted upon', *reality* is a broader genus than existence is. The criterion for what counts as real includes both existence and non-existence.[28] Reality is composed of *both* corporeals and incorporeals. Stoic corporeals and incorporeals are both real, in so far as they are the two kinds of *something*. The difference is modal.

To see how, in Stoicism, the corporeal and incorporeal are not hierarchically organised ontological domains but two modes of reality, consider the Stoics' distinction between principles (ἀρχαί) and elements (στοιχεῖα), which shows again their perversion of Plato and Aristotle.[29] Already in Plato's *Timaeus*, first causes are distinguished from elements.[30] While Timaeus, the character, seems to draw a line between formal and material causes, he places the receptacle (χώρα) in the same list that includes the intelligible paradigm and the demiurge. The strange part is that, as Aristotle notices, the receptacle is considered material.[31] Plato thus slips materiality into a list of causes that are otherwise strictly formal. While Plato distinguishes formal and material causes (or 'first causes' and 'elements'), he undermines the supposition of materiality by trying to make it another sort of formal cause. By contrast, the Stoics, unashamed of matter, make all causation material. Their two principles are: '[1] that which acts and [2] that which is acted upon', and their elements are classic: fire, water, air, earth (DL 7.134). Both are corporeal. 'The principles are bodies and without form, but the elements are [bodies] endowed with form' (DL 7.134). A principle is defined only through its distinction from elements, no through corporeality or lack thereof. Principles are eternal, indestructible and formless, while elements are generated, destroyed (in the cosmic conflagration) and formed. If Stoic principles are material, then there are no immaterial causes, such as intelligible paradigms, the demiurge, or some other incorporeal forms for Stoicism.

Stoic materiality also opposes Aristotelian matter. The Greek word for 'matter' is ὕλη, which is also the word for wood. Ὕλη evokes a wood that carpenters work on as they make tables and houses. Wood from a felled tree is passive; it merely receives the activity of the carpenter. Although the Stoics use the same word (ὕλη), they place it in a different conceptual framework: the egg. The world is an egg, not a tree. The egg is a body of varying zones of intensities and gradients, constantly acting upon itself as it develops. Like an egg, the world is passive *and* active as it unfolds a single embryological development. In Stoic metaphysics, the world is completely corporeal – part active matter, part passive matter. As Jean-Jacques Lecercle puts it, 'the world is the site of a gigantic *corps-à-corps*'.[32] The Stoics thus do not simply flip the Platonic schema or the Aristotelian characterisation of matter; they do not simply make bodies more real than incorporeals rather than making incorporeal forms more real than bodies. For the Stoics, bodies and incorporeals are equally real but modally distinct. As we will see in the next section, these are the two modalities: corporeal existence and incorporeals subsistence.

What differentiates these two modes of reality? A paradoxical surface.[33] This surface is not the Platonic divided line that utterly separates the transcendent realm from the material world through a ranking. Instead, the 'Stoics', writes Deleuze, 'are in the process of tracing out and forming a frontier where there had not been one before' (*LS* 6). Through the construction of this ontological frontier, the Stoics 'transcend the experiential dimensions of the visible without falling into [transcendent] ideas' (*LS* 20). This frontier or surface is how Stoic ontology initiates a new image of philosophy, one that corresponds to an ontological distribution that is oriented like a flat plane; it *both connects and separates* the positions respectively

The Yolk A: Stoic Metaphysics

defended by the Gods and the Giants: for example, the existence of active and passive bodies and the non-existent reality of inactive and impassive incorporeals. While the Giants and the Stoics agree that only bodies exist, the Stoics transform the Giants' blunt materialism by identifying a perverse kind of incorporeality that a full commitment to materialism requires.

Subsistence

Both corporeals and incorporeals are real, although only corporeals exist. While incorporeals do not exist, they are not non-existent; they are just not real in the way in which bodies are real. An incorporeal *subsists* (τὸ ὑφεστός), rather *exists* (τὸ ὄν).[34] What do the Stoics mean by 'subsistence'?

Subsistence designates a mode of reality that evades the classical distinction between being and nothingness. John Rist calls it 'twilight reality', and Deleuze calls 'extra-being', comparing it to the eccentric metaphysics of the Austrian philosopher Alexius Meinong (*LS* 34, 19, 20, 35).[35] Meinong's subsistence (*Bestehen*) echoes the Stoic variety: the 'Stoic discovery presupposed a reversal [or perversal] of the problem of Universals; similarly ... Meinong [presupposed a perversion] against Hegelian logic and its lineage' (*LS* 19).[36] While generations of philosophers laughed at Meinong's eccentric metaphysics and mocked the Stoic theory of incorporeal subsistence, Deleuze argues that this odd theory has an innovative and original force.[37]

According to the *LSJ*, the term ὑπόστασις ('subsistence') conveys, first, different senses of 'under, beneath', in the sense of coming up from underground or below a covering, or the sense of being under political subjection, economic dependence or logical subordination. The term also means 'a placing, setting standing' and refers to things like 'a boxer's standing position, position in relation to a compass', a party formed for seditious purposes, or a statue or decree. In antiquity, ὑπόστασις meant several things: 'standing under, supporting'; the sediment that settles at the bottom of a liquid, a thick soup or jelly; the foundation of a temple, including the architectural plan; substantial nature, actual existence, reality. This is why different scholars translate ὑπόστασις and related forms in different ways. Some use 'substance', some 'potential reality'.[38] While Andreas Graeser thinks that, for the Greeks, '"subsist" clearly signifies what may be called a subordinate or rather dependent mode of existence', this seems wrong because his evidence is non-definitive.[39] In a similar attempt to quell (rather than delight in) Stoic perversity, Victor Caston recommends interpreting incorporeals as 'supervening' on bodily states of affairs.[40] Contrary to Graeser and Caston, we show, through Deleuze, that the Stoic perversion of their predecessors flattens out previous vertical hierarchies by constructing an immanent metaphysics such that bodies and incorporeals erase orders of subordination.

This non-hierarchical order relies on an important principle: *incorporeals are immanent*. Etymologically, 'immanence' comes from *in-* and *manere*, which means 'to stay, dwell, remain, abide, tarry'. Stoic incorporeals are immanent in that they remain within the world; they dwell in the material world, on the surface of bodies. The subsistence of Stoic incorporeals is non-transcendent. 'The Stoics', Calcidius reports,

> criticize Plato for saying that, since exemplars of all things exist of old in another sublime and most excellent substrate, the sensible world was made by god after an immortal exemplar. They say that no exemplar is needed, since seminal reason, pervading a certain nature, which holds and contains it, has created the whole world and everything existing in it.[41]

This insistence on immanence connects these ancient Hellenes and Romans to two great modern Stoics: Spinoza and Nietzsche. 'In truth', writes Deleuze, 'only the philosophies of pure immanence escape Platonism – from the Stoics to Spinoza or Nietzsche.'[42] While the Platonists and the Stoics both describe the ontological character of incorporeality through the concept of 'subsistence', they use the term in very different ways: transcendent versus immanent subsistence.[43]

Incorporeal immanent subsistence leads to more perversity. To see it, consider how Platonic Forms have a causal relation to material particulars. The ideal and primary being of, say, the form of Beauty – beauty-*in-itself* – causally explains the material and derivative existence of particular beautiful things – *a* beautiful body, *a* beautiful painting. For the Stoics, however, existent bodies are not the effects or products of incorporeal causes, which is, perhaps, the ultimate perversion: *bodies are existent causes and incorporeals are subsistent effects.*

Bodies express the maximum of being that is appropriate to that which is a thing, an existing entity, while incorporeals express a 'minimum of being that is appropriate to that which is not a thing, a non-existing entity' (*LS* 5). In Stoic ontology, only existent bodies are causal. Bodies either 'act on' or are 'acted upon'.[44] All causation is corporeal.[45] Incorporeals, by contrast, are not inscribed within

The Yolk A: Stoic Metaphysics

the corporeal causal order; they are (almost) etiologically sterilised, deprived of their causal efficacy. As Marcelo D. Boeri writes, 'according to the orthodox doctrine nothing incorporeal can be a cause'.[46] Since they are not causes, incorporeals must be effects. 'The incorporeal', Sextus reports, 'by nature neither acts nor is acted upon.'[47] Neither active nor passive, they subsist as 'impassive' and inactive (*LS* 20). Ildefonse suggests that 'it was the Stoics who appeared to have introduced the philosophical language of the concepts of "bodies" and "incorporeals"' within a physical analysis of causality.[48]

Contrasting Stoic and Aristotelian ontology shows another perversion. While Aristotelian forms are substantial *beings*, Stoic incorporeals are *becomings*. Aristotle's forms are closer to Platonic forms in that they are perfected ontological objects, identifiable by their unchanging identity. For the Stoics, by contrast, incorporeals are not static beings but subsistent becomings.[49] Deleuze calls this conception of incorporeal becoming a sort of 'Stoic mannerism'.[50] 'The Stoics', writes Deleuze, 'invent a mannerism that is opposed to the essentialism first of Aristotle and then of Descartes.'[51] As we will soon see, these becomings take the form of intensive space, infinitive verbs and infinitively divisible time. In sum, while both Platonic and Aristotelian incorporeals are *existent beings*, Stoic incorporeals are *subsistent becomings*.[52] This account of incorporeal, immanent, subsistent reality marks the beginning of the Stoic system.

The System and the Surface

Both the Stoics and Deleuze place great value in the characterisation of philosophy as a system. 'The Stoics', Goldschmidt claims, 'were the first to use the word σύστημα [*systema*] in the objective sense of a world system' (*SS* 61). Despite the subsequent attacks on system-building, Deleuze believes that '[s]ystems have lost absolutely none of their power'.[53] 'I believe in philosophy as a system,' he proclaims.[54] Hence one of the main reasons for Deleuze's admiration of Stoicism is their original philosophical system.

'The Stoics' strength', writes Deleuze, 'lay in making a line of separation pass – no longer between the sensible and the intelligible, or between the soul and body, but where no one had seen it before – between physical depth and metaphysical surface.'[55] Rather than a vertical ontology that locates two utterly separated and hierarchically ordered domains, the Stoics' system has two interdependent dimensions: physical depths and metaphysical surface. The incorporeal surface is not over and above bodies, but cloaks them. We can think of the surface as the backside of matter, but it is important to remember that it is not another body added to the world. The surface coats the world but does not entail a more primordial domain, either higher or lower. It is better to say that the surface records, rather than reflects, the corporal causal interaction as events. Incorporeals, Bréhier writes, are 'simple effects that play on the surface of being without adding anything' or 'removing anything' (*CAS* 109; *TI* 61). We can think of the surface as a limit of materiality, but it is a limit that does not mark the beginning of another world. It is not another *thing* added to the world of physical things, but is the surface *of* bodies. As Deleuze writes, it is 'another geography, without being another world' (*LS* 99). We might call it a topology or topography rather than a physics. This is perhaps the defining achievement of Stoic ontology: *to construct a fully integrated immanent materialist system composed of causally interacting bodies and an incorporeal surface cloaking them.*

Now we can see how the Stoics also pervert pre-Socratic depth. Calling the ensemble of bodies 'depths' differentiates the structure of corporeal causal relations from the structure of incorporeals effects. The Stoics have a term for the full set of corporeal relations: *fatum*, 'fate'. 'The Stoics', Aëtius reports, '[describe fate as] a sequence of causes, that is, an inescapable ordering and interconnexion' (*HP* 55J). All bodies are causally organised according to fate, which Deleuze calls a kind of 'depth'. 'Causes are referred *in depth* [*en profondeur*] to a unity that is proper to them' (*LS* 169; emphasis added).[56] Among causes there is a unity, composed of their relations, and these relations are characterised by *depth*. The French word for 'depth' is *profondeur*, from the Latin *profundus*, itself rooted in *fundus*, 'ground, bottom'. Depth, profundity, is the primary dimension of corporeal relations. Causal relations run deep; bodies weigh on each other. As we will see in 'The Yolk A', 'depth' refers to the interpenetration of all bodies. Bodies reach deep into each other; they are thoroughly intermixed. Deep interpenetration closes all gaps, making the cosmos a corporeal plenum, a perfect sphere fully packed with bodies, from top to bottom and side to side, a stuffed egg. 'Fate', Deleuze writes, 'is primarily the unity and the *link of physical causes among themselves*' (*LS* 169; emphasis added). When speaking about the composition of the sum total of bodies, the entire set of causal relations, we speak of fate. 'Fate' means that causes are not effects of other causes. Causes are only and always causes.

The Yolk A: Stoic Metaphysics

The surface order of incorporeals is distinct from, but necessarily connected to, corporeal depths. Incorporeals, Deleuze writes, 'maintain *at the surface* specific relations of another sort' (*LS* 169; emphasis added). While the relations among causes are ordered 'in depth', relations among incorporeals organise 'at the surface', *à la surface*. 'Surface' comes from the Latin *superficies*, a combination of *super-*, as in 'above', plus *facies*. At the surface, the organisation of effects composes a flat plane. There is no depth when referring to incorporeals themselves. Depth is corporeal, and surface is incorporeal. The challenge is to see how these are separate but coupled.

The surface relations among incorporeals 'assures them a very special independence, not exactly with respect to fate, but rather with respect to necessity' (*LS* 169). What is the nature of this 'very special independence'? Since incorporeals are effects of corporeal causes, and since causes are subject to fate, incorporeals must follow fate, in some sense. After all, corporeal causes are causes *of* incorporeal effects. Key, here, is that fate does not hold the same sway for bodies and incorporeals, although they both respect fate.

The power of Stoic philosophy, for Deleuze, is that they are 'committing themselves to this line of thought: according to what criteria are events *copulata*, *confatalia* (or *inconfatalia*), *conjuncta*, or *disjuncta*' (*LS* 171).[57] We return to these terms in 'The Yolk A', but the relevant term for us now is *confatalia*, as this illuminates the meaning of incorporeal compatibility. Causes are completely subject to fate; effects are *co*-fated, fated *with* bodies. Effects occur according to fate but are relatively independent of fate. *Confatalia* refers to the interrelation of bodies and incorporeals, but not to the incorporeal effects in themselves. The order of effects in themselves is a question of compatibility, to which we will return in 'The Yolk A'. In short, bodies are fated and incorporeals are co-fated.

This system of incorporeal surface and physical depths is the basic structure of the Stoics' perverse materialism. Their commitment to materialism, immanence and dynamism is what struck Deleuze so forcefully when he encountered the Stoic system. 'If the Stoics are emblematic of Deleuzian thought,' Beaulieu notices, 'it is because they think immanence against the dominant "onto-theology"' of the Platonists and Aristotelians.[58] Boeri agrees that it is necessary to read the corporeal–incorporeal distinction through the whole Stoic system, as he sees this 'distinction as a whole in the different parts of the philosophical discourse (physics, logic, ethics), and not simply as a point belonging just to physics . . . on the Stoic view, we should seriously consider existents and nonexistent in all the fields of research, and that these must be understood as working together'.[59] Stoic metaphysics flattens out the heights of Platonic transcendence and pulls out the interiority of Aristotelian hylomorphism through the construction of an incorporeal surface. No longer is there an ascending movement from depths to height, from particulars to universals, from the darkness of the cave to the bright light of the sun. Instead, the Stoics construct a surface that allows continuous passage from corporeals to incorporeals and back again. 'The hierarchical subordination that characterized the world of Aristotle', writes Bréhier, 'is replaced by the coordination and confederation of all things' (*CAS* 150). The structure of coordination and confederation is the conjunction of surface and depths. Distributing the bottom-up verticality of the pre-Socratics, the top-down verticality of Platonism, and the heights-within of Aristotelianism on a single horizontal plane that twists through bodily depths inaugurates a new style of doing philosophy, one that entails a whole system of physics, logic and ethics.

Intensive and Extensive Faces

Let us now introduce a distinction, which runs throughout Deleuze's writings, in order to make more sense of the Stoic metaphysical system. The Stoic incorporeal surface has two faces: one is full of *extensities*, the other face is composed of *intensities*.

To distinguish between the extensive and the intensive, consider the difference between extensive and intensive measurements. Volume is a standard example of an extensive measurement. Picture a one-gallon bucket of water. If we evenly divide this volume into two buckets that are half the volume, we get two half-gallons of water. Dividing extensive measurements does not bring a real change in kind. A one-gallon bucket of water is not essentially different from a half-gallon or a quarter-gallon or an eighth-gallon bucket of water. We divide without changing *what* is divided. The difference between the measurements of volume is equal. 'Division can', writes Deleuze, 'take place and be continued without any change in the *nature* of what is being divided' (*DR* 237; emphasis added).

Dividing intensities, by contrast, is not like dividing extensities. Consider temperature, a common example of an intensive measurement. If we extensively divide a gallon of water at thirty degrees Celsius, the result is not two buckets at fifteen degrees Celsius but

The Yolk A: Stoic Metaphysics

two buckets of water still at the original thirty degrees. To intensively divide a temperature results in a different *kind* of thing. In a lecture at Vincennes, Deleuze says this 'amounts to saying that when I say "it's thirty degrees", the thirty degree heat is not the sum of three times ten degrees, it's at the level of extensive quantities that thirty is '10+10+10,' but thirty degrees is not three ten degree heats. In other words, the rules of addition and subtraction are not valid for intensive quantities.'[60]

Recall that an intensive measurement is an intensive scale of degrees or gradients, such as the degrees on a thermometer. If there is a significant change in intensity such that the change overwhelms the series of degrees along which a given intensive quantity is distributed, there is a corresponding change in extensity as well, which produces a difference in kind. Now think beyond the heating of a gallon bucket of water to ninety degrees Celsius, and instead imagine using a regular store-bought thermometer, to measure the temperature of the water in a nuclear reactor. The heat generated by a nuclear reaction overpowers a regular thermometer so much that scale breaks. As the temperature increases, there is a point at which there is a distinct *change in kind*, such that what is measured is no longer even a liquid measurable in gallons; it is transformed into a completely different kind of thing: nuclear power.

This distinction between the intensive and the extensive is often attributed to Deleuze's reading of Henri Bergson's distinction between qualitative (or continuous) and quantitative (or discrete) multiplicities.[61] What is less often noticed is that Deleuze and Guattari, in *What is Philosophy?*, connect Bergson back to the Stoics on just this point. Noticing that both the Stoics and Bergson construct two types of multiplicity, Deleuze and Guattari argue that Stoic incorporeals are akin to Bergson's intensive multiplicity, and Stoic corporeals are akin to Bergson's extensive multiplicity. Our suggestion is to think of the Stoic incorporeal surface as composed of both of these two sorts of multiplicities: one face is extensive; the other intensive. The side facing the physical states of affairs is the extensive side, the side facing away from bodily mixtures is the intensive. This is how, write Deleuze and Guattari, the 'Stoics carried to its highest point the fundamental distinction between, on the one hand, states of affairs or mixtures of bodies in which the event is actualized and, on the other, incorporeal events that rise like a vapor from states of affairs themselves' (*WP* 127).

By constructing a single surface with two faces – one extensive, one intensive – the Stoics pervert pre-Socratic depths, Platonic heights and Aristotelian interiority. There is no longer a vertical metaphysical ladder leading back to ideal forms or to an unmoved mover, because Stoicism expels transcendence from reality. This perverse reorientation results in a sort of metaphysical flattening, a setting of everything on an absolutely smooth surface that comprehends two modes of immanent reality: existence and subsistence. The Stoics substitute a veritable plane of immanence for the hierarchy of being; they pervert metaphysical verticality by constructing a strange surface cloaking bodies in depth. With Stoicism, every (some)thing happens as if on a fixed plane, where all things are constantly turning in an infinite cosmic cycle. Hence a tentative Stoic metaphysical proposition: *to extract the concept of reality from the hierarchy of being and project everything onto a fixed, immanent plane*. There is no longer any hierarchy because everything that happens is an immanent expression of single ontological surface cloaking physical depths.

Integration and Differentiation

We can be clearer about what it means to say that the incorporeal surface has two faces by characterising the respective operations of these two sides as integration and differentiation, which allows us to say more about the immanence of Stoicism. It is through the dual operations of integration and differentiation that the Stoics reject the world of transcendent ideas and affirm the materiality of the single cosmos. Let us now specify what we mean by differentiation and integration, and how they respectively organise the two sides of the surface.

While Bréhier strategically uses the term *intégrale* several times, Ildefonse stresses the importance of 'integral' in Stoicism (38, 45, 53). 'The Stoic world', she writes, 'governed [*régi*] by *logos*, is a world of an integral causality [*une causalité intégrale*]. This causality is an efficient, productive, and moving causality ... There is no exception to the causality that integrally governs the world.'[62]

We begin thinking about integration through the integral. According to Lewis and Short's *Latin Dictionary*, 'integral' is a polysemic word derived from *integer*, meaning 'undiminished, whole, entire, complete, perfect'. It is a combination of *in* ('not') plus *tangere* ('to touch, handle, or affect'), and thus literally means 'untouched'. 'Integral' is connected to 'integrate', which means 'rendering something whole or bringing together the parts of (something)'. As an

The Yolk A: Stoic Metaphysics

adjective, 'integral' means 'necessary to the completeness of the whole'. (Recall that an egg is an integrated whole.) Moral 'integrity', too, is related to 'integral', referring to 'completeness, soundness' of body or mind. In arithmetic, an 'integer' is a whole number because it can be expressed as a complete unit, without a fractional component (for example, 0, 25 and −339 are integers, but 6.79, 8½ and √2 are not). The set of all integers is symbolised as the Zahlen (the German word for 'numbers') sign: ℤ.

For calculus, an integral is the inverse of a derivative. A derivative is a representation of change, such as the slope of a curve or a physical rate of change.[63] More precisely, a derivative of y with respect to x represents the change in y over the change in x in so far as the distance between two points becomes infinitely small. A derivative is written as 'dy/dx', where dy represents the change in y and dx represents the change in x; dy/dx represents the *difference* in y divided by the *difference* in x, the ratio or relation of two differences. If derivation is the process of differentiating things into infinitely many, infinitely small differences and articulating how these relate to one another, integration is the process of adding or *integrating* those infinitely many, infinitely small differences. Together, integrals and derivatives form the two basic types of calculus, and their connection is the Fundamental Theorem of Calculus. Similar to how addition and subtraction are inverses of each other, the Fundamental Theorem says that an integral and a derivative are inverse functions of one another. The derivative of x^2 is $2x$; the integral of $2x$ is x^2, which is why an integral is sometimes called an 'antiderivative'.[64] As differentiation refers to the continuous approach towards an infinitesimal point on a curve (the method of exhaustion), integration refers to the summation of the area under that curve. This is why Leibniz introduced the integral sign – ∂ – a stylised 'S' meant to suggest the process of summing, from the Latin *summa*.

Together, integration and differentiation form a causal calculus that helps us understand the two operations of the two sides of the Stoic incorporeal surface. The side facing bodies is organised by integration, wherein the extensive measurements of bodies are continually integrated and reintegrating through causal mixtures and relations. Integration is one way that incorporeals contribute to the genesis of the cosmos, for example by expressing the spatial organisation of bodies in relation to each other and themselves through extensive measurements. Space acts as a part of the genetic conditions by means of which bodies exist. Bodies need space to exist;

without spatial organisation, bodies cannot be. In this sense, materiality requires the immateriality of space for its very existence in states of affairs. The key is that this surface, here seen from the perspective of space, cannot itself exist. If it were to exist, it would be a body, and thus merely defer the required condition. At the same time, it cannot 'be' nothing. So, its ontological status lies between existence and nothingness, or: subsistence. Space subsists as a way to consider the genetic condition through which individuated bodies organise into states of affairs. In considering space as that which organises extensively determined bodies, space is taken as extensive. Bodies are spatially integrated into particular regions of extensive space. In 'The Yolk A' we will argue that place is extensively considered space and void is intensively considered space. That is, place is space in so far as it is related to individuated bodies, and void is space in so far as it is related to unindividuated matter. Place and void, we argue, are the two sides of the single incorporeal surface. One side faces bodies arranged in states of affairs; the other side faces away from this arrangement and towards deranged matter. One side integrates space so that different spaces operate as places for bodies; the other side differentiates space so that it dissolves bodies into pure, blended materiality. Or, yet again, place joins bodies on a flat plane of extensities; void dissolves bodies into an infinite gradation of infinitely divisible materiality.

This same structure holds for the other two incorporeals: λεκτα and time. Each incorporeal is composed of the two faces of the Stoic surface. One side is extensive, faces arranged bodies, and is structured by integration; the other side is intensive, faces away from arranged bodies and towards deranged matter, and is structured by differentiation. 'The Yolk A' looks at how this occurs with space, 'The Shell' does this for λεκτα, and 'The Albumen C' does it for time. Before getting there, 'The Yolk A' thinks more carefully about the nature of incorporeals in Stoicism.

Conclusion

The prominent feature of Stoic physics is what we are calling *perverted materialism*. The structure of perverted materialism falls along the line of separation and combination that passes between the corporeal depths and the incorporeal surface. Through this depth–surface confederation the Stoics pervert their philosophical predecessors and thereby produce a new orientation for thinking and acting. More pre-

The Yolk A: Stoic Metaphysics

cisely, the Stoics take up the depths of the pre-Socratic materialists, pull down on the heights of Plato, and turn inside-out the interiority of Aristotle in order to construct a double-sided surface. The 'Stoics', Deleuze notices, 'establish themselves and wrap themselves up with the surface, the curtain, the carpet, and the mantle' (*LS* 133). They drape the material world in an incorporeal cloak that, in so far it does not add anything to the world but rather acts as a genetic condition for the being of bodies, collapses transcendence into immanence. 'There is nothing behind the curtain except unnamable mixtures, nothing above the carpet except the empty sky' (*LS* 133). There are two sides of one metaphysical surface: integrating extensities and differentiating intensities.

Stoicism thus forms a new image of the philosopher: a surface-dwelling animal. A Stoic philosopher is not a former slave freed of his cavernous chains but 'the animal that is on a level with the surface – a tick or louse' (*LS* 133). The symbol of philosophy is not, for the Stoics, 'the Platonic wing, or Empedocles' lead sandal, but the reversible cloak of Antisthenes and Diogenes' (*LS* 133). Stoicism initiates a new philosophical orientation that opposes pre-Socratic subversion, Platonic conversion and Aristotelian inversion. Deleuze suggests we 'call it "perversion," which at least befits the system of provocations of this new type of philosopher' (*LS* 133). Stoicism, in short, expresses a materialist 'perversion [that] implies an extraordinary art of surfaces' (*LS* 133).

This 'art of surfaces' is not a passive reading or surveying because, as Lapoujade says, it enacts the '*drawing of a plane*'.[65] 'Planes must be constructed,' Deleuze and Guattari write, 'just as concepts must be constructed' (*WP* 27). Under the pressure of their commitment to materialism, and unflinchingly facing the perverse ends to which those commitments lead, the Stoics thoroughly construct a metaphysical surface. Through Deleuze's encounter with Stoicism, he too feels the compulsion to think by plane-making. Consider all the planes in his work. In *What is Philosophy?*, there is a 'plane of immanence', a 'plane of composition', a 'planomen', the 'Cartesian plane', the 'Platonic plane' and more. In *A Thousand Plateaus*, there are 'the plane of consistency', 'the plane of organization', 'a plane of exteriority', 'a plane of expression and a plane of content', 'the plane of the Unconscious', 'Memories of a Plan(e) Maker' and many more. In *Cinema I*, Deleuze includes many of the same, adding 'the plane of matter', an 'acentered plane of pure movement', 'the plane of the movement-image' and others. Lapoujade generalises Deleuze's habit of thinking in planes: 'all his books establish one or several planes ... his thought proceeds by planes, by constructions or sections of planes'.[66] Contrary to grounding in volcanic depths below, heavenly heights above or substantial forms within, plane-making is how the Stoics produce a new philosophical operation. This new mode of philosophical thinking and action strikes Deleuze to the core of his own thought, such that all of his subsequent writings express resonances of this early encounter. Perhaps this is the most resounding effect of the Stoic theory of incorporeals.

Notes

1. Friedrich Nietzsche, *The Gay Science* (1882), trans. Josefine Nauckhoff, ed. Bernard Williams (Cambridge: Cambridge University Press, 2001), 8–9.
2. Seneca, 'Letter to Lucilius', 58.12–13. Admittedly, the language of 'above' or 'primary' is misleading. Our suggestion for getting around this is to place Seneca's comments in the context of inter-school dialogue, which forced various schools to take up each other's language even though that language might not be appropriate to the dogmas of particular schools.
3. Ibid. 58.15.
4. Alexander, *On Aristotle's Topics*, SVF 2.239. Panayiotis Tzamalikos, 'Origen and the Stoic View of Time', *Journal of the History of Ideas* 52.4 (October–December 1991): 535–61. David E. Hahm, *The Origins of Stoic Cosmology* (Columbus: Ohio State University Press, 1977).
5. Jacques Brunschwig, *Papers in Hellenistic Philosophy*, trans. Janet Lloyd (Cambridge: Cambridge University Press, 1994), 105; emphasis in the original.
6. We are using the term 'materialism' in order to place Stoicism in a long tradition of philosophical materialisms, stretching from the ancient atomists, through early moderns such as Thomas Hobbes and Margaret Cavendish, including the later Karl Marx, and up to contemporary new materialists and, especially, Deleuze. Other designations, however, could apply. Some use 'corporealism', and others, such as Julia Annas, use the term 'physicalism'. Julia Annas *Hellenistic Philosophy of Mind* (Berkeley and Los Angeles: University of California Press, 1992), 37–8.
7. Seneca, 'Letter to Lucilius', 58.14–15.
8. Seneca, 'Letter to Lucilius', 58.18. This move is significant, for it prepares the way for the affirmation of the reality only of individuals or singular things, and the denial of the reality of universals. Spinoza, an early modern Stoic and member of Deleuze's so-called 'minor tradition', makes this move in Book II of his *Ethics*.

The Yolk A: Stoic Metaphysics

9. Brunschwig, *Papers*, 92; emphasis in the original.
10. Ibid. 123.
11. Émile Bréhier, *La Théorie des incorporels dans l'ancien stoicism* (Paris: Vrin, 1928; 9th edn 1997).
12. Although we are comfortable with attributing the term 'materialism' to the Stoics, we should be careful to stress the perversity of this term. Jean-Baptiste Gourinat convincingly argues for the dangers of using this term lightly. Conceiving of 'the Stoic doctrine of matter' as a 'reinterpretation of the doctrine of matter or "receptacle" in Plato's *Timaeus* and of Aristotle's theory of matter' leads Gourinat to claim that 'the Stoic theory of matter does not appear as materialistic ... in the sense that things are not explained by the movements and combinations of passive matter.' Jean-Baptiste Gourinat, 'The Stoics on Matter and Prime Matter: "Corporealism" and the Imprint of Plato's *Timaeus*', in *God and Cosmos in Stoicism*, ed. Ricardo Salles (Oxford: Oxford University Press, 2009), 46–70, at 48.
13. Brunschwig, *Papers*, 118.
14. Plato, *Sophist*, 246b.
15. Ibid. 246a; emphasis added.
16. Ibid. 274b.
17. Ibid. 274b–c.
18. It is at this point, Brunschwig notes, that a very interesting ontological space appears, for the Giants now appear to be in a position where it seems just as conceivable either '(1) to limit the domain of existents be ejecting from it any realities they judge not to be bodies, or (2) to extend the domain of bodies by including within it realities that they judge not be non-existents' (Brunschwig, *Papers*, 121). The Giants are a perfectly balanced position, from which there is equal reason to either restrict existence by removing it from incorporeals that seem to be real or to expand corporeality by giving it to non-existent things that seem to be real. It is a question of expanding or contracting the domain of existence or expanding and contracting things the domain of bodies. Plato, however, does not pursue this dilemma further, and instead concludes that the Giants keep the two domains perfectly co-extensive.
19. Plato, *Sophist*, 247d–e, see also 248c; emphasis original.
20. Lucretius, *De Rerum Natura*, 1.440–6. David E. Hahm, *The Origins of Stoic Cosmology* (Columbus: Ohio State University Press, 1977), 11–12.
21. Brunschwig, *Papers*, 123.
22. While Long and Sedley note that 'it is essential to see that the capacity to act or be acted upon, though peculiar to bodes, is not advanced as a defining characteristic of body *per se*', this point does not do very much for the Stoics, and it does even less for Deleuze (*HP 45*).
23. Frédérique Ildefonse, *Les Stoïciens I* (Paris: Les Belles Lettres, 2000), 40.

24. Ibid. 39.
25. Cicero, *On the Nature of the Gods*, 2.24.
26. Ildefonse, *Les Stoïciens*, 37.
27. Cicero, *Academica*, 1.39.
28. While the Stoics boldly accept, though perverting, the *Sophist*'s objections, they find stronger challenges from the Sceptics (*HP* 27E). Responding to the sceptics' arguments will lead the Stoics to posit a different sort of causal efficacy, beyond bodily activity and passivity. As we will see, this is a reason for the Stoic formulation of the incorporeals as quasi-causal.
29. Jean-Baptiste Gourinat, 'Matter and Prime Matter', in *God and Cosmos in Stoicism*, ed. Ricardo Salles (Oxford: Oxford University Press, 2009), 49.
30. Plato, *Timaeus*, 48c.
31. Aristotle, *Physics*, 4.2, 209b11–17.
32. Jean-Jacques Lecercle, *Deleuze and Language* (New York: Palgrave Macmillan, 2002), 113.
33. The Stoics then divide body into four categories: 'the substrate, what is qualified, what is disposed, and what is relatively disposed' (*SVF* 2.369). The scholarly debates on these categorical divisions continue, and there does not seem to be any chance of a consensus in the near future. Since Deleuze does not engage this portion of Stoic physics in any detail, we leave it as something about which the critics can continue to fight among each other. For several important scholarly positions on this, see: Johnny Christensen, *An Essay on the Unity of Stoic Philosophy* (Scandinavian University Books, 1962), 15–16, 25; John Rist, 'Categories and Their Uses', in *Problems in Stoicism*, ed. A. A. Long (London: The Athlone Press, 1971), 38–57, at 40, 51, 53; Gerard Watson, *The Stoic Theory of Knowledge* (Belfast: Queen's University, 1966), 49; Pasquale Pasquino, 'Le statut ontologique des incorporels dans l'ancien Stoicisme', *Les Stoiciens et leur logique, Actes du Colloque de Chantilly, 18–22 séptembre 1976*, ed. J. Brunschwig (Paris: Vrin, 1978), 333–6, at 342; Jacques Brunschwig, 'Stoic Metaphysics', in *The Cambridge Companion to the Stoics*, ed. Brad Inwood (Cambridge: Cambridge University Press, 2003), 206–33; and *SS* 13–25.
34. Galen, *On Medical Method*, 10.155, 1–8.
35. J. M. Rist, *Stoic Philosophy* (Cambridge: Cambridge University Press, 1977), 274. Decades later, Long and Sedley also noticed this similarity among the Stoics, Meinong and Russell (*HP* 164), as does Victor Caston, 'Something and Nothing: The Stoics on Concepts and Universals', *Oxford Studies in Ancient Philosophy* 17 (1999): 145–213, at 152–4.
36. Alexius Meinong, *Über Möglichkeit und Wahrscheinlichkeit. Beiträge zur Gegenstandstheorie und Erkenntnistheorie* [On Possibility and

37. Galen, for example, called this existence/subsistence distinction a mere 'linguistic quibbling' (*tên micrologian ton onomatên*) (Galen, *On Medical Method*, SVF 2.322).
38. For example, Hahm uses 'substance' (Hahm, *The Origins of Stoic Cosmology*, 18). Tzamalikos uses 'potential reality' (Tzamalikos, 'Origen and the Stoic View of Time', 540). Goldschmidt uses 'existence placed in thought' (*SS* 341).
39. Andreas Greaser, 'The Stoic Theory of Meaning', in *The Stoics*, ed. John M. Rist (Berkeley and Los Angeles: University of California Press, 1978), 89.
40. Victor Caston, 'Something and Nothing: The Stoics on Concepts and Universals', *Oxford Studies in Ancient Philosophy* 17 (1999): 145–213, at 207n.126. Although incompatible with a Deleuzian reading, Caston's intrepretation cleverly aligns Stoicism with recent work in philosophy of mind.
41. Calcidius, *In Timaeus*, 298, p. 296, 11–16W., as found in Jean-Baptiste Gourinat, 'The Stoics on Matter and Prime Matter: "Corporealism" and the Imprint of Plato's *Timaeus*', in *God and Cosmos in Stoicism*, ed. Ricardo Salles (Oxford: Oxford University Press, 2009), 54.
42. Gilles Deleuze, *Essays Critical and Clinical* (1993), trans. Daniel W. Smith and Michael A. Greco (Minneapolis: University of Minnesota Press, 1997), 137.
43. For a classic reading, see Robert Todd's essay 'Monism and Immanence: The Foundations of Stoic Physics', in *The Stoics*, ed. John M. Rist (Berkeley and Los Angeles: University of California Press, 1978), 137–60.
44. As clear as it is that the Stoics considered bodies as that which is capable of affection, we should appreciate David Hahm's observation that this idea is not explicitly stated in our sources as a theoretical definition. Instead, it is presupposed in several arguments concerning essential features of corporeality. See Hahm, *The Origins of Stoic Cosmology*, 3. Also see Cicero, *Academica*, 1.39; Sextus Empiricus, *Adversus Mathematicos*, 8.263; DL 7.5; and Seneca, *Letters*, 106, 207.
45. Later, Plotinus attacks Stoic materialism by claiming that activity (*energeia*) or active principles must be incorporeal, for matter is essentially and completely passive. Plotinus, *Ennead*, 2.9, 1 and *Ennead*, 6.1, 26, 11–17.
46. Marcelo D. Boeri, 'The Stoics on Bodies and Incorporeals', *The Review of Metaphysics* 54.4 (2001): 723–52, at 740.
47. Sextus Empiricus, *Against the Logicians*, II, 263.
48. Ildefonse, *Les Stoïciens*, 48.

49. As we will see in our consideration of Stoic logic and philosophy of language in Part II: Logic, *becoming* is tied to *infinitive* verbs, thus: 'infinitive-becomings'. Gilles Deleuze and Claire Parnet, *Dialogues* (1977), trans. Hugh Tomlinson and Barbara Habberjam (New York: Columbia University Press, 1977), 64.
50. Deleuze, *The Fold: Leibniz and the Baroque* (1988), trans. Tom Conley (Minneapolis: University of Minnesota Press, 1993), 53.
51. Ibid. 53.
52. Michael Frede misses this perversity when he says that 'the so-called pneuma ... is the Stoic analogue of an Aristotelian form' (Micahel Frede, 'The Original Notion of Cause', in *Essays in Ancient Philosophy* (Minneapolis: University of Minnesota Press, 1987), 125–51, at 145). Frede is missing the enormous change involved in giving the causal powers of Aristotelian substantial forms (beings) to bodies and the transformation of forms into incorporeal into non-causal becomings. This is more than a simple analogue: it is an ontological perversion, in the sense of 'turning inside-out'.
53. Gilles Deleuze, *Negotiations*, trans. Martin Joughin (New York: Columbia University Press, 1995), 31.
54. Gilles Deleuze, 'Preface' to Jean-Clet Martin, *Variations: La Philosophie de Gilles Deleuze* (Paris: Payot, 1993), 7.
55. Deleuze and Parnet, *Dialogues*, 63.
56. Bennett also notices this: 'fate, for the Stoics, seems like an affair of bodies or causes only, not events or effects.' Michael James Bennett, 'Cicero's *De Fato* in Deleuze's Logic of Sense', *Deleuze Studies* 9.1 (2015): 25–58, at 34.
57. In translation: 'complex, co-fated (or not-co-fated), conjoined, or disjoined'. We admit that including *conjuncta* and *disjuncta* is bit strange, given that these are terms that Deleuze rightly associates with the Epicureans.
58. Beaulieu, 'Deleuze et les Stoïciens', 48.
59. Boeri, 'The Stoics on Bodies and Incorporeals', 751
60. Available at https://www.webdeleuze.com/textes/67 (last accessed 8 February 2019).
61. The theory of two kinds of 'multiplicity' is found in Henri Bergson's *Time and Free Will*, trans. F. L. Pogson (New York: Macmillan, 1910).
62. Ildefonse, *Les Stoïciens*, 47.
63. '[T]he word *differentiation*, itself, is nothing but the mathematical one, which used to refer to the pre-Cantorian mathematical framing, to the operation of writing the infinitesimal variation of some variable, expressed with respect to some others (let us say that if $y=x2+y2$, we differentiate by writing $dy=dx+3y2dy$.' Jean-Michel Salankis, 'Mathematics, Metaphysics, and Philosophy', in Simon Duffy and

Paul Patton (eds), *Virtual Mathematics: The Logic of Difference* (Manchester: Clinamen Press, 2006), 52.
64. Technically, the integral (or the "indefinite integral") is x^2+C, where C is some undecided constant. This is because for any constant C, x^2+C derives to $2x$ because C always derives to zero. People sometimes use this to distinguish integrals from antiderivatives proper (the integral would not include C, while the antiderivative would). Thus to be more exact, x^2 should be x^2+C. I place this technicality in the footnotes in order to keep the cleaner symmetry in the body of the text.
65. Lapoujade, *Aberrant Movements*, 50.
66. Ibid. 51.

2

The Yolk B: Incorporeals

> As long as truths do not cut into our flesh with
> knives, we retain a secret contempt for them.
> Friedrich Nietzsche, *Daybreak*, 460

Introduction

To appreciate the philosophical innovations of Stoic theory – including physics, logic, and ethics – we must better understand their challenging theory of incorporeals. The theory is so wild that many hesitate from fully engaging with its strangeness and instead reach for tamer categories in which such wilds can be domesticated.[1] Marcelo Boeri, for example, avoids this strangeness by categorising incorporeality as 'a *necessary condition* for the existence of bodies', elsewhere calling it the 'indispensable conditions that make up the reality of the corporeal'.[2] While this account grasps the crucial role that incorporeals play in the constitution of the corporeal world, rendering it merely a necessary condition misses the power and perversity of Stoic concepts. To be fair, Boeri correctly characterises the relationship between bodies and incorporeals as one of 'reciprocal dependence' or as 'complementary terms', thereby affirming the need for incorporeality in a materialist ontology.[3] Yet incorporeals are not mere by-products of corporeal causation: they have a strange sort of sense of causal efficacy, which Deleuze calls 'quasi-causality'.

To understand what 'quasi-causality' means, we need to be precise about the Stoics' reconceptualisation of causation. As we will see, this involves severing the connection between causes and effects so that causes are strictly corporeal and effects strictly incorporeal. After this separation is articulated, we look to Clement of Alexandria so as to discover the location and meaning of the quasi-cause. The quasi-cause possesses a wild genetic force that we call 'static genesis', which is a paradoxical order of generation that is impassive and inactive yet efficacious. We conclude 'The Yolk B' by articulating the logic of the incorporeal surface and its power of static genesis through

The Yolk B: Incorporeals

a twist on the logic of Kant's Table of Judgements. With this twist we find a transcendental logic of incorporeality that expresses the distinct organisation of the two-sides – extensive and intensive – of the incorporeal surface. 'The Yolk B' thus determines another feature of the perverse materialism that we find in Deleuze's Stoicism. Let us begin by thinking about how the Stoics' account of causation differs from other ancient etiologies.

Corporeal Causes and Incorporeal Effects

The Stoic theory of incorporeals includes an account of causation that greatly differs from the most prominent causal theories in antiquity. 'In the *Phaedo*, Socrates posits several kinds of cause. Aristotle, following this lead, distinguishes four: material, moving, formal, and final causes.'[4] Contrary to the Platonic–Aristotelian tradition, Seneca writes, the 'Stoics believe in only one cause, that which does something [*facit*].'[5] While some thinkers included non-active causes in their etiological theories – such as Peripatetic final causes or Academic ideas – the Stoics insist that causes are active.

Terminologically, the Stoics speak of 'cause' (αἰτία) in two ways: a general sense and a specific sense. When Chrysippus claims that a cause is 'that because of which', he articulates a sense general enough to cover anything that Plato and others considered causal (*HP* 55A). Clement of Alexandria articulates a narrower, more specific sense that refers to productive or active things: 'that which is the cause and is productive and that *because of which* are the same. Now, if something is a cause and is productive, it is certainly also a *because of which*. But if something is a *because of which*, it does not by any means follow that it is also the cause.'[6] The first sense includes Platonic causes because it allows for non-productive and non-active causes; these are causal simply by their presence. The second sense, however, refers strictly to productive causes, causes that actively produce an effect.[7] Mere presence is inefficacious; things must *do* something to be considered causal. As we argued in the previous chapter, once causes are rendered active, they become corporeal. Stoic causes are bodies that *do* something.

If causes are active bodies, what are these bodies causes *of*. Aristotelians see causes as causes of particular material entities. The Stoics are more ambitious: active corporeal causes produce effects that are not corporeal. *Bodies cause incorporeal effects*. How does this happen? How does a body produce effects that are not bodily?

In Deleuze's metaphor, incorporeal effects 'are *shadows* that play on the surface of bodies, always between two bodies. The shadow is always on the edge.'[8] Bodies cast shadows *on* – not *from* – other bodies. If knowledge concerns the effects that a thing produces, as we will later argue, then we know a body by the shadows cast on other bodies. In short, we know a body due to the effects that are attributed to it. 'The incorporeal', according to Ildefonse, 'lets us accounting for change without attaining the permanence of bodies, and without coming to the position of requiring essences: bodies are defined by a proper quality which absolutely singularize them and that will not stop, if not with the body itself.'[9] In another perversion of Platonism: in contrast to the shadows of Plato's Allegory of the Cave – insubstantial reflections cast by the puppets moved behind the prisoners' heads – Stoic shadows are as real as the bodies casting them.

To make this less metaphorical, we turn to the case of a scalpel cutting flesh, an example of Stoic theory of incorporeality described by Sextus Empiricus: 'the Stoics say that every cause is a body that functions as cause to a body of something incorporeal – for example, the scalpel (a body) as cause to flesh (a body) of the incorporeal predicate "being cut"'.[10] Clement's *Miscellanies* contains a similar example: 'becoming, and being cut – that of which the cause is a cause – since they are activities, are incorporeal' (*HP* 55C). Rather than a scalpel causing a cut to appear in the flesh of an arm, the scalpel is cause of the flesh 'being cut'. Again, Clement: 'causes are causes of predicates, or, as some say, of sayables [λεκτά] – for Cleanthes and Archedemus call predicates "sayables." Or ... some are causes of predicates, for example "is cut," whose [grammatical] case is "being cut"' (*HP* 55C). It is important to see that 'being cut' is *not* another body. The scalpel is a body and the flesh is too, but 'being cut' is *not* corporeal. Cleanthes and others see this as a distinct *type* of incorporeal: λεκτόν. Deleuze calls 'being cut' and other such things as 'logical or dialectical attributes' as opposed to 'physical quantities and properties' (*LS* 5).

Deleuze finds this scalpel imagery in Bréhier, who took it from Sextus.[11] Deleuze quotes Bréhier extensively, giving the longest quotation in *Logic of Sense*, and calling it a 'fine reconstruction of Stoic thought' (*LS* 5). Here is the whole passage from Bréhier, including parts that Deleuze left out:

The Yolk B: Incorporeals

when the scalpel cuts through the flesh, the first body produces upon the second not a new property but a new attribute, that of 'being cut.' The attribute, properly speaking, does not designate any real quality; white and black, for example, are not attributes, nor is any epithet in general. The attribute is always, to the contrary, expressed by a verb, which is to say that it is not a being, but a *manner of being* ... This manner of being somehow finds itself at the limit, at the surface of being, the nature of which it is not able to change: it is right to say it is neither active nor passive, because the passivity presupposes a corporeal nature that undergoes an action. It is purely and simply a result, an effect that is not classed among beings. The results of the action of beings, which the Stoics had been perhaps the first to comment on in this form, is what we call today facts or events: a bastard concept that is neither that of a being, nor one of properties, but that which is said or affirmed of being. It is the singular character of this fact that the Stoics put into the light by saying that it was incorporeal; it excluded incorporeals thus from all real beings in admitting them in a certain measure in the mind. 'All bodies thus become cause for another body (where it acts on it) of something incorporeal.' The importance of this idea for them makes us see them by the concern that they had in expressing always in language, the effect by a verb ... The incorporeal fact is, in some way, at the *limit of the action* of bodies ... The act of cutting adds nothing to the nature and to the essence of the scalpel ... [the Stoics] are as far away as possible from a conception as that of Hume and Stuart Mill, who reduced the universe to facts or events ... [*The Stoics distinguish*] *radically two planes of being, something that no one had done before them*: on the one hand, the deep and real being, the force; on the other hand, the plane of facts, which frolic on the surface of being, and which constitute a multiplicity without links and within ends of incorporeal beings. (*TI* 11–13; emphasis added)

Strictly speaking, Bréhier is not incorrect in saying that the Stoics lay out 'two planes of being'. It is better to say that there is a one two-sided plane and the depths that the plane cloaks. He does, after all, characterise the first plane as 'deep and real'. In depth, bodies interact and intermix; beings dwell down deep.

Out of this profound interaction, writes Deleuze, incorporeal effects emerge to 'play only on the surface, like a mist over the prairie' or 'even less than a mist, since a mist is after all a body' (*LS* 50). When the scalpel cuts, nothing corporeal is added to the nature and the essence of the flesh. A new body (uncut flesh) does not replace another body (cut flesh). It is the same flesh, with the only difference being a new attribute: that of being cut. It is not a new being but a new manner or a way of being. By cutting the flesh, something is expressed, although the expression is not the action. Instead, the expression is, as Bréhier writes, at the *limit of the action*, articulating the way in which the action turns. The attribute is not the scalpel's act of cutting, but the sense of the cut. It is best to think of the attribute by the infinite verb: 'to cut', *couper*, *secāre*, τέμνειν. 'The sky is dark', 'the tree is green', 'the scalpel cuts the flesh' – these are qualitative states of affairs. But what is meant by 'to darken', 'to become green', 'to cut' and 'to be cut' no longer refers to bodies and their states of affairs but instead to incorporeal effects playing along the surface. 'To cut' is an infinitive verb that, when attributed to bodes, is conjugated in various ways: 'being cut', 'having been cut', 'will cut' and so on.

The Stoics, Bréhier continues, 'consider the nature of the predicate completely differently' because, in their judgements about states of affairs, they follow the Megarians' elimination of the copula 'is' (*TI* 20). For example, rather than saying 'the tree *is* green', they say 'the tree *greens*'. They remove the 'is' to emphasise how a certain aspect of a body is expressed. This aspect expresses the corporeal interactivity, that is, when a body acts or is acted upon. The key is that this *aspect of a being* is not itself a being, but instead only the effect of bodily action. This aspect thus does not signify an object or an object relation but rather the 'sense of a verb', which is why the Stoics speak of incorporeal attributes as 'events' or 'facts'. An attribute does not express 'a property like "a body *is* hot," but an event like "a body *heats*"' (*TI* 20–1; emphasis added).

While we will say more about the Stoic theory of predication in Part II, let us review what we have done in this section. Contrary to the Platonic and Aristotelian tradition, which include non-active causes in their etiological theories, the Stoics insist that causes are only active. As we saw in the previous chapter, activity entails corporeality. The question is: what are the effects of corporeal causes? To see this, we turned to the case of a scalpel cutting flesh. Rather than causing a cut to appear in the flesh of an arm, the scalpel is cause of the flesh being cut. Being cut is not another bother but an incorporeal attributed to bodies. Comparing incorporeal effects to shadows and mist, Deleuze sees stoic effects as the expression of bodily action. The attribute is the sense of the action. The perversion here is that attribute is not a predicate. To see how, we need to consider how the Stoics theory of incorporeals connects to their theory of causation.

The Yolk B: Incorporeals

Splitting the Causal Relation

Distinguishing the physical depths and its incorporeal surface reveals, as Deleuze puts it, 'an entirely new cleavage in the causal relation' (*LS* 6). The Stoics' perverse materialism 'begins by splitting the causal relation, instead of distinguishing types of causality as Aristotle had done and Kant would do' (*LS* 6). They sever the relation between 'cause' and 'effect' such that they no longer stand in the common order of causal necessity. Causes turn in on themselves, while effects form a self-enclosed series of effects: causes refer to causes and effects to effects. Notice the prepositional specificity: 'Causes are not *of* each other, but are causes *to* each other' (HP 55D). Ildefonse considers it a '[s]trange scenography of the wound', where a 'body is *for* another body the cause *of* an incorporeal effect'.[12]

Causes and effects are separated along a causal border along which they move in divergent motion. They are divergent because there is no one-to-one correspondence between causes and effects, which means that the relation between them does not follow an order of resemblance. 'The autonomy of the effect is thus defined initially by its difference from the cause' (*LS* 95). This autonomy can be maintained only if effects remain effects, if they do not become causes for other effects. 'One of the boldest moments of the Stoic thought', Deleuze emphasises, 'involves the splitting [*rupture*] of the causal relation' (*LS* 169). Deleuze thinks that this splitting connects the Stoics to Spinoza, the great modern inheritor of this bold Stoic moment. 'Like the Stoics', writes Deleuze, 'Spinoza breaks causality into two distinct chains: effects between themselves, on the condition that one in turn grasps causes between themselves.'[13]

Notice how splitting the causal relation lines up with the split between bodies and incorporeals: the Stoics restrict causes to bodies and effects to incorporeals. This is perhaps the fundamental principal of causation in Stoic physics: 'Nothing incorporeal interacts with a body, and no body with an incorporeal, but one body interacts with another body' (*HP* 45C). Effects express corporeal causes but are, at the same time, irreducible to the causal network.

The Stoic's splitting of the causal relation – locating causes on one side, effects on the other – perverts their predecessors' etiologies. While Plato and Aristotle made metaphysical principles and causes incorporeal, the Stoics restricted causation completely to bodies. The reason is that if causes are active and productive, and only bodies are active and productive, then bodies must be causes, not incorporeals.

On the other side, incorporeals, for the Stoics, are no longer causes and principles. Incorporeals do not subsist on a superior or inferior plane of being because bodies and incorporeals are equally real. They just express reality in different ways: bodies exist, incorporeals subsist. Splitting bodies/causes from incorporeals/effects, according to Deleuze, provokes an *'upheaval in philosophy'* (*LS* 6; emphasis added). None of their predecessors, and few since, have split the causal relation. There must be many questions.

How, for example, can causes and effects be both separate yet still be *causally* related? How can causes produce effects if they form completely different orders of nature – corporeal causes in depth and incorporeal effects on the surface? After all, they are still considered causes and effects, as Deleuze admits: 'events-effects maintain a relation of causality with their physical causes' (*LS* 170).

Here is a difference from the modern notion of causation: a cause, for the Stoics, is not an event. This is their reasoning: *since causes are only corporeal, and events are incorporeal, causes cannot be events.* Further, causes are active, as it is their action that produces effects. Since only bodies can be active (or passive), events cannot be causes. This leads Michael Frede to ask: 'How would an event go about causing something?'[14] As we will see below, the answer is to consider events or effects not causal but quasi-causal.

Recall a line from one of Deleuze's best short works, 'Spinoza and the Three "Ethics"': 'We must also understand "effect" optically and not merely causally.'[15] To understand effects 'optically' is to consider relations among effects themselves, a difficult task indeed.[16] Fortunately, Deleuze shows us how to take on this task: considering effects optically reveals 'extrinsic relations of silent compatibility or incompatibility' among effects themselves (*LS* 170).[17] Independently of corporeal causal relations, incorporeal effects relate in terms of whether or not effects are *compatible* or *incompatible* with each other.

It is important here to notice that compatibility and incompatibility different from logical identity and contradiction. While corporeal causality is captured by logical compatibility and effects are non-causal (because incorporeal), effects relate through 'alogical compatibilities or incompatibilities' (*LS* 171). To understand what it is that makes effects compatible or incompatible in this alogical and non-causal sense, Deleuze turns to the rather awkward term: 'quasi-cause' (*LS* 6). While it might sound more evasive than explanatory, the term 'quasi-cause' reveals something essential about the Stoics' perverse materialism: it opens up space for the development of a

The Yolk B: Incorporeals

kind of immanent and material causality and 'renders ideal causality completely impossible' (*TI* 10).

Stepping back again to survey our path so far, we are in the middle of a discussion of Stoic physics and metaphysics, which Deleuze characterises as a perverse materialism. It is perverse in comparison to other ancient accounts, especially the pre-Socratics', Plato's, and Aristotle's. In this chapter we have looked at how this perversity plays out in the Stoics' theory of causation and their theory of incorporeals. The Stoics, according to Deleuze, provoke a great upheaval in philosophy by splitting the causal from the causal relation such that, on one side, there are corporeal causes, and on the other side, there are incorporeal effects. These form two distinct series, yet they are interconnected as causes and effects. To elucidate this perverse relation, we turn now to one of the strangest concepts in Stoicism and Deleuze: *quasi-causality*. This strangeness of quasi-causality will require us to think more carefully about what counts as causal, and we will unpack Deleuze's use of Kant's Table of Judgements to do this. By the end of this chapter we will have a thorough enough understanding of Stoic causation and incorporeality to investigate, in the next chapter, the first of the three incorporeals: space. For now, we examine the quasi-cause.

Clement of Alexandria and the Quasi-Cause

The quasi-cause only appears in *Logique du sens*, *L'anti-Œdipe* and once in *Dialogues I* and *II*. Few scholars ever mention it, and almost no one connects the Stoics to the 'quasi-cause', as distinct concept.[18]

In Deleuze studies, there is no consensus on how to understand it. James Williams, for example, considers quasi-causality to be 'one of the rare heavy and clumsy concepts of Deleuze's work' which was the result of what 'was always a potential pitfall in Deleuze's return to the Stoics'.[19] Williams is no fan of the quasi-cause or the Stoics. Similarly, Jon Roffe does 'not think that the set of extant claims that Deleuze makes about the quasi-cause are conceptually unified or unifiable ... and so I do not think that they are significant enough to ground a fully-fledged doctrine on their own terms'.[20] Against Williams and Roffe, we do not suppose that Deleuze's return to Stoicism is destined to fail, and we do not think that there are insufficient grounds to create a robust concept of a quasi-cause.[21] While there might not be sufficient grounds within Deleuze's œuvre, we find plenty of material if we dumpster dive in the bins of antiquity.

The concept traces back to the writings of Clement of Alexandria (150–215 CE). Who was Clement? He was born in Athens, later converted to Christianity, and eventually taught at the Catechetical School of Alexandria. Raised by a so-called pagan family, Clement was shaped by early classical Greek writings (especially Plato), Hellenistic philosophy (especially the Stoics), Jewish esotericism and Gnosticism.[22] One of his signature claims was that Greek philosophy originated from non-Greek sources. Plato, Pythagoras and others, he argued, were educated and inspired by Egyptian thinkers.[23]

Full versions of Clement's writings still exist, collectively called the 'trilogy'. The trilogy consists of the *Protrepticus* (*Exhortation*), the *Peaedagogus* (*Tutor*) and the *Stromata* (*Miscellanies* or *Patchwork*).[24] The quasi-cause appears in the last of these: the *Stromata* or *Stromaeis*. As its title suggests, it is less organised and less systematic than the more intellectual *Protrepticus* and the more practical *Peaedagogus*. While Clement had intended to write just one book, the *Miscellanies* soon grew into seven, although even these seven were unable to cover all the topics he had originally intended to address. Given so many topics, scholars such as Eusebius of Caesarea argued that there is an even more fragmentary set of writings, which form an eighth book, and Photios I of Constantinople reportedly found, in the ninth century, extra writings attached to the manuscripts, which he added to the seven canonical books.[25] By the eleventh century, these fragments and excerpts had become an independent eighth book, possibly intended for an exclusive audience.[26] The concept of the quasi-cause thus appears in the last part of a fragmentary and contested section within an unsystematic, final book of a vast trilogy.

Cause (αἰτία) is the theme of the ninth section of Book 8 of the *Miscellanies*. Here Clement reports and evaluates several ancient causal theories, most of which are not identified by name.[27] Still, Clement clearly sees the quasi-cause as a Stoic invention. We translate the relevant passage into English like this:

> (1) they [the Stoics] say that body is a cause properly speaking, but the incorporeal, improperly speaking [καταχρηστικῶς], is also a sort of quasi-cause [αἰτιώδης].[28]

When he introduces the quasi-cause in *Logic of Sense*, Deleuze cites this passage.[29] Unfortunately, as Michael Bennett notices, the precise sense of quasi-causality is lost in both English and French translations.[30] Here is the French:

The Yolk B: Incorporeals

(2) Les Stoïciens dissent que le corps est cause au sens propre, mais l'incorporel, d'une façon métaphorique et comme à la manière d'une cause.

In the French translation of αἰτιώδης, 'quasi-cause' is connected to speaking 'in a metaphorical way [*d'une façon métaphorique*]', suggesting that incorporeals are metaphorically, not literally, causal. This nicely captures the sense of the Latin prefix *quasi-*, meaning 'as if, just as, as it were'. Constantin Boundas's English translation of *Logic of Sense* obscures the quasi-cause even more:

(3) The Stoics say that the body is a cause in the literal sense but the incorporeal, in a metaphysical fashion, poses in the manner of a cause.

In English, an incorporeal is causal because it 'poses in the manner' of a cause.[31] Working backwards through these translations, we see three senses of the quasi-cause: (3) in the English sense of the *manner* of a cause, (2) in the French sense of a *metaphorical* cause, and (1) in the original Greek sense of an 'as-it-were cause'.

Finally, here is the sentence from *Logic of Sense* that cites the elusive Clement passage: 'The Stoics clearly saw that the [incorporeal] event is subject to a double causality, referring on the one hand to mixtures of bodies which are its cause and, on the other, to other events which are its quasi-cause' (*LS* 94). With all this on the table, let us muck around in the Greek to understand the various senses of 'quasi-cause'.

With the help of the *LSJ*, let us go right to the words: οἱ δὲ τὸ μὲν σῶμα κυρίως αἴτιόν φασι. Κυρίως (*kuriôs*), which we translate as 'properly' or 'precisely', originally comes from κυρίως, the word for 'lord' or 'master', thus suggesting a sense of 'dominant' or 'authoritative'. It is not uncommon to see κυρίως used when concerning the 'correct' or 'authoritative' meaning of a term. The real question is: whence the authority? This is especially true when relying on the standard Aristotelian account of causality.[32]

Κυρίως ('properly') is usually opposed to καταχρηστικῶς (*katakhrêstikôs*): 'in a manner of speaking'. But the *LSJ* sees a stronger sense of καταχρηστικῶς: 'by a misuse of language, misapplied words and phrases'. Breaking down κατα-χρηστικῶς into its component parts, the prefix κατα- suggests 'against' and χρηστικος means the 'capacity to use a thing, its usefulness'. If κυρίως means '*according to* the authoritative manner (of speaking or doing something)', then καταχρηστικῶς means '*counter to* the authoritative manner (of speaking or using)'. In sum, only bodies are *properly* called causes because they accord with the authoritative etiology. When we speak of incorporeals as causes, we speak 'in a manner' that goes against that authoritative etiology; it is to speak improperly. We might call this improper speaking *perverse*.

To make sure this perversity is as precise as possible, let us differentiate 'quasi' from a seemingly similar ancient Greek term: *'pseudos'* (ψευδής). *'Pseudos'*, according to Barbara Cassin, 'names, from its origin, and indissolubly, the "false" and the "lie" – the "falsehood," therefore, of one who deceives and/or deceives himself. It is the ethico-logical concept par excellence.'[33] Linking *pseudos* to the figure of the sophist, Cassin points to Plato's characterisation of the sophist as 'an imitation, a feral counterfeit philosopher, because the sophist chooses the domain of the false, the semblance, the phenomenon, opinion – in a word, all that is *not*'.[34] *Pseudos* is a kind of duplicity – a deliberate untruth. A 'pseudo-cause' would be one that claims to be a cause but is not. It is, in every way, not a cause, even though we are sometimes deceived into thinking it is causal. It is a false semblance, a dissemblance. A quasi-cause, by contrast, is causal, but in a different sense. To restrict pure causality to bodies alone, we stipulate a distinction that aligns with other parts of Deleuze's Stoicism: *quasi-causality is genetic rather than properly causal*. Thus, although it is tempting to think that *quasi*-cause is similar to *pseudo*-cause, they are not synonymous.

Let us return to the Greek for 'quasi-cause'. The *LSJ* identifies αἰτιώδης (*aitiôdês*) as the source of 'quasi-causal'. It appears in several post-Stoic texts, including Plotinus and Simplicius, thus apparently having no pre-Stoic provenance.[35] The plausibility that the Stoics invented αἰτιώδης corroborates Deleuze's claim that the Stoics' splitting of the causal relation indeed causes an upheaval in philosophy. Although αἰτιώδης can mean just 'causal', the *LSJ* itself translates it as 'quasi-causal' or 'resembling a cause' .

Breaking it down further, the suffix -ώδης (-*ôdēs*) comes from -ὄζω (-*ozô*), meaning 'I smell', evoking the sense of 'smelling of', as well as 'full of' or 'like'.[36] In short, αἰτιώδης is called a cause because *it smells like a cause*. Αἰτιώδης exudes the full quality of a cause; it is very much like a cause, it reeks of causality, but it is not one, if we are speaking properly. While a pseudo-cause seems like a cause but is not, a quasi-cause emanates causality because it is expresses genetic force. We simply need a special sense to sniff out the distinct causality it exudes, a Stoic sense of smell. If we look at it from the perspective of the dominant thinking about causes, we will smell

The Yolk B: Incorporeals

nothing etiological about it. But if we blur our vision just a bit, if we let the scent of causality waft into our nostrils, we begin to detect a strange, perhaps perverse, generative power. Although little remains of the Stoics' thinking on quasi-causality, Deleuze has a term for this perversity: *static genesis*.

Static Genesis

It is unsurprising that Deleuze's discussion of quasi-cause and Stoicism in *The Logic of Sense* appears amid a discussion of Lewis Carroll's exploitation of logical and linguistic paradoxes. A quasi-cause is paradoxical: it is a non-causal cause.[37] As an incorporeal, it is an effect yet still carries genetic determinativeness. Deleuze calls it 'static genesis' or 'a genesis without dynamism' (*LS* 144; *DR* 183).

There are two characteristics of static genesis: (1) 'impassibility' or 'indifference' and (2) 'productivity' or 'efficacy' (*LS* 144). Impassibility refers to its difference in nature from bodies and their states of affairs. Deleuze also uses other terms: 'impenetrability, sterility, or inefficacy, which is neither active nor passive ... [and] neutrality' (*LS* 95). Unfortunately, to explain what he means by 'impassibility', he confusingly refers to 'several different perspectives', perspectives that he does not explicitly identify. Fortunately, with just a little scratching we see that these 'several different perspectives' correspond to the four logical classes from Kant's Table of Judgements in his *Critiques*: (1) quality, (2) quantity, (3) relation and (4) modality.[38]

1. In its *qualitative aspect*, Deleuze writes, incorporeals are 'entirely independent of both affirmation and negation' (*LS* 101). In Kant's Table, there are three possible qualities for judgement: 'affirmative, negative, infinite'. Describing the impassibility of incorporeals, Deleuze says, they express neither affirmation nor negation. Note that he leaves out 'infinite' without explanation. This will be important later.
2. In its *quantitative aspect*, an incorporeal 'is neither particular nor general, neither universal nor personal' (*LS* 101). In Kant's Table, judgements are quantified as 'universal, particular, and singular'. Note that Deleuze still does not mention the third – 'singular' – because this too will be important later.
3. In its *relational aspect*, incorporeals should not be confused with at least the first two possible relations listed on Kant's Table: the

categorical and hypothetical. Yet again, Deleuze leaves out the third – 'disjunction' – which we should remember for later.
4. In its *modal aspect*, writes Deleuze, 'it is neither assertoric nor apodeictic' (*LS* 101). According to Kant's Table, possible modalities are assertoric, apodictic, and problematic.' While he denies the first two forms of judgment –assertoric and apodeictic – Deleuze again does not mention the third in the Table – 'problematic' – which we should again note.[39]

In sum, Deleuze characterizes the impassibility of incorporeals as indifferent to (1) qualitative determinations of both yes and no, to (2) quantitative determinations of 'both one and all', to (3) relation determinations of both 'categories and conditionals', and to (4) modal determinations of 'actual and necessary'. We might begin to wonder why Deleuze only denies two, not all three, terms in each of the four logical classes in Kant's Table. What about the tacit third term? Begging patience, we here delay answering this question to the end of the chapter. For now, we simply note that the Kantian thirds – infinite, singular, disjunctive and problematic – are markers of static genesis.

Now that we have a sketch of the Kantian logic of the impassivity of static genesis, let us think about its productivity. As we argued, the topology of the Stoic incorporeal surface is composed of an extensive face and an intensive face, both of which correspond to an ontological operation: integration of extensities and differentiation of intensities. These two operations reveal the productivity of static genesis. Incorporeal static genesis is productive in so far as it expresses indirect causal efficacy, rather than the direct causal power of bodies. It is indirect because it moves in two opposite directions at once.

In one direction, static genesis moves *from* corporeal cause *to* incorporeal effect. This is the sense in which we have been talking about incorporeals as effects of corporeal causes. We can call this the direction of *differentiation*, wherein 'having an effect' is tantamount to making a difference. This is the intensive face of what Deleuze calls the metaphysical surface, the side facing away from bodies. It is intensive because it operates by infinitely flattening, that is, by continuously diverging and differentiating along the smooth surface. In the other direction, the side facing bodies, there is a corresponding movement wherein incorporeals are incarnated or contribute to the actualisation of states of affairs. We call this the extensive face of the

The Yolk B: Incorporeals

surface because, as it runs along the surface of bodies, it converges on bodies. It is *integration*, wherein incorporeals non-causally contribute to the generation of corporeal organisation. As we said in 'The Yolk A', integration means synthesising incorporeal effects in the production of corporeal states of affairs. In sum, integration is the operation of the extensive face of the incorporeal surface, and differentiation is the operation of the intensive face of the incorporeal surface. Taken together, the two inverse and inseparable operations explain the productivity of quasi-causality. Static genesis is another name for this double operation.

If this recondite logic is unclear, let think of it is through Deleuze's concept of *expression*, which he repeatedly uses when talking about quasi-causality in Stoicism. The difference is that, between incorporeals and corporeals, there is 'no longer a relation of causality but rather, once again and this time exclusively, a relation of expression' (LS 170). Here is a key claim: *incorporeals are not genetic in so far as they cause this or that particular body, but in so far as they contribute to the full expression of corporeality*. This non-causal expression is a kind of indirect or static genesis because it does not operate according to direct contact, as is the case with corporeal causation. For example, space and time do not 'touch' bodies and bodies do not 'touch' space and time in the way that a scalpel touches flesh. Still, space is incarnated in bodies, which is tantamount to saying that the generation of bodies always expresses a place in which they are produced.

For Deleuze's Stoicism, the arc of static genesis proceeds in three stages:

1. Bodies cause incorporeal effects.
2. These effects infinitely divide or differentiate as they spread along the intensive face of the metaphysical surface.
3. These lines of differentiation reflect or cast shadows on bodies, which is the operation of integrating infinite differences in terms of how they are individuated through various bodies.

It does not matter where you start, as there is constant communication of bodies and incorporeals, causes and effects, physical depths and metaphysical surface. The reason is that the incorporeal surface is *superficial*, a perfectly smooth figure, without depth or height. There is no ascending or descending movement, as there is nowhere else to go, no heaven above to save us. Incorporeals do not add to the world in the way that Platonic forms add a new world to the material world, above or within. For the Stoics, there is only matter and its immaterial surface.

Before ending our discussion of static genesis, notice here another instance of the Stoics' commitment to immanent ontology. In Stoic physics, causes and effects remain two autonomous series that are irreducible to each other '*only* to the extent that the causal relation comprises the heterogeneity of cause and effect' (*LS* 94; emphasis added). 'The fact is', Deleuze admits, 'that these two figures of autonomy hurl us into contradiction, without ever resolving it' (*LS* 96). This causal relation is structured by 'the connection of causes between themselves *and* the link of effects between themselves' (*LS* 94; emphasis original). Causes and effects must be *both* distinct *and* connected. Incorporeals preserve their difference from the corporeal causes only in so far as they contribute to the genesis of states of affairs. There is passage, however perverse, from bodies to incorporeals, from physical depths to metaphysical surface, and back. Deleuze calls this a 'double causality' (*LS* 94).

Double Causality

With this concept of double causality, we can finally see why we have described the two faces of the incorporeal surface as *operations*.

First, Deleuze himself speaks of operation: 'The quasi-cause does not create [*ne crée pas*], it "*operates* [*opère*]"' (*LS* 147; emphasis added). 'Corporeal causes act and suffer [*agissent et pâtissent*] from a cosmic mixture and a universal present which produces the incorporeal event. But the quasi-cause *operates* by *doubling* the physical causality' (*LS* 147; emphasis added). This doubling is not a mirroring or mimicking because the order and connection of bodies and the order and connection of incorporeals do not *resemble* each other. Instead, it is divergent doubling, a doubling that differentiates. The main reason that this doubling diverges is because the relations composing the corporeal depths are strictly causal, while the relations structuring the two faces of the incorporeal surface are effects *and* quasi-causal. The perversity is that these effects are genetic but not causal.

It is only perverse, however, from the perspective of 'formal logic'. To understand the full power of incorporeality requires a 'transcendental logic'. Although formal logic adequately accounts for the causal organisation of bodies, only a transcendental logic expresses how a quasi-cause can be an effect and genetic, but non-causal. 'The

The Yolk B: Incorporeals

opposition between simple formal logic and transcendental logic', writes Deleuze, 'cuts through the entire theory of sense [the logical incorporeal]', and we can add space (the physical incorporeal) and time (the ethical incorporeal) (*LS* 96).[40]

Deleuze's 'transcendental logic' is different from Kant's. Kantian transcendental logic strives to develop a structure of thinking that restricts knowledge claims to that which remains within the bounds of possible human experience.[41] Restricting knowledge claims to what is knowable to creatures like us provides a means for justification that allows us to legitimately make claims about facts of human experience. As the saying goes, Kantian transcendental logic describes the structure of the necessary conditions for the *possibility* (not actuality) of human experience. These conditions connect to human experience because they resemble it.

A major difference from Kant is that Deleuze's transcendental logic does not *resemble* the causal network of corporeal causes. Kantian transcendental conditions, Deleuze argues, are 'traced' from the conditioned, where the conditioned is physical depth or the set of corporeal causes: 'Kant traces the so-called transcendental structures from the empirical' (*DR* 135). This tracing is different kind of doubling. Kant's transcendental logic doubles the structure of corporeal causes by the order to resemblance, while the Stoic quasi-causal doubling *diverges* from the causal corporeal network. In order to be the genetic condition of our world, the incorporeal surface cannot mirror or resemble the empirical. Deleuze has a perverse word to describe how incorporeals are both effects yet genetic: 'transcendental empiricism' (*DR* 143).[42] Transcendental empiricism shows that that which conditions – the incorporeals – is distinct from the conditioned – bodies – yet still contributes their material existence. The incorporeal surface is both the effect and the quasi-cause of bodies. Effects are both independent from physical depths yet also connected to bodies. In short, they are the genetic conditions for corporeal relations. The non-causal set of incorporeal relations composing the metaphysical plane follows a non-causal, non-physical logic. This is a Deleuzian transcendental logic.

To the extent that effects diverge from their causes, the relations composing this incorporeal surface are also different: they are quasi-causal. Effects, Deleuze writes, 'enter into relations of quasi-causality with one another' (*LS* 169; translation mine). Incorporeal *relations are* quasi-causal. In the very next sentence, however, Deleuze seems to confuse the matter. 'Together', he writes, effects *'enter into a relation with* a quasi-cause that is itself incorporeal' (*LS* 169; emphasis added). Something seems amiss. Which is it – do incorporeals enter into quasi-causal relations or is there a separate thing, a quasi-cause, with which incorporeals enter into a relation? As we will soon argue, a quasi-cause cannot be a separate thing, another type of incorporeal, given that there is a distinct set of them. A significant part of the rest of this book is an argument for a shift in the number of types of incorporeal from four to three. According to this reading, rather than adding another type of incorporeal, a quasi-cause describes the nature of the relations among incorporeals.

We are talking about a Deleuzian transcendental logic because it describes the operation of the quasi-cause or non-causal genesis that occurs not between one actual body and another, but between incorporeals and bodies. The relations among bodies themselves are causal, as is the movement from bodies to incorporeal effects. But the movement from incorporeals to bodies is a movement from surface structure to its incarnation in bodies. This is an early instance, perhaps the first in the history of Western philosophy, of static genesis.

Twisting the Table of Judgements

Since the sense of quasi-causality might still be unclear, we can take up the hints that the Stoics and Deleuze left us in order to understand the relations among incorporeals: 'incorporeal compatibility and incompatibility'.[43] To do this, we must first determine the nature of incorporeal of *compatibility*. Incorporeal compatibility is opposed to two other sorts: logical compatibility and corporeal compatibility. Above we said plenty about why incorporeals are non-causal (thus not compatible in the way bodies are), but we have not yet said much about logical compatibility and incompatibility. Let us do that now.

In essence, two things are *logically incompatible* if they are contradictory. Contradiction is a type of conceptual relation. This sense of logical incompatibility (as contradiction) appears in the Stoic's use of hypothetical syllogisms, such as we see in Diogenes Laërtius' account of Stoic logic (DL 7.80).[44] Although Deleuze does not explicitly cite Diogenes Laërtius here, it is clearly his source: 'a True conditional is one the contradictory of whose consequent conflicts with its antecedent. For example, "It is day, it is light." This is true, since "Not: it is day," the contradictory of the consequent, conflicts with "It is day"' (*HP* 35A). As Deleuze notes, 'commentators are certainly right to recall that the question here is not about a relation of physical conse-

The Yolk B: Incorporeals

quence or of causality' (*LS* 69). The contradiction arises not because the physical state of worldly affairs makes it true, but because 'the contradiction must be defined on a single level' – the plane of conceptual containment and entailment (*LS* 170). Contradiction arises because the concept of 'day' entails the concept 'light', and the denial of such conceptual entailment is the contradictory. In sum, logical compatibility and incompatibility is a matter of conceptual inclusion or exclusion, which is used to justifiably describe the physical organisation of the world.

By contrast, incorporeal compatibility and incompatibility is non-causal and alogical. To see how, consider a direct comparison: while rules of formal logic capture the order corporeal causes, transcendental logic (Deleuzian, not Kantian) expresses the relations among incorporeals themselves. To understand this we return to Deleuze's twist on the four classes of Kant's Table of Judgement. When Deleuze explains how the impassibility or neutrality of incorporeals appears from several different perspectives, he explicitly mentioned two of the three terms corresponding to each of the classes, saying that they did not make a difference to the static genesis of incorporeal quasi-causality. The strange thing is that the third term in each class remains tacit.

To refresh, these are the four classes in Kant's Table: (1) quality, (2) quantity, (3) relation and (4) modality. These are the first two terms corresponding to each respective class: (1) affirmative and negative, (2) universal and particular, (3) hypothetical and categorical, (4) apodictic and assertoric. These pairs contribute to the composition of the transcendental grounds that justify the objective validity of Newtonian physics.[45] We can put it in a table:

	Quality	Quantity	Relation	Modality
1st	Affirmative	Universal	Categorical	Assertoric
2nd	Negative	Particular	Hypothetical	Apodictic

In Section Eleven of his *Critique of Pure Reason* (in the B-edition), Kant makes three rather defensive remarks, which he calls '[s]ubtle considerations', about his use of the Table of Categories.[46] In the 'Second remark', Kant writes 'that each class always has the same number of categories, namely three, which calls for reflection, since otherwise all *a priori* division by means of concepts must be a dichotomy'.[47] Taking up the four main classes of formal logic entails a division into two, as in Kant's transcendental logic. Kant continues that 'remark': 'But here the third category always arises from the combination of the first two in its class.'[48] Combining the first two in each class, albeit with a twist, we get the following: (1) 'infinite' is affirmative combined with negative; (2) 'singular' is a particular considered as a universal; (3) 'disjunctive' is categorical in the hypothetical determinations of others; and (4) 'problematic' is existence that is given by apodicticity (necessity) itself.[49] Here is a table of the tacit third terms:

3rd	Infinite	Singular	Disjunctive	Problematic[50]

As incorporeals are effects arising from the interaction of corporeals, it makes sense that the third term in each class arises out of the first two. The first two account for the logic of bodies; the third accounts for the logic of incorporeals. In short, these 'tacit third logical terms' are part of the transcendental logic expressing the metaphysical structure of incorporeals that we find rising in Deleuze's encounter with Stoicism.[51]

To ensure we are all on the same page, let us pause and situate ourselves in the overall story of Deleuze's Stoicism. We have just drawn up the tacit third terms in Kant's Table because we are trying to understand the quasi-causal relations among incorporeals among themselves, as opposed to the causal relations among bodies. We find in Deleuze's transcendental logic a way of understanding the nature of these relations: incorporeal compatibility and incompatibility. We are talking about this because we are, on a more general level, detailing the upheaval in philosophy that the Stoics provoked by splitting the causal relation into corporeal causes and incorporeal effects. All of this is part of our examination of Stoic physics and metaphysics, which we are characterising as a perverse materialism. Now that we are more firmly situated in the overall story, we can now work out the metaphysical structure of the Stoic incorporeal surface.

Transcendental Logic

First we need to articulate the formal structure of corporeal causes according to the first two terms of each of the classes in Kant's Table, which is the structure of the side of the incorporeal surface facing bodies. To do this we need to dive deep into Kant's Table. After this we will extract, according to the tacit third terms, the transcendental structure of the other side of the incorporeal surface.

The Yolk B: Incorporeals

The hypothetical relation is the dominant logical term in Kant's Table. After all, this is where Kant responds to Hume's sceptical challenge to the laws of physical causation by grounding necessity in the transcendental structure of subjectivity. The hypothetical relation – if x, then y – is the logical form of physical causation: if cause x, then effect y. There are four features of this corporeal causal-conditional order, each of which is composed of the first two terms in their respective logical class.

FORMAL LOGIC OF BODIES

First, *Transitive causes (affirmative, negative)*. A transitive cause is one in which causal force is communicated from one body to a different body because each term remains distinct and separate from others. The standard example is mechanical causation, as when a scalpel cuts the flesh. With each body, something can be affirmed of one and not of the other, just as something can be negated about one and not the other. This body is a scalpel, not flesh, and that body flesh, not a scalpel. The scalpel transmits the causal force into the flesh so that a wound appears. Through the transmission of the force, both identities retain what can be affirmed or negated of each alone.

Second, *independent terms (universal, particular)*. In order for the causal force to transmit between bodies, each body must be independent and external to the other. This is encapsulated by a conditional statement: if x, then y. Even if the terms x or y are indeterminate, their existences continue independently of the relations into which they enter. Such identities are derived from forms of judgement that are able to determine bodies as particular instances of universal kinds of things. For example, we can judge that this body here is a particular instance of the universal kind 'scalpel' and that body there is a particular instanced of the universal kind 'flesh'. The forms of universal and particular judgement fix each of their identities as kinds of bodies.

Third, *causal series (hypothetical, categorical)*. Hypothetical judgement captures the logical structure of the scientific laws of causation. The objective validity of this form of judgement grounds the objective validity of the physical laws of nature. This is captured both in the hypothetical judgement – if x, then y – and categorical judgement – all x are y – in so far as the conditional fixes necessity through the hypothetical relation and the universal statement fixes identity through category membership. Further, in an etiological relation, causal force is communicated from the one body to a second body and so on indefinitely. Not only is the force transmitted into a third body, but that first body, the cause, received that causal force from a different body that transmitted causal force to it. An endless chain of causation runs from an indefinite previous time through later times, along a single unidirectional axis that is populated by individual bodies. Hypothetical and categorical relations capture the structure of this causal series.

Fourth, *necessity (apodictic, assertoric)*. The causal relation, as expressed by the hypothetical relation and the identities derived from category membership, locates a necessary connection between antecedent and consequent. A causal relation holds with the force of necessity in so far as necessity marks the difference between causation and correlation. The physical structure of the world is thus organised by what is necessary (apodictic) and what is actual (assertoric). The Stoics calls this *fatum*, fate.

These four physical terms are recorded on the side of the incorporeal surface facing bodies, and they are described by the first two terms in each logical class. The transcendental logical structure of the incorporeal surface facing away from bodies, however, opposes each of the four features of the formal logical hypothetical relation and the corresponding corporeal causal relation. While formal logic captures the structure of bodies, transcendental logic expresses the structure of incorporeals. We now describe the four terms of the side of the incorporeal surface facing away from bodies.

Transcendental Logic of Incorporeals

First, *infinite causes*. Infinite causes correspond to immanent causes. Without distinct, independent terms, as with bodies, transitive causes disappear. The relations between incorporeal effects are immanent in the sense of mutual 'in-dwelling', remaining within each other. They are inseparable and interdependently organised across the entire flat metaphysical surface. This organisation is due to the 'immanence of the quasi-cause' (*LS* 95). The logic of infinite causes corresponds to infinitive verbs – 'to cut, *couper, secāre*, τέμνειν'. 'To cut' and 'to be cut' refer to the incorporeal effects that play along the side of the surface facing away from bodies. Deleuze calls this the 'paradox of infinite identity': 'the infinite identity of both directions at the same time [*deux sens à la fois*]' (*LS* 2). 'To cut' is an infinitive verb that, when attributed to bodies, is conjugated in various ways, such as

The Yolk B: Incorporeals

'being cut', 'having been cut', 'will cut' and so forth. But when unattributed, considered only in relation to themselves, infinitives express the manner in which bodies *can* be conjugated without *actually* being conjugated. Infinitives express *manners of being* but are not themselves beings. On the far side of the incorporeal surface dwell only infinite, immanent quasi-causes.

Second, *singular*. In the logical order of corporeal causality, bodies are independent terms that transmit causal force without losing their identities. In the transcendental logic of the incorporeal surface, however, relations are primary, not the terms that enter into relations. Think of a relation-without-terms as akin to the body-without-organs. When corporeals act on each other, the effect emerges from them, and the effect is recorded on the incorporeal surface. This recording is simultaneously the dissolution of independence and identity; bodies become anonymous and impersonal. The loss of a proper name is the adventure of the surface that is repeated with each incorporeal: space, λεκτα, time. On this surface, there is no larger or smaller body, but only infinite movements of 'becoming larger' or 'becoming-smaller', simultaneously speeding off in opposed (from the perspective of formal causal logic) directions, eluding the fixation of corporeal identities. Deleuze calls this the 'paradox' of the 'simultaneity of becoming': the 'affirmation of both directions at once [*deux sens à la fois*]' (*LS* 1). The surface is an 'impersonal and pre-individual transcendental field' of singularities that are, while logically contradictory and physically impossible, transcendentally compatible on the incorporeal surface (*LS* 102). There is another term for such singularities: intensities, as in the intensive dimensions of an egg. In a passage about kinship identities, Deleuze and Guattari describe the composition of the surface in terms of an egg:

> names do not designate persons, but rather the intensive variations of a 'vibratory spiraling movement', inclusive disjunctions, necessarily twin states through which a subject passes on the cosmic egg. Everything must be interpreted in intensity. The egg and the placenta itself, swept away by an unconscious energy 'susceptible to augmentation and diminution', [becoming-larger and becoming-smaller simultaneously]. (*AO* 158)

Third, *disjunctive*. Quasi-causality is paradoxical: it 'smells' like a cause in so far as it is genetic, but it is unlike a cause in so far as it does not produce transitive causal series. On the surface, categorical (all *A* are *B*) and hypothetical relations (if *x*, then *y*) dissolve into disjunctions ('*either* this *or* this *or* this *or* . . .') (*AO* 12). It is no coincidence that, in *Anti-Oedipus*, Deleuze and Guattari align the physical depths with the 'connective synthesis' and the metaphysical surface (there called the body-without-organs) with the 'disjunctive synthesis'. To say that the Stoic incorporeal surface is organised by disjunctives is to characterise it as pre-personal, pre-individual and asubjective. There is no first or last term. Pre-Socratic hierarchies, Platonic height and Aristotelian interiority flatten out or unfold into an infinitely shallow pool. Only singularities dwell here. Unlike the 'either-or' of the Hegelian dialectic, which Kierkegaard sharply mocks in *Either/Or*, the disjunction of transcendental logic does not return the 'or' back to the first 'either'. There is no categorical return or conditional direction; it only links an infinite series of 'ors' spreading out 'in both directions at once (*deux sens à la fois*)' across the perfectly smooth surface (*AO* 76). Exclusive disjunctions correspond to the heights, depths and interiority, and inclusive disjunctions correspond to the surface. In this incorporeal transcendental logic, disjunction is always 'affirmative, nonrestrictive, inclusive' (*AO* 76). On the incorporeal surface, there subsist '[n]othing but a series of singularities in the disjunctive network' (*AO* 88).

Fourth, *problematic*. This is the odd one out in Deleuze's appropriation of Kant's Table. According to Kant's ordering, 'problematic' is the first, not the third, tacit term; 'assertoric' is the second, 'apodictic' the third. To make sort this out, consider common English synonyms for these three modal types: problematic = possibility, assertoric = existence or actuality, and apodictic = necessity. Although Kant places 'problematic' first in this class, seeing it as a kind of logical 'possibility', we recall Deleuze's critique of Kantian possibility, as doing so gives 'the problem' a Deleuzian sense more appropriate to his Stoic encounter.[52] For Deleuze, a 'problem' is a 'genetic condition' in the sense that problems are essentially productive: problems provoke responses. The productivity of problems is thus a kind of static genesis. Since the incorporeal surface also expresses this sense of static genesis, problematicity is the modality of incorporeality, as opposed to the existence and necessity of corporeality. 'Problematic', as a modal term, characterises something as real as the necessity of fate or the existence of bodies; it is fully real, just modally different. The incorporeal surface is problematic in that it is impassive and productive. While the existence of corporeal causes follows fate, incorporeals express the strange efficacy of quasi-causality or static genesis. The incorporeal surface contributes to the generation of bodies not through actual contact or through the necessity of direct

The Yolk B: Incorporeals

causal relation but as a genetic condition for matter. Put differently, the surface functions as the problem according to which bodies respond.

We twist these two sorts of logical orders, and the metaphysical structures they describe, into a Stoic take on Kant's Table:

Classes	Formal logic of corporeals	Transcendental logic of incorporeals
Quality	Transitive causes (affirmative, negative)	Infinite causes
Quantity	Independent terms (universal, particular)	Singular
Relation	Causal series (hypothetical, categorical)	Disjunctive
Modality	Necessity (apodictic, assertoric)	Problematic

The four terms of the incorporeal transcendental logic depicted in the column on the right articulate the order of incorporeal compatibility and incompatibility, which diverges from the logical and physical compatibilities depicted in the middle column. Incorporeal compatibility does not express a logic of conceptual containment or physical causation, or the order of logical entailment or physical organisation. Instead, it expresses what a body can do, how the physical manifold unfolds along spatial and temporal planes, what it means to exist in space and time. Incorporeal compatibility allows for the organisation of events without prioritisation.

For the Stoics, everything happens on the surface. This incorporeal logic articulates each and every event – from the smallest cut to the great cosmological conflagration of the eternal return. To express the entirety of cosmology, the surface itself must not, on the one hand, be another existent being. On the other hand, the surface cannot be completely separate from this cosmos; it cannot be a transcendent realm existing independently of and ontologically superior to ours. The surface is part of the cosmos; it co-composes and co-organises the one and only world. This strange sense of being a constituting part of the world but in a different manner (or modality) is articulated in this sense of incorporeal compatibility and incompatibility that is expressed by the incorporeal transcendental logic that Deleuze extracts from Kant's Table.

Before concluding the chapter, let us make a comment about this logic. Through *Deleuze, A Stoic*, we are discovering the logic of static genesis or quasi-causality of the incorporeal surface, a logic that escapes corporeal logic, produced in conversation with their predecessors. As committed materialists, they select the material principles from the pre-Socratics – Anaximenes, Empedocles, Heraclitus and so on. They take up this old logic of bodily depth and physical causation without much change. In doing so, however, they see that a different logic emerges; they learn that a full materialist metaphysics entails, perversely, incorporeal conditions. In Lapoujage's words, Stoic materialism is perverse in that it leads to an 'irrational logic of aberrant movements' from corporeal to incorporeal and back.[53] The Stoics and Deleuze come together on just this point. Lapoujade even describes this perverse logic of aberrant movements as 'a preliminary definition of Deleuze's philosophy'.[54] Like the Stoics, logic is what truly interests Deleuze, and this is what differentiates Deleuze from the rest of his generation: 'Deleuze is above all a logician', Lapoujade argues, 'and all his books are "Logics."'[55] Think of all the logics Deleuze produces, especially the text most relevant our story: *Logic of Sense*. What Lapoujade notices as a 'distinct characteristic' of Deleuze's thought can be traced back to what is perhaps the distinct characteristic of Stoic physics: 'a deep perversion of the very heart of philosophy'.[56] The Stoic perversion at the heart of their philosophical system is the drawing of a new metaphysics of causal depths and incorporeal surface. Such a metaphysics entails both a formal logic of causation *and* a transcendental logic of quasi-causality. This logic of quasi-causality is the transcendental logic of the incorporeal surface we just produced by twisting the classic Kantian Table of Judgements, which helps us understand why the splitting of the causal relation in Stoic physics and metaphysics caused such an upheaval in philosophy.

Conclusion

Few scholars fully appreciate what Deleuze, reading the Stoics, means by a quasi-cause. Most thinkers tend to miss the philosophical force that it had for the Stoics, focusing more on what Deleuze selected as the prime examples of quasi-causality: sense and event. To highlight these at the expense of the other incorporeals misses the power of Stoic perversity because it gives a subjective or even human-centric character to Stoic physics and metaphysics. It is a mistake to explain this elusive notion of incorporeal quasi-cause through the meaning of words alone, and thereby overlook the other canonical incorporeals: place, void and time. While Michael Bennett insightfully asks, '[Wh]y does Deleuze treat the Stoic theory of events and causality in

The Yolk B: Incorporeals

terms of sense?' he does not ask a related question: why does Deleuze focus his account of Stoic incorporeality and quasi-cause mostly in terms of sense, and to a lesser degree time?[57] To answer this, while remaining Deleuzian in spirit, we must step beyond Deleuze and develop a full account of the Stoic incorporeals and the quasi-cause. Quasi-causality is Deleuze's expression of the incorporeals genetic power. While Deleuze, and all his commentators, understand this genetic relation through linguistic sense and events, the key to understanding Deleuze's Stoicism requires consideration of the complete cast of Stoic incorporeals. The next chapter will argue that the entire body of scholarship on Stoicism has missed something important about the Stoic cast of incorporeals, and it is only through Deleuze's Stoicism that this is revealed.

Notes

1. A secondary reason why we are characterising Stoicism as *perverse* is to emphasise the strangeness of the school. Recently, Stoicism has enjoyed quite a surge in popularity, especially among pop psychology, cognitive behavioral therapy, scientists and the self-help fad in the tech industry. These modern popularisers often overlook or completely reject any Stoic strangeness. We hope to counteract that whitewashing and commodifying by revealing the Stoics to be perverts.
2. Marcelo D. Boeri, 'The Stoics on Bodies and Incorporeals', *The Review of Metaphysics* 54.4 (June 2001): 723–52, at 730, 734; emphasis added. Seneca distinguishes between causes and necessary conditions in *Letter* 65.
3. Boeri, 'The Stoics on Bodies and Incorporeals', 737, 738.
4. Seneca, *Letter* 57.4–7.
5. Ibid. 57.4.
6. Clement, *Miscellanies*, 8.9.20.3.
7. This might be silly: if the first sense is closer to an explanation, then the second sense is closer to an attribution of responsibility. It follows the adjectival 'αἴτιος', which originally meant that which is 'culpable, responsible, or guilty', Whatever can bear the blame for something is a cause as that which produces, as 'αἰτία' is the accusation of someone who is guilty of having done something and is thus responsible for the consequences.
8. Gilles Deleuze, *Essays Critical and Clinical* (1993), trans. Daniel W. Smith and Michael A. Greco (Minneapolis: University of Minnesota Press, 1997), 141; emphasis original.
9. Frédérique Ildefonse, *Les Stoïciens I: Zénon, Cléanthe, Chrysippe* (Paris: Les Belles Lettres, 2000), 57.

10. Sextus Empiricus, *Against the Physicists*, trans. Richard Bett (Cambridge: Cambridge University Press, 2012), I.211. Sextus also gives the example of 'being burnt': 'And again, the first, a body, becomes the cause to the wood, a body, of the incorporeal predicate "being burnt."'
11. Remember that Sextus was a doctor, which suggests that he might find the scapel imagery very telling.
12. Ildefonse, *Les Stoïciens I*, 54; emphases added.
13. Deleuze, *Essays*, 141.
14. Michael Frede, 'The Original Notion of Cause', in *Essays in Ancient Philosophy* (Minneapolis: University of Minnesota Press, 1987), 125–51, at 130.
15. Deleuze, *Essays*, 141.
16. It is no surprise that Long and Sedley complain that there is '[n]o satisfactory [extant] discussion of the problem' of the relations among incorporeals (*HP* 165).
17. Perhaps unexpectedly, in Cicero's *De Fato*, the main source of Deleuze's thinking about the organization proper to the incorporeals, the English 'incompatibility' is a translation of the Latin *pugnare* and *repugnatia*.
18. Quasi-causality does show up again in *Anti-Oedipus*, but it seems to there take on a new meaning that is only tangentially related to the sense we see in Deleuze's Stoicism; for more on the differences between quasi-causality in *Logic of Sense* and *Anti-Oedipus*, see Emilia Angelova, 'Quasi-Cause in Deleuze: Inverting the Body Without Organs', *Symposium: Canadian Journal of Continental Philosophy* 10.1 (2006): 117–33; and Daniel W. Smith, 'From the Surface to the Depths: On the Transition from *Logic of Sense* to *Anti-Oedipus*', *Symposium: Canadian Journal of Continental Philosophy* 10.1 (2006): 135–53.
19. James Williams, *Gilles Deleuze's* Logic of Sense: *A Critical Introduction and Guide* (Edinburgh: Edinburgh University Press, 2008), 130.
20. Jon Roffe, 'Deleuze's Concept of Quasi-Cause', *Deleuze Studies* 11.2 (2017): 278–94, at 291n.2.
21. Moreover, it is misleading to think of Deleuze as 'returning' to the Stoics, as if he had left them behind early on in his career. *Logique du sens* was published in 1969. While it is unclear when he first started writing the text, many of the themes and concepts can be traced to the earliest stages of Deleuze's thinking. Let us not forget that several of the appendices were lightly revised editions of some of Deleuze's earliest writings.
22. Albert C. Outler, 'The "Platonism" of Clement of Alexandria', *The Journal of Religion* 20.3 (July 1940): 217–40.
23. Gerald A. Press, *Development of the Idea of History in Antiquity* (Montreal: McGill-Queen's Press, 2003), 83.

24. Eric Osborn, *Clement of Alexandria* (Cambridge: Cambridge University Press, 2008), 5. John Ferguson, *Clement of Alexandria* (New York: Twayne Publishers, 1974), 17.
25. John Kaye, *Some Account of the Writings and Opinions of Clement of Alexandria* (London: J. G. & F. Rivington, 1835), 221.
26. Osborn, *Clement*, 8.
27. For a careful, detailed account of the understanding of 'cause' in this section of Clement's *Miscellanies*, see Frede, 'The Original Notion of Cause'. There Frede sorts out the complexities between the distinction between 'perfect and principal [*perfectae et principales*]' causes and 'auxiliary and proximate [*adiuvantes et proximae*]' causes in Cicero's *De Fato* (41) and Clement's distinction between *autoteles aition*, *sunaition* and *sunergon* (8.9.33). Frede argues that Clement's *autoteles aition* and *sunaition* roughly correspond to Cicero's *causae perfectae et principals* while Clement's *sunerga* almost match up with Cicero's *causae adiuvantes et proximae*. We do not step into this complexity because it is not relevant to Deleuze's Stoicism. Deleuze is interested more in the strange concept of quasi-cause.
28. The Greek reads: 'οἱ δὲ τὸ μὲν ϛῶμα κυρίως αἴτιόν φαϛι, τὸ δὲ ϛώματον καταχρηϛτικῶς καὶ οἷον αἰτιωδῶς.' Clement of Alexandria, *Miscellanies*, 8.9.26,1.
29. First footnote, 'Fourteenth Series'.
30. Michael Bennett, 'Deleuze's Concept of "Quasi-Causality" and its Greek Sources', an invited talk at the Classics Department Lecture Series, Dalhousie University, Halifax, Canada, 30 November 2014.
31. Recall Bréhier's above description of incorporeals: 'The attribute is always, to the contrary, expressed by a verb, which is to say that it is not a being, but a *manner of being*' (*TI* 11).
32. Matyáš Havdra, *The So-Called Eighth* Stromateus *by Clement of Alexandria* (Leiden: Brill, 2017), 275.
33. Barbara Cassin, 'The Muses and Philosophy: Elements for a History of the *Pseudos*', in *Contemporary Encounters with Ancient Metaphysics*, ed. Abraham Jacob Greenstine and Ryan J. Johnson (Edinburgh: Edinburgh University Press, 2017), 13.
34. Barbara Cassin, 'The Muses and Philosophy: Elements for a History of the *Pseudos*', in *Contemporary Encounters with Ancient Metaphysics*, ed. Abraham Jacob Greenstine and Ryan J. Johnson (Edinburgh: Edinburgh University Press, 2017), 13.
35. Plotinus, *Enneads*, 6.8.14; Simplicius, *in Aristotelis physicorum libros commentaria*, 17.25.
36. See the Perseus Project: http://www.perseus.tufts.edu/hopper/text?doc=Perseus:text:1999.04.0007:smythp=833.
37. For those more familiar with *Difference and Repetition*, Deleuze also claims that static genesis 'may be understood as the correlate of the

notion of *passive synthesis*, and which in turn illuminates that notion' (*DR* 183; emphasis original).

38. Immanuel Kant, *Critique of Pure Reason*, trans. Paul Guyer and Allen W. Wood (Cambridge: Cambridge University Press, 1999), A70/B95. In the First *Critique*, the order goes: quantity, quality, relation and modality, but the Third *Critique* starts with quality, thus making the order: quality, quantity, relation and modality. Kant explains this change in order of the first two classes: 'In seeking the moments to which this power of judgments [of taste] attends in its reflection ... I have considered the moment of quality first, since an aesthetic judgment on the beautiful takes notice of this first.' Immanuel Kant, *Critique of the Power of Judgment*, ed. Paul Guyer and Eric Matthews (Cambridge: Cambridge University Press, 2000), 5:203. Since the Deleuze's reading of Kant is rooted in the Third *Critique*, we list the order of the logical classes according to that organization.
39. To be fair, Deleuze seems to includes a third modality – the 'interrogative' – but he does not explain much of this, and this does not appear in Kant's Table.
40. 'While formal logic describes the first aspect of stoic events (their being dependent and derived),' Michael Bennett writes, 'the quasi-causal power of sense (animated by paradoxical instances) to generate other events, propositions, and state of affairs implies moving to transcendental logic.' Bennett, *Deleuze and Ancient Greek Physics* (London: Bloomsbury Academic, 2017), 111.
41. Kant, *Critique of Pure Reason*, A50–64/B74–88.
42. Joe Hughes suggests that Deleuze gets this idea of 'transcendental empiricism' from one of Paul Ricœur's accounts of Husserl. See Joe Hughes, *Deleuze and the Genesis of Representation*, (New York: Continuum, 2008), 39; Paul Ricœur, *Husserl: An Analysis of his Phenomenology*, trans. Edward G. Ballard and Lester E. Embree (Evanston: Northwestern University Press, 1967), 107.
43. In one place in *Logic of Sense*, there is a strange reference to astrology. 'Astrology', writes Deleuze, 'was perhaps the first important attempt to establish a theory of alogical incompatibilities and noncausal correspondences' (*LS* 171). As elusive and mysterious as this statement is, on our reading, astrology is not particularly illuminating. Michael Bennett, however, takes the astrology reference much further, and provides a clever interpretation of the relationship between incorporeal compatibility and incompatibility and astrology. See his 'Cicero's *De Fato* in Deleuze's Logic of Sense'.
44. This Stoics' use of the hypothetical structure, and propositional logical altogether, was, in itself, a great break with the traditional categorical logic of the Peripatetics, but we will wait to address the Stoics' innovations in logic in Part II on Stoic logic

45. For the full story, see Immanuel Kant, *Metaphysical Foundations of Natural Science*, ed. Michael Freidman (Cambridge: Cambridge University Press, 2004).
46. To be sure, Kant is referring to the Table of Categories, not the Table of Judgements. But given the structural isomorphism of the two tables, it makes sense to infer that what he says about the former applies to the latter.
47. Kant, *Critique of Pure Reason*, B110.
48. Kant, *Critique of Pure Reason*, B110. He then details the exact manner in which the tacit third category or term arises. Using the terms in the Table of Judgements, Kant writes: 'allness (totality) is nothing other than plurality considered as a unity, limitation is nothing other than reality combined with negation, community is the causality of a substance in the reciprocal determination of others, finally necessity is nothing other than the existence that is given by possibility itself.' Kant, *Critique of Pure Reason*, B111.
49. The twist is that we are applying this to the Table of Judgements, not the Table of Categories.
50. A second twist is that we are treating the first term in 'modality' as if it were the third term. The main justification for this is that it is the one term in this class that Deleuze does not mention. Hopefully, a different scholar could say explain this twist in Deleuze's thinking. If nothing else, while it is true that Kant actually lists 'problematic' first under the 'modality' hearing, it still seems to function as the odd one out, the uncomfortable third (Kant, *CPR*, A70/B95).
51. If there is any doubt as to whether or not Deleuze is actually relying on Kant's Table, consider that Deleuze refers to all four classes of the Table at least four separate times in *Logic of Sense* (LS 32–4, 101, 165, 175).
52. Deleuze's critique of possibility in Kant is largely based on Solomon Maimon's critiques of Kant's conception of transcendental conditions of possibility. For Maimon, Kant needed a conception of the genetic conditions of actual experience not the conditions for the possibility of experience. I explain this in more detail in a recent article. I write, for example: 'While the method of mere conditioning, as Kant construes it, takes a presupposed unity of the manifold as the necessary condition for the possibility of experience and the objects of experience in general, the genetic method contends that differentials structure the genetic conditions of actual experience. Demonstrating how differentials produce extensive magnitudes, Maimon shows how his account engenders appearances rather than merely maps onto them.' Ryan J. Johnson, 'Homesickness and Nomadism: Traveling with Kant and Maimon', *Polish Journal of Philosophy* 10.2 (Fall 2017): 14–15.
53. Lapoujade, *Aberrant Movements*, 27.

54. Ibid.
55. Ibid.
56. Ibid.
57. Michael James Bennett, 'Cicero's *De Fato* in Deleuze's *Logic of Sense*', *Deleuze Studies* 9.1 (2015): 25–58, at 29.

3

The Yolk C: Space

Introduction: The Canonical Incorporeals

Having considered Deleuze's engagement with the Stoic theory of incorporeality and how it relates to their perverse physics of causality and quasi-causality, we can now begin elaborating a heterodox account of Stoicism, the full account of which spans the rest the book. Let us restate the heterodoxy at the start.

According to all scholarship on Stoicism – from their Hellenistic and Roman contemporaries to twenty-first-century philosophers and classicists – it is agreed that there are four types of incorporeals: void, place, λεκτα and time. For example, Jacques Brunschwig calls these the 'canonical incorporeals', and Émile Bréhier considers them 'the four species of incorporeals admitted by the Stoics'.[1] Bréhier continues: these four 'constituted, on the side of real beings, bodies, something fleeting and elusive, a "nothingness"' (TI 60). Despite what Brunschwig and Bréhier write, in fact, contrary to what everyone says about Stoic physics, we argue for a different understanding of the set of Stoic incorporeals. Without simply saying that the canonical reading is completely wrong, we tap into the perverse power of Stoic materialism in order to develop a new reading, one that appears only through Deleuze's Stoicism. Hence our heterodoxical claim: *there are three, not four, incorporeals*. Hence the heterodoxical list of incorporeals: space, λεκτα and time. On our reading, void and place are folded into space, and this chapter will argue for this folding.

We begin by considering reasons for and advantages of our heterodoxical claim. We then turn to the first of the three incorporeals – space – by demonstrating how and why the two canonical incorporeals – place and void – are really two articulations of spatiality in Stoic metaphysics. This requires thinking through ancient accounts of infinite divisibility, Aristotle's discussion of place in his *Physics*, and Epicurus' account of void, including the Stoic responses to Epicurus' atomism. This leads us into delicate interpretations of vague passages on Stoic physics, before we fold place and void into a single incorporeal: space. Space, as one perspective of the incorporeal surface, has two sides: place is the side facing bodies because it is extensively organised, and void is the side facing away from bodies because it is intensively organised. We conclude 'The Yolk A' by showing that the double-sided structure of space also applies to λεκτα and time. All three incorporeals share the same double-sided (extensive/intensive) structure. The next two sections of our book – 'Logic' and 'Ethics' – corroborate the claim that the repeated structure of the incorporeal surface is at the heart of the heterodoxical account emerging from the Deleuze's Stoicism.

A Heterodox Reading: Three Reasons and Three Advantages

There are at least three reasons for and three advantages of our heterodoxical reading. Together, they open a space into which our heterodoxical reading takes hold. First, the reasons.

The first reason for our heterodoxy stems from textual paucity. Almost all early Stoic writings were lost. None of the actual writings of Zeno, Cleanthes, Chrysippus, Panaetius, Posidonius, or any the early or middle Stoics still exist. What survived from those periods does not come directly from the Stoics themselves but through hostile opponents and often undiscerning doxographers, such as Cicero, Stobaeus, Sextus Empiricus, Diogenes Laërtius and Plutarch. The positions ascribed to the Stoics were frequently set up only in order to attack or mock. Since we must rely on the words of the critics and opponents of the Stoics, we must remember that these authors regularly assumed partisan, polemical and uncharitable, perspectives. It is almost certain that there are significant differences between what the Stoics themselves thought and what their critics said about them. Furthermore, many of these critical texts include *generalised attacks*, which were aimed at several philosophical schools at once, without regard for their differences. For example, Brad Inwood notes that reading Alexander's writings gives 'the impression . . . that this target is a mixed Stoic-Epicurean account'.[2] Such non-specific critiques lump together, and thus distort, the nuanced positions of the Stoics, the Epicureans and other ancient schools. The effect of generalised reports is that the schools seem to share a philosophical position that might have, in actuality, been a serious point of contention. Thus, the number of incorporeals in Stoicism could be different from the canonical four that the Stoics' critics and doxographers mention.

The second reason for our heterodoxy is that there is great variation among the Stoics themselves, especially concerning what does or does not count as an incorporeal. Cleomedes' *De Motu* (I.1.139–44), for example, uses the word 'surface' (επιφάνεια) instead of 'place' (τόπος): 'Everything that is limited has its limit in something different in kind . . . [thus] our bodies also similarly border onto something different in kind, their surface, which the particular application of this reasoning Plutarch, though hostile, also accepts that the Stoics thought bodies touch one another by means of an incorporeal limit.'[3] Moreover, rather than closing off the types of incorporeals at four, Cleomedes leaves the list open-ended with an '*et cetera*'. Sextus Empiricus, by contrast, reports that 'they [the Stoics] count four forms of incorporeals: sayable, void, place, and time'.[4] This strange combination of rigor (strictly four incorporeals) and fluidity (possibly fewer or more incorporeals) might further express the perversity of the Stoics' philosophical orientation. As Claude Imbert says, 'the most dogmatic in appearance, the Portico, is also the least dogmatic in fact . . . their arguments were always of sufficiency, never of completeness'.[5] Thus, the disagreement among the Stoics themselves suggests that there is sufficient space for our heterodoxy.

The third reason is that the list of the canonical incorporeals still puzzles contemporary philosophers. Here are a few examples. Bréhier expresses both appreciation and confusion at the oddity of this list when he writes that the 'profound originality of this theory is to have associated within the same group such very different beings' (*TI* 60). It might seem odd to give both time and λεκτα identical ontological status when they seem so different. Long and Sedley share Bréhier's concern: 'Why are they [λεκτα] grouped together with place, void, and time whose incorporeality seems unproblematic' (*HP* 199)? Since place and void (or space) and time seem similarly incorporeal, we might not question a list consisting of these. But it seems strange to include these four things, given their dissimilarity, in a list that is organised as including things 'of the same type'. Victor Goldschmidt shows similar puzzlement by noticing: '[i]ncorporeals are not all inexistent to the same degree' (*SS* 26). Although we may consider place and time, for example, either inexistent or non-existent (as opposed to existent bodies), they seem to in-exist or not-exist in very different ways. Frédérique Ildefonse poses it as a question and lets it ring: 'Why the four incorporeals: void, place, time, λεκτα?'[6] Jacques Brunschwig, Ildefonse's teacher, attempts to answer this question by locating 'two cleavages' that unsettle the list of incorporeals. The first cleavage divides the three that are 'continuous and infinitely divisible, namely time, place, and the void from the fourth [λεκτα], which is not'.[7] The second cleavage divides the two that 'are both unique and infinite (namely time and the void) from the other two that are multiple and finite (places and the λεκτα)'.[8] Vanessa de Harven also admits that 'it has been unclear what this *motley crew* of immaterial entities have in common ... the incorporeals look like left over entities that don't fit the corporeal mold, but aren't quite dispensable either'.[9] This suggests her tentative conclusion: 'the Stoics worked with an open-ended list of incorporeals according to the principle of body*less*-ness'.[10] As we can see, contemporary scholars of Stoicism are still confused by this list, as no one has provided a truly convincing account yet.

In addition to these three reasons, there are at least three advantages of our Deleuzian reading of Stoic incorporeals, each corresponding to one of the three incorporeals.

First, our reading allays the confusion as to why place and void are considered separate types of incorporeal when they seem to be rather two ways of understanding space. Although several scholars notice this, none seems particularly interested in sorting it out. Long and Sedley, for example, admit that the 'Stoics, unlike Epicurus, do not seem anxious to treat place and void as merely terms which pick out different aspects of the same concept' (*HP* 296). Contrary to Long and Sedley, Kiempe Algra is one of the few scholars who recognises that the 'Stoics differed from Aristotle in so far as they no longer defined the void as a *kind* of place (namely as *unoccupied* place), but instead regarded both place and void as species of a more general "entity", namely what we might call "space".'[11] Our reading will support and further develop Algra's claims by showing that the Stoics were indeed quite anxious to see place and void as two dimensions of the same concept. One reason for this anxiety was grounded in the limits of the Greek language.

Second, our reading also clarifies the clever account of the Stoics' materialist theory of language. As Ildefonse insightfully notices, there is debate as to whether or not the Stoics had a fully worked-out grammar.[12] Whether or not Stoic grammar was complete, it is clear that they strove to formalise the dynamic structure of language, especially in so far as it expresses their original metaphysical concerns. Given their commitments to immanence and rejection of transcendence, the Stoics had to explain how incorporeal language is both the effect *and* the quasi-cause of states of affairs. We sorted out the general logic of this in 'The Yolk B', and in 'The Shell A' we will

The Yolk C: Space

show how rational speech (λόγος) comes from unintelligible noises (Φωνή) and the emergence of linguistic sense itself. In short: how do meaning and matter relate? In 'Logic A' we will see that the answer comes from a strange double-sided surface. Using grammatical categories from 'The Yolk A', the formal logic of bodies captures the relations among nouns, and the transcendental logic of incorporeals expresses the relations among verbs.

Finally, our reading addresses some of the concerns arising from the Stoics' seemingly paradoxical accounts of time. Noticing 'the apparently conflicting account Chrysippus gave of the past, present, and future', A. A. Long distinguishes what he calls 'physical time and psychological time'.[13] Long does not, however, given all the argumentation offered in support of his distinction, and given that thoughts are physical, this distinction is not convincing. Further, our distinction between two senses of time better addresses conflicting accounts of time in Chrysippus because it does not smuggle in the non-physical connoted by comparing the psychological to the physical (which is an issue because the Stoics saw the psychological as physical).

Combining these reasons and advantages creates enough space in ancient and contemporary accounts of Stoic metaphysics through which our heterodoxical claim emerges. Despite the scholarly misgivings listed above, no one, to my knowledge, has satisfactorily explained *why* the number of incorporeals is four and not three, five or any number. Or, if it is an ever-increasing or open-ended list, no one has yet explained *why* this is the case, as opposed to a finite set. We, however, will explain why there are exactly *three* types of incorporeals – no more, no less. The way we make this argument is to locate a distinct, double-sided structure in one incorporeal – space – and then demonstrate how this structure is repeated in the other two incorporeals – λεκτα and time. We will go into more detail about λεκτα and time in 'The Shell A' and 'The Albumen C', respectively. Space is the incorporeal that falls within the study of physics, while λεκτα is the incorporeal proper to logic, and time concerns ethics. Let us now see how void and place form only one, not two, incorporeal: space.

The Whole, the All and Infinite Divisibility

To begin, let us review some of our Deleuzian account of Stoic physics from the last two chapters. The highest category, *something*, divides into corporeals and incorporeals. Corporeals are existents and are divided into two principles: active and passive. All bodies, from the infinitesimally small to the largest, are constantly acting and being acted upon. The Stoic universe is one self-affecting body, a cosmic egg self-unfolding according to eternally repeated cycles. The egg imagery connotes plenistic physics, a finite world of constant corporeal contact. The Stoic world is completely full, without gaps – a stuffed egg. The entire cosmos is crammed with bodies through spatial dimensions: front to back, side to side and top to bottom, or what Diogenes Laërtius calls 'length, breadth, and depth' (DL 7.135). *There are* (*Il y a*) bodies all the way down. Bodies composed of bodies, composed of bodies, composed of bodies, ad infinitum. Everywhere only bodies. The Stoic cosmos is a *corporeal continuum*.[14]

Complete corporeal continuity entails *infinite divisibility of matter*, thereby opposing the Stoics to the atomists. A hallmark of atomic theory is the limitation of the material division. The word *a-tom* (ἄ-τομον) means 'uncuttable, indivisible'. Atomists from Democritus to Epicurus to Lucretius agreed that there are physical and conceptual minima. For all atomists, matter 'bottoms out' at a limit.

The Stoics' attack on the atomic thesis of the indivisibility of matter echoes Aristotle's arguments from *Physics*, Book IV, Chapter One. As indivisibles, the argument goes, atoms must be partless. If they had parts, they could be divided into those parts and thus would not truly be indivisible. The Stoics' 'favorite objection to the champions of partless magnitudes', Plutarch reports, 'is that there must then be contact neither of wholes with wholes nor of parts with parts' nor of part to whole (*HP* 50C6). If the atoms touch whole to whole, then they would not be two distinct bodies but instead collapse into one. This 'produces', Plutarch continues, 'not contact but blending' (*HP* 50C6). Atoms also cannot touch part to part (or part to whole) 'because partless magnitudes do not have parts' (*HP* 50C6). Thus, atoms cannot touch or combine. Since atomism explains the cosmos through the atomic combination, if atoms cannot combine, then the atomic cosmology fails to fulfil its promise. The Stoics thus reject atomic indivisibles and embrace the principle of the indivisibility of matter.

Chrysippus is careful to forestall the later objection of Lucretius.[15] If bodies were infinitely divisible, the objection goes, and thereby every body would be composed of infinitely many parts, then every body would be composed of the same number of parts – infinite – and the same size – also infinite. In response, Chrysippus argues that,

The Yolk C: Space

although a body is infinitely divisible, this does not entail an actual infinity of elemental composing parts (*HP* 50C3). Division does not proceed 'to infinity [εἰς ἄπειρον]', in the sense of ending up at an actual infinite entity. Instead, Chrysippus merely claims that there will be a continuous process of dividing as long as we care to divide. Every answer given to the question as to how many parts compose a body is strictly arbitrary.[16] The Stoic thesis of the infinite divisibility of matter thus avoids Lucretius' eventual objection.

While there is no limit to how far bodies can be broken down, there is a largest body: the cosmos (κοσμος). The cosmos, as an egg, is singular and finite, whole (ὅλον) and complete unto itself. The universe does not expand infinitely in all directions but instead exhausts the cosmological curve of the eggshell. Diogenes reports: 'The world, they say, is one and finite, having a spherical shape' (DL 140). Within the shell, there are only bodies. Outside the shell, there is still something. As it is imprecise to say that an incorporeal *is* beyond the whole cosmos, we say that this incorporeal something *subsists* extracosmically. What is this subsisting something beyond the whole cosmos? Void, κενόν (literally: 'empty').

Sextus notices a distinction:

> Stoic philosophers suppose that there is a difference between the 'whole' [ὅλον] and the 'all' [πᾶν]. For they say that the world is *whole*, but the external void together with the world is *all*. For this reason they say the 'whole' is finite, since the world is finite, but the 'all' is infinite, since the void outside the world is such. (HP 44A; emphases added)[17]

'The whole' designates the cosmos, the finite sum of bodies swarmed together, the egg. 'The all' designates the cosmos *plus* the extracosmic void. Beyond the bodies composing the whole, void is utterly incorporeal. There are no bodies in the void, as bodies are always in a place. We should be precise about the genealogies of the ancient senses of place and void, starting with *place*.

Place

According to Bréhier, the Stoics follow Aristotle's thinking about place in his *Physics*, especially in so far as it responds to Zeno of Elea's paradoxes.[18] Aristotle entertains four possible candidates for the proper meaning of place: (1) form, (2) matter, (3) the extension or interval between the extremities, or (4) the extremities themselves. Aristotle selected the fourth, the Stoics the third.[19]

To define place as (3) the 'extension between the extremities' of a body entails the fullness of what is extended. A filled extension connects directly to the Stoic account of matter. 'Chrysippus', reports Stobaeus, 'declared place to be what is occupied through and through by an existent, or what can be occupied by an existent and is through and through occupied whether by one thing or by several things' (*HP* 49A). Place is 'made equal to what occupies it', defined completely by the body or bodies that occupy it (*HP* 49B). Connecting place to bodies also connects place to motion. Since bodies constantly move, place is like a transition marker for the bodies passing into and out of it. 'Place', writes Bréhier, 'is the point of passage common to several bodies which succeed one another' (*TI* 38). Aristotle describes this account of place – the replacement of one body by another body – by comparing it to a vase. Although different kinds of bodies can fill up a vase, the place of the vase persists. Move wine, sand or coins into or out of it, the interval between the sides of the vase (its place) remains unchanged.[20] 'The problem of place', Bréhier notices, 'is thus connected, as in Aristotle, to the problem of movement' (*TI* 39).

The reason why Aristotle selected the fourth candidate in his list is due to his objections to the third. 'If there were an extension which were such as to exist independently and be permanent,' Aristotle objects, 'there would be an infinity of places in the same thing.'[21] If wine is poured out of a vase and sand replaces it, it would seem that either there are two bodies in one place or, if a place is defined completely by the occupying body, then there are two places in one place. Yet more than just two, a potentially infinite number of bodies would be in the same place. Even worse, an infinite number of places would be in *one and the same place*.[22] Still, the Stoics openly select the third candidate because they think they can avoid their sting of his objections.

The Stoics strive to evade Aristotle's challenges through, first, their account of the infinite divisibility of bodies. Aristotle's hypothesis of space as the extension between extremities assumes two things: (1) a clear independence of the containing body (vase) and the contained body (wine), and (2) a clear point of contact between the extremities of each body. The Stoics, however, erase complete corporeal independence and inter-bodily contact. Since bodies are infinitely divisible, there is no last bodily extremity that determines its complete independence from other bodies. Since there are potentially infinitely many parts of every body, Plutarch notes, there always remains the possibility of further division, resulting in more and more bodies

The Yolk C: Space

below (*HP* 50C). This leads to what Bréhier considers an 'essential, paradoxical, and very profound' consequence of Stoic materialism, which he calls the 'thesis of the interpenetrability of bodies' (*TI* 40). If there is no precise and final point at which one body stops and another begins, then *all bodies reciprocally and perpetually interpenetrate*. Each body is *in* other bodies and other bodies are *in* each body; no particular body is completely independent. Everything corporeal is in the corporeal everything. The correlate of this thesis is the porousness of bodily extremities. As bodies are constantly interpenetrating, there is no clear point of inter-bodily contact. The Stoic cosmos is a totally blended mixture.

Despite Aristotle's misgivings, it also seems that two bodies can be in the same place. As Brunschwig notes, 'it is not strictly true that one body corresponds to each place; for in Stoic physics, which is known to admit total mixture, a single place may be occupied by several bodies'.[23] Without complete corporeal independence, we cannot strictly speak of a containing vase or the contained wine. Bréhier connects this to a famous Leibnizian thesis: 'The "all [*tout*] is in the all [*tout*]" of Leibniz represented here by the "total mixture"' (*TI* 41). Deleuze's Leibniz book echoes Bréhier: 'As the Stoics stated, nothing is either separable or separated, but everything conspires [*conspire*], including substance.'[24] Diogenes Laërtius sums it up with an evocative metaphor: 'According to Chrysippus, blendings (κράσεις) occur through and through, and not by surface contact and juxtaposition. If a little drop of wine were cast into the sea, it will be equally diffused over the whole sea for a while and then be blended with it' (DL 7.151).

Other ancient thinkers take issue with this account of material mixture. Plutarch, for example, thought that seeing the active part of matter, which the Stoics call God or Λόγος, as neither pure nor simple means that it must be composite or a mixture. As a mixture, the thinking goes, it must be dependent on something else. But this is a false dichotomy. More than merely simple or composite (*mutatis mutandis*, active or passive), the Stoics strive to conceive of principle itself as essentially composite. Strong resonance holds between Stoic mixture and Deleuzian multiplicity in so far as they both designate a organisation belonging to the many, as Deleuze writes: 'multiplicity must not designate the many and the one, but rather an *organisation belonging to the many as such*, which has no need whatsoever of unity in order to form a system' (*DR*, 182; emphasis added).[25] Beyond the simple or composite, the pure or the sullied, the Stoic active principle (God, Λόγος) is a manifold that organises without unifying, uniting or homogenising, a form of organisation that is essentially composed. Rather than an utterly distinct vase and wine, the Stoics see a thoroughly blended oenological ocean, a single sea of wine.

If we connect the thesis of the interpenetrability of bodies and total mixture to the Stoic selection of Aristotle's third candidate for the meaning of 'place', we see that all bodies form a single cosmos occupying a single place. Beyond the cosmos, there is no place; the shell of the cosmological egg is the limit, not void. Void cannot limit the universe because it is not physical, and only physical things can limit other physical things.[26] Bréhier, too, notices this: 'the limit of a body, and in particular that of the world, is given by the internal reason that extends in space, without encountering there the least resistance, and not by space itself' (*TI* 47). Beyond the egg, there are no limits. The shell of the egg functions as the limit of the extension of the world. As incorporeal, place cannot act or be acted upon. It subsists simply as the place 'where' corporeal interaction occurs. The interval within the shell (logic) is the place of the cosmos, which is where the yolk (physics) and the albumen (ethics) hold sway. The shell is the limit of the world. All bodies, being infinitely divisible, thus occupy one and the same place. There is only one place, as there is only one world. Beyond, only void subsists.

Atomic Void

The atomists are the most ardent thinkers of void. Their thinking on this is likely a response to the Eleatic notion of non-being.[27] From Leucippus to Lucretius, void is essential to ancient atomic theory. Despite the nuanced variations in their respective accounts of void, we here focus only on Epicurus.[28]

Risking uncharitable reduction, Epicurean atomism is grounded on two elemental principles. 'The totality', writes Epicurus, 'is made of bodies (ἄτομα) and void (κενόν) . . . Beyond these two things nothing can be conceived.'[29] The key difference from the Eleatics is that, for Epicurus, both bodies and void *exist*; they are existent beings. Through these two elements, Epicurus explained the nature of things, starting with what is arguably the most important atomic principle: movement.[30]

To explain the undeniably real movement of the world (while simultaneously rejecting Parmenides' arrest of motion), Epicurus argues that bodies and void are equally necessary because movement is impossible without void. In his account of motion, Epicurus equalises four terms: 'room' (χώρα), 'place' (τόπος), 'intangible substance' (ἀναφὴς φύσις) and 'void' (κενόν).[31] In Epicurean atomism, 'void' functions as the 'room' through which bodies move; 'place' is where bodies are as they move.[32] Epicurus characterises void as 'intangible substance' in order to avoid Aristotle's challenge: the interaction of occupied void and occupying body is impossible, Aristotle argues, if both are substantial (and thus mutually excluding) beings.[33] In response, Epicurus makes void substantial *yet* intangible. Making void an intangible, immaterial and submissive substance means that void cannot be acted upon, and thus cannot impede bodies. Void is more like a three-dimensional extensive space that can only be occupied or unoccupied. When occupied, it is 'place'; when unoccupied, it is 'void'. The atomists thus define void in terms of giving way, relenting or submitting. It is 'the nature of the void which separates each of them [atoms] and is not able to provide resistance'.[34] In short, void yields. Yielding to atomic bodies is atomic movement. Without void, the argument goes, all bodies would be packed together, thereby arresting motion and leaving a completely static universe, similar to what Parmenides describes. Since there is void, however, motion is not only possible but actual. As Lucretius says, 'if there were no place and space [*locus ac spatium*] which we call void [*inane*], bodies could not . . . move anywhere at all'.[35]

Stoic Void

Stoic void is different in at least four ways. One difference: they do not equalise void and place, or any of the four terms listed above. As we will see, although void and place are distinct in Stoicism, they are two dimensions of one species of incorporeal. Another difference: Stoic void does not exist because it is ontologically different from body. Bodies and void express two different ontological natures: bodies exist, void subsists. As incorporeal, void subsists, like place, time and Λεκτα. A third, perhaps most important, difference: Stoic void is intensive, not extensive. We explain this below. A fourth difference: atomists and Stoics provide different accounts of motion. For the atomists, void is what makes motion possible. For the Stoics, void immobilises. Void and bodies mutually exclude each other in Stoic theory; wherever a body is, the space occupied is place, not void. Thus, bodies cannot move through void.[36] Empty space arrests bodies, rather than mobilises them. In Stoic physics, the nterpenetrability of bodies allows for motion, not void. Stoic movement is always and fully corporeal. Bodies never move through nothingness; they move through each other. In the cosmos, bodies are constantly swirling, churning and turning into, out of and through the whole body of the world. The cosmological egg is a swarming, spinning bodily mass.[37]

As an incorporeal, Stoic void is negatively defined. We can divide Cleomedes' account of void into seven negative qualities and one positive quality. Void, he writes,

> is incorporeal and without contact [ἀσωμάτου] and intangible [ἀναφοοῦς], has neither shape [σχῆμα] nor takes on shape [σχηματιζομένου], is neither acted upon in any respect nor acts, but is simply capable of receiving body [δέχεσθαι οἷόν τε ὄντος]. (HP 49C)

Grouping the seven negations together, void subsists as (1) incorporeal, (2) without contact, (3) intangible, (4) shapeless, (5) unshapeable, (6) inactive and (7) impassive. Cleomedes identifies one positive quality: the *capacity to receive a body*. This capacity does not conflict, but aligns, with the negative qualities. As Goldschmidt recognises, void's capacity 'is neither an action, nor even a passion', nor a tangible shape (*SS* 28). We have a term, which we discussed in the previous chapter, to describe this capacity: quasi-causality.

With this quasi-causal capacity, void is extremely minimal, hence Cleomedes characterises it as 'the simplest thought' (*HP* 49C). Void is the Stoic concept closest to nothingness without disappearing completely, which is especially relevant when we consider the canonical list of incorporeals. Place, time and Λεκτα all clearly relate to bodies. Place gains determinateness from the limits of bodies, and we will see how determinateness is also transferred from bodies to time and to Λεκτα. At least here, void is the odd one out. 'Void is', Bréhier notes, 'among all the incorporeals that we have studied until now, in an absolutely special situation' (*TI* 49). Goldschmidt agrees: 'Void ... is a pure incorporeal' (*SS* 27). As the furthest from existent body, void is the incorporeal furthest from existence. As the *least* bodily, it subsists as the *most* incorporeal, the *most* non-existent. Brunschwig agrees, 'void is ... the incorporeal par excellence'.[38]

With these Stoic accounts of place and void in hand, we can begin to make the argument that void and place are not two separate kinds of incorporeals, but two articulations of a single type: space. We think of space as the single double-sided incorporeal surface, with place and void as its two sides.

The Yolk C: Space

Something Else Unnamed

Let us recall our heterodoxical claim. Place and void are not two distinct types of incorporeal, but two sides of a single incorporeal surface: space. Recalling also the three reasons for and advantages of this claim, and having distinguished Stoic void and place from other ancient accounts, we can now fully motivate it. With this we will have in hand our first full Stoic incorporeal – space – the one studied by physics and metaphysics.

To begin, note that there are at least two places where the Stoics suggest that place and void are specifications of a broader category. Stobaeus reports that Chrysippus pointed to a 'third thing', a 'nameless thing' that gathers place and void: 'if what can be occupied by an existent is partly occupied by something and partly unoccupied, the whole will be neither place nor void, but *something else unnamed* [οὐκ ὠνομασμένον]; for void is spoken of almost in the manner of empty containers, while place in the manner of full ones' (*HP* 49A; emphasis added).[39] Chrysippus seems to have conceived of a broader category, a 'something else unnamed' into which place and void are folded. The 'something else unnamed', we argue, is the spatial consideration of *both* place *and* void. There is the space with bodies – place – and the space without bodies – void; or: occupied and unoccupied space. Although Chrysippus did not name it, we can: 'space'. The key is that this becomes evident through Deleuze's Stoicism.

While it might sound strange to modern ears, Keimpe Algra, the scholar who has done the most work on space in antiquity (having written *the* book on it), corroborates our claim several times: 'I would like to point out that there was a kind of general concept of what we might call "space" underlying the various concepts of topos, chôra, and kenon' and 'the Stoics . . . regarded both place and void of a more general entity, namely what we might call "space."'[40] Vanessa de Harven adds an important caveat, 'I don't take extension [her name for space] to be a *further* incorporeal entity but the mode of incorporeal reality that place, void and room all share; it is the principle of their subsistence.'[41] The caveat is that there is not a third type of incorporeal, either the whole or extension, in addition to the place and void (and Λεκτα and time). Space is not a fifth incorporeal, but a *single incorporeal composed of two different faces*: place and void.

Consider this passage from Galen: 'The Stoics are compelled to admit that extension in three dimensions [τὸ τριχῇ διαστατόν] is common to body and void and place' (*HP* 49E). Galen thus also identifies a third thing. But, rather than leave it unspoken, a nameless thing, Galen calls it 'extension [διάστημα]'. According to Deleuze's Stoicism, extension is not completely accurate.[42] Extension is an essential component of space, to be sure, but it only applies to place, not to void. We argue that there is a single incorporeal that folds (rather than adds to) place and void into a single surface. It is wrong, on our account, to see extension as this one incorporeal. Space subsists as the true incorporeal. The reasoning is straightforwardly Deleuzian: place is extensive space while void is intensive space.

Space: The First Frontier

Before recasting place and void as, respectively, extensive space and intensive space, we should pause to consider an important question: why did the Stoics not just talk about space directly? If place and void are really two sides of a single spatial surface, why did they not just use a Greek word for it? Why go to the trouble of saying something that should easily be encapsulated in a single term? Our answer is simple: *there was no word for space in ancient Greek*.[43]

Algra notices that the 'Greek language did not have a terminological distinction matching the conceptual distinction between place and space'.[44] There were conceptual distinctions, but the lack of a clearly articulated term for 'space' is striking. After all, the Greeks and Romans were usually very careful about their terminology.[45] They rarely passed up an opportunity to formulate or invent technical terms in order to make, match or change fine conceptual distinctions and definitions.[46] Still, they did not have a 'univocal term exclusively denoting space'.[47] It makes sense that Algra entitled his book *Concepts of Space in Greek Thought*, with 'Concepts' plural, rather than *The Concept of Space in Greek Thought*. Even in Aristotle, the ancient thinker most likely to develop a concept of space distinct from other spatial concepts (place [τόπος], the category of 'where' [ποῦ], the sense of locomotion, and so on), there was, Edward Hussey writes, an 'almost total absence of any concept of *space*'.[48] We can see this etymologically, too. The English 'space' comes from the French *espace*, which derives from the Latin *spatium* and further to the Greek σπάω, meaning 'to draw, to pull (a sword [ξίφος[49]])', as when Achilles pulls out his sword in battle. 'Space' does not connect to a Greek word, but instead turns into swordfights. There was no name, in the singular, for 'space' in antiquity.

The Yolk C: Space

This lack of a univocal, singular and independent concept of space allowed, Algra notes, 'the early Stoics to "isolate" the notion of space' for the first time.[50] Part of our claim is that the Stoics' perverted materialism pushed the commitment to matter further than any other ancient thinkers. The closest Plato comes to thinking of space, as a self-subsistent something, is the 'receptacle' in the *Timaeus*, and Aristotle somewhat follows Plato on this, as Hussey notes: Aristotle, 'does have a substitute for space in some of its roles – namely the notion of matter'.[51] Before 'the Hellenistic schools', writes Algra, 'neither Greek common parlance, nor the early philosophical Greek had a term which *exclusively* denoted space. The *early Stoics and rival schools were important innovators.*'[52] We argue that these innovations were part of the Hellenic turn to materialism, away from the Platonic–Aristotelian affinities for ideas and forms. Moreover, we argue that the Stoics, more than the atomists, were the more sophisticated thinkers of matter, and their account of incorporeal space expresses this. From the perspective of a Deleuzian reading, the Stoics' innovation in spatial thinking is the formulation of a single, double-sided incorporeal surface. Hence a simple formula: place + void = space. The difference between the two sides is the difference between the extensive and the intensive.

Intensive and Extensive Space

In 'The Yolk A', we considered the vocabulary of extensive and intensive in terms of measurements. To remind us, if we divide an extensive measurement of one metre in length into two half-metres, there is no change in kind. *What* is measured remains essentially the same – length – regardless of subtractions or additions. But if we change an intensive measurement, such as heating up the temperature of water beyond 100 degrees Celsius or cooling it below zero, there is a change in kind: water becomes steam or ice.

To take another example, consider Manuel DeLanda's description of this difference.[53] Extensive space consists of a certain amount of fixed lengths, such as the acreage of a farm, which are defined by certain limits or frontiers, such as the fence of a farmer's field. Acreage, as extensive, is additive. Adding more space to a farm results in more of the same; on either side of the fence, there is just more soil to till. An intensive space, by contrast, is not measured in acres but is 'marked by *critical points* of temperature, pressure, gravity, density, tensions'.[54] A critical threshold indicates the point at which there is a change in kind. Think of the discomfort that is felt when one enters our personal space or when a newsperson reports along the hazy edges of a hurricane. DeLanda cites 'weather maps that have become common in television news' and 'made intensive spaces very tangible (zones of high and low pressure, cold or warm fronts defining the sharp temperature transitions)'.[55] Such thresholds are not evenly spaced like millimetre marks on a metre stick because they are not preset. Instead, these thresholds emerge due to the emergent organisation of the intensities composing the spaces. Intensive space is not there, ready-made, but emerges out of the intensification of space.

Considering this difference, in Deleuze's Stoicism extensive space is place and intensive space is void. Extension here is a question of occupation. 'The Stoics', writes Sextus, 'say that void [κενόν] is what can be occupied by an existent [body] but *is not occupied*, or an empty interval [διάστημα ἔρημον], or an interval unoccupied by body. Place is what *is occupied* by an existent [body] and made equal to what occupies it.'[56] In short, place is occupied space; void is empty space. Where bodies are, space subsists; where bodies are not, void subsists. Since place is defined in relation to bodies and bodies are finite, place is finite; place subsists equal in dimension to the occupying body. By contrast, void subsists beyond bodies, functioning as the empty space outside corporeality. Beyond the totality of 'what is', void spreads out infinitely from the corporeal cosmos in all directions at once. While place is finite and limited and void is infinite and unlimited, both articulate space.

Place is extensive because extension refers to the spatial coordinates of our physical universe: height, width and depth. Everything that is, is a body, and can thus be described according to these three dimensions. Even though bodies can be infinitely divided, at each stage of the division, the body, however small, still expresses a finite height, width and depth. In contrast to place, void is intensive. Devoid of bodies, Cleomedes reports, height, depth or any other dimensions cannot be said of void.[57] Since void is space considered independently of bodies and their finite, limited dimensions, it is infinite and unlimited.[58] As Chrysippus reportedly argued:

> Void is said to be infinite. For what is outside the cosmos is like this, but place is finite because no body is infinite. Just as the corporeal is finite, so the incorporeal is infinite, for both time and void are infinite. For just as non-being is no limit, so too there is no limit to non-being, which is the kind thing void is [a non-being]. For according to its own subsistence

The Yolk C: Space

[κατὰ γὰρ τὴν αὐτοῦ ὑπόστασιν], it is infinite. But it is made finite by being filled up. But if that which fills is taken away, a limit to it cannot be conceived.[59]

Thus 'according to its own subsistence', void is intrinsically infinite. Void subsists as unlimited space. Place is limited due to its occupying body; void is unlimited.

Recalling our above discussion of place and the infinite divisibility of bodies, this sense of limited and unlimitedness suggests we should pay special attention to a repeated phrase: 'to infinity [εἰς ἄπειρον]'. While Chrysippus denies that division of bodies *actually* proceeds 'to infinity', Cleomedes describes void with this very phrase. Given that place and bodies are necessarily linked, and given that there is no actual infinity at which conceptual division arrives through divisions, we cannot actually divide *place* 'to infinity'. Void, however, does divide 'to infinity'. This echoes the void's proximity to nothingness, implying that *void is more incorporeal than place* and *place is more corporeal than void*. Void comes closest to disappearing into nothingness without disappearing completely. 'Void', Bréhier writes, 'is thus considered as a sort of body attenuated until it has lost all its properties, but is nevertheless existent, since it is separated from bodies' (*TI* 49). Void is still something, but it is something in so far as it nearly vanishes to infinity (εἰς ἄπειρον).

Deleuze's term to describe this sense of a nearly vanishing something is: intensity. Intensity is closely related to Deleuze's appropriation of Leibniz's infinitesimals. An infinitesimal is, in essence, a disappearing difference, a difference that tends to, but does not actually, disappear. It is called an 'infinite*simal*' (*infinitesimus*) because it is an infinitely small difference, a difference smaller than any quantity or extension.[60] Infinitesimals have 'neither sensible form nor conceptual signification, nor ... assignable function' (*DR* 183). They are still something, while they are almost, but not yet, nothing. Notice the important similarities between the nature of infinitesimals and that of Stoic void. As void lacks determined extensive measurements, it is composed of infinitely dividing spaces, that is, spaces that are infinitesimal. Infinitesimal spaces are covered up by the extensive intervals spanning the cosmos. Like infinitesimals, void has 'neither existence, nor value, nor signification'.[61] Although it seems equal to nothingness, void is not yet nothing. As the measurement of the void, since it is intensive, it is smaller than any quantifiable difference. Intensive spatial measurements infinitely approach but never reach zero; they subsist as vanishing without having vanished, disappearing but not yet disappeared.

We also see another sense of the term 'unlimited', ἄπειρον, a term that Chrysippus and others use to describe void. As Inwood says, 'for Chrysippus ἄπειρον seems to invoke a qualitative rather than a quantitative notion'.[62] The sense of the intensive nature of void is closer to a qualitative than a quantitative notion in so far as qualitative infinity is more intensive and quantitative infinity more extensive. Inwood is very close to getting this, but then takes a wrong turn, just as he is about to make this claim: 'Place is occupied body', he writes,

> in so far as a body has a limit, place does too. Void is not so occupied, and hence cannot have a limit ... it gets its limits from the body which comes to occupy it ... where no body is found limits are impossible. That, simply put, is the metaphysical case for the unlimitedness, not the 'infinity,' of the void.[63]

While this resonates well with our claims, we go further. Although void might not be an actual existent infinity, it is a surface composed of infinitesimals, which is why void is not extensive but intensive. In short, the unlimitedness (ἄπειρον) of the void is an intensive or qualitative unlimitedness.

One reason to think of void as intensive is to reveal its quasi-causality. While bodies are causal, which we will call in 'The Yolk A' a kind of dynamic genesis, incorporeals are quasi-causal, which we will called a kind of static genesis. Conceiving of space as completely devoid of bodies reveals its genetic structure. While not 'causing' bodies or the cosmos, void, as intensive space, give rise to extensive spaces; that is, unoccupied and unlimited void contributes to the emergence of occupied and limited place. Put differently, the genetic condition for striated or extensive space is smooth space.

As we have repeated, the Stoic commitment to materialism leads them to consider the conditions for material existence, and one of these conditions is that bodies occupy space. This space cannot be corporeal, for it would then be another body, thus entailing infinite regress. Space must thus be incorporeal. As an incorporeal, however, it can be considered two ways – either in relation to or devoid of bodies – both of which are necessary to conceive space. If we think of space in relation to bodies and their limits, it is extensive; if we think space devoid of bodies, it is intensive. As the cosmos is populated by individual bodies, void is composed of pre-individual singularities, ever-changing gradients, continuous variation. Twisting Deleuze's

The Yolk C: Space

words, the intensive side of the surface is 'the *spatium* of the egg' (DR 251). In the void, there is no depth or height, no up or down. There subsists only the smooth arc of infinitely dividing, in opposed directions, or: void.

Put differently, a commitment to materialism must engage the incorporeal conditions for corporeals, and specifying the nature of this incorporeal condition is perhaps the most perverse task of Stoic metaphysics. The incorporeal cannot resemble corporeals without risking circularity or by rendering bodies subordinate to active, causal incorporeal principles (as Plato and Aristotle do). Echoing 'The Yolk B', incorporeals also cannot resemble the corporeals by postulating a material depth without entering an infinite regress of matter all the way down into cavernous depth (as pre-Socratics do). Incorporeals thus must be dissimilar from the corporeals but not completely separate. They must subsist as something but not as some beings. They must be effects and quasi-causal, but not causes. In another language, incorporeals, especially void, do not function as a new ground but as a groundlessness (*un sans-fond*) that acts as the genetic condition for bodies. Stoic incorporeals do not form a new grounding but an ungrounding (*effondement*). The point is not to discover a groundlessness below, like the infinite depths of a volcano, for depth is a given in Stoicism. We are bodies, and that is all we *are*. Corporeality is what we assume about our world. But we are not given the smooth surface that cloaks our existence. What Deleuze most admires about Stoicism is their art of constructing surfaces. Thus what Lapoujade says of Deleuze also applies to the Stoics: 'the important thing for Deleuze is not discovering new depths, but rather *producing new surfaces*'.[64] In sum, space is that single double-sided surface that the Stoics construct; place and void are its extensive and intensive faces.

Conclusion: The Structure of the Three Incorporeals

In the chapter on Stoic physics and metaphysics, we have focused mostly on making our heterodoxical claim: void and place are not two distinct kinds of incorporeals, but two faces of a single concept: space. Space is the incorporeal proper to physics, which we are calling a perverted materialism partially because it caused a great upheaval in ancient philosophers. We now conclude this discussion of the Stoics' metaphysics of something, their theory of incorporeality and corporeal causation, and space by showing how this same double-sided, intensive/extensive single surface structure repeats for Stoic logic and ethics.

The difference between the two sides of space is that place is space considered in terms of the finitude and limitedness of occupying bodies, and void is space considered independently of bodies, and so as infinite and unlimited. Space is *one* incorporeal surface, composed of two sides: void and place. Space functions as that border without thickness separating and connecting void and place. Here is a new diagram based on the one found in Victor Goldschmidt's *Le Système stoïcien et l'idée de temps* (SS 39):

$$\text{SPACE} \begin{array}{c} \text{Void (infinite in all its parts)} \\ \hline \text{Place (limited)} \end{array}$$

Space is the incorporeal proper to Stoic physics; the other two belong to the other two parts of the Stoic egg: Λεκτα and logic, time and ethics. Parts II and III will engage these. In preparation, we extend the structure of space to Λεκτα and time.

Λεκτόν is the second kind of incorporeal. Much of *Logic of Sense* focuses on Λεκτα and sense, and we engage with this discussion in 'The Shell A'. Here we simply note that Λεκτα is also double-sided, respectively composed of conjugated verbs and infinitive verbs. Infinitive verbs are infinite and unlimited Λεκτα; conjugated verbs are finite and limited Λεκτα. Bringing them together and keeping them apart is that same ever-so-thin frontier that enters 'into the propositions themselves, between nouns and verbs, or, rather, between denotations and expressions' (LS 182).[65] Extending the language above, infinitive verbs are intensively considered Λεκτα and conjugated verbs extensively considered Λεκτα. We twist that same Goldschmidtian diagram to articulate the structure of Λεκτα:

$$\text{Λεκτα} \begin{array}{c} \text{Infinitive verb (infinite)} \\ \hline \text{Conjugated verb (limited)} \end{array}$$

Time is the third type of incorporeal, and it belongs to the domain of ethics. In Deleuze's Stoicism, there are two readings of time: chronos and aion. Chronos is finite and limited time, wherein only the present exists to a certain length and the past and future subsist. Aion, by contrast, is infinite and unlimited time, wherein the present,

The Yolk C: Space

past and future do not exist; all subsist. Put differently, chronos is corporeal time and aion is incorporeal time. In Deleuze's terms, chronos is extensive time and aion intensive time. What connects and separates them is that same paradoxical surface without thickness that runs throughout the whole Stoic egg. Here is a simplified version of Goldschmidt's actual diagram (*SS* 39):

$$\text{TIME} \begin{array}{c} \text{Aion (infinite)} \\ \hline \text{Chronos (limited)} \end{array}$$

Let us twist these diagrams one more time. Imagine this: take the 'ends' of the intensive and extensive faces of each flat incorporeal surface, twist them, and glue the twisting ends together. The result: three Möbius strips, three paradoxical surfaces, each turning in unison. One side of each is the extensive face – place, conjugated verb, chronos – the other side the intensive dimension – void, infinitive verb, aion. Each side constantly turns into and out of each other as the whole surface twists through the world, covering individual bodies and the entire cosmological egg.

In sum, as place is occupied space and void unoccupied space, chronos is filled time and aion empty time. As Deleuze says, 'Chronos is filled up with states of affairs and the movements of the objects that it measures. But being an empty and unfolded form of time, the aion subdivides ad infinitum that which haunts it without ever inhabiting it' (*LS* 64). To this we can add: conjugated verbs are filled Λεκτα and infinitive verbs are empty Λεκτα. Conjugated verbs are filled in so far as they are conjugated by bodily states of affairs (for example, when a denotation corresponds to a state of affairs, it is considered 'true'), while infinitive verbs endlessly empty or displace themselves. Taken together, space, time and Λεκτα are the three incorporeals in Deleuze's Stoicism. Stoic metaphysics, expressed through the encounter with Deleuze, constructs a genetic organisation composed of intensive and extensive dimensions that are separated and connected by a single surface. While Bréhier correctly observes that the 'tendency toward dualism is . . . rather strong in Stoicism', we should not understand such dualism too simply (*CAS* 139–40). Instead, we should remember that the way in which Stoicism constructs a dualism is quite different from the dualisms deployed in the other ancient schools. The Stoics construct a dualism that is actually a monism, as perverse as it is. The Stoic monism is a single double-sided surface, with extensive and intensive faces.

As we will see in Part II, the surface shows how the paradoxes that are provoked in Stoic theory are not explained away but are instead retained for their power to produce a new distribution of thought. The Stoic refusal to insist on retaining the productivity of paradoxes without recourse to transcendent forms is what, Deleuze argues, makes them initiators of a new image of the philosopher, one that runs counter to Platonism and Aristotelianism. This 'new image', Deleuze continues, 'is already closely linked to the paradoxical constitution of the theory of sense', and (we can add) space and time (*LS* xiv). These three incorporeals are paradoxically structured by the surface separating and connecting their respective extensive and intensive dimensions. It is through this perverse account of the incorporeals in Stoic ontology that the Stoics initiate a new image of philosophy that spawned a lineage of thought leading, eventually, to Deleuze himself.

Notes

1. Jacques Brunschwig, *Papers in Hellenistic Philosophy*, trans. Janet Lloyd (Cambridge: Cambridge University Press, 1994), 92.
2. Brad Inwood, 'Chrysippus on Extension and the Void', *Revue internationale de philosophie* 45.178 (1991): 245–66, at 263.
3. Cleomedes, *Comm. Not.* 1080e, and see Brunschwig, *Papers*, 96.
4. Sextus Empiricus, *Against the Physicists*, II.218.
5. Claude Imbert, *Pour une histoire de la logique. Un heritage platonicien* (Paris: Presses universitaires de France, 1999), 30.
6. Frédérique, Ildefonse, *Les Stoïciens I: Zénon, Cléanthe, Chrysippe* (Paris: Les Belles Lettres, 2000), 57.
7. Brunschwig, *Papers*, 134.
8. Brunschwig, *Papers*, 134.
9. Vanessa de Harven, 'How Nothing Can be Something: The Stoic Theory of Void', *Ancient Philosophy* 35.2 (2015): 405–29, at 406; emphasis added.
10. Ibid. 424.
11. Kiempe Algra, *Concepts of Space in Greek Thought* (Leiden: E. J. Brill, 1995), 270n.28; emphasis original.
12. Ildefonse, *La Naissance de la grammaire dans l'Antiquité classique* (Paris: J. Vrin, 1997), 138–44.
13. A. A. Long, 'The Stoics on World-Conflagration and Everlasting Recurrence', *Southern Journal of Philosophy* XXIII, Supplement (1985): 13–37, at 28.
14. We delay speaking of the temporal continuum until 'Albumen A' because the incorporeal time belongs to ethics not physics.

15. Lucretius, *De Rerum Natura*, 1.615–22.
16. This is also how the Stoics respond to the Zenoian objection that an infinite divisible continuum prevents motion. Since, the objection goes, every distance that a body would cross can be infinitely divided and subdivide, there is not first motion and thus motion cannot commence. The Stoic response, Proclus reports, is that such mathematical limits 'subsist in mere thought'; they are merely thought constructions, and so does not prevent the movement of actual bodies' (HP 50D).
17. Sextus Empiricus, *Against the Professors*, 9.332.
18. Aristotle, *Physics*, IV.3.6.
19. Ibid. IV.4.6.
20. Ibid. IV.2.4
21. Ibid. 211b19–211b29.
22. For more on this Aristotelian criticism, see chapters 5–6 of Richard Sorabji, *Matter, Space and Motion* (Ithaca: Cornell University Press, 1988).
23. Brunschwig, *Papers*, 137.
24. Gilles Deleuze, *The Fold: Leibniz and the Baroque* (1988), trans. Tom Conley (Minneapolis: University of Minnesota Press, 1993), 56.
25. Emphasis added. Robin Durie argues that Deleuze's uses the Riemannian multiplicity (by way of Bergson's modifications) to think Spinozist ontology that does not fall prey to the difficulties of thinking the relationship between the One and the Many. Durie, 'Immanence and Difference: Toward a Relational Ontology', *Southern Journal of Philosophy* 40.2 (2002): 161–89, at 169–70.
26. We must admit that there is no agreement as to the status of 'limit' in the Stoic theory of incorporeals, mostly due to Cleomedes inclusion of 'surface' (επιφάνεια), instead of 'place' (τόπος), in the list of incorporeals. For example, Brunschwig inclines towards including limits or surfaces in a third ontological class that he calls '*not something* (οὔτι = NST)', which 'denotes the ontological status of concepts (ἐννοήματα)'. Brunschwig, *Papers*, 92.
27. Keimpe Algra, *Concepts of Space in Greek Thought* (Leiden: E. J. Brill, 1995), 32.
28. For the history and genealogy of Epicurus' thinking about void, see Brad Inwood, 'The Origin of Epicurus' Concept of Void', *Classical Philology* 76 (1981): 273–85.
29. Epicurus, 'Letter to Herodotus', 39–40; see also Lucretius, *De Rerum Natura*, 1.429–44.
30. See Thomas Nail's *Lucretius I: An Ontology of Motion* (Edinburgh: Edinburgh University Press, 2018) for more on Lucretian atomism's prioritisation of movement.
31. Epicurus, 'Letter to Herodotus', 39–40. For differing accounts of this, see David Sedley, 'Two Conceptions of Vacuum', *Phronesis* 17.1:

175–93; Algra, *Concepts*, 44–53; and C. C. W. Taylor, *The Atomists, Leucippus and Democritus* (Toronto: University of Toronto Press, 2010), 184–6. We will return to this, but notice that 'space' is not on the list.

32. Sedley points out that the Greek word for 'room', χώρα, is etymologically linked to the Greek verb χωρεῖν, meaning 'to go'. David Sedley, 'Epicurean Physics', in *The Cambridge History of Hellenistic Philosophy*, ed. Keimpe Algra, Jonathan Barnes, Jaap Mansfeld and Malcolm Schofield (Cambridge: Cambridge University Press, 1999), 362–81, at 367.
33. Aristotle, *Physics*, IV.8.
34. *Epicurus: The Extant Remains*, ed. and trans. Cyril Bailey (Oxford: Clarendon Press, 1926), 44.
35. Lucretius, *De Rerum Natura*, 1.426–9. We will also return to this, but notice that Lucretius uses the word 'space (*spatium*)' even though Epicurus does not.
36. This is part of the reason why we have not dealt with the other spatial concept: 'room (χώρα)'. Although Sextus and others include room in their discussion of space in Stoicism (HP 49B), it seems to be included only in order to leave room for comparison to other accounts of space in antiquity. In terms of the logic of Stoic physics, however, it either plays little role or is excluded from describing nature. Furthermore, in that same article, Inwood astutely notes that χώρα is not in the canonical list of corporeals. This suggests, to Inwood and to us, that χώρα has no special importance and so is not found in the list of incorporeals' (Brad Inwood, 'Chrysippus on Extension and the Void', *Revue internationale de philosophie* 45.178 (1991): 245–66, at 254n.28).
37. Moreover, movement, in Stoic physics, also opposes Aristotelian motion. 'Movement', writes Bréhier, 'is not the passage of a power to act, but really is an act that always repeats anew' (TI 45). Since movement is fully corporeal, and bodies are only causes and never effects, movement is the same cosmological act again and again. As we will see in 'Albumen B', this repeated movement is the great conflagration or what Nietzsche will later call 'the eternal return'.
38. Jacques Brunschwig, 'Stoic Metaphysics', in *The Cambridge Companion to the Stoics*, ed. Brad Inwood (Cambridge: Cambridge University Press, 2003), 206–33, at 213. De Harven repeats Brunschwig's phrase: 'Void is', de Harven notices, 'the incorporeal par excellence being defined purely in terms of lacking body ... which is why one might be tempted to think of it as nothing at all.' De Harven, 'How Nothing Can be Something', 14.
39. Full reference is at Stobaeus, 1.161, 8–26.
40. Algra, *Concepts*, 270, 270n.28.
41. De Harven, 'How Nothing Can be Something', 17.

The Yolk C: Space

42. The reason why many scholars refer to space as 'extension', I take it, is due to the overwhelming success of early modern accounts of space as *extensio*.
43. For a fairly exhaustive bibliography on this topic, see Fransisco Caruso, *Sources for the History of Space Concepts in Physics: From 1845–1995* (Rio de Janeiro: Centro Brasileiro de Pesquisas Físicas), 1996.
44. Algra, *Concepts*, 32.
45. Think about Plato's grammatical nuance in his writing the names of the forms or of Cicero's endless attention to composing a distinctly Latin philosophical vocabulary.
46. Inwood seems mistaken on this point. 'This nameless entity never made the list [of canonical incorporeals], because although fundamental to the other two [place and void] it is exhausted by them; as long as they have been mentioned there is no need to add it to the established list' ('Chrysippus on Extension and the Void', 254). This is strange because, if this third term (which we argue is 'space') could exhaust or gather both place and void, then it would seem, especially given the Stoics' usual nominalism (something that Inwood admits in a footnote on that same page), that the Stoics should just use the term rather than repeat two separate terms over and over again. As we now see, they did not use the term because they did not have the term in the Greek language.
47. Algra, *Concepts*, 32.
48. Edward Hussey, *Aristotle's Physics Books III and IV* (Oxford: Clarendon Press, 1983), xxviii. To be fair, Hussey argues that this is not an embarrassing oversight, but 'is a mater of deliberate policy on Aristotle's part, and one for which he has good reasons'. Yet even if this is deliberate, the absence of a word for 'space' is question provoking.
49. ξίφος is the word Homer uses that we translate as 'sword'.
50. Algra, *Concepts*, 32.
51. Hussey, *Aristotle's Physics*, xxxi.
52. Algra, *Concepts*, 38; emphasis added. While I do not necessarily endorse this view, it is interesting to see scholars identify the Stoics as precursors of what became, in the modern period, 'absolute space'. The 'Stoics posit there to be absolute space, anticipate Newton and his allies in the modern period' (Powers, 'Void and Space', 430).
53. Manuel DeLanda, 'Space: Extensive and Intensive, Actual and Virtual', in *Deleuze and Space*, ed. Ian Buchanan and Gregg Lambert (Edinburgh: Edinburgh University Press, 2005), 80–8.
54. Ibid. 80.
55. Ibid. 80.
56. Sextus Empiricus, *Against the Professors*, 10.3–4; emphasis added.
57. Found in Bréhier, 'Theory of Incorporeals', 47 but originally in *SVF* 173.9.

58. Perhaps we should comment on the scholarly confusion on this point. Some miss the point completely, others are partially correct. Nathan Powers, for example, is correct to say that, 'for Chrysippus . . . [taking] together place and void imply a notion of space', but he is wrong to call space 'extension'. Nathan M. Powers, 'Void and Space in Stoic Ontology', *Journal of the History of Philosophy* 52.3 (July 2014): 411–32, at 418. Even Algra is mistaken to consider the general category 'space' as extension. Algra, *Concepts*, 270. Algra also unfairly doubts what he calls Inwood being 'unnecessarily skeptical about the Chrysippean (or in general: early Stoic) credentials of the term "extension" (διάςτημα)'. Alga, *Concepts*, 271n.30. Inwood is right to doubt the use of διάςτημα, since, we are aruging, only place is extensive, but not void. Similarly, Robert Todd's account of void is on the right track but ultimately never arrives. He claims, following Cleomedes' report, that void has no extension. Robert B. Todd, 'Cleomedes and the Stoics Concept of the Void', *Apeiron: A Journal for Ancient Philosophy and Science* 16.2 (December 1982): 129–36. Todd's argument rests on Cleomedes' claim that space lacks shape. This is correct if 'shape' refers to extensive measurement – length, breadth, height – but not intensive measurement.
59. Stobaeus, *Eclogae*, I.161, 17–26 (*SVF* II.503).
60. Deleuze, *Cours Vincennes* transcript, 'Sur Leibniz', 22/4/1980, http://www.webdeleuze.com/php/texte.php?cle=51&groupe=Leibniz&langue=1> (last accessed 8 February 2019).
61. Deleuze, 'How Do We Recognize Structuralism?', in *Desert Islands*, 176.
62. Inwood, 'Chrysippus on Extension and the Void', 264.
63. Ibid. 265.
64. David Lapoujade, *Aberrant Movements: The Philosophy of Gilles Deleuze* (2014), trans. Joshua David Jordan (South Pasadena: Semiotext(e), 2017), 50.
65. For more on Deleuze's account of denotation, as well as the corresponding features of the proposition – manifestation, signification, sense – see the 'Third Series of the Proposition' in *Logique du sens*.

PART II
Logic

4

The Shell A: Λεκτα

Introduction: Cracking Open the Shell

We now begin Part II, moving from physics to logic. As parts of the egg, we are leaving the yolk and cracking open the shell. What we find in the shell are mysterious things called λεκτα (or λεκτόν, singular). While it is better to leave this term in the original Greek, for now we can at least say that it has something to do with linguistic meaning or sense.[1] This might make us wonder why sense is grouped alongside space and time as the three incorporeals. Although an affinity between space and time seems plausible, certainly one that allows for their easy classification in a single category, λεκτόν seems like the odd one out. As we will see, λεκτόν is grouped alongside space and time because it shares – alongside space and time – the same double-sided structure of Stoic incorporeality.

In this chapter we first must hunt down the origins of λεκτα in the early days of the Stoa, where we find that the Stoics' full commitment to materialism entails a serious challenge, one Deleuze, too, faces: the emergence of language out of meaningless materiality. Through Deleuze's Stoicism, we map this emergent movement and find that there are *two kinds* of genesis – dynamic and static – that operate between *three stages* of language – primary order, secondary organisation, and tertiary ordinance. After detailing these kinds and stages, we compare Epicurean grammar to Stoic grammar, where we reveal a difference in prioritisation: Epicureans privilege nouns, Stoics privilege verbs. We conclude by showing how λεκτα has the same double-sided structure of all Stoics incorporeals.

The remaining two sections of Part II – 'The Shell B' and 'The Shell C' – round out our examination of Stoic logic. 'The Shell B' considers the Stoics' development of propositional logic and the correlative art of paradoxes. 'The Shell C' offers a *Handbook* or training manual of logic, as was wont in the Stoa. This *Handbook* connects with the transcendental logic of incorporeals from 'The Yolk B' and the Stoic paradoxes from 'The Shell B' in order to offer a regiment for cultivating a Stoic form of life. With this logic book in hand, we will turn to Part III of the Stoic egg: 'The Albumen', or ethics.

Origin of Λεκτα

To convey the full breadth of meanings contained in this term, let us first consider the breadth of different English and French translations, do some etymology, and then characterise its origin.

TRANSLATION

Consider some ways that French- and English-speaking scholars have translated λεκτα. Bréhier, Goldschmidt and Thomas Bénatouïl prefer *l'exprimable* ('expressible').[2] Ildefonse uses *dits* ('said, expressed').[3] Andreas Graeser and Brunschwig like 'what can be and what is said'.[4] Mates and Kneale select 'what is said or what is meant'.[5] Gerard Watson prefers 'judgments that can be expressed'.[6] Dam Drozdek chooses 'meaning'.[7] Michael Bennett uses 'sayable'.[8] Although none is perfect, each captures something important about 'λεκτόν'. As we proceed, we retain all these shades of meaning in hand, while prioritising Deleuze's *sens*.

Although he does not explicitly translate the term, what Deleuze means by 'sense' (*sens*) in *Logic of Sense* corresponds to the Stoic λεκτόν, along with an intimate connection between sense and the event (*l'événement*).[9] 'The Stoics', writes Deleuze, 'discovered it [sense] along with the event: sense, the expressed of the proposition, is an incorporeal, complex, and irreducible entity, at the surface of things, a pure event which inheres or subsists in the proposition' (*LS* 19). Sense is part of a whole logic of expression. 'Such a logic', Deleuze says elsewhere, 'is the outcome of a long tradition, from *the Stoics* down through the Middle Ages' into Spinoza and up to Deleuze.[10] The logic of expression captures the structure of the process of bodies expressing λεκτα and λεκτα quasi-causing bodies. We will soon see how the logic of expression spans Deleuze's logic of sense and the Stoics' theory of λεκτα.

ETYMOLOGY

In ancient Greek theatre, λεκτόν was closely associated with speech.[11] In Euripides' *Hippolytus*, for example, the leader of the chorus uses the term when he bides Theseus to '*Speak*, if I may hear it.'[12] Or when a leader of the chorus in Aristophanes' *Birds* bids some 'clever

The Shell A: Λεκτα

men' 'to *speak* and *speak* quickly', he also uses λεκτόν. This association between λεκτόν and speech is strong, as λεκτόν derives from λέγω, 'to say, speak'.[13] According to the *LSJ*, λέγω also means 'to choose, select, pick up', as well as 'what is gathered, chosen, picked out, selected'. The reference here is to the selection of stones, as in the *Odyssey*: Homer uses λέγω when Eurymachus talks to Odysseus of 'picking out stones for building walls' (αἱμασιάς τε λέγων).[14] In philosophy, Plato often uses λέγω to convey a search for the meaning of what a person is saying, as when Socrates asks Theaetetus, 'what can they possibly mean by *saying* [ποῖόν τί ποτε ἄρα λέγοντές φασι]?'[15]

Moreover, Michael Frede notes that the ending of λεκ-τόν – the -τόν or -τα – is a verbal adjective, which can be used in at least three ways: '(i) they can indicate a *passive* state: thus *agraptos* means "unwritten"; (ii) they can indicate a *passive* possibility: thus a *haireton* is something which can be chosen ... (iii) they can have an *active* sense: thus *dynatos* means capable'.[16] It is important to the Stoic account of λεκτόν that it slips between passive and active senses because incorporeals are neither active nor passive; they are inactive and impassive, that is, neutral.

Λεκτα in Stoicism

In Stoicism, the neutrality of λεκτα conveys independence and objectivity beyond any particular utterance or expression.[17] Λεκτα are inactive and impassive because they designate *what is expressed* in an expression, not the *act* of expressing or the *expression* itself. Consider the difference between *what* is expressed and the expressing *expression*. When Zeno speaks, what is expressed is not simply a swarm of sounds, but something else, something both beyond yet within the sounds. As bodies are beings and what is expressed is non-bodily, *what is expressed* is something between being and non-being, which the Stoics call subsistence and Deleuze calls 'extra-being' (*LS* 31). Whatever its name, it is not transcendent because it does not exist completely beyond the expression. It is both within yet without any particular expression. We might say λεκτα *inhere* in expressions. Here is another example of the double causality that we first mentioned in 'The Yolk B': the expression causes what is expressed but what is 'expressed makes possible the expression' (*LS* 186). This 'making possible' is another take on quasi-causality. *What is expressed* inheres or subsists in the expression but remains neutral.

Where and when did λεκτόν first appear on the Stoic scene? With some etymology and selected scholarly translations in hand, we seek to find its first appearance in history. Clement of Alexandria writes that Cleanthes is the first Stoic known to use it, who reportedly used it when discussing his ontology, not his philosophy of language, thus reflecting the Stoics' materialist commitments in their philosophy of language.[18] Importantly, contrary to the teachings of his master Zeno, Cleanthes said that bodies cause λεκτα. Gourinat, however, says that it was Clement himself who 'invented the term "expressible"'.[19] By contrast, Margherita Parente writes that while 'Zeno and after him Cleanthes conceive the incorporeals as physical realities: time, place, void', it was Chrysippus who 'added to this series a fourth incorporeal': λεκτόν.[20] Assuming that Clement was just reporting, not inventing, and given that Chrysippus was the Stoic master who made the most significant contributions to Stoic logic and linguistics, we infer that, while Cleanthes likely invented the notion of λεκτόν, it was Chrysippus who made something special.[21] Now that we know the different ways to translate λεκτόν, its etymology, and how it came about in the Stoa, let us see how λεκτόν emerges out of matter.

The Voice

Stoic philosophy of language takes up a major problem, one that derives from any committed materialism: how do incorporeal λεκτα emerge out of corporeal causation? The answer is one half of Stoic double causality, and it is essential that this answer involves a true genesis, not a mere repetition of the same at a higher or lower level.

As always for the Stoics, everything begins and ends in bodies. We start with the voice, in its utter physicality: 'voice [Φωνή], according to the Stoics, is something corporeal' (*DL* 7.55).[22] 'In their theory of dialectic', Diogenes continues, 'most of them see fit to take as their starting point the topic of voice' (*DL* 7.55). The theory of λεκτόν, like the logic of sense, begins with the voice conceived as the material production of articulated sound, which we call 'speech' (λόγος). At its base, speech involves two bodies: voice and mouth. Deleuze cites one of Chrysippus' paradoxes on this topic: 'If you say something, it passes through your lips: now you say wagon [ἄμαξα], consequently a wagon passes through your lips' (*DL* 7.187). Notice that this paradox rests on the ambiguity between the thing – an actual, wooden wagon – and the word 'wagon'. We delay addressing this paradoxical ambiguity until 'The Shell C' in order to focus on the matters at hand: mouth and sound.

The Shell A: Λεκτα

When Chrysippus speaks to his students in the Stoa, breath emerges from his throat, is shaped in his mouth, and echoes through the bodies of the students and the columns of the portico under which he walks and talks. These particular sounds are connected to several bodies: (1) to the intention *manifested* in the minds of the speaker, (2) the actual wagon *denoted*, and (3) the *concept* of the wagon and other concepts logically connected to it. Deleuze calls these the 'three dimensions of the proposition' (*LS* 17). Beneath these three, or cloaking this bodily interaction, there is a 'fourth dimension': 'what is said' or 'what is expressed', λεκτόν (*LS* 19). While 'voice' (Φωνή) in Greek, refers to both humans and animals, speech differentiates the human voice from feral sounds. 'There is a difference between voice and speech', reports Diogenes: 'voice may include mere noise, speech is always articulate' (*DL* 7.57).[23] Humans do not just make noises; humans speak, and speech expresses sense. Λεκτόν marks the separation of speech from mere noise, sense from nonsense. The question becomes: how does this separation occur?

As is the case with every body, voice is composite. According to Stoic grammar, (the ancient Greek) language is composed of twenty-four basic elements or letters (*DL* 7.56). Depending on the order of composition, elements can be meaningless or meaningful. When it is meaningful, it is discourse (λόγος). The question is: how do noises thrown off of clanging bodies become rational discourse? Since it is difficult to imagine, Deleuze offers four analogies for the emergence of incorporeal sense from corporeal depths: a '[1] faint incorporeal mist which escapes from bodies, [2] a film without volume which envelops them, [3] a mirror which reflects them, [4] a chessboard on which they are organized according to a plan' (*LS* 5). The explanation for this seemingly immaculate construction involves the incorporeal surface that subsists between voiced sounds and voicing mouth.

Consider two references to Λεκτα from Seneca's *Letters*: 'walking' and 'being wise':

> 'There are,' it is said, 'certain natural classes of bodies; we say: 'This is a man,' 'this is a horse.' Then there attend on the bodily natures certain movements of the mind which declare something about the body. And these have a certain *essential quality which is sundered from body* [*proprium quiddam et a corporibus seductum*]; for example: 'I see Cato walking.' The senses indicate this, and the mind believes it. What I see, is body, and upon this I concentrate my eyes and my mind. Again, I say: '*Cato walks*.' 'What I say [in this],' they continue, 'is not body; it is a certain *declarative fact concerning body* [*enuntiativum quiddam de*

corpore] – called variously an 'utterance [*effatum*],' a 'declaration [*enuntiatum*],' a 'statement [*dictum*].' Thus, when we say 'wisdom,' we mean something *pertaining* to body; when we say '*he is wise*,' we are *speaking concerning body* [*de corpore loquimar*].[24]

Seneca here distinguishes three things: (1) the λεκτόν that Cato is walking, (2) the expression 'Cato is walking', and (3) Cato, a human being who walks. The first is incorporeal, the last two bodies.

'To walk' and 'being wise' are not bodies because, when Cato walks, there is not another body – an 'ambulatory body' – that is added to Cato's physical form, just as 'being wise' is not a new body – a 'sagacity body' – that is added to him. Instead, 'to walk' or 'being wise' is, as Seneca claims, a 'declarative fact concerning a body'.[25] These are incorporeal λεκτα, like 'to cut' or 'being cut'. They concern bodies, they are about bodies, but they are not bodies themselves. Bodies exist and λεκτα subsist as their surface, in accord with Stoicism's immanent materialism. Although λεκτα are non-physical, they haunt physical depths like a mist, for they do not exist outside of their corporeal expressions. Speech is about bodies and their mixtures, but when voice becomes meaningful, sounds become more than merely properties attached to bodies. A new form of relation opens up within bodies: attribution.

From Predicates to Attributes

Sounds become expressions when attributes ('to walk', 'being cut') are distinguished from predicates ('is green', 'is tall'). According to Bréhier, the reason why Stoics distinguish attributes from predicates is to pervert Platonism. Let us make this distinction clear.

Predication is the process of joining predicates to subjects through a copula – 'is, *est*, ἔστιν' – or copulation. For example, 'the tree *is* green'. Copulation is possible because predicates and subjects are said to be 'of the same kind': corporeal. But this raises a difficulty: how can two different things – subject and predicate – copulate without collapsing their differences into identity? That is, how can two bodies copulate without merging into a single body? Plato's metaphysics of participation seeks to resolve this difficulty. In Platonic participation, subject and predicate are rendered different in kind. The subject is a material object, the predicate a transcendent form, and participation is a kind of operative resemblance between them. Participation allows two things to be both similar (resemblance) yet different (material and transcendent).

The Shell A: Λεκτα

In accord with their overall rejection of transcendence, the Stoics reject the metaphysics of participation. Following the Megarians, they reject the copula '*is*' (a conjugated, indicative form of the verb 'to be, *être*, εἶναι') in favour of the infinitive or non-finite forms of the verb.[26] As Bréhier puts it, the Stoics replace the Platonic proposition – 'the tree is green' (*L'arbre est vert*) – with what the Stoic proposition – 'the tree greens' (*L'arbre verdoie*) (*TI* 20). In the Stoic proposition, the subject – 'the tree' – is not 'predicated *of*' but is attributed: '*is* green' becomes 'greens', or 'to green' (*verdoyer*). The attribute, Bréhier continues, now considered as 'the whole verb, appears thus no more as expressing a concept (object or class of objects), but only a fact or event' (*TI* 20).[27] On Deleuze's Stoicism, 'the whole verb' assumes a distinct verbal form: the infinitive.

One advantage of the Stoic proposition is that it does not need to explain the mysterious interpenetration of one being – a tree – by referring to another being – a transcendent form. Instead, it expresses only a certain *aspect* of an object, a *manner* of being, rather than trying to join two distinct beings. This aspect or manner is not a second object, another body, but an effect or event that rises out of the interaction among bodies. 'The attribute is always', Bréhier writes, 'expressed by a verb, which is to say that it is not a being, but a *manner of being*' (*TI* 12; emphasis added). The content of the proposition – 'what is expressed' – is neither a body nor a bodily relation but an incorporeal. It is no surprise that Deleuze describes the invention of incorporeals, especially λεκτα, as a 'new way of getting rid of the [copula] IS: the attribute is no longer a quality related to the subject by the indicative "is", it is any verb whatever in the infinitive which emerges from a state of things and skims over it'.[28] The Stoics fold up copula and predicate into the infinitive (grammatical) form of an attribute.

This shift from predicates to attributes (which Helen Palmer calls a 'shift from substantive to infinitive') leads to a new order of classification.[29] In the *Organon*, Aristotle categorises predicates in terms of their relation to the subject. Whether a predicate is essential or accidental, affirmative or denying, depends on the kinds of relations that may obtain between a predicate and the subject of the predication.[30] By contrast, the Stoics' classification does not centre on possible relations to the subject of a proposition but instead, Bréhier writes, 'is even identical to, the grammatical classification of verbs' (*TI* 21). The attribute is neither a being nor a concept; it subsists as an incorporeal event or effect. Deleuze agrees with Bréhier: the 'essential part of the λεκτόν is the attribute or the event' (*TI* 22).³¹ The Stoics replace a logic of concepts with a logic of events. While attributes are one kind of λεκτα – 'incomplete λεκτα' – we will see below that incomplete λεκτα correspond to infinite verbs, as opposed to complete λεκτα, which correspond to finite conjugations of the verbs and subjects of determinate conjugation. The classification of attributes corresponds to the structure among infinitives.

While attributes (as incomplete λεκτα) are effects emerging from corporeal mixtures, they remain generative. Quasi-causally, incorporeals contribute to the generation of bodies in a distinct way: they provoke the transformation of some bodies – sounds – into meaningful statements or propositions and thereby effectuate change in bodies – the ears and souls of an audience. Λεκτα mark the change of noise into words, that is, they are the sense that is expressed in sensible bodies as the double-sided surface between bodies. With the appearance of language, however, there is a new principle of organisation.

In a purely material world, there are only bodies, all the way down into the deep dark depths of corporeality. And yet, amid our world, a separation occurs: there are bodies and there are words. Words remain bodies, but they also express sense. Words are bodies become expressible entities. When Seneca says, 'Cato walks', the words 'Cato' and 'walks' signify two bodies: the spoken name and Cato's actual body, moving through the world step by step, the object bearing the name. Λεκτα is the incorporeal surface organising these two series by separating them into bodies and words, things and propositions ('to walk', 'to cut').

Before moving on, we should stress the simultaneous independence and objectivity of λεκτα. Although the Stoics sometimes talk as if a λεκτόν is a thought or cognition manifested by spoken sounds, λεκτα is not just a thought because thoughts are corporal and λεκτα incorporeal. Everything that exists in the material world is corporeal, including bodies, minds and thoughts. Since thoughts are dispositions of the brain, thoughts are physical. Thus λεκτα are neither the thoughts in a speaker's mind nor those produced in a listener's. Instead, λεκτα *subsist* in thoughts, speech, text and any physical body capable of expressing them. As Michael Frede notes, λεκτα 'should not be confused with our thought ... but rather conceived of as something *subsisting alongside* our thought'.³² Although different people have different thoughts, the use of language directs us to the same objective plane where λεκτα subsist. Λεκτα are not manifested

The Shell A: Λεκτα

thoughts, denoted objects or signified concepts. The theory of λεκτα, like the ethics we will see in Part III, is not simply linguistic; it is primarily metaphysical. Λεκτα are objective metaphysical objects connected to, though independent of, the bodies on which they subsist.

A Final Task

We call the emergence of sense out of bodies, or the attribution of λεκτα to corporeals, the *genesis of language*. Accounting for this genesis is important for both Deleuze and the Stoics because of their shared insistence on the necessary materiality of sound and immateriality of meaning. Deleuze calls it '*a final task*: to retrace the history that liberates sounds and makes them independent of bodies' (*LS* 186; emphasis added). Let us see how Deleuze takes up this final task in the *Logic of Sense*.

Although Deleuze admits it is a 'convoluted story', we can reveal its architectonic symmetry by dividing *Logic of Sense* in half (*LS* xiv). The first half (First to Seventeenth Series) examines static genesis; the second half (Eighteenth to Thirty-Fourth Series) analyses dynamic genesis. The first half connects Stoicism to Lewis Carroll, the logician of words, in order to study the metaphysical surface. The second half conjoins Stoicism to Antonin Artaud, the screaming poet of bodies, in order to mine the corporeal depths. The question is: how do the two halves of this convoluted story combine? The genesis of language is an important part of this answer. For Deleuze, there are three stages of this genesis: (1) *primary order*, (2) *secondary organisation* and (3) *tertiary ordinance*.

Primary order (*ordre primaire*) refers to brute matter, to the noisy depths of the cave, to the guttural cries, cracklings and explosions of 'bodies burst[ing] and caus[ing] other bodies to burst *in* a universal cesspool' (*LS* 187). This is the order of 'bodies taken in their undifferentiated depth and in their measureless pulsation' (*LS* 124). Bodies here are apersonal and unindividuated; in fact, we cannot even speak of a single body here. Rather than a cosmos, we use the term Deleuze appropriate from *Finnegans Wake*: 'chaosmos', cosmos in chaos (*LS* 176; *ATP* 313).[33] There is no *my* body or *your* body because a body is just a *thing* that 'penetrates another and coexists with it in all of its parts, like a drop of wine in the ocean', to evoke an image from 'The Yolk C' (*LS* 5–6).[34]

The best examples of primary order are infant noises. An infant's body is an amorphous, pudgy, mass of soft tissue, or, in more

Deleuzian language, a screaming, farting, pissing, oozing gob of intensities. Sounds emitted are nonsense, mere bodily noises. The infant is not an individuated 'ego', but an anonymous 'id' or 'it', *ça*. Recall the opening scene of *Anti-Oedipus*, featuring 'the nursing infant, beginning with his or her first year', which comes from the 'theatre of terror whose unforgettable picture Melanie Klein painted' (*LS* 187).[35] In this Kleinian scene, the function of the infant's mouth is indeterminate, wavering between several functions: *it* eats, *it* vomits, *it* screams, *it* drools, but it does not yet speak. In primary order, one either eats or is eaten, a distinction matching the Stoics' characterisation of corporeal interaction: to eat is to act, to be eaten is to be acted upon. The mouth, breast and each body in the whole cosmos is terrifyingly intermixed 'in the abyss' where 'everything is passion and action' (*LS* 188, 192). The sounds of an infant are not yet expressive of sense because they are mere meaningless materiality. Deleuze characterises the primary order as a cave of schizoid psychosis, and only nonsense echoes through this cave (*LS* 187).[36]

Secondary organisation (*organisation secondaire*) rises from primary order. Deleuze calls it 'secondary' in order to locate an element of language that lies after the terrifying noise of primary order but before the meaningful language of tertiary ordinance. Meaningful language is made possible by means of a distinct function that appears in secondary organisation. This function assures that 'sounds are not confused with the sonorous bodies of things' by 'separate[ing] sounds from bodies and organiz[ing] them into propositions, freeing them for the *expressive function*' (*LS* 181; emphasis added). That which separates are the sections of the incorporeal surface, which emerge out of the intermixing of bodily fragments and begin to organize into spatial, temporal and meaningful units – the three incorporeals. Secondary organisation marks the emergence of sense out of the clanging, incoherent noise of the infant as its screams sharpen through the sections of the superficial sieve of secondary organisation.

Amid the terrifying noise, the infant begins to notice repeated, similar-sounding noises. Through their repetition, chunks of sounds detach themselves from the swirling chaos, as they become elements of language beyond the elements of bodies.[37] Grammarians call these material fragments 'the three formative elements of language: phonemes, morphemes, and semantemes' (*LS* 232).[38] These formative elements take their organisation from the voice of a parent emerging as a 'voice from above' (*LS* 232). Secondary organisation marks

The Shell A: Λεκτα

the movement 'from noises as ... passions of bodies in depth, to the voice as the entity of the heights' (*LS* 229). Although the child does not yet have access to the domain of sense lurking within this 'familial hum of voices', it discerns a hint of a pre-existing system of sounds (*LS* 229).

Lost in the undifferentiated abyss of primary order, there was little chance of discerning up from down, left from right. Now in secondary organisation, orientations emerge. Rather than one 'bottomless depths', '[t]wo depths are opposed: a hollow depth ... [and] full depth' (*LS* 187, 188–9). These two depths (or two territories) are surface effects corresponding to 'two mixtures: one is made of hard and solid fragments that change; the other is liquid, fluid, and perfect' (*LS* 189). It creates a distinction between the threat of apersonal and unindividuated amorphous matter and the safety of the promise of formed personae and identifiable individuals. This distinction later emerges in full through tertiary ordinance.

As primary order (the site of depths) are populated by apersonal and unindividuated material intensities, secondary organisation (the emergent surface) is composed of impersonal and pre-individual events. Unlike the activity and passivity of depth, the surface is neutral, inactive and impassive. Above all, this incorporeal surface is produced by corporeal causation. Still, the surface is also generative, though this is a different order of generation, one that leads to tertiary ordinance. Secondary organisation is the domain of perversion.

Tertiary ordinance (*ordonnance*[39] *tertiaire*) is the domain of formed speaking subjects, which Deleuze characterises as the domain of neurosis or depression (*LS* 192). One reason why it is called 'tertiary' is that it refers to the three dimension of the proposition: (a) denotation, (b) manifestation and (c) signification (*LS* 12). Drawn together, they form 'the circle of the proposition' (*LS* 17).[40] We need to first explain the circle of the proposition before explaining tertiary ordinance.

1. *Denotation* refers to the relation of the proposition to an 'external state of affairs (*datum*)' that is '*individuated*' (*LS* 12; emphasis original). Also called 'indication', denotation is the relation of the proposition in so far as it indicates or points out an individual thing in an individuated context. Daniel W. Smith considers it a 'theory of reference'.[41] The proposition 'Dion walks', for example, indicates the body of Dion walking through the Stoa.
2. *Manifestation* refers to the 'relation of the proposition to the

person who speaks and expresses herself', that is, the relation between the internal psychology of a speaker – the one who says 'I' – and the speech that 'I' make (*LS* 13). The speaker has 'desires and beliefs' that may or may not correspond to the proposition, which speech manifests (*LS* 13).
3. *Signification* refers to the relation of the proposition to the inferential connection of its conceptual content. When we say 'Dion walks', the meaning of that proposition refers to the concepts Dion, the Stoa through which he walks, and likely includes relation concepts such as the Athens, Zeno and so on. This is the domain of formal logic, with its laws of implication and demonstration.

The three dimensions of the propositions refer to three types of propositional relations: (1) relation to the denoted object, (2) to the subjects that speak them, or (3) the interrelations among propositions themselves. As Deleuze puts it, (1) 'what one talks about is the denotatum', (2) the 'one who begins to speak is the one who manifests', and (3) 'what one says are the significations' (*LS* 181). The three dimensions compose the tertiary ordinance of language, as it continuously circles from 'denotation to manifestation, then to signification, but also from signification to manifestation and to denotation, we are carried along in a circle' (*LS* 16–17).

Inspired by the Stoic theory of λεκτα, Deleuze's intervention in the philosophy of language is to show how the circle of the proposition presupposes its own genesis, and thus requires a superior genesis. In the circle, the genesis of language is endlessly deferred. From the perspective of denotation, manifestation seems primary, but from that of manifestation, signification seems primary. From the respective perspectives, another dimension seems to come first. The three dimensions of the propositions circumscribe themselves and thus assume, but do not account for, the genetic element. If we think of the circle as *conditioned*, then we need to seek its *condition*.

As Deleuze shows us, however, simply seeking the conditions does not sufficiently explain the genesis of the circle. Here Deleuze echoes his critique of Kant's conditions of possibility. Merely seeking what conditions make it possible for, say, denotation to successfully refer to a denotatum does not explain its actuality but only its possibility. Explaining an actual conditioned by referring to the possible condition leads to a vicious circle because the conditioned and the condition presuppose each other. To avoid such circularity, Deleuze claims, the condition 'ought to have an element of its own, distinct from the

The Shell A: Λεκτα

form of the conditioned. It ought to have *something unconditioned* capable of assuring a real genesis' of the circle of the proposition (*LS* 19; emphasis original). Explaining the genesis of language requires a fourth dimension: sense. Sense is the genetic element of language, and Deleuze knows that it was the 'Stoics who discovered it along with the event' (*LS* 19). To understand how the Stoics discovered the genetic element of language, Deleuze distinguishes between two sorts of genesis: dynamic and static geneses.

Given all complex distinctions we just made, let us pause for a moment to situate ourselves so that we do not lose track of the overall story. Part I focused on Stoic physics and metaphysics, especially in so far as their theories of causation and incorporeality contribute to their perverse materialism. From this Deleuze inspired us to make a heterdoxical claim – there are three, not four, incorporeals. Part I took up the incorporeal proper to physics – space – and Part II takes up the incorporeal proper to logic – λεκτα. So far in Part II, we have considered the breadth of various English and French translations of λεκτα, its etymology, and then characterised its origins in Stoicism. This led to consideration of the materiality of the voice, to which the Stoics responded with their theory of attributes, as opposed to predication. Next we considered what Deleuze calls the final task: to explain the genesis of meaning out of matter. To do this, we examined Deleuze's logic of the genesis of language – which includes *primary order*, *secondary organisation* and *tertiary ordinance* – as well the three dimensions of the proposition – denotation, manifestation and signification. We mention all of this in order to consider how Stoic λεκτα informs Deleuze's account for the genesis of language. Echoing concepts from 'The Yolk B', we will now examine Deleuze's distinction between the two types of genesis involved in language and logic: dynamic and static geneses.

Two Distinct Geneses

The three stages of the genesis of language convey the *structure* of this genesis, but they do not express the *relations* among them. In Deleuze scholarship, there is a disagreement as to how to conceive of these genetic relations. Daniel W. Smith claims that 'Deleuze distinguishes three different stages in *the dynamic genesis*' of language, and that dynamic genesis spans all three.[42] Joe Hughes, however, argues that 'for these three stages there are *two geneses*: a static genesis and a dynamic genesis'.[43] According to Hughes, dynamic genesis *moves* from primary order to secondary organisation, and static genesis *leaps* from secondary organisation to tertiary ordinance. There are two reasons why Hughes seems correct.

First, Deleuze not only consistently makes this distinction but also emphasises its importance. When he first introduces the concept of dynamic genesis in *Logic of Sense*, Deleuze writes: '[i]t is no longer a question of a static genesis . . . [because] it is a question of a dynamic genesis . . . which *must not in any way implicate the other genesis*' (*LS* 186/217; emphasis added). Earlier in the text, Deleuze identifies 'the entire tertiary ordinance' as 'the object of the static genesis, *not* dynamic genesis' (*LS* 126).

Second, conceiving of the genesis of language as following two geneses between three stages reveals something important about the quasi-causality of the incorporeal surface. As we know, incorporeals are quasi-causal because they are effects of corporeal causes and yet contribute to the genesis of states of affairs. If we think of the *dynamic genesis moving* from primary order to secondary organisation as distinct from a *static genesis leaping* from the secondary organisation to tertiary ordinance, we see that the incorporeal surface of the secondary organisation is both the effect of the bodily depths of primary order and yet generative of corporeal states of affairs. In short, the difference between the two geneses corresponds to the difference between the double causality of causal corporeals and quasi-causal incorporeals that we saw in 'The Yolk B'. We thus agree with Hughes: there are two geneses – one dynamic, the other static.

Dynamic and Static Geneses

Dynamic genesis refers to how corporeal causes 'lead directly from states of affairs to events, from mixtures to pure lines, *from depth to the production of surfaces*' (*LS* 186; emphasis original). This type of genesis is called 'dynamic' because it refers to the dynamism of the depths, and dynamism consists of moving bodies caught in tensions of acting and being acted upon, eating and being eaten (to evoke an image that Deleuze draws from Lewis Carroll). 'This depth', writes Deleuze, 'acts in an original way, *by means of its power* [or dynamism] *to organize surfaces and to envelop itself within surfaces*' (*LS* 124; emphasis original).

Static genesis, by contrast, refers to the way in which the quasi-causality of the incorporeal surface is both the effect and the generative condition of bodies. It is called 'static' because it refers to the fixed flatness of the incorporeal surface. We are using the language of 'leaping' from secondary organisation to tertiary ordinance in order to distinguish it from 'moving' (think: δύναμις) from primary order to secondary organisation.

In between dynamic and static geneses is the incorporeal surface, that non-bodily border separating *and* connecting two bodily orders: the undifferentiated mass of primary order and the well-ordered state of affairs of tertiary ordinance. The key is that this surface is not itself a body, but an incorporeal surface composed of sense or λεκτα. 'The surface', writes Deleuze, 'is the transcendental field itself, the locus of sense and expression', opening into the two geneses (*LS* 125). Perhaps it is more accurate to say that onto the two sides are projected shadows of two corporeal phases: the corporeal cesspool of primary order and the corporeal state of affairs of tertiary ordinance. This might be why Lecercle speaks of an '*inter*face' rather than a *sur*face.[44] From the perspective of the surface, it looks back 'down' the wake of dynamic genesis, down into the depths, and 'up' the path of static genesis, up to the heights. As we will soon see, on one side of the surface, differentiation and intensities project diverging shadows, and on the other side, integration and extensities project converging shadows.

Phases of Dynamic and Static Geneses

Deleuze details distinct phases in dynamic and static geneses. First we will explain dynamic genesis, which is organised as three syntheses: (1) connective, (2) conjunctive, (3) disjunctive; or '*conexa, conjuncta, disjuncta*' (*LS* 174).[45] We turn to static genesis after we finish the three syntheses of dynamic genesis. To make it easier to follow along, here is a diagram:

PRIMARY ORDER		*Corporeal chaosmos*
Dynamic genesis		Connective synthesis
		Conjunctive synthesis
		Disjunctive synthesis
SECONDARY ORGANISATION		*Incorporeal surface*
Static genesis		Differentiation
		Integration
TERTIARY ORDINANCE		*Bodily states of affairs*

Connective synthesis marks the beginning of the transformation from the abyss of clanging bodies into shards of meaning. We see this when the infant begins to extract pure phonemes from the 'gnashings, cracklings, explosions, shattered sounds . . . and the inarticulate howls breaths [*cris-souffles*]' (*LS* 193). These phonemic shards are extracted along two axes: 'the *concurrence* of simultaneous entities [associative axis] and the *concatenation* of successive entities [syntagmatic axis]'.[46] 'Concatenation' (from *concatenare*) means to form a chain (*cateno*) by binding together (*con-*); 'concurrence' (from *concurrere*) means to run (*cursus*) together (*con* + *currere*). Connecting both axes, chunks of formerly meaningless noise run together to form a sonorous chain. To imagine this, think of the first sounds of infant makes: 'ba ba ba', 'ma ma ma', 'da da da'. These repeated chunks – 'ba', 'ma' or 'da' – are not discrete, individuated, self-constituting units of language but are closer to what Deleuze calls 'differential elements' in so far as they have significance not in themselves but only through the differences between them. Differential elements only exist in so far as they reciprocally determine each other. Considered in themselves, beyond their differential relation, they are inarticulate nonsense – just: 'ba ba ba'.

Logic of Sense calls these differential elements of language 'partial surfaces', although Deleuze is cautious about the use of 'partial' (*LS* 197). It is not exactly correct to speak of a 'part' of a surface here because the surface, taken in its entirety, does not exist before the parts. Instead, the surface *results from* corporeal causes. Before a completed, whole surface, each partial surface revolves around singular points, often plosives such as 'b' or 'd' sounds.[47] Organising the 'vicinity of another zone depending on another singularity', the entire surface is the product of this connection of partial surfaces (*LS* 197). We speak of a 'partial zone', then, only from our current perspective, 'within' language, after its genesis. We can only view a part or zone in so far as it is projected onto the completed surface.

Conjunctive synthesis is a synthesis *of* connective syntheses, not a totally new synthesis. It conjoins phonemes previously extracted from the noise and connected through unorganised concatenation and concurrence. While connective synthesis 'involves the construction of a single series' or chain through incremental addition, conjunctive synthesis brings about the convergence of multiple sonorous chains in order to produce the complete integration of partial surfaces (*LS* 174). More than merely added together, several chains converge as the first hints of a full organisation begin to emerge. The synthesis

The Shell A: Λεκτα

is called 'conjunctive' because it conjoins or converges connections. Through the convergence of these assorted phonemic chains, elements are coordinated, and through such coordination, connections start to form the breadth of a single continuous surface.

Deleuze's examples of the type of pre-linguistic sounds heard in conjunctive synthesis are esoteric or portmanteau words.[48] Lewis Carroll, a fiendish master of such esoteric words, creates them by conjoining chains of heterogeneous propositions. 'Snark', for example, results from conjoining two words – 'snail' and 'shark' – which, in their conjunction, denote, manifest, and signify a monstrosity.[49] The conceptual monstrosity to which the word 'Snark' points also corresponds to the material monstrosity that would be created were the actual bodies of a snail and a shark conjoined like the word is conjoined. 'Snark' is thus an empty signifier, which is why the map that the head of the snark hunt, the Bellman, uses to lead them to the snark is a blank sheet of paper:

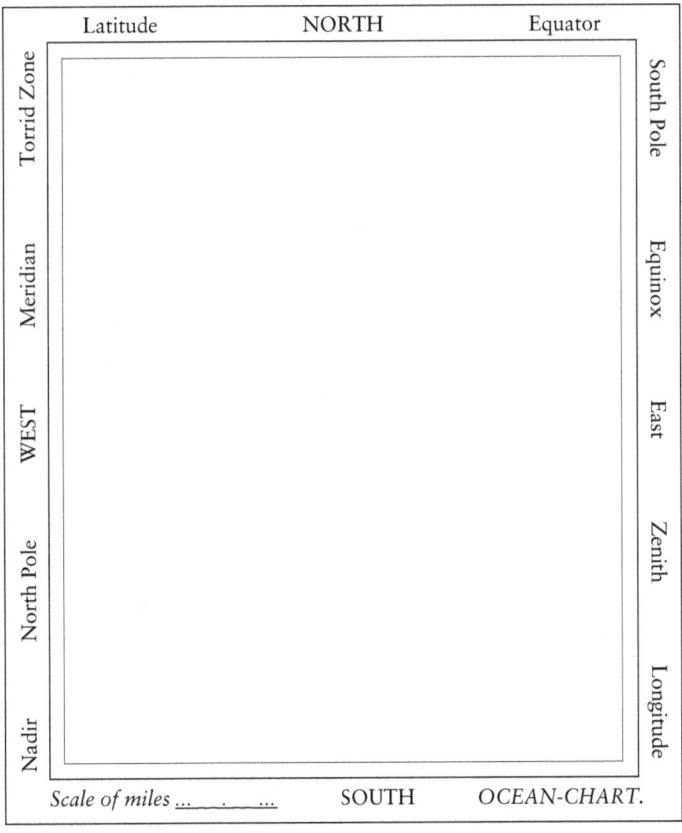

Though the hunting party persistently pursues it, the Snark forever slips away, as seen in the last lines of the poem:

> In the midst of the word he was trying to say,
>   In the midst of his laughter and glee,
> He had softly and suddenly vanished away—
>   For the Snark *was* a Boojum, you see.

Just as differential elements vanish when taken by themselves, outside of their differential relations, the Snark vanishes beneath its articulation. As they approach their prey, and finally seem to seize it, the hunting party finds that it was a not a Snark at all, but what W. H. Auden calls 'the dreadful Boojum of Nothingness'.[50] What is the Boojum? Noting but another invisible meaningless monstrosity. In the Snark hunt, the pursuit of one fantastical creature slips into another fantastical creature because both converge on the same esoteric word. It is not simply a snail in itself or a shark in itself, but a snail *and* a shark *and* a Boojum *and* . . . It is a monster that has sense. It is no coincidence that children, in the earliest stages of learning a language, conjoin disparate words and sounds to create jungles of fantastical creatures, as Carroll lasciviously and logically appreciated. Infants babble, but children speak nonsense. Carving that line that leads from inside to outside the circle of the proposition, the Snark is just such a shard of nonsense.

We should be precise here: nonsense *is not* senseless. Nonsense has a sense, albeit a specifically paradoxical one. The sense of nonsense is what happens when a sound is reduced to such an extent that *what* it expresses is only *that* it expresses. There is no *what is expressed* beyond the brute act of expressing. This is its paradox: nonsense says its own sense.[51] As Lapoujade puts it, 'the specificity of nonsense is *to have nothing but sense*'.[52] The Snark is nonsensical because it has both too much sense ('an excess of sense' that exceeds the circle of proposition, slipping through multiple bodies at once) and too little sense (because it 'says the sense of what it says') (*LS* 71, 67).

The function of an esoteric word like 'Snark' is to coordinate multiple heterogeneous chains. In short, coordination is the operation of conjunction. Conjunctive synthesis coordinates disparate partial surfaces of connective synthesis in order to contribute to the composition of a whole incorporeal surface. On this coordinated surface, a third synthesis happens: disjunctive synthesis.

Disjunctive synthesis bears upon conjunctive synthesis. If connective syntheses are synthesised by conjunctive synthesis, and

The Shell A: Λεκτα

conjunctive syntheses are synthesised by disjunctive synthesis, then disjunctive synthesis is a synthesis of the prior two. It is a global synthesis that is 'the truth and the destination of the others' in so far as disjunction attains its positive use through the affirmation of difference (*LS* 229). We can think of this affirmation of difference through disjunctive synthesis.

In formal logic, disjunctive synthesis is often considered intolerable, if not downright fallacious. Jean-Jacques Lecercle points to the oxymoronic nature of the phrase itself: 'the Latin prefix "*dis-*" contradicts the Greek prefix "σύν-"'.[53] Disjunctive synthesis is a failed action because it disrupts the convergence of the connective chains produced by the two other syntheses. Just as the connective chains are coordinated with the aim of forming a complete and coherent surface, disjunction is the subterranean force that undercuts the completion of a global synthesis. Thus disjunctive synthesis is the inversion of conjunctive synthesis: the latter produces convergences, the former divergences. Although the three syntheses remain incomplete, the divergence composes the incorporeal surface. The surface is complete *because* of its incompleteness; it succeeds *in so far as* it fails; it converges *through* its divergence. Deleuze calls this resonance or ramification.[54] Disjunctive synthesis makes divergent series 'resonate and ramify' through their divergence (*LS* 234). Through the differences of the conjoined heterogeneous chains, a resonance collects the sounds being separated from bodies into an incorporeal surface. As two chains converge on a point, they produce a paradoxical instance, or what Deleuze calls 'an aleatory point with two uneven faces', which crosses the divergent series in so far as they diverge (*LS* 174). This provokes a resonance that arises because of, not despite, their differences. The surface produced out of these three syntheses is not a new plane that exists unto itself, but is rather an unresolved problem consisting of aberrant and deviating movements infinitely ramifying and contracting along the smooth incorporeal plane. Deleuze is very clear on this: 'The line-frontier brings about the convergence of divergent series; but it neither abolishes nor corrects their divergence. For it makes them converge not in themselves ... but around a paradoxical element ... This element is the quasi-cause' (*LS* 183). Incorporeality is composed through disparity and difference, not through identity and similarity.

Hence the call for a new logic of sense, a transcendental logic of what Lapoujade calls 'aberrant movement', or what we (twisting the Kantian Table) have called a transcendental logic of incorporeals.

The movement is aberrant because it is convergent *and* divergent, convergent *because of* its divergence. The logic of sense developed in Deleuze's *Logic of Sense*, is isomorphic to the theory of the Stoic λεκτα, and the theory of λεκτα structurally corresponds to the logic of the two other incorporeals – space and time.

In sum, dynamic genesis is composed of three phases: '[1] the connective synthesis on a single series, [2] the conjunctive synthesis of convergence, and [3] the disjunctive series of resonance' (*LS* 229). Put differently, (1) connective synthesis produces contraction, (2) conjunctive synthesis produces coordination, and (3) disjunctive synthesis produces ramification. This is the movement of the dynamic genesis leading from primary order to secondary organisation. We can describe this movement in other ways: from nonsense to sense, from noise to speech, from bodies to language, from corporeal depth to incorporeal surface. To make sure we are all on the same page, let us put this organise the phases of dynamic genesis in a table:

Synthesis	Phases	Effects	Word
Connective	Single chain	Contraction	'Ba ba ba'
Conjunctive	Convergence	Coordination	Esoteric
Disjunctive	Divergence	Ramification	Λεκτα

Now back to static genesis. While dynamic genesis moves through these three phases, static genesis is the 'leaping in place (*saut sur place*)' from secondary surface to tertiary heights (*LS* 149). If dynamic genesis is the construction of the incorporeal plane out of corporeal depths, static genesis is the return to bodies. This return, however, does not simply lead back to the cesspool of unindividuated monsters screaming terrifying nonsense. Instead, it is the production of individuated and determined bodies. Although the plane emerges out of the corporeal chaosmos, it returns to a well-formed cosmos that follows the hierarchical ordinance of general and specific states of affairs. This is the structure of static genesis, of leaping in place. Since we already covered this in great detail in 'The Yolk B', we can simply repeat the stages: (1) Bodies cause incorporeal effects, which are infinitely divide or differentiate as they spread along the intensive face of the metaphysical surface or the operation of differentiation; (2) These lines of differentiation reflect or cast shadows on bodies, which is the operation of integrating infinite differences in terms of how they are individuated through various bodies. It does not matter

The Shell A: Λεκτα

where you start, as there is constant communication of bodies and incorporeals, causes and effects, physical depths and metaphysical surface. For the Stoics, there is only matter and its immaterial surface. What we now see, which is different from 'The Yolk B', is that there are two ways in which bodies exist – as the corporeal chaosmos of primary order and as bodily states of affairs of tertiary ordinance. These are not two different worlds but the same corporeal world. The difference is that the bodily states of affairs are organised by the quasi-causal surface, while the corporeal chaosmos is the order of bodies conceived of independently of their surface effects. Without the surface, there is just brute matter, only guttural cries, cracklings and explosions of a corporeal cesspool. Out of this chaos, however, organisation emerges as surfaces form along bodies that individuate themselves. The surface then marks the organisation among bodies, out of which states of affairs emerge. Yet all of these can collapse into the primary order at any time, as we will see below. For now, the key is to recall that this as a true, immanent genesis.

Let us pause again to take stock of where we are in the overall story of Deleuze's Stoicism. As part of our heterodoxical claim – there are three double-sided incorporeals, with intensive and extensive sides – we have been looking at the incorporeal proper to logic: λεκτα. Early in this chapter we looked at the translations, etymology and origins of the concept, before then taking up what Deleuze calls the final task of any materialism, especially a perverted one like Stoicism: to explain the genesis of meaning out of meaningless matter. This explanation involved distinguishing between dynamic and static genesis. We saw that dynamic genesis moves from primary order to secondary organisation, and a static genesis leaps from the secondary organisation to tertiary ordinance. Dynamic genesis is organised as three syntheses – connective, conjunctive and disjunctive. Static genesis is organised by the movements of integration and differentiation, the logic for which we explained in 'The Yolk B' by twisting Kant's Table of Judgements into a transcendental logic of incorporeals. In a moment, we will conclude this chapter by considering that familiar double-sided structure of the incorporeal surface. In order to see it fully, though, we must first compare two competing ancient philosophies of language: Epicurean and Stoic.

Epicurean and Stoic Philosophies of Language

Λεκτα function as the incorporeal surface subsisting between bodies, and which distributes states of affairs into words and things, cosmos and chaosmos. Λεκτα make it possible for certain bodies to stand out from the corporeal mixture, to organise into propositions, and to take on an expressive function. We have just told the story of this separation. Yet there is another important point to make. Λεκτα do not merely mark the separation of expressions from the mixture; λεκτα also enter into propositions themselves. It is as if λεκτα crack open the world into sounds and things in order insert themselves therein. While sounds are still bodies – articulated breaths – when λεκτα subsist within them, they are words. The separation between words and things creates a second separation within propositions: a separation 'between nouns and verbs, or, rather, between denotations and expressions. Denotations refer always to bodies ... expressions refer to expressible meanings' (*LS* 183). The separation between nouns and verbs is made possible because of the prior separation between things and propositions. These two separations 'operate ... on both sides [of the surface] by means of one and the same incorporeal power': quasi-causality (*LS* 183). Quasi-causality generates both denotations and expressions. As denotations refer to bodies or beings, they take the form of nouns; as expressions refer to events or manners of being, they take the form of verbs.

To see how nouns and verbs form λεκτα's two faces, let us follow Deleuze's abbreviated analysis of the respective Epicurean and Stoic philosophies of language. As ancient materialisms, these 'two great ancient systems' strove to discover what, in bodies, makes language possible (*LS* 183). According to Deleuze, the main difference between the two systems corresponds to the second separation: Epicureans privilege nouns and adjectives, and the Stoics verbs and adverbs.[55] Deleuze here exploits the interwoven play of grammar and metaphysics in these Hellenic–Roman schools:

> Epicureans created a model based on the *declension of the atom*; the Stoics, on the contrary, created a model based on the *conjugation of events*. It is not surprising therefore that the Epicurean model privileges nouns and adjectives; nouns are like atoms or linguistic bodies which are coordinated through there declension, and adjectives like the qualities of these composites. But the Stoic model comprehends language on the basis of 'prouder' [*plus fiers*] terms: verbs and their conjugation, in relation to the links between incorporeal events. (*LS* 183; emphasis added)[56]

The Shell A: Λεκτα

On this reading, the Epicurean model begins and ends with atoms and void. Epicurean cosmology builds the universe out of basic bodily building blocks, denoted by nouns and adjectives. It makes sense that almost all the atomists, and many of their critics, talk of the analogous way in which atomic and linguistic worlds are produced through combinatory processes: atoms are to composite individuals as letters are to words and sentences. The seventeenth-century Christian atomist Pierre Gassendi calls this 'the similitude of letters'.[57] The idea is that a finite set of basic types produces indefinite atomic and linguistic worlds through various combinations and changes. Composite bodies of the atomic world and meaningful words of the linguistic world are the results of various combinations.

Furthermore, just as Greek and Latin nouns are organised by *declensions* into various cases (nominative, genitive, dative and so on), atoms are organised in so far as there are infinitely small *declinations* or deviations from the regular rectilinear direction of atoms speeding through void. The diversity of divergent worlds is produced through the relations into which atoms enter because of a slight shift away (a de-cline) from rectilinear motion. An analogous declination thus operates in Epicurean cosmology and philosophy of language. It is no coincidence that Lucretius repeats *declinare*, *inclinare*, *declinado* and, of course, *clinamen*, each of which refers to the Greek root κλίνω, meaning 'to lean, to recline, to slope, to decline, to inflect'.[58] Nouns are similarly organised into meaningful sentences through the declension, albeit into cases rather than by swerving away from rectilinearity. Nouns decline according to number and case, and pronouns and adjectives also decline according to gender. For example, a certain noun functions as the subject or object of a sentence when it declines into, respectively, the nominative or accusative case. These various declensions compose empirical descriptions of the material world. The point is that *atoms and nouns decline*: atoms through the swerve, a physical inflection, and nouns through the inflected grammar of Greek or Latin.

By contrast, the Stoic philosophy of language prioritises infinitive verbs and their conjugations. Rather than declining into various subjects and objects in so far as they correspond to states of affairs, verbs conjugate according to the events that arise from them. To conjugate according to events connects verbs to the continuous movement of time and to the discontinuous movements of bodies. Recall that, in Latin, *coniugāre* means 'to yoke together'. In addition to the sense of conjoining or uniting in, say, marriage or biology (such as when bacteria temporarily fuse together by exchanging DNA), 'conjugation' has a grammatical sense: the formulation of verbal derivations from a principal part (often the infinitive) specifies an activity or state of being.[59] A verb is conjugated according to person, gender, number, tense, mood, voice, aspect and sometimes categories such as possession and politeness. If we conjugate the English 'to cut', we get the following conjugated forms (in present tense, active voice, indicative mood): 'I cut, you cut, he/she/it cuts, we cut, you (all) cut, they cut'. In Latin, *secāre* conjugates into *secō, secās, secat, secāmus, secātis, secant*.[60] Each conjugation is individuated by person (first, second, third) and number (singular, plural). Conjugations thus limit the unlimitedness of the infinitive. Since Stoic grammar and metaphysics overlap, conjugation is the grammatical correlate of metaphysical actualisation.

The infinitive, by contrast, does not conjugate. Here Deleuze's thinking about infinitives seems to come from Luce Irigaray's early essay 'Du fantasme et du verbe'.[61] As Irigaray points out, there is no subject or object position of infinite verbs because there is no such division. Without gender, number or other grammatical determination, Keith W. Faulkner writes, infinitives apply '*to* no one, *at* no time, and *in* no place'.[62] Infinitives are impersonal, subjectless and neutral, neither active nor passive. At most, they express what Beat poet Lawrence Ferlinghetti calls (in his 'surreal semi-autobiographical blackbook record' *Her*) 'the *fourth person*' of phrases such as 'it rains' (*il pleut*) or 'it snows' (*il neige*).[63] Deleuze echoes Ferlinghetti on this point: 'the *they* [*on*] of the pure event wherein *it dies* [*il meurt*] dies in the same way that *it* rains [*il pleut*]' (*LS* 152; emphasis original). The fourth person is only personal in the way that Deleuze and Guattari speak of the proper name (*nom propre*). The proper name does not refer to an individual subject, but to a non-personal agent 'of a pure infinitive comprehended as such in a field of intensity' (*ATP* 37). A proper name is the designation of an *effect* or result that spreads across the incorporeal surface. Deleuze mentions proper names in modern physics (the Kelvin or Doppler effects) and medicine (Alzheimer's or Parkinson's) as examples of the fourth person of infinitives, and *Logic of Sense* speaks of 'the Chrysippus effect', perhaps naming the form of Deleuze's encounter with Stoicism (*LS* 70). There is no subject of the Chrysippus effect, even though it has a proper name; the most that we can say that it expresses the fourth person 'it': *it* subsists as effect or the effect subsists as *it*.

Deleuze claims that the verb oscillates between 'two poles: [1] the

The Shell A: Λεκτα

present, which indicates its relation to a denotable state of affairs in a view of a physical time characterized by succession; and [2] the infinitive' (*LS* 184). We can think of these two poles as corresponding to corporeal depths and incorporeal surface, which means that conjugation articulates a distinct tense, person and so on, while the infinitive corresponds to sense and λεκτα. Put differently, the infinitive represents the circle of the proposition unwound. The infinitive does not indicate a denotatum, manifestation or signification; it expresses only sense. An individuated conjugated form, on the contrary, closes the circle of the proposition so that an object is denoted, intention manifested and concept signified. Between these two poles, 'the verb curves its conjugation in conformity with the relations of denotation, manifestation, and signification – the aggregate of times, persons, and modes' (*LS* 184).[64]

The Two Faces of Λεκτα

Dorothea Frede appreciates how λεκτα 'straddle the *borderline* between the mind-dependent and the mind-independent in an awkward enough way'.[65] What Frede calls an 'awkward enough way', we call perversity. The mind-dependency to which she refers appears in the relation of λεκτα to states of affairs, where this relation takes the form of tertiary ordinance and the circle of the proposition. The mind independency appears in the relation of λεκτα to the terrifying depths of brute materiality churning beneath our words in the primary order. The surface is this 'borderline between', and its two faces form what Deleuze calls secondary organisation: one side faces the primary order of corporeal chaos; the other side faces the tertiary ordinance of state affairs. One side surveys the articulated arrangement of individuated speakers and propositions; the other side peers into the undifferentiated depths of bodies swirling, interpenetrating and exploding. We see this in the following table of vocabulary:

Primary order	Nonsense	Φωνή	Apersonal and unindividuated	Corporeal mixtures	Chaosmos	Schizophrenic
Secondary organisation	Sense	Λεκτα	Impersonal and pre-individual	Incorporeal surface	Surface	Pervert
Tertiary ordinance	Denotation, manifestation, signification	Λόγος	Egos and individuals	States of affairs	Cosmos	Neurotic

Notice that primary order and tertiary ordinance are two ways of conceiving of the same thing: matter. Primary order refers to matter in its chaotic mixture wherein it is impossible to distinguish one body from any other body, unlimited material madness. By contrast, tertiary ordinance refers to matter in so far as it has been arranged into individuated states of affairs, each of which is composed of distinct bodies; it is a realm differenciated by distinct bodily limits. What differenciates them is the incorporeal surface that disjoins and conjoins matter to itself. Although we talk about two sides of the surface, we know that both sides face one world, similar to a Möbius strip. Viewed from the perspective of logic, we call this double-sided surface λεκτα: one side faces the unlimited depths of the chaosmos, and the other the limited heights of the cosmos.

The two faces of λεκτα match the two faces of space that we saw in 'The Yolk C': conjugated and infinitive verbs correspond to place and void.[66] As we noted above, Diogenes Laërtius reported a distinction between two kinds of λεκτα: incomplete λεκτα correspond to infinitive verbs, and complete λεκτα correspond to conjugated verbs and their subject position. 'Incomplete' can thus mean unconjugated, and 'complete' means conjugated. Incomplete λεκτα are Stoic attributes – 'to green' or 'greens' – and complete λεκτα correspond to the predicates that that we see in the Platonic theory of predication – 'the tree is green'.[67] Incomplete λεκτα refer to incorporeal events; complete λεκτα refer to corporeal subjects and states of affairs. As Michael Frede notes, in Stoicism there is 'an analogue of the whole verbal system on the level of the λεκτα'.[68] Conjugated verbs are finite and limited λεκτα because they refer to limited and differentiated bodies arranged in states of affairs. By contrast, infinitives are infinite and unlimited λεκτα because they refer to the unlimited and undifferentiated depths of the primary order.

Recall that the word *infinitivus* itself means 'unlimited, countless, endless', as in the Greek ἄπειρον, which is extensively explored in Plato's *Philebus*. In the *Philebus*, Socrates compares unlimited (ἄπειρον) to limit (πέρας), citing predicates such as 'the hotter and the colder'. Plato writes, 'these things never had an end' because there is always something hotter than some hot body, or colder than the coldest body.[69] Since unlimited things 'always contain the more and less', they are 'always in flux', ever exceeding 'all definite quantity'.[70] If they did take on definite quantity, such as 133 degrees Celsius, they would no longer be hotter or colder. There would be just a hot or cold thing. Unlimited would convert to limited; becoming would seize into being.

The Shell A: Λεκτα

We mention this because Deleuze refers to the *Philebus* in the first scene of *Logic of Sense*. Lewis Carroll's description of Alice's paradoxical becoming is the prime example of the unlimited and the infinitive. When Carroll writes, 'Alice becomes larger', he is saying that Alice is simultaneously (*à la fois*) becoming larger and smaller. It is not that she is both bigger and smaller at the same time, but rather that *now* she is larger, *before* she was smaller. Hence this paradox: It is 'at the same moment that [she] becomes larger than [she] was and smaller than [she] becomes' (*LS* 1). *Becoming* thus eludes the present; it cannot seize into being, no more than unlimitedness can convert into limited. Hence the perverse essence of becoming: 'to move [*aller*] and to pull [*tirer*] in both directions [*sens*] at once [*à la fois*]' (*LS* 1). Notice that the French word used here for 'directions' is *sens*. *Sens* denotes 'sense, meaning, direction'. In so far as becoming spreads in two opposed directions, it is expressed by infinitive verbs endlessly dividing or differentiating across the intensive face of the metaphysical surface in two directions.

In different language, infinitives are intensively considered λεκτα and conjugations are extensively considered λεκτα. The side facing tertiary ordinance is extensive in so far as it denotes extensively determined bodies, and bodies are extensively determined in so far as they are finite, limited, and quantitative. The side facing primary order is intensive in so far as it expresses incorporeal intensities endlessly dividing in two directions at once (*à la fois*). In between conjugations and infinitives is the surface, although it is more accurate to say that the surface is composed of two unequal faces in constant disequilibrium. We repeat the diagram from the last chapter:

$$\Lambda\varepsilon\kappa\tau\alpha \quad \frac{\text{Infinitive verb (infinite)}}{\text{Conjugated verb (limited)}}$$

Intensive and extensive faces correspond to differentiation and integration. Differentiation is the process of infinitives dividing without end, and integration is the process through which conjugations are differenciated into determinate persons, genders, numbers and so on. On the backside of the surface is projected the movement from primary order to secondary organisation. Put differently, differentiation is the amorphous shadow of the dynamic genesis cast from the chaosmic depths shaping the paradoxical play of sense and nonsense. Differentiation is a way of conceiving of the relations among infinitives themselves. Infinitives mark the process of continuously and infinitely dividing or differentiated without conjugating. On the front side of the surface is projected the leap from secondary organisation to tertiary ordinance. Put differently, integration is the clear silhouette of the static genesis of language into the circle of the proposition.

Conclusion

To say that Stoicism prioritises verbs in their philosophy of language does not mean they ignore nouns, conjunctions, articles or other parts of speech.[71] That would, after all, be a very sparse grammar.[72] Instead, the Stoics had an innovative account of noun inflection (declensions are not simply features of words but correspond to what is signified or meant), and considered conjunctions and articles to be parts of speech (unlike many other ancient thinkers).[73] Yet, for our purposes, the prioritisation of verbs reflects the Stoic perversion of their predecessors. While Plato and Aristotle locate nouns and beings in the domain of truth, Stoics locate truth in verbs and becomings. Two very different metaphysics, logics and ethics follow from such grammatical prioritisation.

From the perspective of Platonic heights or Aristotelian interiority, the Stoic incorporeal surface expresses a logic that is paradoxical and perverse. Several Hellenistic contemporaries, and many commentators afterwards, thought the Stoics proffered nonsense, especially in their account of λεκτα. Although Deleuze considers the Stoic theory paradoxical, he claims that this very paradoxicality proves, rather than refutes, the Stoics' philosophical ingenuity. 'The genius of the Stoics was to have taken this paradox as far as it could go, up to the point of insanity and cynicism, and to have ground it in the most serious of principles: their reward was to the first to develop a philosophy of language' (*ATP* 86). 'The Shell A' has focused mostly on the Stoic philosophy of language, which forms half of Stoic logic. The other half is what looks to us moderns more like logic as a form of systematic inference. 'The Shell B' turns to this other half. As we will see, at the heart of Stoic logic, at least on Deleuze's Stoicism, are paradoxes.

The Shell A: Λεκτα

Notes

1. We are not translating the Greek into English in order to retain the specific meaning that the Stoics attribute to this term, and to avoid secreting in any inappropriate connotations.
2. *TI*; *SS*; Thomas Bénatouïl, 'Le système stoïcien', in *Philosophie antique*, ed. Jean-François Pradeau (Paris: Presses universitaires de France, 2010), 13–49.
3. Frédérique Ildefonse, *Les Stoïciens I: Zénon, Cléanthe, Chrysippe* (Paris: Les Belles Lettres, 2000).
4. Andreas Graeser, *Zenon von Kition: Positionen und Probleme* (Berlin: de Gruyter, 1975). Jacques Brunschwig, *Papers in Hellenistic Philosophy* (Cambridge: Cambridge University Press, 1994).
5. Benson Mates, *Stoic Logic* (Berkeley: University of California Press, 1961). William Kneale and Martha Kneale, *The Development of Logic* (Oxford: The Clarendon Press, 1962).
6. Gerard Watson, *The Stoic Theory of Knowledge* (Belfast: Queen's University, 1966).
7. Adam Drozdek, '*Lekton*: Stoic Logic and Ontology', *Acta antiqua Academiae Scientiarum Hungaricae* 42.104 (2002): 93–104.
8. This is what Michael James Bennett uses. Bennett, *Deleuze and Ancient Greek Physics: The Image of Nature* (London: Bloomsbury Academic, 2017).
9. Though *Logic of Sense* suggests that Deleuze is taking the word *sens* from Husserl's Ideas, the conceptual framework and larger philosophy of language is resoundingly Stoic (*LS* 20–1; Edmund Husserl, *Ideas Pertaining to a Pure Phenomenology and to a Phenomenological Philosophy*, First Book, trans. F. Kersten (The Hague: Martinus Nijhoff, 1983), 309–16.
10. Gilles Deleuze, *Expressionism in Philosophy: Spinoza* (1968), trans. Martin Joughin (New York: Zone Books, 1990), 62; emphasis added. On the connection between Stoic λεκτα and medieval thought, see Giorgio Pini, *Categories and Logic in Duns Scotus* (Leiden: Brill, 2002), 158n.48.
11. Aristophanes, *Birds*, ed. and trans. Jeffrey Henderson (Cambridge, MA: Loeb Classical Library, 1995), 423.
12. Euripides, *Hippolytus*, in *Euripides: Children of Heracles. Hippolytus. Andromache. Hecuba*, ed. and trans. David Kovacs (Cambridge, MA: Loeb Classical Library, 1995), 875.
13. All these etymological flights of fancy rely on the *LSJ*.
14. Homer, *The Odyssey: Books 13–24*, ed. George E. Dimock, trans. A. T. Murray (Cambridge, MA: Harvard University Press, 1919), 18.359.
15. Plato, *Theaetetus*, 181c. See also: *Gorgias*, 480b, *Phaedo*, 60e, *Gorgias*, 489d, and *Phaedrus*, 265c.

16. Michael Frede, 'The Stoic Notion of a *Lekton*', in *Companions to Ancient Thought: 3 Language*, ed. Stephen Everson (Cambridge: Cambridge University Press, 1994), 109–28, at 109; emphasis original.
17. Adam Drozdek argues: 'For the Stoics, comparison of [subjective] thoughts is possible because there is a *tertium comparationis*, namely the objective meaning of the thought, the *lekton*.' Adam Drozdek, '*Lekton*: Stoic Logic and Ontology', *Acta antiqua Academiae Scientiarum Hungaricae* 42.104 (2002): 93–104, at 95.
18. Clement, *Miscellanies*, 8.9.26.3.
19. Jean-Baptiste Gourinat, *Le Stoïcisme* (Paris: Presses universitaires de France, 2014), 11.
20. Margherita Isnardi Parente, 'La notion d'incorporel chez les stoïciens', in *Les Stoïciens*, ed. Gilbert Romeyer Dherbey and Jean-Baptiste Gourinat (Paris: J. Vrin, 2005), 176.
21. The reason why Chrysippus is most likely the source of λεκτα is due to his fascination with logic and language. This association of Chrysippus as *the* Stoic logician is the standard view. For a summary of the standard view, see F. H. Sandbach, *The Stoics* (Indianapolis: Hackett Publishing Company, 1994), 95.
22. Chrysippus included his discussion on voice in his book on *Physics* (DL 7.55). Brunschwig notes that this is an interesting way to define the vocal sound 'because it seems to be a self-conscious inversion of Plato's and Aristotle's descriptions of vocal sound as "a blow of/on the air".' Brunschwig, *Papers*, 133.
23. Another distinction to draw between saying (λέγειν) and uttering (προφέςθαι). For more on this, see Catherine Atheron, *The Stoics on Ambiguity* (Cambridge: Cambridge University Press), 283–4.
24. Seneca, *Letters of Lucilius*, 117.
25. Ibid.
26. To be fair, Bréhier does not explicitly make the move to infinitives, while Deleuze openly does. Still, since '. . . greens' does seem to be a non-finite form of the verb, similar to a participle or gerund, the move seems well motivated.
27. This is how Bréhier, in a different text, characterizes the 'Stoic dialectic': it 'does not further decompose the verb, as Aristotle does, into a copula and an attribute designating a general notion; it takes the verb in its unity, in so far as it expresses an event,' such as 'to green' or 'to cut' (*CAS* 70).
28. Gilles Deleuze and Claire Parnet, *Dialogues* (1977), trans. Hugh Tomlinson and Barbara Habberjam (New York: Columbia University Press, 1977), 64.
29. Helen Palmer, *Deleuze & Futurism: A Manifesto for Nonsense* (London: Bloomsbury Academic, 2014), 49.
30. Remember that the word 'category', κατηγορία, means 'predication'.

The Shell A: Λεκτα

31. Diogenes reports that the Stoics see two kinds of λεκτα: complete and incomplete (DL 7.63). incomplete λεκτα are attributes, such as 'greens' or 'to walk'. They are incomplete because they do not refer to a subject. Complete λεκτα include a subject and an attribute, such as 'the tree greens' or 'Dion walks'. Stoics distinguish between different kinds of complete λεκτα: propositions, interrogations, invocations, oaths and imperatives (DL 7.66). What distinguish these different kinds of λεκτα are the different effects produced by each of them. For example, propositions and imperatives are distinguished by what follows from the act of asserting or the act of commanding, respectively. Here we see the strange quasi-causality of λεκτα: they are passive effects of the expressed imperative or interrogation, but they also contribute to the organisation of states of affairs. Moreover, there is some debate about the importance of incompete λεκτα. Marc Baratin says that incomplete λεκτα are the prime forms of λεκτα, while Ildefonse disagrees. For this debate, see Marc Baratin, *La Naissance de la syntaxe à Rome* (Paris: Éditions du Minuit, 1989), 384–5; Frédérique Ildefonse, *La Naissance de la grammaire dans l'antiquité grecque* (Paris: J. Vrin, 1997), 146–7.
32. Frede, 'The Stoic Notion', 118; emphasis added.
33. Ildefonse also speaks of a 'chaosmos' in Stoicism. Ildefonse, *Les Stoïciens*, 206.
34. Although he does not cite Diogenes Laërtius here, notice Deleuze's use of Chrysippus' 'ocean of wine' imagery (DL 7.151).
35. On our reading, Deleuze turns to psychoanalytic concepts and vocabulary not simply because they were dominant in France at the time, but also because psychoanalysis, especially the Kleinian variety, engaged with the same problem that Deleuze was engaging with in the second half of *Logic of Sense*. This is the shared problem: how to explain the production of a meaningful psychology out of a meaningless material world. In *Deleuze, A Stoic*, we are pushing aside the psychoanalytic language in order to reveal Deleuze's continued engagement with Stoicism that appears throughout the *Logic of Sense*. We only see this Stoic encounter once we strip away the psychoanalytic vocabulary. One reason to justify this downplaying of psychoanalysis is that Deleuze himself suggests this when he wrote a preface to the Italian translation of *Logic of Sense* in 1976, about seven years after its original publication. He writes, 'What is it that was just not right in *Logic of Sense*? Apparently it still refelcts a naïve ang tuilty sense of self-satisfaction with respect to psychoanalysis. My only excuse for such self-satisfaction would be this: I was then trying, very timidly, to render psychoanlaysis *inoffensive*, presenting it as a surface art, one which deals with Events as surface entities.' Gilles Deleuze, *Two Regimes of Madness: Texts and Interviews 1975–1995*, ed. David Lapoujade, trans. Ames Hodges and Mike Taormina (New York: Semiotexte, 2006), 65.

36. 'Melanie Klein describes it as the paranoid-schizoid position of the child' (*LS* 187).
37. Recall that the Greek word that we translate a 'elements' – *stoichea* – means both physical elements and linguistic elements or the alphabet.
38. Deleuze develops a whole psychoanalytic account of the correspondence of the geneic structure of these three elements to three psychoanalytic locales: 'phonemes referring to the erogenous zones, morphemes to the phallus of coordination, and semantemes to the phallus of castration' (*LS* 232). We are not using this language because we are focusing on the Stoicism lurking below.
39. We translate *ordonnance* as 'ordinance', rather than Lester and Stivale's 'arrangement' in order to retain the sense of the Latin *ordo*, which can mean several senses of ordering, including: (1) putting things into order with rows, lines or series; (2) ordering people in classes, stations or ranks; (3) arranging soldiers into military formations for the most efficient forms of attack; (4) rhetorical organisation of a speech for most effective speaking. In French, according to Larousse's *Encyclopedia*, *ordonnance* refers to a 'legal text legislated by the king or an act taken by the government, with Parliamentary authorisation in domains normally covered by the law'.
40. Sean Bowden suggests that Deleuze gets the three dimensions of the proposition from Bertrand Russell. Sean Bowden, *The Priority of Events: Deleuze's Logic of Sense* (Edinburgh: Edinburgh University Press, 2011), 26.
41. Daniel W. Smith, 'From Surface to the Depths: On the Transition from *Logic of Sense* to *Anti-Oedipus*', in *Gilles Deleuze: The Intensive Reduction*, ed. Constantin V. Boundas (New York: Continuum, 2009), 84.
42. Daniel W. Smith, 'From Surface to the Depths: On the Transition from *Logic of Sense* to *Anti-Oedipus*', in *Gilles Deleuze: The Intensive Reduction*, ed. Constantin V. Boundas (New York: Continuum, 2009), 83; emphasis added.
43. Joe Hughes, *Deleuze and the Genesis of Representation* (New York: Continuum, 2008), 24; emphasis added.
44. Jean-Jacques Lecercle, *Deleuze and Language* (New York: Palgrave Macmillan, 2002), 114.
45. Although we are stripping these geneses of their psychoanalytic terminology, we can still connect the three phrases of dynamic genesis to their psychoanalytic correlates. Connective corresponds to the 'pregenital sexuality', conjunction corresponds to 'phallic coordination', and disjunctive corresponds to 'castration' (*LS* 225, 225, 208). According to Lecercle, Deleuze follows 'Serge Leclaire, the psychoanalyst who theorised erogenous zones and their differential values'. Jean-Jacques Lecercle, *Badiou and Deleuze Read Literature* (Edinburgh: Edinburgh

The Shell A: Λεκτα

University Press, 2010), 19. We should also note that these three syntheses correspond to the three syntheses in Kant's First *Critique*: 'synthesis of apprehension in the intuition', 'synthesis of reproduction in imagination' and 'synthesis of recognition in the concept' (Immanuel Kant, *Critique of Pure Reason*, trans. Paul Guyer and Allen W. Wood (Cambridge: Cambridge University Press, 1999), A98–110). If we are tempted by even more architectonic correspondence, we might see it in the three syntheses that start out Hegel's *Phenomenology of Spirit*: sense-certainty, perception, and force and the understanding.

46. Deleuze cites 'what linguists sometimes call "a concatenation of successive entities, but not the concurrence"'. The 'linguists' to whom Deleuze refers is most likely Roman Jacokson. Roger D. Woodard and David A. Scott, *The Textualization of the Greek Alphabet* (Cambridge: Cambridge University Press, 2014), 170. Interestingly, this text cites Lewis Caroll when discussing these issues.

47. Another way to think of this is through information theory, which recognises that certain letters or sounds 'pull' and 'push' on each other. In English, for example, the 'q' sound pulls on a 'u' sound to come after it, while a 't' sounds pushes a 'c' sound away from it coming directly afterwards. See Jimmy Son and Rob Goodman, *A Mind at Play: How Claude Shannon Invented the Information Age* (New York: Simon & Schuster, 2017).

48. Deleuze actually distinguishes three types of portmanteau words: 'contracting', 'circulating' and 'disjunctive', each of which correspond to one of these three syntheses (*LS* 47). We are overlooking this distinction because the Snark most clearly applies to the second synthesis.

49. Lewis Carroll, *The Annotated Hunting of the Snark* (New York: W. W. Norton & Co., 2006), 15n.4. Interestingly, Deleuze says that 'Snark' is a combination of 'shark + snake', contrary to what Beatrice Hatch, the child muse of Charles Dodgson, reports in her article on Lewis Carroll appearing in *The Strand* (April 1989). Carroll said that Snark is a conjunction of snail and shark. Others, however, suggest different conjoined terms. Phyllis Greenacre thinks that it was 'snake', not 'snail', and Stephen Barr suggests it was a combination of 'snarl' and 'bark'. Carroll, *The Annotated Hunting of the Snark*, 15n.4. But, given that the point of conjunctive synthesis rests with the conjoining, not the conjuncts, it is not important which are the true identity of the conjuncts. Synthesis is prior to the synthesised elements.

50. Adam Gopnick, 'Introduction to *The Annotated Hunting of the Snark*', in Carroll, *The Annotated Hunting of the Snark*, xxxix.

51. In a 17 March 2017 Lecture at *Cours Vincennes,* Deleuze reflect this paradoxical logic: 'We cannot simultanesouly say something and explain what we are saying.' https://www.webdeleuze.com/textes/43 (last accessed 8 February 2019).

52. Lapoujade, *Aberrant Movements: The Philosophy of Gilles Deleuze* (2014), trans. Joshua David Jordan (South Pasadena: Semiotext(e), 2017), 134–5; emphasis original.
53. Lecercle, *Badiou and Deleuze Read Literature*, 17.
54. Deleuze might not have been as careful in his word selection here as he could have been, especially considering the critique of 'trees' that we later see in *A Thousand Plateaus*. The word 'ramify' comes from the Latin *ramificare*, meaning 'to branch, spread', and further back to *rāmus*, which means 'branch, bough, twig', connoting the tree, the 'first type of book' (*ATP* 5). *Rāmus* itself comes from *rādix*, from which we get 'radicle', as in 'the second figure of the book' (*ATP* 5). A better word than 'ramify' would have to do with the 'rhizome'.
55. Here we might link up the Epicureans with Parmenides, in so far as they privilege nouns, and the Stoics with Heraclitus, in so far as they privilege verbs. As a personal pedagogical aside, I used to teach an ancient philosophy class in which I turned pre-Socratic philosophies into experiential learning exercises. On the Parmenides day, the class sat as still as possible and tried to conduct our class conversation only in nouns and adjectives. The next class day, when we covered Heraclitus, the class kept moving and tried to discuss Heraclitan philosophy speaking only in verbs and adverbs.
56. Deleuze calls verbs 'prouder' because of what Humpty Dumpty says in *Alice Through the Looking-Glass*. Speaking of how he uses words, he says: 'They've a temper, some of them – particularly verbs: they're the proudest – adjectives you can do anything with, but not verbs.' Lewis Carroll, *Alice Through the Looking-Glass* (New York: Bloomsbury, 2001), 113.
57. Gassendi's adaptation of the similitude of the letters and its afterlife throughout the seventeenth century is covered in Daniel Selcer, *Philosophy and the Book: Early Modern Figures of Material Inscription* (London: Continuum, 2010).
58. *Depellere*: Lucretius, *De Rerum Natura*, ed. and trans. Cyril Bailey (Oxford: Clarendon Press 1947), 2.219; *depellere* is used in a different sense at 3.321, where Lucretius discusses the capacity of reason to overcome our faults: 'illud in his rebus video firmare potesse, usque adeo naturam vestigial linquiparvola quae nequeat raio depellere nobis ut nil inpediat dignam dis degree vitam' (Ibid. 3.319–22). *Declinare*: Ibid. 2.221, 2.250. *Inclinare*: Ibid. 2.243; at 6.563 and 6.573, Lucretius uses related terms (*inclinata* and *inclinatur*), but these terms refer to the lean of buildings and the tilt of the earth rather than the clinamen. *Declinado*: Ibid. 2.250; *declinamus*, the first-person plural present indicative active form of *declinare*, appears a few lines later at 2.259, but refers to the movement of human will as it swerves away from certain desires rather than the atomic swerve. *Clinamen*: Ibid. 2.292.

The Shell A: Λεκτα

59. Although there are four basic parts of Latin verbs (first-person singular of the present indicative act, present infinitive active, first-person singular of the perfect indicative active, perfect passive participle), we focus on the infinitive form because Deleuze considers this the core sense of a verb.
60. Deluzes uses *conjugaison* several times in *Logic of Sense*, for example, 'the *conjugation* of effects', 'the art of *conjugation* (see the *confatalia* or series of events that depend on one another)', 'verbs and their conjugation incarnate reaction', 'the Stoics . . . created a model based on the *conjugation* of events . . . verbs and their conjugation, in relation to the links between incorporeal events', 'effects refer to effects and form a *conjugation*, whereas causes refer to causes and form a *unity*' (LS 6, 8, 183, 184, 270; emphases original)
61. Luce Irigaray, 'Du fantasme et du verbe', *L'Arc* 34 (1968).
62. Keith W. Faulkner, *Deleuze and the Three Syntheses of Time* (New York: Peter Lang Inc., International Academic Publishers, 2005), 28; emphasis original. See Jean-Jacques Lecercle, *Deleuze and Language* (New York: Palgrave Macmillan, 2002), 117; Faulkner, *Deleuze and the Three Syntheses of Time*, 27.
63. Lawrence Ferlinghetti, *Her* (New York: New Directions, 1960). On the back cover, Ferlinghetti describes *Her* as 'A surreal semi-autobiographical blackbook record of a semi-mad period of my life, in that mindless, timeless state most romantics pass through, confusing flesh madonnas with spiritual ones.' For more on the how Deleuze appropriates the concept of 'the fourth person' from Ferlinghetti, see Jeff Bradley, 'The Eyes of the Fourth Person Singular', *Deleuze Studies* 9.2 (2015): 185–207. At the end of Bradley's essay, he gestures towards uses of the fourth person in what Deleuze might call now 'minor languages'. For example, some Native American languages (Algonguain, Navaho) have what linguists call the 'obviative' because such languages 'have four rather thant three distinctions in the catgory of person' (204). There is also the 'Finnish passive', which 'is usually called the fourth person' but can include '[s]entences containing the zero person', where 'the gramamtical subject is omitted' (204).
64. 'It is from the verb too that we infer what the ring [of denotation-manifestation-signification] conceals or coils up, or what it reveals once it is split, unrolled, and deployed over a straight line: sense or the event as the expressed of the proposition' (*LS* 184).
65. Dorothea Frede, 'Fatalism and Future Truth', *Proceedings of the Boston Area Colloquium in Ancient Philosophy* 6.1 (1990), pp. 195–227, at 217; emphasis added.
66. While we must admit the bold Eurocentrist, or at least Indo-European, assumptions that arise whenever linguistic grammar is made to match ontological structures, this seeming bias might also be an opening for

encounters with different grammars. In particular, I am thinking about any language that does not inflect or conjugate verbs for tense, person, number and so on. Regardless of temporal differences, these verbs do not change. They are truly neutral or sterile, similar to infinitives.

67. Michael Frede also realises this: 'Diogenes discusses ... incomplete λεκτα of a kind, which correspond to verbs, but which are explicitly distinguished from verbs as the corresponding λεκτα.' Michael Frede, *Essays in Ancient Philosophy* (Minneapolis: University of Minnesota Press, 1987), 304.
68. Frede, *Essays in Ancient Philosophy*, 307.
69. Plato, *Philebus*, 24b. Deleuze also cites the discussion of unlimited and limit in Plato's *Parmenides*.
70. Plato, *Philebus*, 24c.
71. Hence the discussion of cases appears in the larger study of λεκτα (DL 7.64–5, 70).
72. Still, Deleuze and Guattari do flirt with a very sparse grammar consisting of only three forms: 'Indefinite article + infinitive verb + proper name' (*ATP* 263).
73. Frede, *Essays in Ancient Philosophy*, 329–30.

5

The Shell B: Paradoxes

Introduction

Now that we have considered Stoic perversity in their materialist physics (especially the theory of incorporeals) and their materialist philosophy of language (especially the theory of λεκτα), we can examine how the Stoics developed a perverse logic. This perversity is due to the Stoics' fascination with the power of paradoxes.

We begin this chapter by acknowledging that Stoic logic was almost forgotten due to the 2,000 years of dominance of Aristotelian logic. From the perspective of Aristotle's categorical reasoning, the Stoics' system of propositional system perverted, especially its exploitation of paradoxes. To consider Stoic propositional logic, we will first consider how it harnesses absurdity, especially in so far as it perverts good and common sense. We then specify the structure and purposes of paradoxes in their propositional system. We will focus on the four paradoxes that are essential to the type of transcendental logic of incorporeals that we have been developing since 'The Yolk B': (1) The Heap, (2) The Liar, (3) The Master and (4) The Nobody. Each of these four express the structure of ambiguity, which turns on what Deleuze calls the 'aleatory point'. We conclude by comparing two ancient types of inference – *ergo* and *igitur* – and ask whether it is enough to study Stoicism or whether Stoic theory necessitates a *becoming-Stoic*. At the very end of this chapter, before turning to 'The Shell C', we will pause to ask what Deleuze considers an essential question for anyone who takes seriously the history of philosophy: 'How much have we yet to learn from Stoicism' (*LS* 158)?

A Forgotten Logic

For much of the history of philosophy, Stoic logic was widely panned, partly due to the Stoics' fascination with paradoxes. Given this fascination, it is not surprising that Zeno reportedly paid 200 drachmas for seven versions of one paradox: 'The Reaper' (DL 7.25).

Depending on time and rates, this might just under $10,000 (current USD) in order to acquire just one logical paradox. Sextus Empiricus describes what he sees as the absurd allure of paradoxes to Stoics: when a Stoic

> has made a collection of such trash he draws eyebrows together and expounds Dialectic and endeavours very solemnly to establish for us by syllogistic proofs that a thing becomes, a thing moves, snow is white, and we do not have horns; although it is probably sufficient to confront the trash with the plan fact in order to smash up their positive affirmation by means of the equipollant contradictory evidence from appearances.[1]

Even 2,000 years later, scholars still pan Stoic logic, including Carl Prantl:

> it must have been a frightfully decadent and corrupted age that could designate so hollow a head as Chrysippus as its greatest logician, continuing, Chrysippus created nothing really new in logic ... his activity consisted in this, that in the treatment of the material descended to a pitiful degree of dullness, triviality, and scholastic quibbling; or in this, that they created a technical expression for every possible detail, e.g., for the triflings of sophistries and paradoxes.[2]

To Deleuze, however, Stoicism marked a totally new way of doing philosophy, philosophy as 'perversion, which befits the system of provocations of this new type of philosopher' (*LS* 133). Paradoxes were necessary to that perverse new type of philosopher

Most philosophers have forgotten or just ignored Stoic logic. For over two thousand years, Aristotle's logic was so dominant that it seemed there was nothing more to say. Kant expressed this sentiment in the 'Preface to the second edition' of his *Critique of Pure Reason*: 'What is remarkable about logic is that until now it has been unable to take a single step forward [from Aristotle], and therefore seems to all appearance to be finished and complete.'[3] This was a common perception of the history of logic for the 150 years after Kant. Even today many still are ignorant of the Stoics' logical innovations. It was not until 1927, when the Polish logician Jan Łukasiewicz noticed that the Stoics had developed an alternative, seemingly forgotten, logic.[4] Yet, even after Łukasiewicz, Stoic logic was the minor logic to Aristotle's major logic.[5] Even Benson Mates, who wrote the most formative text on *Stoic Logic*, spends just over two pages on paradoxes in Stoicism, saying that most 'Stoic paradoxes, though slightly amusing, are too weak to be worth mentioning here'.[6]

Back in antiquity, however, Chrysippus, the third head of the

The Shell B: Paradoxes

Stoa, was described as the greatest logician of them all, and arguably the reason why Stoicism survived its early shaky foundations.[7] 'So renowned was he for dialectic that most people thought, if the gods do dialectic, they would adopt no other system than that of Chrysippus' (DL 7.180). Deleuze recognises Stoic logic is forceful because they are 'amateurs and inventors of paradoxes' (*LS* 8). According to Deleuze's Stoicism, all those nay-sayers miss out on the true creativity and force of Stoic logic. In so far as the incorporeal surface is the fundamental figure of the paradox, the Stoic 'extraordinary art of surfaces' is also 'an extraordinary art of paradoxes'. Let us now see how this art perverts good and common sense.

Perverting Good and Common Sense

To see how the Stoics practised this art of paradoxes, we must remember that what we mean by term 'paradox' in the twenty-first century is different from what paradoxes were for the ancient Greeks and Romans. For us, paradoxes often denote logical puzzles. For the ancients, 'paradox' (παράδοξος) was opposed to *doxa* (δόξα).

As opposed to δόξα, παράδοξος is something contrary to everyday assumptions. Etymologically, παράδοξος is composed of παρά- ('beyond, beside, against, contrary to') plus δόξα ('expectation'). For example, the way of truth revealed by the goddess to Parmenides is considered 'paradoxical' because it is contrary to commonplace opinions.[8] In so far as the Stoics constructed a form of life that conflicted with the common practice of the typical citizen, they were boldly paradoxical. In this sense, paradoxes were not merely logical fancies, but articulated ways of living. For the Stoics, paradoxes were as much a matter of living as thinking. More than a means for clarifying arguments or speech, the Stoics used paradoxes in a new manner: 'both as an instrument for the analysis of language and as a means of synthesizing events' (*LS* 8). As we will soon see, synthesising events is the activity proper to the Stoic master.

On a Deleuzian reading, we can specify two ways in which paradoxes oppose δόξα: 'good sense' and 'common sense' (*LS* 75). *Good sense [bon sens]* is distinguished by its unidirectional orientation at one of two opposed terms: truth not falsity, veracity not illusion, goodness not evil, and so on. Given that the French phrase *sens unique* refers to a 'one-way street', as does *seul sens*, we might say that good sense is the 'unique sense' [*sens unique*] (*LS* 75). Since *sens* connotes direction, good sense is the single-minded directedness towards the good. Singularly focused, good sense sorts everything into opposed categories – 'on the one hand and on other hand' – and selects only one as what is *good*.

While paradox opposes good sense, it is not exactly correct to say that it simply moves the other way because Stoic opposition is perversion, not inversion. 'The power of the paradox [*la puissance du paradoxe*]', writes Deleuze, 'does not all consist in following the [opposite] direction, but rather in showing that sense always takes on both senses or directions simultaneously' (*LS* 94; translation mine). The art of paradoxes demonstrates that two opposed directions are inseparable, that it is impossible to establish, once and for all, a single direction or *sens unique*. The art of paradoxes uncovers the brute sense below good or unique sense. Sense, too, goes in both directions at once – towards the primary order *and* towards tertiary ordinance. Think of the flatness of space and the bi-directionality of infinitive verbs. The essential paradox of sense is '*subdivision ad infinitum*' or '*indefinite proliferation*' (*LS* 75, 29; emphasis original in both).

In addition to perverting good sense, paradox also perverts common sense. *Common sense* [*sens commun*] concerns 'an organ [*organe*]', not a direction (*LS* 77). By 'organe' Deleuze means a faculty of identification, as we see in standard interpretations of Cartesian and Kantian subjectivities, which is used to identify objects by recognising them as similar to other things; all these similar things belong to a universal class. The effect is stamping the marker of 'the Same' on corporeal diversity. If the aim of good sense is to orient our focus on the good and true, common sense is a means for developing con-*sens*-us.

Consensus arises through distributing stable identities between two fixed poles: the subjective and the objective. *Subjectively*, common sense stabilises the identity of the 'I' by harmonising the various subjective faculties. Think of the passage in Descartes' *Meditations* in which the meditator gathers his diverse faculties through the commonality of 'one and the same I' which 'doubts, understands, affirms, denies, is willing, is unwilling, and also imagines and has sensory perceptions'.[9] As Deleuze says, '[o]ne and the same self perceives, imagines, remembers, knows, etc.; one and the same self breathes, sleeps, walks, and eats' (*LS* 78). *Objectively*, common sense stabilises the identity of the form of the object. Any object is forced to submit to the Procrustean form of objectivity that corresponds to the form of subjectivity. Corresponding to '[o]ne and the same [that] self perceives, imagines, remembers, knows' and 'one and the same self

The Shell B: Paradoxes

[that] breathes, sleeps, walks, and eats', there is one and the 'same object that I see, smell, taste, or touch ... one and the same object that I perceive, imagine, and remember' (*LS* 78). Common sense establishes consensus by stabilising these poles of identity: subject and object. We see why common sense is the logical condition of manifestation. Good sense and common sense work together to establish a general orientation that passes from subjects to objects on the way towards a sedentary distribution through which everything is 'arrested and measured, attributed and identified' (*LS* 78/96).

Paradox is the perversion of both good and common sense.[10] Perverting good sense, the paradox affirms two contradictory directions at once, which is, from the perspective of logic and physics, a 'becoming-mad' (*LS* 78). Perverting common sense, the paradoxical object is unrecognisable, just a heap (*sorites*, σωρίτης) of nonsense. No universal class fits the unruly object, such as Alice's simultaneous becoming-larger and becoming-smaller. As Alice goes in opposite directions/senses, her identity subdivides endlessly into absurdity. She is unable to answer a basic question: who am *I*? Without a subject that manifests a soul in speaking, without an object to denote, without universal classes or predicates to signify, language and subjectivity seem impossible.

But just as meaning disintegrates into utter absurdity, it is exactly here that Deleuze sees the genetic condition for language. Prior to good sense, prior to common sense, 'language attains its highest power [*plus haute puissance*]' through a paradoxical element (*LS* 79). While good sense excludes both directions by affirming one-way passage, this exclusion is possible *because* the 'two directions are inseparable' (*LS* 79). At the frontier between two incompatible directions, when we ask, 'Shall we go left or right, forwards or backwards', the Stoic madly answers, 'Yes, left and right, forwards and backwards, both at once!' Although it is physically and logically impossible, sense subsists. Alice does not grow without shrinking, nor shrink without growing, but both at the same time, *à la fois*. The paradox is located in neither direction alone but in 'between' [*l'entre-deux*]' both at once (*LS* 80). Either ... or, both ... and, 'one is always mad *in tandem*' (*LS* 79). The smooth incorporeal surface generates left and right by joining and disjoining both simultaneously; it subsists as that insubstantial border between contradictions, that border without thickness between *x* and *not-x*, the excluded middle out of which stable identities are produced. In short, the surface subsists paradoxically, which is why the Stoics insist on paradoxes in their logic.

It is thus no surprise that Plutarch writes an essay entitled 'The Stoics Talk More Paradoxically than the Poets'.[11] Rather than recreational fancy, the Stoics' passion for paradoxes is rooted in the specific way in which paradoxes both undermine and provoke thinking. Paradoxes do not simply shake the façade of certainty; they produce the shake, the face and the certainty. While '[g]ood sense and common sense are *undermined* by the principle of their production', paradoxes do more than muck up our deductions; they explain the geneses of language and logic (*LS* 171). The Stoic, Deleuze claims, 'holds a new discourse, a new logos animated with paradox' (130). In short, paradoxes generate language and the three dimensions of the proposition with what Deleuze calls the 'gift of sense' [*donation de sens*] (*LS* 79, 81). Sense, like λεκτα, 'is that which can be expressed by propositions but does not merge with the propositions that express it' (*LS* 81). Sense subsists in propositions without reducing to any propositional dimension.

Let us pause here to step back and see the broader project. Although Stoic logic was panned and almost forgotten through history, Deleuze notices a great innovation to the history of logic: the art of paradoxes. While other philosophers and logicians shied away from paradoxes, striving only to resolve or dissolve them in order to maintain logical consistency, the Stoics embraced paradoxes because they appreciated their generative force. Although, or perhaps because, paradoxes pervert good and common sense, they generate thought, and it is this generative power that connects the Stoics' theory of λεκτα and Deleuze's notion of sense. We are thinking about λεκτα and sense in this chapter because we are, in whole of Part II, considering the incorporeal proper to logic. We are considering the logical incorporeal in particular in order to make the heterodoxical claim that is produced from Deleuze's' Stoicism: there are three, double-sided incorporeals, where one side is intensive, the other extensive. Let us now consider the history and details of the Stoics' propositional system, first by comparing it to Aristotle's categorical system.

A New Logic in Antiquity

To see how the art of paradoxes forms the heart of Stoic logic, consider the way in which they organised their system. According to Diogenes, the Stoics divided logic into two parts: 'rhetoric and dialectic' (DL 7.41). We are interested in dialectic not only because it resonates with modern formal logic, but also because it involves much

The Shell B: Paradoxes

more than formal reasoning. Dialectics includes not just logic, but also epistemology, grammar and linguistics. As Goldschmidt notes in his review of Benson Mates' *Stoic Logic*: 'the Stoics completely ignored the difference between logic and epistemology'.[12] Since 'The Shell A' was mostly devoted to examining λεκτα, we will not spend as much time on linguistics in 'The Shell B'. We are hunting paradoxes. Before we capture them, we will describe the Stoics' great contribution to the history of logic: the formulation of a propositional system. To understand the greatness of this contribution, we need to recall Aristotle's logic and compare them.

Before Zeno, Aristotle's logic reigned supreme because he was the first to formalise inferential rules of arguments. These rules form a 'categorical system' or 'term-logic' in so far as it takes categories – such as 'human being' or 'animal' – as basic logical elements and determines forms of categorical interrelations through formal operators. The result is a system of deductive inference built from categorical sentences and centred on validity. Risking oversimplification, categorical operators appear in four basic sentence forms:

1. A-type or Universal affirmative: 'Every person is just'
2. I-type or Particular affirmative: 'Some persons are just'
3. E-type or Universal negative: 'No person is just'
4. O-type or Particular negative: 'Some persons are not just'[13]

Propositional logic was the alternative system, the first articulations of which trace back to the Megarians, a philosophical school founded by a student of Socrates, Euclides of Megara. While Euclides mostly propounded ethical doctrines that combined Socratic and Eleatic teachings, some of his followers splintered off into what became known as the 'Dialecticians [Διαλεκτικοί]' (DL 2.104). The earliest Dialecticians included Clinomachus of Thurii, supposedly 'the first to write about propositions and predicates', and Eubulides of Miletus, who famously unleashed many of the most lasting and powerful paradoxes (DL 2.112, 2.108). The second generation of the Dialecticians included Diodorus of Cronus and Stilpo, both of whom worked intensely on 'conditionals'. According to the reports, these were serious logicians. For example, while attending a banquet, someone posed a paradox to Diodorus that struck him so forcefully that he went home, wrote a treatise on it and died from despair.[14] Logic was not a dry formality for the Megarians or Stoics, but a matter of life and death. Later, Stilpo (and possibly Diodorus) taught Zeno, founder of the Stoa, their propositional system (DL 7.2, 7.16).

Yet it was Chrysippus who developed logical innovations so crucial to Stoicism that, Diogenes reports, 'if it were not for Chrysippus, there would have been no Stoa' (DL 7.183).

Aristotelian logic is called 'categorical' because it takes categories as the basic elements, and Stoic logic is called 'propositional' because it takes complete propositions as the basic elements. Different elements entail different operators. In Stoic logic, there are three basic operators: conditionals (if . . . then . . .), conjunctions (. . . and . . .), disjunctions (either . . . or . . .). Chrysippus developed the five basic types of 'undemonstrated' arguments using these operators.[15] They are called 'undemonstrated' because their obvious validity excludes the need for demonstration. We know more about the undemonstrables than anything else in Stoic logic.[16]

Here are the Five Types in three columns: argument on the left, formal schema in the middle, explanatory terms on the right. *First Type* is a 'hypothetical syllogism':

If it is day, then it is light.	If the first, then the second.	(Conditional proposition)
It is day.	The first.	(Antecedent)
Thus, it is light.	Thus, the second.	(Consequent)[17]

Second Type places the contradictory of the consequent in the second premise and then infers the contradictory of the antecedent:

If it is day, then it is light.	If the first, then the second.	(Conditional proposition)
But it is not light.	Not the first.	(Contradictory of consequent)
Thus, it is day.	Thus, not the second.	(Contradictory of antecedent)[18]

Third Type involves a conjunctive proposition and denials:

Not both: it is day and night.	Not both: first and second.	(Negated conjunctive)
It is day.	The first.	(First conjunct)
Thus, it is not night.	Thus, not the second.	(Contradictory of other conjunct)[19]

Fourth Type employs a disjunctive proposition and the contradiction of one disjuncts (DL 7.81):[20]

The Shell B: Paradoxes

Either it is day or night.	Either the first or second.	(Disjunctive)
It is day.	The first.	(First disjunct)
Thus, not: it is night.	Thus not: the second.	(Contradictory of other disjunct)

Fifth Type deploys a disjunctive and contradictories:

Either it is day or night.	Either the first or second.	(Disjunctive)
Not: it is day.	Not: the first.	(Not first disjunct)
Thus, it is night.	Thus, the second.	(Second disjunct)

These are the five basic indemonstrable syllogisms. From these, all valid forms in the Stoic propositional system follow. Since λεκτα insist in all propositions, the sense of each syllogism is also incorporeal. The key for Deleuze's Stoicism is to determine that these propositional arguments are located on the side facing the states of affairs, the material articulations of propositions. We might think of these five types as the five dimensions of sense that are projected on the surface by propositionally arranged bodies. They form the genetic material for the fully formed language that the Stoics use to argue and converse with rival philosophers and schools.

However, these five basic forms, like everything, must be generated, for they assume, rather than explain, their own geneses. Such geneses require the other side of the surface, the side facing the corporeal chaosmos. As is the case for all of Deleuze's encounters, genesis is *the* question. We thus ask: whence the five forms? The Stoics have an answer: paradoxes.

Why Propositional Logic?

Before delving into the story of the genesis of propositional logic, we should consider three goals for and advantages of the propositional system: (1) introduction of time into logic, (2) denial of universals, and (3) resolution of problems categorical logic could not solve.

The Stoics were very interested in thinking about time, as we will detail in Part III. While Aristotle offered an engaging meditation on time at the end of his *Physics* Book IV the Stoics developed a different, equally fascinating and confusing, account of time.[21] In their thinking about time, the Stoics show that a convincing theory of time requires thinking with propositions, not categories. Conditional statements seem essential to the development of a temporal logic because they can consider changes according to 'before' and 'after'. While universal ('all') or particular ('some') operators, in themselves, are atemporal, 'if . . . then . . .' operators can be used to formalise temporal considerations. In short, conditionals allow propositions to become functions of time. It is safe to say that Diodorus Cronus is the formulator of the beginnings of temporal logics, and the Stoics unfolded it further. In sum, the Stoic theory of propositions, especially conditionals and related modal concerns, lead to the introduction of temporal dimensions into logic.

Another reason why the Stoics might have developed a propositional system comes from their *denial of universal categories*. To see how, let us compare it to Spinoza's critique of universals. For Spinoza, a universal arises when the senses are overwhelmed. Amid the swarm of overpowering sensory experiences, our vision tends to blur, thereby forcing us to guess which traits are essential to a sensed object. In doing so, we must disregard many contributing factors, traits or capacities. As Spinoza says, 'when the images in the body are completely confused, the mind also will imagine all the bodies confusedly, without any distinction, and comprehend them as if under one attribute, namely, under the attribute of Being'.[22] The universal concept 'Being', for example, is a result of something to which many ascribe transcendent value. What happens is that we substitute an unclear and confused image in place of clear and distinct encounter with corporeal particulars. Rather than paying attention to the particular ways in which bodies affect and are affected by each other, a confused category is used to mask our inability to grasp the complexity of the composition of corporeals. A universal is a sort of conjectural trash bin that arises from the abstraction of one or two sensory characteristics (such as erect stature, featherlessness, bipedality), and which is used to impose artificial boundaries and thereby establish classes, genera, species and a whole categorical system. As Spinoza writes, universal 'terms signify ideas that are confused in the highest degree'.[23] Long before Spinoza, the Stoics wholeheartedly enacted a thorough critique of universals. Propositions allow them to do this because, while categorical operators imply a commitment to the existence of universals like 'human in general', propositional operators do not. The Stoics attack universals with a paradox: the 'Nobody' [οὖτις] paradox, which we will detail below.

A third suggestion as to why the Stoics developed their propositional system is to allow them to resolve some logical problems that plagued Aristotelian logic. In an attempt to win argumentative combats with their rival schools, Stoics diligently trained themselves to navigate linguistic and logical slippages and mistakes so that they could speak clearly, precisely and soundly. Below we will look at Chrysippus' retort to Aristotle's formulation of the 'Sea Battle' with the formulation of the Master paradox. The Master paradox engages time in ways Aristotle never could. Propositions became sharply honed weapons in heated logical battles.

Genesis of the Contradictory

In order to win arguments, the Stoics embraced paradoxes because logic and paradoxes co-necessitate each other. To understand how to speak well and win arguments, the Stoics spent much time and effort focusing on the ways in which language-use goes awry. Dialectics, they thought, must cover its virtues *and* vices, reason *and* its treason.[24] The Stoics thus developed taxonomies, lists, and tables, of examples and types of logical and linguistic errors. Chrysippus alone wrote about sixteen books on 'ambiguity' (ἀμφιβολία), at least six on fallacies, and many more that addressed paradoxes (DL 7.190–202). What may appear like an upstanding affinity for grammatical and logical correctness thus includes a perverse fascination with errors, mistakes, slip-ups and gaffes. Stoicism strives to see what happens when language and logic stutter and sputter.[25]

Both the Stoics and Deleuze are attuned to the strange ways in which language is in perpetual flux and instability, weaving in and out of synchronicity with itself, constantly varying and vibrating. 'Language trembles from head to toe', Deleuze writes, just beneath the surface, even when communication seems to be functioning well.[26] The appearance of linguistic facility that aligns with winning arguments rests directly atop an infinitely thin surface that constantly threatens to collapse into bumbling thought and babbling speech.

The lesson here is that the art of paradoxes belongs to the study of dialectics just as much as the science of propositional logic does. This is part of a general ethics of thought, or as Deleuze and Guattari put it: 'those who criticize without creating, those who are content to defend the vanished concept without being able to give it the forces it needs to return to life, are the plague of philosophy' (*WP* 28). Part of Stoic dialectics shows that language is not possible without the operation of paradoxical elements, that paradoxes are the forces that give life to concepts.

To the Stoics, paradoxes are not merely fancies of logical amusement, but fundamental features of living, thinking and acting. Their thirst for paradoxes expresses what Deleuze calls a '[p]assion for thought' (*LS* 74).[27] Beyond the propositional articulation of logical and causal compatibility, the art of paradoxes leads to a confrontation with *both* 'what can only be thought' *but* is 'unthinkable', *both* 'what can only be spoken' *but* is 'ineffable' (*LS* 74). In *Difference and Repetition*, Deleuze calls these, respectively, the '*cogitandum*' and the '*loquendum*', which he connects to a higher or 'transcendental exercise' of the faculties (DR 141, 143, 140). We might think of this higher exercise as training for one to encounter the backside of the surface. The drive to thoroughly think through paradoxes 'force[s] each faculty to its respective limit, thereby forcing each to encounter what properly belongs to it': its own paradoxical object (DR 193). In Deleuzean language, we could say that the Stoic art of paradoxes is a transcendental exercise of the faculties.

When logic short-circuits, when language stutters, when physics falls silent, the transcendental exercise of thinking is forced to begin. Paradoxes communicate the violence of that which forces thought to become unhinged and disoriented, unable to tell which way is up or down, inside or out. Confronting paradoxes face-on leads to the uncoiling of the circle of the proposition as it smooths out across the incorporeal surface. From the perspective of bodies, the backside of the surface seems absurd and contradictory, as in the 'Liar's Paradox', wherein articulating one proposition simultaneously articulates its opposite. But from the perspective of the surface, which is the point of view of the Stoic sage, we discover that the 'force of paradoxes is that they are not contradictory; they rather allow us to be present at the *genesis of the contradictory*' (*LS* 74; emphasis added). Being present at the genesis of the contradictory is a way of viewing the static genesis leaping from secondary organisation to tertiary ordinance, as we discussed in 'The Yolk B'. Looking 'down' from tertiary ordinance – from the perspective of denotation, manifestation and signification – secondary organisation looks absurd. Each of the three perspectives of the circle of the proposition reveals a different dimension of absurdity, which we now examine.

Three Dimensions of Absurdity

'Absurdity' is the name of the relation between a meaningful body of language and the paradoxical surface that both undermines and generates it. Deleuze says this is the relation between the three dimensions of the circle of the proposition and the fourth dimension: sense. His *Logic of Sense* characterises absurdity in three ways, each of which corresponds to the perspectives of the three propositional dimensions: (1) Denoting Absurdity, (2) Manifesting Absurdity and (3) Signifying Absurdity.[28]

Denoting Absurdity. In denotation, a word *directly* picks out a denotatum. If the denoting word successfully indicates its denotatum, the denotation is true; if it misses or picks out nothing, it is false. Truth and falsity equal successful or unsuccessful reference. Absurdity perverts denotation by means of 'propositions that designate contradictory objects' (*LS* 35). Absurd propositions refer to objects that are impossible from the perspective of logical and causal compatibility. Deleuze offers several examples of *impossible objects*: 'square circles, matter without extension, *perpetuum mobile*, mountain without valley' (*LS* 35). As physically and logically impossible, impossible objects find their home always elsewhere, outside of the order of corporeality. The denotation cannot be fulfilled because its denotatum is an 'empty square', that is, 'place without an occupant and . . . occupant without a place' (*LS* 47, 41).

Located in this extra-cosmic outside, however, impossible objects do still 'have a precise and distinct position' (*LS* 35). Although they cannot be realised in any given state of affairs, they remain something, they do have a sense. It is just that, in relation to denotation, absurdity 'may be neither true nor false' (*LS* 15). Impossible objects express 'extra-being', an ontological 'minimum common to the real, the possible, *and the impossible*' (*LS* 35; emphasis original). In short, impossible objects denote events, not things. Deleuze calls absurd denotation the *'paradox of the absurd'* or 'Meinong's paradox' (*LS* 35; emphasis original).[29]

Manifesting Absurdity.[30] Manifestation concerns the relation between a spoken proposition and the person speaking it. Desires and beliefs of the speaker are manifested, and the task is to understand them. Following Kant, Deleuze defines desires and beliefs as types of 'causal inferences': desire is an 'internal causality' and belief an 'external causality' (*LS* 13). In Kant's words, desire is the 'faculty which by means of its representations is the *cause* of the actuality of the objects of those representations'.[31] Desire is the internal power of making an imagined object into a real thing, and belief is the inverse: the imagined expectation of an object in so far as it has been produced by an external object or context. At the centre of it all is the first-person subject position, which 'constitutes the domain of the *personal*' or 'I' (*LS* 13; emphasis original). If the proper name is a standard form of denotation, '"I" is the basic manifester [*manifestant*]' (*LS* 13). While the logical value of denotation is truth or falsity, the logical value of manifestation is 'veracity and illusion' (*LS* 14). Absurdity perverts this subject-centred structure of manifestation in so far as absurdity reveals not the self-subsistent and coherent Cartesian Cogito, but the madman whom the meditator (from Descartes's First *Mediation*) fears he might become. Absurdity manifests 'the dissolved self, the cracked I, the lost identity' (*LS* 141).[32] Absurdity reveals a terrifying chaos at the heart of subjectivity, where desire and belief are inverted and the separation between internality and externality collapse into a schizophrenic interpenetration of bodies in depth. The manifestation of absurdity reveals the 'paradoxes of becoming-mad' haunting us whenever we say 'I' (*LS* 33).

Signifying Absurdity. In terms of signification, absurdity is, Deleuze writes, 'that which is without signification' (*LS* 15, 35, 135).[33] Signification concerns the relation between a proposition and a general concept and the set of concepts that are implied or entailed therefrom. The prime example is the conditional operator of a hypothetical syllogism. For the Stoics, the premises are conditions and the conclusion is the conditioned; signification establishes the order of demonstration between the conditions and the conditioned. The significance of a conclusion is an indirect process of implication. Rather than truth and falsity, signification concerns the 'condition of truth', that is, the logical value of signification is determined in so far as it establishes the 'aggregate of conditions under which the proposition "would be" true' or false (*LS* 14). Signification concerns the possibility, not the actuality, for truth or error. As such, conditions of truth are 'not opposed to the false, but to the absurd' (*LS* 14–15).

In sum, absurdity is how secondary order appears from the perspective of the circle of the proposition. Looking down from denotation, manifestation and signification, the surface seems absurd. But if we flip the perspective and assume a surface point of view, absurdity evaporates, as Alice finds when, while wandering through Wonderland, she asks the Cheshire Cat for directions (*sens*), hoping to find some good and common sense. To her dismay, his response affirms both directions:

The Shell B: Paradoxes

'In *that* direction,' the Cat said, waving its right paw round, 'lives a Hatter: and in *that* direction,' waving the other paw, 'lives a March Hare. Visit either you like: they're both mad.'

'But I don't want to go among mad people,' Alice remarked.

'Oh, you can't help that,' said the Cat: 'we're all mad here. I'm mad. You're mad.'

The Cheshire Cat is the embodiment of the impossible object. As the cat vanished slowly, Alice glimpsed its absurdity:

'Well! I've often seen a cat without a grin,' thought Alice; 'but a grin without a cat! It's the most curious thing I ever saw in all my life!'

Yet it is more than curious; it is absurd. Like the Hatter's tea party, everyone is mad on the surface.

We pause here again in order to review what we just discussed and to grasp how it relates to the overall story of *Deleuze, A Stoic*. After recovering the Stoics' propositional logic from the shadows of the history of philosophy, we compared it to the logical system that put it in the shadows: Aristotle's logic. Contrary to his categorical system, the Stoics, we saw, grounded their system in five propositional forms, and we considered three goals for and advantages of the propositional system over Aristotle's: (1) introducing time into logic, (2) denial of universals, and (3) resolution of problems that categorical logic could not handle. Next we saw how paradoxes are generative of these five fundamental propositions and of the whole of language and thinking, which we called the genesis of the contradictory. Then we looked at the three dimensions of absurdity, which correspond to the three dimensions of what Deleuze calls the circle of the propositions: denotation, manifestation and signification.

In terms of the overall story of Deleuze's Stoicism, issues of paradoxes, absurdity and the creation of propositional logic are part of the story of the λεκτα, the logical incorporeal. One of the defining features of the Stoics' incorporeals is their perverse status as both effects and yet quasi-causes. We are continuing to explain this perversity by considering the generative nature of quasi-causality, with the current emphasis on incorporeality in so far as it appears in logic. All of this is part of our overarching heterodoxical claim that there are only three, double-sided incorporeals; one side is intensive, the other extensive. With the sense of paradoxes as generative of logic and language, we will next look at the structure and purpose of paradoxes, before looking directly at what we consider the four fundamental Stoic paradoxes. We will see that each of these four paradoxes repeats the double-sided structure of incorporeality, the logical character of which is ambiguity. To get there, we need to consider the structure and purpose of paradoxes, which we do next.

Structure and Purpose of Paradoxes

The Stoic incorporeal surface is paradoxical because, Deleuze writes, it composes two 'dissymmetrical faces of the paradoxical element' (*LS* 81). We have seen different examples of such dissymmetrical faces: void and place of space, infinitives and conjugations of λεκτα. In Part III we will see aion and chronos as these two faces of the surface conceived according to the incorporeal proper to ethics: time. When speaking from the perspective of Stoic logic and their art of paradoxes, sense and nonsense are oppositional but complementary; they form two sides of one and the same plane. 'Nonsense and sense', writes Deleuze, 'have done away with their relation of dynamic opposition in order to enter into the co-presence of a static genesis – as the nonsense of the surface and the sense that hovers over it' (*LS* 141).

Recalling distinctions from 'The Shell A', static genesis is the production of the circle of the proposition, the leap from secondary organisation to tertiary ordinance. As sense is the genetic condition for denotation, manifestation and signification, sense forms the side of the incorporeal surface facing actualised propositions and the fully formed language of the Voice. Nonsense lives on the backside of that surface, facing away from well-formed propositions, towards the terrifying noise of primary order. As this matches the double-sided structure of the incorporeal surface, we apply the same concepts. The side facing meaningful propositions and the well-ordered cosmos is the extensive face of integration or conjugation, while the side facing the delirious depths and senseless scream of corporeal chaosmos is the intensive face of differentiation and infinitives.

For Deleuze's Stoicism, paradoxes are important because they are the means for accounting for the genesis of language and logic. To be fair, the Stoics were not the first to understand the importance of paradoxes and absurdities. Simply recall the aporetic endings of many Platonic dialogues or Aristotle's clarification of perplexities (turning ἀ-πορία into εὐ-πορία) and the wonder that spawns his investigation into the first causes in his *Metaphysics*. Both of these orientations, however, quell such perplexities by postulating fixed immaterial and eternal beings, either above or within. The Stoics, by contrast, render incorporeals paradoxical and then cloak the entire world with that

The Shell B: Paradoxes

paradoxical incorporeal surface. While the Platonic or Aristotelian transcendent forms account for the genesis of the material world, the Stoics replace forms with paradoxes. Here the Stoics rely more on Heraclitean notions of fiery flux and chiasmatic (χιασμός) logic, as we will see in their ontogenetic accounts of the great conflagration (or the eternal recurrence) in Part III and the role of the seminal *logos* (λόγος) therein. Through Stoicism, Deleuze understands that true genesis must be necessarily paradoxical, or: *op*-position is at the heart of the *pro*-position.

The Paradoxes

It is difficult to know how the Stoics organised their paradoxes because scholars do not agree on the proper classification of them. Diogenes alone offers different classifications. In one, he describes two basic types of paradox, which correspond to the two halves of Stoic dialectics: '[1] the signified and [2] the utterance'. But Diogenes also describes a different classification: paradoxes are '[1] defective, [2] aporetic, or [3] conclusive' (DL 7.44).[34] Still, it is not surprising that a classification of ambiguities and confusions is unclear. In the absence of clarity, we articulate the following four fundamental paradoxes. In 'The Shell C', these four paradoxes will correspond to the four classes in the transcendental logic of incorporeals and to four Deleuzian paradoxes that we detail therein. For now, here are what we see as the four fundamental paradoxes of Stoic logic: (1) The Heap, (2) The Liar, (3) The Master and (4) The Nobody.

THE HEAP

Ancients called it the *sorites* (σωρείτης) because it comes from the Greek word for 'heap' (σωρός). Most agree Zeno of Elea was the first to articulate it.[35] Galen refers to it as the 'argument of little-by-little'.[36] Modelled on Galen's formulation, we will phrase it as a series of questions and responses.[37]

Does one grain of wheat make a heap? No, one grain is too few. If one grain does not make a heap, do two grains? No, two are too few. If two grains do not, do three grains? No, still too few. What about three or four or . . . (skipping ahead) . . . 9,998 or 9,999? If 9,999 grains of wheat do not make a heap, what about 10,000 grains? Since we have moved one by one from one to 10,000 but never reached a determinate limit as to what makes a 'heap', we never have end up with a heap, even though it sure looks like one. The same series of questions goes in descending order, from 10,000 to 9,999 down to three, two and one grain.[38] Also called 'The Bald Man', we can formulate the Heap like this: can we call a person with one hair on her head 'bald'? Probably. Can we describe a person with two hairs on her head 'bald'? Most likely. Skipping ahead, if we can describe a person with ten thousand hairs on her head as bald, where should we draw the line between a bald person and a person with a full head of hair? We cannot definitively draw the line separating bald and non-bald. Thus everyone and no one is bald, which is absurd.

THE LIAR

Arguably the most famous and influential paradox in history, its formulation is attributed to the Dialectician Eubulides (DL 2.108). The Stoics were fascinated with this paradox. Chrysippus himself reportedly wrote six books on the Liar paradox (DL 7.196–7). Philitas of Cos was reportedly so perplexed by it that, after hearing it, he never slept again, and so died.[39] There are plenty of versions of it, but Cicero probably puts it best. Addressing the Stoics, he writes: 'A basic principle of dialectic is that anything asserted . . . is either true or false. Well, in that case, are examples like this true or false? If you say that you are lying and what you say is true, you are lying and saying something true.'[40] Thus truth and falsity converge and diverge in the Liar.

THE MASTER

Diodorus formulated the Master, although it is unclear why it has a magisterial name. It is partially a response to Aristotle's problematisation of *future contingents* in the Sea Battle.[41] The Sea Battle goes like this: either 'there will be a sea battle tomorrow' or 'there will not be a sea battle tomorrow'. One these is true, the other false. If it is currently true that there will be a sea battle tomorrow, then the sea battle is inevitable, and there is nothing we can do to stop it. But this seems absurd because tomorrow has not yet come.

Although widely circulated in antiquity, let us use Epictetus' formulation: 'The Master Argument is evidently based on the mutual incompatibility of the following three propositions: (1) everything past that is true is necessary; (2) an impossibility cannot follow a possibility; (3) something that is neither true nor ever will be true

The Shell B: Paradoxes

is possible.'[42] Diodorus' solution to this inconsistency, Epictetus continues, is 'to concede the truth of the first propositions, but maintain (in defiance of the third) that nothing is possible which neither is nor ever will be true'.[43] While Diodorus resolved the paradox by rejecting the third proposition – 'something that is neither true nor ever will be true is possible' – the Stoics offered different solutions by selecting or rejecting different propositions. Cleanthes rejected the first – 'everything past that is true is necessary' – while Chrysippus attacked the second – 'an impossibility cannot follow a possibility'.[44]

Chrysippus' reasoning pivots on a hypothetical proposition: 'If Dion is dead, *this* man is dead.'[45] The antecedent – 'If Dion is dead' – is possible because Dion will eventually die. But the consequent – '*This* man [pointing out Dion] is dead' – is impossible because whatever either is not true now or can never be true in the future is impossible. That is, since Dion is currently alive and well, '*this* one is dead' is false. Later, when Dion actually is dead, the proposition '*this* one is dead' will also be false (because there will be nothing to point at when Dion is gone). But this destroys the hypothetical proposition because we then have a true antecedent followed by a false consequent, which is false. As we will see in 'The Shell C', this leads to the affirmation of contradictory propositions: everything happens according to fate (*fato omnia fiunt*) but humans act freely. For Deleuze, this is why 'the Stoics can oppose fate and necessity' (*LS* 6). In Part III, we will spend plenty of time on this perverse affirmation of this opposition.

4 The Nobody [οὔτις]

Diogenes reports two versions of this argument. Zeno's version: 'If anyone is here, he is not in Rhodes; but there is somebody here, therefore there is nobody in Rhodes' (DL 7.82). Most scholars understand this paradox as an attack on universal kinds or categories, as we saw above when we discussed Spinoza's critique of universals.[46] For the Stoics and Spinoza, there is no 'human' in general, such as a transcendent form of humanness; every thing is particular for them. Playing on language, the Greek word we translate as 'nobody' is οὔτις, which means 'not something', thus placing it outside the Stoic metaphysical schema. Universal categories are nothing, mere figments of the imagination, like centaurs, giants and Platonic forms. There is nothing beyond corporeal depths and incorporeal surface, no transcendent heaven above and beyond.

Structure of Ambiguity

Each of these four paradoxes repeats the double-sided structure of incorporeality. The logical character of this double-sidedness is *ambiguity*.

The meaning of 'ambiguous' is, fittingly, complicated. The *Oxford English Dictionary* tells us it can mean 'obscure, indistinct, doubtful, questionable, wavering'. The obscurity or dubitability of ambiguous things is due to a specific source: duplexity or duplicity, that is, their unbalanced openness to distinct meanings, which is due to their placement on a boundary between both. The Latin *ambigere* from which the English word originates is composed of *amb-* ('both ways') plus *agere* ('to lead, drive').[47]

'Amphiboly' is a type of ambiguity that results from grammatical ambiguity, as opposed to the ambiguity of a word or phrase (often called 'equivocation'). 'Amphiboly' is the transliteration of the Greek ἀμφιβολία, usually translated into English as the more general sense of 'ambiguity'. Thucydides describes a concrete amphiboly in which the Athenians occupy the island of Pylos 'with the object of causing the enemy the greatest possible embarrassment; for they [the Spartans] would be surrounded *on all sides and have no single direction* through which to counterattack; instead they would always be exposed to great numbers in *both directions*'.[48] The German word for 'ambiguity' is *Doppelsinn*, as in *doppel-* ('dual, counterpart, duplicate, double) plus *Sinn* ('sense, meaning').[49] Catherine Atherton (who wrote *The Stoics on Ambiguity*) locates five senses of 'ambiguity':

> [1] *imprimis*, cases of obscurity, in which no single determinate meaning (use, sense, *etc.*) will or can be assigned to a bearer; [2] cases of vagueness, where the criteria for correct application of an expression are imprecise, [3] cases of generality or non-specificity; [4] cases of multiple applicability (to any of a set of particular objects; and [5] perhaps metaphorical usages too.[50]

Again and again, we see the figure of an unstable two-faced surface.

From ancient Greek and Latin to modern English, German, French (*ambiguïté*), and more, ambiguity repeats the same structure: double-sided, bi-directional, two-sensed. Diogenes reports it thus: 'verbal ambiguity arises when a word properly, rightfully, and in accordance with fixed usage *denotes two or more things*, so that *at one and the same time* we may take it *in several distinct senses*' (DL 7.62; emphasis added). This sort of paradoxical ambiguity expresses the two-faced structure of the incorporeal surface that winds through Stoicism, which is important for Deleuze's Stoicism because ambiguity expresses the genetic element of paradoxes.

The Aleatory Point

The genetic element of paradoxes is an 'aleatory point' (*LS* 56). In fact, Deleuze makes aleatory and ambiguity synonymous, most likely because they both express the intensity of this double-sided structure (*LS* 114, 116). As usual, let us start with etymology.

'Aleatory' comes from the Latin *aleator* ('dice-player, gambler'), and further from *alea* ('a die'), which originally meant 'pivot-bone' or 'joint-bone' because bones were likely used as dice. *Alea* links to *axis*, as in an axle around which something turns, such as a wheel, clock or the earth. Think of Julius Caesar's (supposed) quoting of Menander – 'The die is cast!' – when he led his army across the Rubicon in 49 BC, thus marking the beginning of Caesar's civil war.[51] In Latin, die is *alea*, as in '*Alea iacta est*'.[52] Caesar himself is a paradoxical figure who marks a boundary line: on one side was the Republic, on the other, the Empire. In between, Caesar, a non-imperial emperor, the king who was not *rex* of Rome.

The aleatory point is genetic because it is the site of the contraction of incompatible, contradictory or opposite sides, and thus because it is the axis around which the momentum of thought builds. Such a churning contraction forces two sides tighter and tighter together, which creates a stronger, more concentrated tension. This intensification of the contraction reaches a singular point – a singularity – that marks the release of the tension – an explosion. When the tension extends out, things settle into a calm, sedentary distribution. Paradoxes are the propositional presentation of the aleatory point, which compels an audience to hold two concepts in great tension. Put differently, paradoxes compel thought to confront implicated intensities. As intensities are held in thought, as contradictory poles are forced tighter and tighter together, the mind stutters and splits.[53]

From the perspective of logic, the aleatory point organises the surface without thickness, the depthless passage between dissymmetric sides. As a two-faced surface, both sides of the aleatory point are unequal and in disequilibrium: one facing the states of affairs and the meaningful circle of the proposition, the other the terrifying depths and nonsensical babble. On the side facing the states of affairs, Stoic logic organises sense by silently matching a denoting proposition to a denoted body and to the two other dimensions of the proposition. On the side facing the chaosmos, paradoxes run wild as the aleatory point speeds across the surface. The 'aleatory point', the infinitely thin threshold separating and connecting the two sides of the surface, is not in the centre but is 'endlessly displaced', writes Deleuze (*LS* 65). Peripherally it dwells. The aleatory point cannot be at the centre because there is no centre of the surface; there are only two flat sides spreading out infinitely in all directions. One is always on one side or the other, never in the centre. The aleatory point is always missing, already evacuated, never present. When approaching the aleatory point, one finds one has already passed through to the other side without noticing.

Ergo *and* Igitur

With the Stoic science of propositional logic and art of paradoxes now placed back to back, we introduce another logical distinction: *ergo* and *igitur*. In 'The Yolk B', we introduced two logical tables: the formal logic of corporeals and the transcendental logic of incorporeals. These logics correspond, respectively, to the side of the surface facing the well-ordered states of affairs and to the side facing away from bodies, towards the chaotic depths of complete material mixture.

The formal logic of corporeals is encapsulated by the propositional logic detailed above. Starting from the five basic types – the three main operators (conditional, conjunctive and disjunctive) and fully formed propositions – we can capture the causal order of the physical cosmos. This is what Kant offered in his Table of Judgements, as we saw in 'The Yolk B'. Formal propositional logic cannot, however, describe the chaos on the other side. Unlike the relatively ordered and individuated states of affairs, the chaotic and unindividuated cesspool of materiality twists and splits well-formed propositions. Propositional logic falters and fells in the face of the chaosmos. Only paradoxes can express such nonsense. Propositional logic corresponds to the formal logic of corporeals, and paradoxical logic corresponds to the transcendental logic of incorporeals.

As with any logic, everything turns on the movement from premises to conclusion: inference. If these two logics – propositional and paradoxical – are indeed different, they must express different sorts of inferences. Fortunately, Latin has a terminological distinction that allows us to distinguish two different orders of inference: *ergo* and *igitur*.⁵⁴ Most often, *ergo* and *igitur* are translated by the same English word – 'therefore, hence, thus' – which is why, Caroline Kroon writes, 'generations of scholars have implicitly or explicitly considered ... *igitur* and *ergo*, to be more or less synonymous'.⁵⁵ While the distinction between these terms is easily overlooked and never thoroughly analysed, we notice an important difference.⁵⁶ To see it, let us consult some scholars of Latin and Greek.

While '*igitur* and *ergo*', Kroon continues, 'often seem to be interchangeable from a syntactic and semantic point of view. *Pragmatically*, however, they are *always clearly distinct*.'⁵⁷ According to *Allen and Greenough's New Latin Grammar*, '*ergo*, therefore, is used of things proved formally ... *Igitur*, then, accordingly, is weaker than *ergo* and is used in passing from one stage of an argument to another'.⁵⁸ *Ergo* is a bit stronger and typically follows the unidirectional movement of logical deduction, from premises to conclusion, which is why *ergo* appears in the five basic forms of propositional syllogisms in the Stoic system. *Ergo*'s etymology is contested. Some, such as Valpy's *Manual of Latin Etymology*, trace it to the Greek ἔργον, meaning 'work, deed'.⁵⁹ Others, such Halsey's *Etymology of Latin and Greek*, claim it originated from *e-rego*, meaning 'to extend upwards or outwards', a contraction of *ex-* ('out of') plus *rego* ('to direct, guide, keep straight, conduct'). Both etymologies suggest correctness and work, as in the direct work of deductive inference. In short, *ergo* marks the inferential movement in propositional logic.

Igitur marks the movement of the unstable leap across an aleatory point. According to Fischer's *Latin Grammar*, '*igitur* represents the predicate as a *natural* consequence of the previous proposition'.⁶⁰ *Gildersleeve's Latin Grammar* corroborates: *igitur* is 'said of *opinions*, which have their ground in the preceding statement', while *ergo* 'denotes *necessary consequence*, and is used especially in arguments, with somewhat more emphasis than igitur',⁶¹ Rather than strict logical consequence, *igitur* is both broader and weaker than *ergo*. *Igitur* applies less to formal validity and more to the movement from one opinion to another, usually sidestepping or breaking formal rules of deduction, which is why *igitur* often takes the place of *ergo* but not the reverse.⁶² The etymology of *igitur* is even less clear than *ergo*'s. Antilla's *Greek and Indo-European Etymology* claims that *igitur* itself is a 'bleached out [that is, enclitically weakened] variant' of the third-person singular of *agitur*, meaning 'it is done, it is made'. *Agitur* comes from *agere*, meaning 'to lead, drive', which is also the root of *ambiguitas*. Lewis and Short's *Latin Dictionary* breaks *igitur* down into the stem *is*, the third-person pronoun ('he, she, it; this, that'), and the mere adverbial ending *-tus*. Whichever is correct, the etymology of *igitur* does not have the directedness or rectilinear movement of *ergo*, but instead hinges on the anonymity of the third-person pronoun – it, *ça*, *id* – and a leap already leapt. Rather than a direct line leading from the premises to the conclusion, *igitur* conveys the sense of a movement already accomplished, as if we had already passed, unconsciously, to the other side of the surface, without us noticing. Deleuze, though, is unsurprised: 'There is nothing astonishing in the fact that the paradox is the force of the unconscious: it occurs always in the space between consciousness, contrary to good sense or, behind the back of consciousness, contrary to common sense' (*LS* 80).

If we call the movement of *ergo* in propositional 'logic cognitive deduction', then we can call the leap of *igitur* the 'production of cognition'. *Ergo* marks the valid propositional inference from true premises to true conclusion, the defining movement of the formal logic organising the side of the surface facing states of affairs. By contrast, *igitur* marks the paradoxical in(ter)ference across the infinitely thin aleatory point that both separates and connects two contradictory and physically incompatible (no)things. It is no surprise that Deleuze connects *Igitur* ('from the Book of Mallarmé') to the aleatory point (*LS* 65).[63]

Before concluding, let us pause one last time in Part II in order to review our discussion so far in this chapter and to situate ourselves in the overall story of *Deleuze, A Stoic*. After recovering the Stoics' propositional logic from the shadows of the history of philosophy, and comparing it Aristotle's categorical logic, we articulated the five main propositions and considered how paradoxes are generative of the whole of language and thinking. We then looked at three dimensions of absurdity and noticed that the structure of ambiguity is that same unstable two-faced surface that characterises the Stoic incorporeals. Then we claimed that Deleuze's Stoicism emphasises ambiguity because it expresses the logic of the genetic element of paradoxes: the 'aleatory point'. From a logical perspective, the aleatory point organises the surface without thickness, the depthless passage between dissymmetric sides, which generates thought by pressing together two incompatible or contradictory propositions. We then distinguished two kinds of inference, which correspond to the Stoics' propositional logic and their art of paradoxes: movement of *ergo* in propositional as a logic cognitive deduction, and the leap of *igitur*

The Shell B: Paradoxes

as the production of cognition. We are looking at this Stoic art of paradoxes in order to further grasp our overarching heterodoxical claim: there are only three, double-sided (intensive and extensive sides) incorporeals. We now conclude by stepping back even further and noticing something about Deleuze's appreciation of Stoicism: the tenuousness of sense and λεκτόν.

Standing on the Shore

To conclude, reflect on where we have been and where we are going in Part II. 'The Shell A' detailed the genesis of sense out of bodies, the dynamic movement and static leap that follows the path into the domain of a sense-laden world. While this story seems right, we must make a comment in order to stave off false senses of security.

Once we have access to sense, once we are able to discern what is expressed in an expression and express ourselves, we do not thereby have full and secure access to the entirety of sense. The sense that is accessed when we learn to communicate in English does not entail the same access to the sense of French or Latin, for every language has its own means for accessing sense. Sextus describes it like this:

> we apprehend [λεκτόν] as it subsists in accordance with our thought, whereas Barbarians do not understand, even if they hear the vocal sound; the bearer of the name is the external object, such as Dion himself. Of these, two are bodies – the vocal sound and the bearer of the name – the third is incorporeal, namely the thing signified, that is, what is said [καὶ λεκτόν].[64]

Think about what it is like for a person who does not understand French to witness two French speakers chatting.[65] This non-francophone person knows that there is a sense to the French conversation, and she knows that the French speakers are accessing what subsists in these sounds, but she cannot access it. It was the Greeks' inability to access the sense of the language of the so-called 'Barbarians', as Sextus mentioned above, that lead to the appellation βάρβαρος. When they heard non-Greeks speak, the Greeks, with their sophisticated tongues, only heard incomprehensible 'bar-bar-bar' (βαρ-βαρ-βαρ) sounds.[66] Outside of Greek, all languages – Egyptian, Persian, Phoenician – sounded like gibberish. It is as if such 'vulgar' peoples were closer to the primary order, repeating phonemic chains like the onomatopoeic babbling of infants. As they used the pejorative term 'Barbarians' to mean 'foreign, non-Greek, strange', all other languages sound barbaric to the Greeks. The point is that, when we speak, when anyone speaks, although we express sense with every word, we never say it all. There will always be things unsaid, a sense that remains silent.

In addition to being unable to access the sense of foreign tongues, we are often in danger of becoming foreign to our mother tongues. Who is not aware of the fragility of the surface separating and connecting the organised state of affairs from the chaosmos lurking below, as we see in, for example, the *jamais vu* phenomenon? *Jamais vu* (French for 'never seen') is the opposite of *déjà vu* ('already seen'), and is often associated with aphasia and amnesia. It is the eerie sense of feeling like we are experiencing something for the first time, even though we know it is familiar. Consider what happens if we repeat a single word over and over until its meaning evaporates, leaving an empty signifier. *Jamais vu* is that feeling of foreignness at home, evoking Deleuze's description of those minor writers who 'carve out a kind of foreign language within language'.[67] The collapse into the corporeal chaos that threatens to rise up out of those depths and unsettle our seemingly secure states of affairs is due to the infinitely thin nature of the incorporeal surface. Deleuze's *Logic of Sense* is full of literary examples of writers who slipped and fell into 'the undifferentiated abyss of a groundlessness that only permits the pulsation of a monstrous body', including Seneca and '[Joë] Bousquet's wound, [F. Scott] Fitzgerald and [Malcolm] Lowry's alcoholism', 'Nietzsche and Artaud's madness' (*LS* 120, 157). Yet within the safe confines of language, we find security from 'remaining on the shore', staring out into the abyss lurking just below the surface (*LS* 157).

Stoicism prevents us from sitting comfortably on the safety of the shore because the shore is the threshold between the depths of the watery abyss and the heights of the rising heavens. The Stoic art of paradoxes teaches how to live on the shoreline, on the border between land and sea, fate and freedom, sense and nonsense. By training ourselves to not only sort through the twisted *igitur* of the various paradoxes, but to become accustomed to living with such irresolution, we become resolute. The Stoics use paradoxes not to simply to entrap or infuriate, but to train the capacity to live resolutely through irresolution. As we will see in 'The Shell C', Stoic logic is not just about formal validity or consistency. It is about living with the dangers, uncertainties and irresolvable differences composing our world. Stoic logic concerns living because of, not in spite of, such irresolvable differences.

The Shell B: Paradoxes

Here is the first example of the Stoic imperative to confront the crack opening between our feet, the cut dividing ceaselessly in both directions as we teeter on the edge of the sea of nonsense. The Stoic imperative calls out from across the millennia to us. Deleuze knows this well; in fact, he seems almost struck dumb by it. This call aims at each of us, as we read these words in Deleuze's self-proclaimed logical and psychological novel: *Logic of Sense*. Take the series of questions that lead to be a pause, or perhaps it is a stutter, near the middle of the text. Considering what to do with the Stoic imperative, Deleuze asks if we should become boring scholars who go to conferences, 'give talks', read in monotonous tones, and rehearse the same old arguments again and again (*LS* 157). Should we become professors who 'take up collections and create special journal issues', or should we pass through that incorporeal limit between words and things in order to live precariously yet precisely, according to the course of the cosmos (*LS* 157)? Is it enough to study Stoicism or must we *become-Stoic*? Must we risk disrupting our aims and desires in order to really understand how to make oneself a Stoic? It is a dangerous deed indeed, and Deleuze does not pretend to have understood it. Yet he takes it seriously enough to pause in the middle of the text, after posing the question that haunts any encounter with Stoicism: 'How much have we yet to learn from Stoicism . . .' (*LS* 158).

In 'The Shell C', the final chapter of Part III, we will answer Deleuze's question. We can still learn from Stoicism the craft of producing concepts. Inspired by an ancient tradition of Stoic texts, 'The Shell C' offers a new handbook of logic in order to see if, for just a moment, we might discover what we can learn from an encounter with Stoicism.

Notes

1. Sextus Empiricus, *Outlines of Pyrrhonism*, 313.
2. Carl Prantl, *Geschichte der Logik im Abendlande* (Leipzig: S. Hirzel, 1855), 404, 408, cited in Benson Mates, *Stoic Logic* (Berkeley: University of California Press, 1961), 87.
3. Kant, *Critique of Pure Reason*, trans. Paul Guyer and Allen W. Wood (Cambridge: Cambridge University Press, 1999), Bvii.
4. Mates, *Stoic Logic*, 2.
5. *The Development of Logic* was one of the few English publications that saw great value in Stoic logic. 'It is tantalizing that tradition has preserved so little of the work of these latter philosophers [Megarians and Stoics]; for what little remains suggests that they were highly intelligent

and deserving of better treatment than they have received from historians.' William Kneale and Martha Kneale, *The Development of Logic* (Oxford: The Clarendon Press, 1962), 113.
6. Mates, *Stoic Logic*, 85.
7. Ibid. 7. While Zeno was a charismatic and successful philosopher, his successor Cleanthes, a man known more for his fighting abilities than his intellect. By contrast, Chyrsippus was reportedly a decent marathoner (DL 7.179).
8. A. A. Long, *From Epicurus to Epictetus: Studies in Hellenistic and Roman Philosophy* (Oxford: Clarendon Press, 2006), 14.
9. René Descartes, *The Philosophical Writings of Descartes, Vol. II*, trans. John Cottingham, Robert Stoothoff and Dugald Murdoch (Cambridge: Cambridge University Press, 1984), CSM 19/AT VII 29.
10. Although Deleuze here speaks of a 'reversal [*renversement*]', it would be more accurate to call it a 'perversion' for reasons we have already given.
11. Plutarch, *Stoic Essays*, 1056D–1058D.
12. Goldschmidt, '*Stoic Logic* par Benson Mates', *Revue de métaphysique et de morale* 59.2 (April–June 1954): 213–14, at 213. Goldschmidt raises the important danger of trying to match ancient ideas to contemporary ones. Deleuze, it seems, does not do this. Instead, he seeks to release the power for producing ideas that occurs when ancient and modern ideas are conjoined.
13. Based on Aristotle, *De Interpretatione*, 17a25–18a13.
14. Mates, *Stoic Logic*, 5–6.
15. Both Diogenes and Sextus claim Chrysippus invented the five indemonstrables. DL 7.79 and Sextus, *Against the Logicians*, 2.223.
16. Mates, *Stoic Logic*, 69.
17. Sextus Empiricus, *Against the Logicians*, 2.224.
18. Ibid. 2.225.
19. Ibid. 2.226.
20. Here we switched from citing Sextus to citing Diogenes because, in *Against the Logicians*, Sextus only details the first three Stoic indemonstrables, although he reports that there are five. Mates suggests this is intentional, explaining that Sextus did not need to detail all five given that he had other goals to achieve. See Mates, *Stoic Logic*, 73n.56.
21. We should also appreciate the whirlwind of thinking about time that Aristotle offers after he provides his famous definition of time ('number [ἀριθμὸς] of motion [κινήςεως] with reference to before and after'). Aristotle, *Physics*, IV.11, 219b1–2. The rest of Book IV is some of the most honest thinking in all of Aristotle.
22. Spinoza, *Ethics*, IIP40S1.
23. Ibid. IIP40S1.
24. We might think of reason and treason as two faces of one plane.

The Shell B: Paradoxes

'Reason' traces back to the Latin *ratio*, meaning 'reckoning, numbering, calculation; business affair, procedure', and to *reri*, meaning 'to reckon, calculate', as in counting chunks of limestone (*calx*) in order to sum the cost of a heap of wheat. By contrast, 'treason' comes from *traditionem*, meaning 'deliver over, a give up, surrender', itself coming from *tradere*, meaning 'to deliver, hand over', which is combines *trans* 'over' + *dare* 'to give'. This connects to *traditor*, which means 'one who delivers', and to *traitor*, which likely comes from the Christian Bible passage in which the traitor Judas hands over Jesus to the chief priests and temple elders (Luke 22:52). The side of reason operates through counting and reckoning, while the side of treason gives up on counting and gives over to endless division.

25. Gilles Deleuze, 'He Stuttered', in *Essays Critical and Clinical* (1993), trans. Daniel W. Smith and Michael A. Greco (Minneapolis: University of Minnesota Press, 1997), 108.
26. Ibid. 109.
27. For a contemporary example of this passion, see P. D. Magnus's ongoing collection of idiosyncratic or 'one-off' fallacies, such as the 'Wittgenstein Fallacy', wherein inferring 'that the profession of philosophy as currently practiced is somehow flawed, because a modern day Wittgenstein would not receive recognition or employment'; or the 'fallacy *ex homine*', which is the 'opposite of *ad hominem*. A sense of decorum stops anyone from making accusations of some particular dark motive, such as racism, while charges of other dark motives are still hurled around. The result is that the unspeakable dark motive gets a free pass.'
28. Although Deleuze identifies 'two forms of the absurd', he does not determine that these are *the* only forms of the absurd. Further, when he mentions these 'two forms', he is using them to compare them two 'two figures of nonsense' (*LS* 69).
29. Deleuze continues, '. . . for Meinong knew how to draw from it the most beautiful and brilliant effects' (*LS* 35).
30. While Deleuze does not say much about this form of absurdity, it lurks within his texts.
31. Kant, *Critique of Judgment*, trans. Paul Guyer and Eric Matthews (Cambridge: Cambridge University Press, 2000), 178n. Also see Immanuel Kant, *The Metaphysics of Morals*, trans. Mary Gregor (Cambridge: Cambridge University Press, 1991), Ak. VI, 356–7. Daniel W. Smith makes a typically fascinating claim about this: 'Interestingly, *Anti-Oedipus* can be read as an explicit attempt to rework the fundamental theses of Kant's *Critique of Practical Reason*. Daniel Smith, *Essays on Deleuze* (Edinburgh: Edinburgh University Press, 2012), 187.
32. For a great reading of a philosophical absurdist reading of Descartes,

see Kyoo Lee, *Reading Descartes Otherwise: Blind, Mad, Dreamy, and Bad* (New York: Fordham University Press, 2012).
33. Deleuze repeats this definition at least three times.
34. Mario Mignucci suggests that 'there is here the superimposition of two different and possibly unrelated classification of sophisms'. Mario Mignucci, 'Logic', in *Cambridge History of Hellenistic Philosophy*, ed. Kiempe Algra, Jonathan Barnes, Jaap Mansfield and Malcolm Schofield (Cambridge: Cambridge University Press, 1999), 158.
35. Simplicius, *In Aristotelis de Physica Commentarii* 1108.18–28, in Mario Mignucci, 'The Stoic Analysis of the Sorites', *Proceedings of the Aristotelian Society* n.s. 93 (1993): 231–45, at 231.
36. Galen, *Three Treatises on the Nature of Science*, trans. Michael Frede (Indianapolis: Hackett Publishing Company, 1985), 74.
37. Ibid. 75.
38. Diogenes put is this way: 'It cannot be that if two is few, three is not so likewise, nor that if two or three are few, four is not so; and so on up to ten. But two is few, therefore so also is ten' (DL 7.82).
39. 'Philetas', in *Encyclopædia Britannica* 21, 11th edn, ed. Hugh Chisholm (Cambridge: Cambridge University Press, 1911), 375–6.
40. Cicero, *On Academic Scepticism*, 2.95.
41. Aristotle, *De Interpretatione*, Ch. 9. For an impressive treatment of how the Sea Battle argument relates to time, see Richard Gaskin, *The Sea Battle and the Master Argument: Aristotle and Diodorus Cronus on the Metaphysics of the Future* (Berlin: De Gruyter, 2011).
42. Epictetus, *Discourses*, II.19.1.
43. Ibid. II.19.1.
44. Ibid. II.19.2–5. Also: 'Cleanthes devoted a whole treatise to [The Master]' and 'Chrysippus has written on the subject in the first Chapter of his book *On Possibles*'. Ibid. II.19.9.
45. Emphasis is added to stress the sense of pointing at a single, actual person: Dion.
46. Jacques Brunschwig, 'The Stoic Theory of the Supreme Genus and Platonic Ontology', in Brunschwig, *Papers*, 92–157; Victor Caston 'Something and Nothing: The Stoics in Concepts and Universals', *Oxford Studies in Ancient Philosophy* 17 (1999): 145–213.
47. *Amb* relates to *ambio*, which means 'to go around or about a thing' or 'to envelope', synonymous with *circumeo*. 'To drive' (as in: cattle), 'to conduct, impel' (as in: humans), 'to chase, pursue' (as in: drive off on a line of flight).
48. Thucydides, *History of the Peloponnesian War*, ed. M. I. Finley, trans. Rex Warner (Harmondsworth: Penguin Classics, 1972), IV.32; emphasis added.
49. This is the word Hegel uses to describe the double-sided structure of the lordship–bondsman dialectic. G. W. F. Hegel, *Phenomenology of*

Spirit, trans. A. V. Miller (Oxford: Oxford University Press, 1977), 111.
50. Catherine Atherton, *The Stoics on Ambiguity* (Cambridge: Cambridge University Press, 1993), 21–2.
51. Plutarch reports that Caesar said it in Greek (ἀνερρίφθω κύβος).
52. Plutarch, *Parallel Lives*, 'Alexander and Caesar', 32.8; Suetonius, 'The Life of the Deified Julius', paragraph 33.
53. Think of the wren from J. A. Baker's *The Peregrine*, who 'trembled on its perch in an agony of hesitation, not knowing whether to fly or not, its mind in a stutter, splitting up with fear.' Baker, *The Peregrine* (New York: New York Review of Books, 1967), 87.
54. There are other Latin words for concluding markers – such as *itaque, proinde, idcirco, propterea, ideo, ita* – but we are focusing on these two because of their popularity and because Deleuze makes much of Mallarmé's *Igitur*.
55. Caroline Kroon, 'Causal Connectors in Latin: The Discourse Function of Nam, Enim, Igitur and Ergo', *Cahiers de l'Institut de linguistique* 15, no. 1–4 (1989): 231–43, at 231.
56. Ibid. 236.
57. Ibid. 241; emphasis added.
58. *Allen and Greenough's New Latin Grammar* (Newburyport: Focus Publishing, 2001), 194.
59. Francis Valpy and Edward Jackson, *A Manual of Latin Etymology, as Ultimately Derived, with but Few Exceptions, from the Greek Language* (London: Longman & Co., 1852).
60. Fischer, *Latin Grammar*, 284.
61. Gildersleeve and Lodge, *Gildersleeve's Latin Grammar*, 311; emphasis original.
62. Gustav Fischer, *Latin Grammar: Etymology and an Introduction of Syntax* (Schermerhorn, 1879), 284.
63. Deleuze mentions Mallarme's *Igitur* in three other texts: AO 106; WP 177; *Nietzsche and Philosophy* (1962), trans. Hugh Tomlinson (New York: Columbia University Press, 1983), 32, 33.
64. Sextus Empiricus, *Against the Logicians*, 2.11–12.
65. In recent example of a long tradition of songs that 'sound' like another language without actually meaning anything, something very interesting happened in pop music and comedy beginning in post-war Italy. There was a burst of American songs, films and jingles inspired by a diverse range of 'American-sounding' products. My personal favorite is 'Prisencolinensinainciusol', a number-one hit song composed in 1972 by the legendary Italian entertainer Adriano Celentano (arguably the person to introduce rock 'n' roll to Italy). On top of driving, heavy drums, Celentano sings lyrics that sound, to an Italian audience, like American English but are actually gibberish. The lyrics mimic

how verbalised English sounds to non-English speakers but were senseless.
66. 'Barbarian' (βάρβαρος) was the opposite of 'citizen' (πολίτης), although Plato rejects this division as unilluminating of the meanings of each group. Plato, *Statesman*, 262d–e.
67. Deleuze, *Essays Critical and Clinical*, 71.

6

The Shell C: Living Logic

> The 'paradox of Stoicism' is 'to make of this dialectic a theory of proof and demonstration . . . as a privilege of wisdom'.
>
> Émile Bréhier [*CAS* 79]

Introduction

To conclude our study of Stoic logic let us dwell on Deleuze's question with which we ended last chapter: how much have we yet to learn from Stoicism? We should chew on this for a few moments before starting into 'The Shell C'.

One Stoic lesson that we might yet have to learn from Stoicism is this: Stoic philosophy must be put into action, not merely studied. We cannot just study Stoicism from a disengaged distance; we must actually *do* something Stoically to learn from Stoicism. In this final section of *Part II* we will try to do something: we will construct a *Handbook of Paradoxes*.

There is a long tradition of logical handbooks in the Stoa. Such handbooks are meant to train one's thinking so that students acquire the disposition and capacity for constructing concepts for living and acting. Rather than teaching propositional logic, however, our *Handbook* teaches the power of paradoxes. As we saw in 'The Shell B', paradoxes produce thought and language, the two branches of dialectics. In 'The Shell C' we exploit this productivity in order to generate our *Handbook* by combining (1) the transcendental logic from 'The Yolk B', (2) the four Stoic paradoxes from 'The Shell B', and (3) the four Deleuzian paradoxes from the 'Fifth Series' of *Logic of Sense*. Here is a table to help us stay organised through the complexities in this chapter:

Transcendental logic of incorporeals	Stoic paradoxes	Deleuzian paradoxes
Infinite	The Heap	Infinite regress
Singular	The Liar	Sterile division
Disjunctive	The Master	Neutrality
Problematic	The Nobody	Absurdity

Combined these form four practical acts. Acts are important because our *Handbook* is a field guide, and so must be used or performed, like a tool or sword. Our *Handbook* consists of four acts: (1) Infinite Act, (2) Singular Act, (3) Disjunctive Act and (4) Problematic Act. Performing these acts contributes to a concrete goal of Deleuze's Stoicism: constructing concepts for living. Our *Handbook of Paradoxes* teaches us how constructing such concepts with each of these acts contributes to developing the disposition for affirming the necessary cosmic path of life, wherever it leads. As living itself is the domain of ethics, we will take up those themes in Part III. As Deleuze closed out *Logic of Sense* with appendices, our *Handbook* is appended to the end of Part II.

Handbooks for Thinking

Let us sketch a first draft of a *Handbook of Paradoxes* (Ἐγχειρίδιον παραδόξων), adding to the long Stoic tradition of logic handbooks; we might also call them workbooks, manuals, guidebooks, field guides or how-to instructions. According to doxographical bibliographies and extant literature, handbooks were some of the most prominent textual genres in the Stoa. From Chrysippus' 'Introduction to Logic' textbooks (εἰαγωγὴ διαλεκτική) to Epictetus' *Manual* (Ἐγχειρίδιον) to Marcus Aurelius' *Meditations* (Τὰ εἰς ἑαυτόν) – handbooks were common in Stoic pedagogy. The Greek title of Epictetus' *Manuel* – Ἐγχειρίδιον – is illuminating because, according to the *LSJ*, it can also mean 'sword' or a general term for hand tools, such as those used for cutting stone. As Simplicius says:

> It is called Ἐγχειρίδιον because all persons who are desirous to live as they ought, should be perfect in this book, and have it always ready at hand (πρόχειρος); a book of as constant and necessary as the sword (which commonly went by this name, and from whence the metaphor seems to be taken) is to a soldier.[1]

The Shell C: Living Logic

Jean-Baptiste Gourinat suggests that, since this was the time of papyri rolls, an Εγχειρίδιον rolled up in a hand would have looked like a tool or small sword.² Stoic theory was always ready at hand (πρόχειρος), easily deployable in any situation. The handbook genre thus has clear practical aims. As Sellars says, 'the *Handbook* is a book designed to be used to exercise (γυμνάζειν, ἀσκεῖν) the soul (ψυχή) analogous to the way in which one might exercise the body'.³ Notice here the resonances with what Deleuze sees as the 'ethical task properly so called' in Spinoza's *Ethics*: 'the *Ethics* takes the body as model'.⁴ Stoic logic is intended not simply to win philosophical contests with rival schools but to initiate a becoming-Stoic, a process that is modelled on the body.

For the Stoics, then, logic was not just a mere logical *organon*, as it was for the Peripatetics, but an integral part of the whole philosophical form of life, just as the shell is an integral part of the whole egg. Victor Goldschmidt echoes this point in his critique of Benson Mates's attempt to compare Stoic logic and twentieth-century logic: 'The Stoics ... fought against any conception of a logic that was not integrated to philosophy (hence their polemic against the logic-*organon* of Aristotle).'⁵ In this Stoic spirit, we place our book in that ancient tradition of Stoic texts by concluding the Part II with our own *Handbook*.

The 'Twentieth Series on the Moral Problem in Stoic Philosophy' of *Logic of Sense* begins with the Stoics' characterisation of philosophy as an egg. Evoking Diogenes, Deleuze writes: 'The shell is Logic, next comes the albumen, Ethics, and the yolk in the center is Physics' (*LS* 142). Now that we are in the last section of Part II, at the far edge of 'The Shell', about to enter 'The Albumen', we can articulate the real purpose of this egg-imagery: pedagogy. The integrated distribution of the egg is designed to help students comprehend the integrated organisation of the Stoic system. While Aristotle saw dialectics as the means for discovery or invention of new theses, Stoics saw logic as pedagogical in nature and purpose. 'The Stoics', Bréhier claims, 'transformed logic completely into dialectic' and for pedagogical purposes (*CAS* 63). As Bréhier reminds us, the Stoics were pedagogues first, scholars second.⁶

Remember back to our 'Introduction', where Deleuze was asking us to imagine a teaching scene – consisting of a student and a Stoic sage – in which the student posed a 'question of signification: O master, what is ethics?' (*LS* 142). The Stoic sage responded by pulling out an egg from beneath his cloak and pointing at it with his staff. The answer to the question of ethics, it seems, is: a real egg.

But this is not all, as there are actually two imagined scenes. Deleuze describes the second scene thus: 'Or, having taken out the egg, he [the Stoic sage] *strikes the student with his staff*, giving him to understand that he himself must provide the answer' (*LS* 136). For Deleuze, the 'staff is the universal instrument, the master of questions'; the student thus 'takes the staff and breaks the egg in such a manner that a little of the white remains attached to the yolk, and a little to the shell' (*LS* 136, 142). The first painful lesson of becoming-Stoic is the sting of the master's staff.

Under the Stoa, the lesson continues: 'Either the master has to do all of this himself, or the student will have come to have an understanding only after many years' (*LS* 142). The final lines of Spinoza's *Ethics* echo this Stoic lesson:

> If the road I have pointed out as leading to this goal seems very difficult, yet it can be found. Indeed, what is so rarely discovered is bound to be hard. For if salvation were ready to hand and could be discovered without great toil, how could it be that it is almost universally neglected? All things excellent are as difficult as they are rare.[7]

What should we make of this painful scene? While the sage might literally strike a student's skull, it also means striking with paradoxes. As Quintilian reports, experiencing the blunt force of a paradox is essential to a full Stoic education.[8] Paradoxes are not harmless abstract puzzles, but tenacious problems that compel existential response. To ensure that the lessons enhance, rather than diminish, living, Stoics wrote manuals. We evoke this pedagogical practice with our own *Handbook of Paradoxes*. With our *Handbook* we can hit Stoic apprentices with paradoxes, or maybe roll it up and literally strike them on the head as if it were a staff because Stoic logic has both physical and conceptual effects.

Handbooks endow students of Stoicism with dialectical skills and prowess. As highly trained dialecticians, Stoics evade the attacks of rival philosophers and thwart the positive positions other schools proposed. 'The dialectic is thus', writes Bréhier, 'a defensive weapon used to escape adversaries' (*CAS* 64). In this sense, the time of Hellenistic Athens was even more athletic or agonistic than what Jean-Pierre Vernant depicts in the earlier decades of the city. Vernant sees the agora has having 'the form of ἀγών [*agon*]: an oratorical contest, a battle of arguments whose theatre was the agora, the public square, which had been a meeting place before it was a marketplace'.[9] More than political rivalries, the Hellenes carried this competitive spirit into philosophical contests. Stoics, Epicurean, Academics, Peripatetics and other schools would roam the city in packs of philosophers, each seeking to win impromptu or planned debates. While many claim that philosophy began in ancient Athens, with Socrates and Plato, and others identify the land occupied by Ionia (modern-day Turkey) as its birthplace, we claim that *philosophies*, in the plural, begin in the Hellenistic Ages.[10]

Logic was often taught through handbooks called simply 'Introduction to Logic' (εἰαγωγὴ διαλεκτική).[11] On a Deleuzian reading, these were sets of exercises for sculpting and honing the creation and use of concepts. Although nearly all of the Stoics' writings on logic were lost, fragments of handbooks survived. According to Mates, all of these fragments 'have one characteristic in common: the more interesting the logic becomes, the more corrupt the text becomes'.[12] Is this not the mark of a powerful concept? – the more interesting it becomes, the more it evades our grasp. Our *Handbook* is a means for keeping the force of these fragments alive as we unfold them through Deleuze's Stoicism. We have one goal: to construct concepts for living.

Constructing Concepts for Living

Constructing concepts for living is both very Deleuzian and very Stoic. It is very Deleuzian because he and Guattari define the philosophical operation as 'the art of forming, inventing, and fabricating concepts', and it is very Stoic because Stoicism is about practical life (*WP* 2). We combine these to formulate a definition of a Deleuzian Stoicism: *creating concepts for living*. Logic is a necessary part of that practice. Before we attempt to actually create concepts, to truly *do* philosophy, we should make three comments about concepts and their construction.

First, *concepts structure our lives and thoughts*. 'Logic', according to Pierre Hadot, 'was not limited to an abstract theory of reasoning, nor even to school exercises in syllogistics; rather, there was a daily practice of logic applied to the problems of everyday life. Logic was thus the mastery of inner discourse.'[13] Rather than assuming that formal logic is the true, unadulterated account of the structure of thinking, Stoic logic includes sorting out the array of thoughts and emotions composing one's form of life. 'Dialectic', Catherine

Atherton notes, 'is no intellectual exercise, and no mere tool of philosophy; it is an intrinsic part of the technique of living a happy and successful life as a rational animal.'[14] Taking up a perversion of Socratic intellectualism, the Stoics thought that passions and emotions resulted from mistaken judgements or misunderstandings. We are emotionally overwhelmed due to an error in reasoning, and logic is a means for monitoring our inner discourses in order to discern whether or not erroneous value judgements occurred. A common method of this use of logic is to place an object before one's eyes, strip away externally imposed value judgements derived from an overly human perspective, and reveal its bare materiality. This logical move is not simply a reduction to abstract structures but an insistence on the necessary materiality of our lives. Logic is a process of revaluating the values structuring of our world in order to initiate a purely material relation: a material subject engaging a material object.

Second, *concepts are bodies*. Stoics' full commitment to materialism entails the corporeality of concepts. Concepts are part of our corporeal composition, like our hair, nails, legs or lungs. If philosophy is the practice of creating concepts for living, then philosophy is a direct intervention in matter. The form of this intervention is the confrontation with the incorporeal surface that connects and separates bodies. Confronting this surface, the spatio-temporal and meaningful incorporeal structure of the world is brought face to face with the chaotic depths of corporeal interpenetration. Stoic handbooks contain sets of exercises for practising this corporeal confrontation with the surface. If the whole of Stoic logic includes the entire set of such exercises, then logic functions similarly to an abstract machine for constructing concepts. Concepts are constructed in terms of shadows that bodies project onto the surface, and logic is the mapping of these projections, that is, the determination of the events and singularities composing the structure of matter. Put differently, Stoic logic trains the extraction of the event from a state of affairs. This is one way to think about what Deleuze calls 'counter-actualisation', or the process of unearthing the event embedded in states of affairs (which we will discuss in Part III).[15] The corresponding movement – actualisation – is the actualisation of the event in bodily networks reaching out through the entire cosmos. For the Stoics, concepts are bodies that correspond to the expression of events on the incorporeal surface.

Further, if concepts are bodies, and if philosophy creates concepts, then the practice of philosophy is also the creation of bodies. This includes inter-corporeal causality and the quasi-causality involved when sense shifts states of affairs. Out simply, concept creation is the provocation of *incorporeal transformations* on the surface of the world. Creating concepts does not mean adequate representation of a state of affairs, but intervention in the world along the lines of a 'speech act', as we see in Sextus' description of how a teacher affects the student (*ATP* 86). The Stoics

> say, just as the trainer or the drill sergeant sometimes takes the boy's hands to drill him and to teach him to make certain motions, but sometimes stands at a distance and moves to a certain drill, to provide himself as a model for the boy – so too some impressers touch, as it were, and make contact with the commanding-faculty to make their printing in it ... whereas others have a nature like that of the incorporeal λεκτα, and the commanding-faculty is impressed *in relation to them*, not *by* them. (*HP* 27E)

Without impressing a student's body like a hand moves a soldier through the movements of a drill, λεκτα quasi-cause corporeal changes. Thus, the effect of a speech act is quasi-causal, and creating concepts is akin to such an *act*. While acts are incorporeal, they happen in the world, amid bodies and things. Concepts do not speak *of* bodies because they *are* bodies, and their creation is a cosmological event, occurring at a specific place and time. Deleuze and Guattari notice this: 'Hence the significance of dates for the Stoics. From what moment can it be said that someone is bald [as in The Liar paradox]? In what sense does a statement of the type "There will be a naval battle tomorrow" [as in The Master paradox] constitute a date or order-word?' (*ATP* 86). Concept creation is the provocation of events in so far as a 'concept', writes Deleuze, 'should express an event'.[16]

Third, concepts are not just created, willy-nilly, whenever someone feels like it. 'You don't say one day, "Hey, I am going to invent this concept" and then whip it up out of nowhere.[17] A philosophical "creator" is not a preacher working for the fun of it.'[18] The philosopher creates what she *must* create. Concepts are created because of a compulsion that emerges out of concrete contexts. Our *Handbook* is a set of imaginative and physical exercises that attune us to the compulsion to which we must respond by creating concepts for living; it is a practical prolegomena for doing philosophy in our singular lives in the singular cosmos.

Constructing our Handbook

Consider four paradoxes from *Logique du sens*: (1) Paradox of Infinite Regress, (2) Paradox of Sterile Division, (3) Paradox of Neutrality and (4) Paradox of the Absurd. Each of these embodies a paradoxical operation: (1) Indefinite Proliferation, (2) Dry Iteration, (3) Essence's Third Estate and (4) Impossible Objects. To construct our *Handbook*, we align these four Deleuzian paradoxes and their paradoxical operations with the four Stoic paradoxes from 'The Shell B': (1) The Heap, (2) The Liar, (3) The Master and (4) The Nobody.[19] (4). Finally, we align these two sets with the four classes from the Transcendental Logic of Incorporeals we sketched out in 'The Yolk B': (1) infinite, (2) singular, (3) disjunctive and (4) problematic. With this, we can construct our *Handbook*:

Transcendental logic of incorporeals	Stoic paradoxes	Deleuzian paradoxes	Paradoxical operation
Infinite	The Heap	Infinite Regress	Indefinite Proliferation
Singular	The Liar	Sterile Division	Dry Iteration
Disjunctive	The Master	Neutrality	Essence's Third Estate
Problematic	The Nobody	Absurdity	Impossible Objects

HANDBOOK OF PARADOXES

INFINITE ACT

Infinite Act is first in our *Handbook*. Picture this: you are a walking with a friend through a college campus on graduation day when you notice a group of students walking in the opposite direction. They are singing a song with Latin lyrics. When this happens, attempt this conversation with your friend:[20]

> *You*: 'The name of the song they are singing is *called* [1] '*Gaudeamus Igitur*.'
> Your friend may ask, with a curious facial expression: 'That is the name of the song?'
> *You*: 'No, that is what the *name* of what the song is *called*. The *name* really is: [2] "Let Us Thus Rejoice".'
> Your friend, with a curiouser expression on his face, may respond: 'I should have said "That is what the *song* is called?"'

The Shell C: Living Logic

You: 'No, you should not have. That is a completely different thing. The song is called [3] "On the Shortness of Life". But that is only what it is *called*.'

Your friend, now curiouser and curiouser, may retort: 'Well! What *is* the song, then?'

You: 'I was just getting to that. The song really *is* [4] "De Brevitate Vitae".'

... (Continue on indefinitely.) ...

This short conversation distinguishes a potentially infinite series of names that follow an indefinite progression.

To see what is going on pedagogically, let us work backwards, starting with: (4) the last thing you said, 'The song *really* is "De Brevitate Vitae".' The song itself is a proposition, a name, n_4: 'De Brevitate Vitae' is the name that this song is. (3) But this is not the name *of* the song. The song itself is a name, whose meaning is designated by a different name, n_3: 'On the Shortness of Life'. 'On the Shortness of Life' is the name that designates *what the song is called*, which has a meaning that forms a new name, n_2: 'Let Us Thus Rejoice'. This name, however, must be designated by yet another name, n_1: 'Gaudeamus Igitur'. To recap, the meaning of n_4 is designated by n_3, the meaning of n_3 is designated n_2, and the meaning of n_2 is designated by n_1. This first name – n_1 – is *what the name of the song is called*: 'Gaudeamus Igitur'. In case this is getting confused, here is a table, based on Lewis Carroll's break:

n_1	n_2	n_3	n_4	n_n
What the *name* of the song is *called*:	What the *name* really *is*:	What the *song* is *called*:	What the *song* really *is*:	Ad infinitum
'Gaudeamus Igitur'	'Let Us Thus Rejoice'	'On the Shortness of Life'	'De Brevitate Vitae'	Etc.

There are four names, each of which is a 'real name' in so far as it designates a 'reality'. The first reality is the song that the students are singing, and there is a name that designates this reality, n_1: 'Gaudeamus Igitur'. But this designating name is itself a reality, for which there is a different name, n_2, which designates it: 'Let us Thus Rejoice'. This, too, is a reality, for which there is another name, n_3: 'On the Shortness of Life'. And this is also a reality with a further name, n_4: 'De Brevitate Vitae'. And this is yet a fourth reality for which there is another name – n_5 – and on and on infinitely approaching n_n.

Deleuze calls it 'Carroll's Paradox', although he also describes a simpler version that he calls it 'Frege's Paradox' (*LS* 29). Frege's Paradox is 'a regress of two alternating terms: [1] the name that denotes something and [2] the name that denotes the sense of this name' (*LS* 30). Put differently: reference and sense. The paradoxical operation here is infinite proliferation or regress, which is the paradoxical operation in 'The Heap'. We can keep adding one more grain of wheat but we never reach a heap or vice versa.

The paradox of infinite regress is first because it 'is the one from which all the other paradoxes are derived' (*LS* 36). As a regress, its form is *serial*. Each denoting term in the series has a sense that must be denoted by another term in a series ad infinitum. If we focus solely on the terms of the series, we only notice a chain of homogeneous terms: $n_1 \rightarrow n_2 \rightarrow n_3 \rightarrow n_4 \ldots n_n$. Each term is distinguished from the preceding one by degree or ordinal rank – first, second, third, fourth ... nth – not a difference in kind. Deleuze calls this 'a synthesis of the homogenous' (*LS* 36). Infinite Act is its articulation.

Such infinite proliferation corresponds to the 'infinite proposition' from Kant's Table of Judgements.[21] Although an infinite proposition is controversial in the history of logic, Kant values it highly. It is controversial because it contains a negation operator but only negates one term in the proposition. As Kant puts it, 'infinite judgements [or propositions] are affirmative, because the negation affects only the predicate ... nonetheless, there is always a negation in there, not of the proposition, that is, of the relation of the concepts, but of the predicate'.[22] Deleuze describes sense just this way: 'Sense brings about the suspension of both affirmation and negation' (*LS* 31). Infinite proposition is both affirmative and negative at the same time, which is the ambiguous structure of a Stoic paradox.

Here is an example of an infinite proposition: 'The grain is a non-heap.'[23] This proposition articulates a 'quality' that is proper to our transcendental logic of incorporeals. The formal logic of corporeals uses affirmative propositions – 'The grain is a heap' – and negative propositions 'The grain is not a heap.' Affirmative and negative propositions both employ a positive predicate – 'x is a heap' – in so far as they ascribe positive predicates to a subject, and simply affirm or deny this predication; as mirror inversions of each other, there is no difference in kind between them. Infinite propositions, however, 'ascribe no positive quality, no definite connotation, to their subjects'.[24] They affirm something of a subject, but what they affirm is not something that is reducible to the limitations of the states of affairs and the propositions that describe them. Perhaps it is not even correct to call it a predicate; it is closer to an attribute, an event or a sense. An attribute is *in* the world, it is *in* the grains, but it infinitely proliferates across them; it subsists as the border of bodies without being a body itself. It is neither a heap nor not a heap, but a non-heap. Hence the paradoxical status of incorporeals: neither beings nor non-beings, but still something. Put differently, it neither exists nor does not exist, but non-exists or subsists. Infinite proposition is that which is proper to Infinite Act: that infinitely thin border that connects and separates two heterogeneous series. To commit an Infinite Act is to identify oneself with this border position, and the Stoic sage acts directly on this paradoxical border.

Singular Act

Perhaps this conversation is confusing your friend (or you). This confusion is addressed by Singular Act in so far as it cuts off the infinite regress of Infinite Act by freezing the movement of a proposition along an infinitely proliferating series just long enough to extract its sense. Consider how this freezing and extracting of sense occurs in Singular Act.

Return to the conversation above, but rather than focusing on the terms in the series – $n_1 \to n_2 \to n_3 \ldots n_n$ – focus on the relations between them – xà x à x à etc. This is where sense subsists, between the terms, in 'that which alternates in the succession' (*LS* 36). Put differently, if we prioritize the relations rather than the terms themselves, we notice that sense generates the series. To use semiotic vocabulary, each term is a 'signifier' designating a body in the world or 'signified'. What the signifier signifies, however, is not just the denoted object but also the *sense* of the object. Sense exceeds the signified object, or as Deleuze puts it, 'there is always a blurred excess of the signifier' over the signified (*LS* 40). Signified and sense are thus distinct; the signified is corporeal (even if it is a concept, since concepts are bodies) and sense incorporeal. The sense of the first signifier, then, becomes the signified of another signifier. This second signifier also has a sense, which becomes the signified of third signifier, and so on indefinitely. In short, there are two different series – a series of signifiers and a series of signified – and sense subsists in between. We only glimpse the interserial sense if we see that the signifieds and the signifiers form not one but *two different series*.

Acting out the above dialogue is intended to reveal the relation between the terms, and Deleuze is adamant about specifying the exact nature of this relation: difference. Singular Act shifts our focus from the terms to the relations between them. This difference is seen, at first, as the difference between series that are different *in kind*, not just degree, which is why Deleuze calls it 'a synthesis of the heterogeneous' (*LS* 36). Sense subsists as that paradoxical, two-sided surface enabling these two different series to resonate because, not in spite, of their differences. Sense, writes Deleuze, 'ensures the relative displacement of the two series, the excess of the one over the other, without being reducible to any of the terms of the series or to any relation between these terms' (*LS* 40). Singular Act attunes us to these differential relations in the series.

Through these differential relations, Singular Act connects words to actions. When we speak – naming a song or stating an ethical proposition – we assume easy access to the sense of our speech. Sense is just there, already understood, 'always presupposed as soon as *I* begin to speak' (*LS* 28). By assuming sense, we do not have to say the sense of what we are saying, as this is a necessary feature of language. In order to speak the sense of what we were saying, we must make it the object of another proposition. Trying to name the sense of a name – that is, saying, simultaneously, something and its sense – leads to an infinite regress. This inability to say the sense of what we say testifies to a strange asymmetrical potency: 'the great impotence of the speaker' and 'the highest power of language' (*LS* 28–9). As will see in Part III: Ethics, this asymmetrical potency is the structure of a Stoic ethical act.

When speaking of an ethical reality, we must use propositions, but this leads to the infinite proliferation of propositions. Since a proposition cannot say its own sense, it requires another proposition, thus leaving behind the original ethical element. Speaking of an ethical reality does not bring us closer to a real ethical act but actually enters us into an infinite regress drifting away from acting. Just as language would be impossible if we had to continuously say the sense of what we say, action would be impossible if we had to continually and exhaustively determine the fixed ethical proposition justifying an act. There is an unbridgeable gap between ethical reality and the sense of the proposition. And yet, Stoic ethics demands that we do *both*: that we infinitely strive and fail to speak the moral of a proposition *and* that we refuse to get swept away by the indefinite progression, and just act, *hic et nunc*, at every instant. A Stoic imperative aims directly at the paradoxical threshold between fully justifying an act prior to action and simply acting. We might call this paradoxical threshold a singularity, hence the name: Singular Act. For Deleuze, the singularity 'is a two-sided entity . . . [that] guarantees, therefore, the convergence of the two series which it traverses, but precisely on the condition that it makes them endlessly diverge' (*LS* 40). As a paradoxical entity, a singularity is 'always displaced in relation to itself' (*LS* 40). Deleuze is quit insightful here, for he notices 'the possibility of a profound link between the logic of sense and ethics, morals, or morality, is confirmed' (*LS* 31). He is suggesting that we, students of Deleuze and Stoicism, strive to realise this possibility and make the connection between the logic of sense and ethics, which is one of our main goals of our *Handbook of Paradoxes* and the ethics of Part III.

Through the Paradox of Sterile Division, which Deleuze calls 'the Stoics' paradox', Singular Act connects with The Liar paradox in so far as The Liar paradox is a means for extracting sense. To refresh us, let's take Paul of Tarsus' formulation of The Liar paradox: 'One of Crete's own prophets [Epimenides] has said: "Cretans are always liars, evil brutes, idle bellies."'[25] While this paradox is very well known, let us specify the details. If the proposition – 'All Cretans are liars' – is true, and the person speaking this proposition is Cretan, then the speaker is not lying. Thus, not all Cretans are liars and the proposition is false. But if the proposition is false, then the speaker is lying, thus making the statement true. The proposition is neither true nor false, or both true and false. The truth, if that is what we seek, endlessly turns in a dizzying circle. However, what appears to be endless movement is really static. Although an affirmation of a contradiction, the proposition is meaningful; while paradoxical, we discern a sense lurking within. With regards to veracity and validity, it remains neutral. A 'splendid sterility of the expressed', Deleuze calls it, 'constitutes its peculiarity' (*LS* 32). It is peculiar because it combines two seemingly incompatible things: the sterility of sense (which we extracted from the heterogeneous series) and the genetic condition (which produces the series). Deleuze calls this peculiarity 'dryness'; later on in *Logic of Sense* he calls it 'impenetrability'; we call it perversion (*LS* 32). The paradoxical operation of Singular Act, as in The Liar paradox, is 'dry iteration', another name for 'static genesis' in so far as it opposes the wetness of dynamic genesis. 'One of the most remarkable points of Stoic logic', writes Deleuze, 'is the sterility of sense-event' (*LS* 31).

Singular act connects to the singular proposition in Kant's Table of Judgements. Neither particular nor universal, singularity suspends both particularity and universality, serving as their 'evanescent double' (*LS* 32). This logical class in Kant's Table is called 'quantitative' because it concerns 'how much' of a predicate is included. In a universal proposition, the subject is '*wholly in*cluded in or *ex*cluded from the notion of the predicate'; in a particular proposition, the subject 'is only *in part in*cluded in or [*in part*] *ex*cluded from it'.[26] In a singular proposition, however, the subject is neither included nor excluded, beyond whole and part, because it is absolutely unequal to anything else. Here is how.

On the one hand, singular propositions are both *similar and dissimilar to universal* ones in so far as the predicate applies to the subject completely. For example, 'All Cretans are liars' is a universal proposition because the entirety of the subject – 'Cretans' – is included in the predicate – 'liars'. 'Epimenides is lying' is a singular proposition because the entirety of 'Epimenides' is included in the predicate, but 'Epimenides' is not a universal like 'Cretans' because 'Epimenides' is completely unique. Put differently, universal propositions tell us something about an indefinitely large number of objects, while singular propositions only tell us something about one single thing.

On the other hand, singular propositions are both *similar and dissimilar to particular* ones. Although the subject's inclusion in the predicate is complete, the inclusion does not refer to the entirety of a class because the subject is not a member of any class. For example, 'Some Cretan are liars' is a particular proposition because, Arthur O. Lovejoy writes, it 'tells us something about a number of objects more than one, and less than an indefinite whole number of objects constituting the extension of the class'.[27] Similarly, 'Epimenides is lying' is a singular proposition because it tells us something about only one object. More precisely put, it is not an object but an *act*: the act of lying. A singular proposition refers not to a whole person (Epimenides) but to what is most impersonal and pre-individual: an act. The Liar must be enacted, or at least it must refer to an act of articulating the paradox. Thus 'Epimenides' is a proper name in the sense that we discussed in 'The Shell A'. The singular element is the self-referential act of lying, echoing Cicero's formulation: 'If you say that you are lying and what you say is true, you are lying and saying something true.'²⁸ By enacting the proposition, truth and lies split in two opposite directions, although the act remains dry and static. A singular proposition is that which is proper to a Singular Act because it expresses an absolutely singular thing – an act – and The Liar is the paradox corresponding to a Singular Act because it expresses the infinitesimal singularity of an act.

DISJUNCTIVE ACT

Deleuze claims that the first two paradoxes form a disjunction. Infinite Regress/The Heap and Sterile Division/The Liar 'form the two terms of an alternative: one *or* the other' (*LS* 32). The disjunctive paradox concerns the neutrality of sense because it is 'indifferent to affirmative and negation', as well as to universality and particularity. For example, the sense of The Liar paradox remains untouched and unchanged in relation to either truth or falsity.

Disjunction appears in The Master paradox, especially Chrysippus' interpretation. To remind ourselves, The Master paradox is Diodorus Cronus' response to Aristotle's 'Sea Battle' argument and the problem of future contingents. Here is the opening disjunction: '*Either* there will *or* there will not be a sea battle tomorrow.' Whichever is true, we seem currently unable to change the future course of events. The question is thus whether or not future events confer necessity 'backwards in time' to the present. Diodorus' response affirms absolute necessitarianism: if something is possible, it is necessary. Chrysippus, however, denies necessity by affirming fate. In Cicero's words, 'Chrysippus, rejecting necessity, yet believing that nothing can happen without antecedent causes, distinguishes causes into two kinds, in order to preserve the doctrine of fate and yet avoid that of necessity.'²⁹ Chrysippus subscribes to three positions: (1) everything happens according to fate, (2) every proposition is either true or false, and (3) everything happens due to 'antecedent causes' (*causae antecedentes*). And yet, humans are free. There seems to be a blatant contradiction between necessity and freedom. Chrysippus' response: the doctrine of fate.

Remember what we said in 'The Yolk A': bodies are *subject to* fate, while incorporeal events happen *according to* fate. This relation to fate – 'according to . . .' rather than 'subject to . . .' – shows that events subsist both inseparably and independently of bodies; corporeals and incorporeals compose two distinct causal series, although they form an immanent relation. Incorporeal events are distinct because they *in*directly contribute to states of affairs, which we call quasi-causality. Since propositions are incorporeal λεκτα, propositions about future events cannot directly cause bodies to do anything. The proposition 'There will be a sea battle tomorrow' cannot make ships, oars, sailors, the sea and so on actually fight. The Stoic doctrine of fate draws a line that corresponds to the line between corporeal depths and incorporeal surface. While bodies are subject to fate, events happen 'according to' fate, but are not 'subject to' fate. In 'The Yolk A', we called this order of events 'co-fated' (*confatalia*). Thus, Deleuze writes, the sea 'battle *hovers over* its own field [the sea], being neutral in relation to all of its temporal actualisations' (*LS* 100). It makes no sense to ask 'Where is the battle?' because a battle, as an event, never is some*where* or some*when*. *The* battle is never present in a state of affairs, but remains 'always yet to come and already passed' (*LS* 100). Whether a sea battle will take place or not, the battle floats on top of the sea in so far as it is propositionally attributed to battling bodies, like a morning mist before the (true) start or false start of a war.

Distinguishing between fated bodies and co-fated events splits the modality of possibility from necessity, thereby making room for 'contingent possibilities': a proposition that is currently true may become true in the future or it may become false. Possibility, Diogenes reports, thus means: that 'which is admits of being true, there being nothing in external circumstances to prevent it being true' (DL 7.75). We see this account of possibility in the shift to disjunctive propositions. 'Chrysippus insists', Deleuze claims, 'on the transformation of hypothetical [and categorical] propositions into ... disjunctives' (*LS* 170). In a hypothetical proposition such as 'If a cause is present, then there will be an effect', two judgements are related: 'there is a cause' and 'there will be an effect'. The relation between them carries *uni*-directional necessity (*if* the antecedent, *then* the consequent), rather than the bi-directional disjunctive (*either* one *or* the other *or* another *or* . . .). In a categorical proposition such as 'Humans are mortal', two categories are related: the subject category – 'humans' – belongs to the predicate category – 'mortals'. In a disjunctive proposition – 'Either there will or there will not be a sea battle tomorrow' – opposed propositions 'constitute everything that can be said' of the proposition without determining the direction of the relation.[30] It merely constructs the plane of incorporeal compatibility and incompatibility.

A disjunctive proposition spans the sense of contradictory propositions because of its neutrality. Since disjunction 'excludes all depth and elevation', hovering at the surface, 'the relation with regard to sense is always established in both directions at once' (*LS* 183, 33). Events, like battles, do not cause each another or states of affairs, but 'enter relations of quasi-causality', which Deleuze calls an 'unreal and ghostly causality' (*LS* 33). In regards to the future and the past, the event 'divides its presence ad infinitum. If the event is possible in the future and real in the past, it is necessary that it be both at once, since it is divided in them at the same time' (*LS* 33). Here Deleuze says he is 'reminded of the paradox of contingent futures and its importance in Stoic thought', and thus appreciates that the 'Stoics went to astonishing lengths in order to escape necessity and to affirm the "fated" without affirming the necessary' (*LS* 33–4). The escape route: inclusive disjunctive synthesis.

The synthesis of inclusive disjunction holds contradictory propositions in productive tension, as we saw in 'The Shell B' with that portmanteau or esoteric words of which Lewis Carroll was master. The sense of 'Snark', we recall, comes from the resonance of conflicting terms. From the perspective of formal logic, a snail and a shark cannot combine: either it is a snail or a shark, but not both. Inclusive disjunctive synthesis, however, adjoins conflicting terms and thus presents sense through impossible objects. As Lapoujade says, 'the impossible object' – Snark, Nobody, wooden iron, square circle – '*includes the disjunction within itself*: it is at once a circle and a square'.[31] Hence inclusive disjunctive synthesis is essential for the transcendental logic of incorporeals and the Stoic art of paradoxes.

Finally, when Deleuze calls the logical operation of this paradox 'Essence's Third Estate', he is referring to Avicenna's 'three states of essence' (*LS* 34). The first state is essence in so far as it is thought in relation to other universal concepts (essence as signification). The second state is essence in so far as it is embodied by particular things (essence as designation or manifestation). 'But the third state of essence is essence as sense, essence as expressed – always in . . . this splendid sterility or neutrality' (*LS* 34–5). It is through this indifference to opposite relations that sense contributes to the genesis of universal propositions and particular states of affairs, a cold indifference that Deleuze finds chilling. Sense 'is more terrible and powerful in this neutrality, to the extent that it is all of these things at once' (*LS* 35). Since the conflicting and contradictory things are included in disjunction, the resultant proposition is quite monstrous. Disjunctive Act affirms the neutrality of sense event, however threatening and powerful it may be. Another name for this frightening power: *fatum*. Disjunctive Act is the affirmation of what happens according to fate, whether or not we battle at sea tomorrow.

Problematic Act

Problematic Act follows from Disjunctive Act and the paradox of Neutrality. In 'The Shell B', we looked at absurdity and impossible objects, and we continue that investigation in this discussion of Problematic Act.

Recall The Nobody [οὔτις] paradox. In 'The Shell B' we gave Zeno's version. Here we give Chrysippus': 'If anybody is in Megara, they are not in Athens: now there is somebody in Megara, therefore there is nobody in Athens' (DL 7.187). 'Nobody' is an impossible object because its denotation can never be fulfilled; the denotatum of 'nobody' is empty. For example, think of the scene from Homer's *Odyssey* in which Odysseus and his men are stuck in Polyphemus' cave. After intoxicating the Cyclops with 'heady wine', Odysseus queries,

> 'you ask me the name I'm known by, Cyclops? I will tell you. But you must give me a guest-gift as you've promised. *Nobody* – that's my name. *Nobody* – so my mother and father call me, all my friends.' But [Polyphemus] boomed back at me from his ruthless heart, '*Nobody*? I'll eat Nobody last of all his friends. I'll eat the others first! That's my gift to *you*!'[32]

Polyphemus' proposition is formally absurd. The 'you' to whom he refers is empty because the denotation of 'Nobody' cannot be fulfilled (in word or food). Polyphemus never eats Nobody because it is impossible to eat nobody. Later, after Odysseus has stabbed the Cyclops' eye and fled the cave with his band, the blinded giant chasing after them, Polyphemus sounds even more absurd. When 'his neighbor Cyclopes ... asked what ailed him', he responds, '*Nobody*, friends ... Nobody's killing me ...!'[33] As Polyphemus continues spouting nonsense, his neighbours walk away, chortling at his absurdity. When Polyphemus begs his friends to hunt for Nobody, they ridicule him, knowing it would be a fool's errand. Wherever they would look, they could never find Nobody. 'Nobody' is an impossible object from the perspective of denotation because it is 'always displaced in relation to itself', and from the perspectives of manifestation and signification because there is no belief or desire that can be manifested or concept to be signified (*LS* 40). An impossible object never shows

The Shell C: Living Logic

its face because it is never self-identical or even self-similar, but 'an extremely mobile *empty place* ... an *occupant without a place*' (*LS* 41; emphasis original). Nobody is nowhere, nowhen, perpetually '"without a home," outside of being' (*LS* 35).

While impossible objects subsist outside of being, 'they do have a precise and distinct position within this outside', and that position is its sense (*LS* 35). Impossible objects exceed the circle of the proposition but still have sense. They are impossible but not meaningless. We mean *something* when we talk about Nobody. Although we are unable to understand what such a name means, we are not just babbling senselessly. It is just that impossible objects are 'unable to be realized in a state of affairs' (*LS* 35). Impossible objects have a sense, but they cannot be actualised; they are problems, not resolutions. Thus 'problematic' is the modality of impossible objects.

'Problematic' means that they *concern problems*, not that impossible objects are problematic *objects*. For example, a square circle is not an object because it cannot be spatio-temporally actualised. It is an 'event'. 'The event by itself is problematic and problematising,' Deleuze writes (*LS* 54). Problems are defined by the singular points that articulate their structures, and states of affairs are the solutions that problems generate. In different language, the determinacy of problems is due to the operation of *differentiation*; the determinacy of solutions is due to the operation of *integration*. Problems are not, for Deleuze, 'a subjective category of our knowledge' but are objective (*LS* 54). Deleuze learns that 'Kant was without doubt the first to accept the problematic not as a fleeting uncertainty but as the very *object* of the Idea, and thereby as an indispensable horizon of all that occurs ...' (*LS* 54; emphasis added). Notice the precise terminology here: although they are not sensible objects, problems are *objective*. Their objectivity refers to the incorporeal structure that constitutes sense and grounds the circle of the proposition.

Deleuze learns from Kant how to apply truth and falsity to problems, rather than solutions (*DR* 161). 'What is essential is that there occurs at the heart of problems a genesis of truth ... The only way to take talk of "true and false problems" seriously is in terms of a production of truth and falsity by means of problems, and in proportion to their sense' (*DR* 162). The productivity of problems echoes the productivity of sense. Just as Deleuze shifts questions of true and false from solutions to problems, he makes the same shift in moving from propositions to sense. Problems and sense are measured by their generative capacities.

> The genetic element is discovered only when the notions of true and false are transferred from propositions to the problem these propositions are supposed to resolve, and thus alter completely their meaning in this transfer. Or rather, it is the category of sense that replaces the category of truth, when 'true' and 'false' qualify the problem instead of the propositions that correspond to it. (*LS* 120)

The transfer thus changes the determinations from veracity to sense. Beyond true and false, there subsists the problem of sense or the sense of the problem, and the problem of sense 'is a matter of production, not of adequation' (*DR* 154).

In Kant's Table, modality concerns 'the *way in which* something is maintained or denied' in a proposition.[34] There are three types of modality: assertoric, apodeictic and problematic. An assertoric proposition conveys how something is determined in so far as it is *actual*, an apodeictic proposition conveys truth of a proposition in so far as it is *necessary*, and a problematic proposition conveys the *possibility* of settling a proposition's truth *or* untruth. Put differently, an assertoric proposition is possible and empirically found to be true, an apodeictic proposition is true because conceiving of the subject necessitates conceiving of the predicate, and a problematic proposition may or may not be true. Assertoric and apodeictic propositions are both true; it is *how* they are true that distinguishes them. Problematic propositions, however, are neither true nor false but the condition for both, or as Kant puts it: a 'problematic proposition is a *contradiction in adjecto*'.[35] A *contradiction in adjecto* means 'a contradiction between parts of an argument' (where *adjectum* means 'thrown forward, brought about'), as when that which is 'brought forth' by an adjective contrasts or contradicts the noun it modifies, as when Schopenhauer mockingly calls some of Kant's central concepts instances of 'wooden iron' (*hölzernes Eisen*).[36] Even though 'wooden iron' brings together two mutually excluding terms – organic wood and inorganic iron – the phrase still has sense.

In Problematic Act, the Stoic student confronts the problematic state of the incorporeal surface through the paradox of Absurdity or The Nobody. In response to such perplexity, the student becomes the body through which a question is formulated. 'The question', writes Deleuze, 'is developed in problems' (*LS* 56). The question emerges when the mind stutters and thought intensifies, as it squeezes together two contradictory ideas. This stuttering and intensifying is precisely the experience of taking paradoxes seriously, as well as the act of confronting problems in so far *as* they are problematic, not in so far as they can be resolved. Questions do not quell the intensity of the problem, but envelop it. Here is the act of the Problem: to hold in tension contradictory poles so as to provoke questions. Deleuze describes such an act as 'the objective equilibrium of a mind situated in front of the horizon of what happens' (*LS* 57).

Conclusion: A Profound Link

Let us place our *Handbook of Paradoxes* in the tradition of Stoic handbooks. While many earlier handbooks likely contained exercises for sharpening capacities for argument, a perverse fascination with paradoxes lurked below. Deleuze appreciates this because 'a *profound link* between the logic of sense and ethics, morals or morality, is confirmed' (*LS* 31; emphasis original). This profound link is the shared concern for the genesis of 'the given'. Rather than simply accepting what is true at face value, the student of Deleuze's kind of Stoicism demands a genetic account. Rather than deferring the truth of a denotation to manifestation or to signification, a viciously circular deferral that endlessly pushes the truth further around the circle of the proposition until it gets back to the denotation with which it started, an education in the art of paradoxes confronts the genetic conditions for the existence of meaningful language. As Michael Bennett puts it, paradoxes drive us into 'the midst of the productive simmer at the boundary itself'.[37]

'The force of paradoxes', Deleuze writes, 'is that they are not contradictory' in themselves (*LS* 74). Contradictoriness is a feature of formal logic and physics in so far as contradictions are given. The danger is that myopic focus on their givenness obscures the genetic processes that produced those contradictions. The Stoic student knows that contradictions are produced, which is exactly what our *Handbook of Paradoxes* is meant to teach. It is a training manual that 'allow[s] us to be present at the genesis of contradiction' (*LS* 74). Put differently, paradoxes are underground passageways leading to what lies beyond the circle of the proposition and the system of propositional logic, and our *Handbook* guides the student of Stoicism to navigate these twisted passageways, as the Stoic dialectic intends.

According to Diogenes, 'the study of dialectic ... enables [the student] to distinguish truth from falsehood' (DL 7.47). Yet to make this distinction, the student must learn *how* truth and falsity are produced, which includes another ability: 'to discriminate what is merely plausible and what is ambiguous' (DL 7.47). And to make this distinction, the student must know how ambiguity works, which requires the perfection of the art of paradoxes. If truth and falsity are two sides of one topic, then knowing what these two sides are includes intimate knowledge of *both* sides. To know both sides is to know ambiguity inside out and outside in. Knowing double-sidedness intimately requires a confrontation with the incorporeal surface and the aleatory point that connects and disconnects the two sides. Our *Handbook* cultivates all of these abilities and kinds of knowledge through the training in four acts.

We can now clarify a misunderstanding in ancient attacks on Chrysippus. Sextus reports that, in the face of the undecidability of The Heap or similar paradoxes, Chrysippus conceded, a 'wise person will hold fast and keep quiet', and eventually pass out and sleep.[38] While Sextus interprets this as acquiescence to the sceptical attitude, Deleuze thinks he 'does not seem to understand this response very well' (*LS* 80). Rather than conceding to scepticism, Chrysippus enacts the attunement to the aberrant movements that animate logic and language. They are aberrant because they fall between the propositions and the corresponding formal logic. The art of paradoxes leads to the confrontation with a silent yet powerful force of thinking: that which is unthought in thought, the *cogitandum*. Rather than inducing sleep, 'paradox is the force of the unconscious' (*LS* 80).

Our *Handbook* is now part of an education in the Stoic art of paradoxes because it trains the capacity to harness the power of paradoxes. This power is confronted at the surface of the mirror, as Alice felt when passing through the looking glass. Deleuze described this scene from *Alice Through the Looking-Glass* in *Logic of Sense*, as 'a surprising conquest of surfaces' in which 'one no longer sinks, one slides; it is the flat surface of the mirror'.[39] It is no coincidence that Deleuze characterises the double-sidedness of incorporeal surface as 'two sides of a mirror, only what is on one side has no resemblance to what is on the other' (*LS* 25).[40] Passage through the mirror is disorienting and destabilising, for the other side is not the inversion but a perversion of the original side, the world turned inside out and flattened. More than simply the reversal of left and right, up and down, front and back, the cosmological orientation is *pulled through* so that the inside is on the outside and the outside on the inside, and so on, thus transforming the entire distribution of ancient philosophy. In 'The Yolk A', we saw this redistribution through the four ancient philosophical orientations: the Platonic height, the Pre-Socratic depth, the Aristotelian height-within and the Stoic surface.

The Shell C: Living Logic

Deleuze took these orientations seriously, as he repeats in his 'Note for the Italian Edition of *The Logic of Sense*': 'In *Logic of Sense* I am trying to explain how thought organised itself according to similar axes and directions.'⁴¹ In a Stoic education, thought is takes on the surface. As Stoics are plane-makers, our *Handbook* is a training manual for plane-making. According to Deleuze's Stoicism, logic necessitates the confrontation with such planes.

With our *Handbook* complete and our training well under way, we now turn from logic to ethics, from the shell to the albumen. The four acts in our *Handbook* together form a single act: constructing concepts for living. We have begun constructing concepts with each of these acts, but the overall orientation of this concept construction is life, wherever it leads. Living, however, is the domain of ethics. Let us now leave the shell and begin the ethics of *Deleuze, A Stoic*.

Notes

1. Simplicius, *In Epicteti Enchiridion*, Praef. 18–20, quoted in John Sellars, *The Art of Living: The Stoics on the Nature and Function of Philosophy* (London: Bristol Classical Press, 2009), 130.
2. Jean-Baptiste Gourinat, *Premières leçons sur le Manuel d'Epictète: comprenant le texte intégral du Manuel dans une traduction nouvelle par Jean-Baptiste Gourinat* (Paris: Presses universitaires de France, 1998), 140.
3. John Sellars, *The Art of Living: The Stoics on the Nature and Function of* Philosophy (London: Bristol Classical Press, 2009), 131.
4. Gilles Deleuze, *Expressionism in Philosophy: Spinoza* (1968), trans. Martin Joughin (New York: Zone Books, 1990), 269.
5. Victor Goldschmidt, 'Stoic Logic par Benson Mates', *Revue de métaphysique et de morale* 59.2 (April–June 1954): 213–14, at 214.
6. Consider this, for example. While the division of philosophy into three parts – physics, logic and ethics, or yolk, shell and albumen – was something Aristotle already did in his *Topics* (105b19), 'explicit recognition and use of it in teaching seems to be a novelty of the Stoics'. William Kneale and Martha Kneale, *The Development of Logic* (Oxford: The Clarendon Press, 1962), 139.
7. Baruch Spinoza, *Spinoza: Complete Works*, ed. Michael L. Morgan, trans. Samuel Shirley (Indianapolis: Hackett Publishing Company, 2002), VP42S.
8. Quintilian, *Institutio Oratoria*, 1.10.5.
9. Jean-Pierre Vernant, *Origins of Greek Thought* [1962] (New York: Cornell University Press, 1984), 46–7.
10. For an account that locates Ionia as the birthplace of philosophy, see

Isonomia and the Origins of Philosophy, trans. Joseph A. Murphy (Durham, NC: Duke University Press, 2017), 12–17.
11. Mates, *Stoic Logic* (Berkeley: University of California Press, 1961), 8.
12. Ibid. 10.
13. Pierre Hadot, *What is Ancient Philosophy?* trans. Michael Chase (Cambridge, MA: Belknap Press, 2004), 135. Ian Buchanan echoes this: 'It is easy to see why Deleuze's ethics are so inspired by the Stoics. What their ethics considers the essential moral task of the individual to be, we recognize as the vocation Deleuze attributes to philosophers by right: the invention of concepts. On this view, philosophy patently is a style of life, too, as Deleuze often insists ... It is in this sense that it might be said concepts must have an ethics.' Buchanan, *Deleuzism*, 73.
14. Catherine Atherton, *The Stoics on Ambiguity* (Cambridge: Cambridge University Press, 1993), 69. Atheron, however, does seem to miss the generative force of ambiguities and paradoxes when she says, '[a]mbiguities are obstacles' that 'stand in the way of the achievement of a firm, internally coherent, and correct conceptual scheme' (Ibid. 69).
15. We will say more about counter-actualisation in 'Ethics C'.
16. Gilles Deleuze, *Negotiations* (1995), trans. Martin Joughin (New York: Columbia University Press, 1990), 25.
17. Gilles Deleuze, *Two Regimes of Madness Two Regimes of Madness: Texts and Interviews 1975–1995*, ed. David Lapoujade, trans. Ames Hodges and Mike Taormina (New York: Semiotexte, 2006), 318.
18. Ibid.
19. Connecting these two sets of paradoxes is not arbitrary, as Deleuze speaks about each of the Stoic paradoxes.
20. This is a modified version of the conversation between Alice and the White Knight in Lewis Carroll's *Alice Through the Looking-Glass*.
21. Kant calls them 'infinite judgements' but I will use 'infinite proposition' in order to keep our vocabulary consistent.
22. Immanuel Kant, *Lectures on Logic*, trans. J. Michael Young (Cambridge: Cambridge University Press, 2004), 370.
23. Kant's example of an infinite proposition is,'*Anima est non mortalis*' or 'The Soul is non-mortal'; his example of affirmative propositions is '*Anima est moratalis*' or 'The soul is mortal'; and a negative propositions is,'*Anima non est mortalis*' or 'The soul is not mortal'. Kant, *Lectures on Logic*, 370.
24. Arthur O. Lovejoy, 'Kant's Classification of the Forms of Judgment', *The Philosophical Review* 16.6 (November 1907): 588–603, at 597.
25. Paul, Epistle to Titus 1:12–13. Clement of Alexandria refers to this passage: 'In his epistle to Titus, Apostle Paul wants to warn Titus that Cretans don't believe in the one truth of Christianity, because "Cretans are always liars".' To justify his claim, Apostle Paul cites Epimenides, a Cretan man. Apparently, Paul was not a very astute logician. Clement,

The Writings of Clement of Alexandria, Vol. II: Miscellanies, trans. The Rev. William Wilson (Edinburgh: T. & T. Clark, 1867), 1.14.
26. Kant, *Lectures on Logic*, 598; emphasis original.
27. Lovejoy, 'Kant's Classification of the Forms of Judgment', 593.
28. Cicero, *On Academic Scepticism*, 2.95.
29. Cicero, *Treatises of Cicero*, XVII.
30. Kant, *Lectures on Logic*, 372.
31. David Lapoujade, *Aberrant Movements: The Philosophy of Gilles Deleuze* (2014), trans. Joshua David Jordan (South Pasadena: Semiotext(e), 2017), 135.
32. Homer, *The Odyssey*, trans. Robert Fagles (London: Penguin Classics, 1999). 408–11. The same impossible object plays out in any use of the Latin *Nemo* as in Jules Verne's adventures or some recent popular films such as *Finding Nemo* or *Mr Nobody*.
33. Homer, *The Odyssey*, 446–55.
34. Kant, *Lectures on Logic*, 604.
35. Kant, *Lectures on Logic*, 605.
36. Arthur Schopenhauer, *The World as Will and Representation, Vol. 1*, trans. E. F. J. Payne (New York: Dover Publications, 1966), 523.
37. Michael James Bennett, *Deleuze and Ancient Greek Physics* (London: Bloomsbury Academic, 2017), 82.
38. Sextus Empiricus, *Against the Logicians*, I.416.
39. Deleuze, *Two Regimes of Madness*, 64.
40. Although Deleuze is here talking about the 'duality in the propositions', it corresponds to the incorporeal surface because it is the surface as seen from a linguistic perspective.
41. Deleuze, *Two Regimes of Madness*, 64.

PART III
Ethics

7

The Albumen A: Time

Introduction: Goldschmidt and the Idea of Time

We now enter the final part of the Stoic egg. We are leaving the shell and entering the albumen, moving from logic to ethics. As we do, let us recall the warning from the introduction: we are not referring to ethics in the traditional sense of normative theory or applied morality, where the focus is on issues of right and wrong, virtue and vice, good and evil. Deleuze's Stoicism, instead, begins from the perspective of time, ontology and action in order to later reach the more recognisable concerns of moral philosophy. The reason is that such moral concerns are not given, pre-made, but must be generated *as* concerns. Like everything else, ethics too is generative.

As space is the incorporeal proper to physics and λεκτόν that proper to logic, time is the incorporeal proper to ethics. Like space and λεκτόν, time, for the Stoics, expresses a double-sided surface structure. Although Deleuze does not articulate this double-sidedness exactly as we do, he makes much of the two faces of time; he even gives them provocative names: chronos and aion. Deleuze gets these terms and the corresponding conceptual distinction between chronos and aion from Victor Goldschmidt's *Le Système stoïcien et l'idée de temps*.

For Goldschmidt, though there are two faces of Stoic time, the conceptual distinction between them is obscured because of a lack of terminological distinction.[1] 'Without doubt', writes Goldschmidt, 'the theory would have been more scholarly intelligible if, as in the case of void and place, Chrysippus had used two different terms in order to distinguish the two times' (*SS* 39). In 'Albumen A', we explain Deleuze's Goldschmidtian account of the two faces of time in Stoicism. Beginning with a comparison among three ancient theories, we next consider different meanings of the present in terms of the two faces of time. We then consider the twisted genealogy of chronos and aion, question their role in Stoic texts, and explain how time is a single surface with chronos and aion as, respectively, the extensive and intensive sides. In short, time is the third incorporeal. We close by connecting time to ethics and the act. In 'Albumen B', we consider what Goldschmidt meant by the Stoics' 'two methods and two moral attitudes' by explaining the meaning of the act and the event. 'Albumen C' concludes the Stoic egg by considering the two different eternal returns in Stoicism.

Through Goldschmidt's account of the two faces of time in Stoicism, Deleuze also notices that Stoic time directly connects to two other important doubles: two ethics and two eternal returns. First double, ethics: Goldschmidt 'demonstrates that there exist for the Stoics two methods [of interpretation] and two moral attitudes' (*LS* 340n.3). Although Deleuze does not claim to find in Goldschmidt evidence of a correlation of the two moral attitudes with the two faces of time, the correlation is real. Second double, eternal return: Goldschmidt raises 'the question of two very different eternal returns', which Deleuze sees as 'corresponding to the two times' in Stoicism (*LS* 340n.3). In sum, Deleuze thinks the two returns correspond to the two times, but not necessarily the two moral attitudes. This seems odd because, as Deleuze puts it, neither correlation 'appear[s] (at least directly) in Stoic thought' (*LS* 340n.3). But why does Deleuze affirm the second correlation but not the first? Why does he give up and admit that 'whether these two [moral] attitudes correspond to the two times is still obscure' (*LS* 340n.3). He gives an argument for why the second double correlates to the two faces of time but not the first. Instead, all he says is: 'We shall return to these points' (*LS* 340n.3). But he does not fully return, either to the two different eternal returns or the two moral attitudes. We, however, will return. To ensure clarity, here is a table:

Faces of time	Two methods	Moral attitude	Eternal returns
Aion	Divination	Singular perspective	Straight line
Chronos	Use of representations	Cosmos perspective	Cycle

Three Ancient Theories of Time

In antiquity, it was perverse to consider time an object of ethics. Plato viewed time from a metaphysical perspective, while Aristotle made time a matter for the natural sciences by placing most of his comments on time in his *Physics* Book IV.[2] '[F]or the ancients,' writes Goldschmidt, 'the problem of time falls exclusively to physics' or metaphysics (*SS* 49–50). The Stoics, however, develop a theory of time that passes 'from cosmic time to lived time', from physics to ethics (*SS* 55). To their contemporaries, this 'passage risks appearing like quite a leap, perhaps even an artifice'; we call it perverse (*SS* 55). Goldschmidt suggests a pedagogical reason for this perverse passage from physics to ethics via time: it is intended to draw us into a particular movement of nature whose momentum picks us up and carries us into accord with the cosmos. The Stoics' ethical account of time marks, as we might expect, a perversion of both Platonic time and Aristotelian time.[3] Panalyiotis Tzamalikos almost seems to appreciate this perversity when he claims that the Stoic theory of time 'is in fact a third and alternative understanding [of time] . . . to the extent that the Platonic definition of time is a metaphysical as well as a theological one, while Aristotle's is more of a scientific character'.[4] It is not that Stoic time is neither metaphysical (à la Plato) nor scientific (à la Aristotle), but that it is both and neither simultaneously. They are two faces of a single temporal surface: one metaphysical, one scientific. One faces away states of affairs, the other towards them. And yet, time is an ethical concern. To see how, we start with Zeno, founder of the Stoa.

Since 'the thesis of Zeno', Bréhier claims, 'is singularly closer to that of Aristotle', we should compare it to the Stagirite (*TI* 54). Aristotle's *Physics* famously claims: time is the 'number of motion [ἀριθμὸς κινήσεως] in respect of "before" and "after"'.[5] The key word is ἀριθμὸς, from which we get the English 'arithmetic'. Aristotle specifies his terms: ἀριθμὸς 'is used in two ways – both of [1] what is counted or countable and also [2] that with which we count'.[6] Common English translations include 'number, account, sum, quantity, unit, measure'.[7] In both senses, Aristotle prioritises *what* is counted (meaning ἀριθμός applies to both space and time). Time counts motion and change but does not itself move or change in so far as time gives number to physical changes. There is something, a determinate unit or body that is counted, and a specific period of time is a determinate measurement of time. Time is about quantifying some temporal discrete quantity of bodily movement.

Compare Aristotle's definition to extant formulations of Zeno's definition. According to Stobaeus, Zeno says: 'time is an extension of motion [κινήσεως διάστημα] and the criterion of *fastness and slowness*'.[8] But, according to Simplicius, Zeno says: 'time is in general the extension of any motion [πάσης ἁπλῶς κινήσεως διάστημα]'.[9] While both Aristotle and Zeno define time in relation to motion, Zeno does not count discrete quantities but 'places more emphasis on continuous motion'.[10] Perhaps this is why Zeno used διάστημα ('dimension'), rather than ἀριθμὸς ('number'). Time, for Zeno, is the continuous dimension of speed. While Aristotle's account relies on the act of counting what came before and what came after, Zeno sees time as the measurement of how fast or slow bodies move some determinate distance.[11] Zeno contributes to the Stoic perversion of Aristotelian time by shifting the ancient thinking of time from what Deleuze might call the movement from extensive to intensive measures of time.

After Zeno, 'Chrysippus said time is', Stobaeus reports, 'the dimension of motion accompanying the world's motion [παρακολουύοῦν διάστημα τῇ τοῦ κόσμου κινήσει]' (*HP* 51B). While some scholars do not think Chrysippus makes an 'essential modification of Zeno's view', we argue that he pushed Aristotle and Zeno in at least two important ways.[12] The first way was to render time more objective. Aristotelian time is more subjective because such time would not exist without human souls.[13] While it is unclear whether or not this account of time is as phenomenological as it sounds, it is clear that time, for Aristotle, does not exist beyond the act of counting because there must be a soul present to tally temporal units; otherwise, time would not exist. The Stoics, by contrast, render time more objective, echoing the objectivity of space and λεκτα. Incorporeals are not mere subjective entities because they objectively subsist beyond any person's experience. Zeno ascribes some objectivity to time by rendering it the dimension *of* motion, and Chrysippus ascribes more objectivity to time by making it the dimension *accompanying all* motion. Chrysippus thus makes time highly objective and relatively independent of discrete bodies and units. With Chrysippus, time becomes continuous, a perfectly smooth surface. This objectivity of time reflects the quasi-independence of the incorporeal surface from corporeal depths.

Chrysippus' second modification of Zeno's definition corroborates the objectification of time: time connects to the *world's motion*, the movement of the cosmos. Note the differences with Plato and Aristotle concerning conceptions of cosmological infinity. For Plato, time is linked to the infinite in so far as it is the 'moving image of eternity'.[14] We call this a circular infinity because it refers to the eternal revolution (περιφορά) of the Platonic heavenly spheres. Aristotle, too, connected time to the eternal circular motion of the heavens (though he shies away from positing an actual infinity). Aristotle writes, 'time itself is thought to be a circle'.[15] Chrysippus, however, connects time to world *cycles*, thus formulating a *cyclical* infinity. Here is the difference: *circular infinity is materially continuous, but cyclical infinity is materially and structurally continuous*. Plato and Chrysippus agree time is *materially continuous*, meaning that there are no gaps in time. Time is a smooth and unending surface. But Chrysippus also posits time as *structurally continuous*, meaning that time is infinitely divisible. Contrary to the atomists, the Stoics posit no end to continuously dividing time.[16] 'Chrysippus said that bodies are divided to infinity, and likewise things comparable to bodies', that is, incorporeals.[17] For Chrysippus, time is both structurally and materially continuous.

Time expresses a kind of cyclical infinity in so far as the cosmos is destroyed in the cycle of cosmic conflagrations. Cosmoi exist in between conflagrations, meaning conflagrations are not *in* time. They act as limits marking the beginning and end of the temporal continuum, as Turetzky notes: 'Chrysippus was the first to understand the concept of a limit to which an infinite series converges.'[18] Hence Rist suggests that this is how the 'Stoic theory of the beginning and end of each cosmic cycle gave Chrysippus an opportunity to explain events in a continuum that was not available to Plato and Aristotle.'[19] The Stoics construct an account of infinity that was *intensively infinite*. This sense of cyclical, intensive infinity appears in Borges's 'The Babylonian Library', and Deleuze repeats Borges's words from his short story about the logic of cyclical time: '*The ignorant suppose that an infinite number of drawings requires an infinite amount of time; in reality, it suffices that time be infinitely subdivisible*, as is the case in the famous parable of the Tortoise and the Hare' (*LS* 61; emphasis original in both Borges and Deleuze).[20] A continuum has fixed limits and yet is infinitely subdivisible, as in Chrysippus' account of time.

The Adventures of the Present

THE PRESENT OF AION

The principle of the infinite divisibility of time produces a paradoxical adventure of the present. If time is an infinitely divisible continuum, then every part of it, including the present, can be divided endlessly. Chrysippus says most clearly that no time [Χρόνος] is wholly present [ὅλως ἐνίσταται]. For since continuous things are infinitely divisible, on the basis of this division every time too is infinitely divisible. Consequently *no time is present exactly*, but it is broadly [κατα ρλάτος] said to be so. (*HP* 51B; emphasis added)[21]

Strictly, not broadly, speaking, time is never present. The effect: present time never exists or time is never presented.

To say that the future and the past never exist in the present makes some sense because they cannot, by definition, be present. If they could, they would become present. The rub is that this infinite divisibility does apply to the present. Although the present, broadly speaking, seems constituted by part of the past and part of the future, these parts can be divided endlessly. Continuous division implies that the present never *is*. Hence the paradoxical conclusion: the present is never present, now is never now. As Deleuze says, the present 'is subdivided ad infinitum into something that has just happened and something that is going to happen, always flying in *both directions at once*' (*LS* 63; emphasis added).[22] Note the double sense or direction. The present never exists in so far as it remains the non-existent limit endlessly decomposing into past and future; it 'is' simply the border at which past and future join and disjoin. The present 'is the instant without thickness and without extension, which subdivides each present into past and future, rather than vast and thick presents which comprehend both future and past in relation to one another' (*LS* 164). Hence a provocative conclusion: since present, past and future do not exist, time does not exist. We call this account of time 'aion', the untimely backside of chronos. We connect aion to the untimely because both are 'neither temporal nor eternal' (*DR* 130). From the perspective of Deleuze's Stoicism, the reason for this untimely undermining of time is simple: aion is the side of the incorporeal surface facing away from corporeal states of affairs and towards corporal chaos.

The Present of Chronos

The Stoics add a further complication to the paradoxes of time. As soon as they claim that the present never exists, they say the opposite: 'only present time belongs [ὑπάράχειν]' (*HP* 51B). The Greek for what translates as 'belongs' is ὑπάράχειν, 'the literal meaning of which', Rist points out, is 'to be present, to be there, to be available'.[23] Only the present is there, available to us, *hic et nunc*. Only

The Albumen A: Time

the present really exists, not the past or the future because the 'past and future subsist [ὑφεστάναι]', Chrysippus continues, 'but belong in no way' (*HP* 51B). The present thus has a limited extension or duration into which past and future are absorbed. '[P]art of the present is future and the other past' (*HP* 51C). Plutarch reports: 'the part of time which is past and the part that is future subsists but do not belong [οὐχ ὑπάρχειν] and only the present belongs [ὑπάρχειν]' (*HP* 51C). As Deleuze puts it, 'whatever is future or past in relation to a certain present (a certain extension or duration) belongs to a more vast present which has a greater extension' (*LS* 162).

From the perspective of chronos, the present exists in so far as it belongs to bodies. Since existence is the ontological quality of bodies and the present belongs to bodies, the 'present is *in some manner* corporeal' (*LS* 162; emphasis added). As bodies are always intermixing and blending, the chronological present is 'the time of mixtures or blendings' (*LS* 162). Temporalisation, or placing in succession, is 'the very process of blending' bodies (*LS* 162). Notice the similarities with Aristotle here: the extended present measures bodily interaction, as Aristotelian time measures of bodily motion. The extensiveness of bodies transfers to the extensiveness of time. As bodies continuously expand and contract, the extension of the present also expands and contracts, expanding out to the present day, month, year, decade out until it encompasses the 'greatest present, the divine present ... the great mixture, the unity of corporeal causes among themselves' (*LS* 163). Every present is somewhat corporeal in that each is relative to bodies, and since every body is mixed with others, at smaller and larger scales, 'each present refers to a relatively more vast present', expanding out to 'an absolute movement proper to the most vast of presents' (*LS* 163). There is thus a movement of expansion and contraction of bodies intermixing in depth in order to cycle all presents and bodies in a single 'play of cosmic periods' (*LS* 163).

Expanding outwards from some extended present to the entire cosmological present is straightforward because the finitude of the Stoic cosmos offers a definitive measurement of corporeal interaction: bodily extension. Contracting down from any relative present or body, however, entails a deeper problem, one deriving from the Stoics' principle of a corporeal continuum that we saw in Part I: bodies can be subdivided infinitely. As we divide, corporeality vanishes because there is no minimal finite extension, such as a temporal atom. In Stoicism, the ground of corporeality slips away without the support of a fixed ground. The fundamental trouble of the present is a 'ground that overthrows and subverts [*subvertit*] all measure, a becoming-mad of depths, which slips away from the present' (*LS* 163). At the core of corporeality is ground that is not grounded, 'a groundlessness (*un sans fond*) in which original Nature resides in its chaos' (*DR* 243). Think of Deleuze's 'universal *ungrounding* [*l'universel effondement*]', often connected to the eternal return (*DR* 67, 91, 194, 202, 230). At their limits, bodies blend together, forming into a corporeal cesspool of apersonal and unindividuated depths where it is impossible to cleanly distinguish one body from others. For imagery, recall the infant's amorphous, pudgy, soft mass of a body from 'The Shell A'. This is precisely what we mean by the language of 'depth'. At the base of bodies is a deep cavern, but beyond that there is another cavernous depth, and another beyond that, and another ad infinitum. There is 'always another [cave] in which to hide' (*DR* 67). These endless cavernous depths contract the present to a point at which a present extension disappears. Chronos, the time of individuated beings, is subverted by a 'becoming' below. Each extensive measurement contains a 'pure and measureless becoming of qualities [that] threatens the order of qualified bodies from within' (*LS* 164). The unlimitedness of past and the future are unleashed; they 'take their revenge, in one and the same abyss which threatens the present and everything that exists' (*LS* 164). Hence the paradox of the present.

The measureless becoming within extensive bodies is thus always threatening. The present is real, but barely. Deleuze here points to the second deduction of Plato's *Parmenides*. Plato writes: 'But if nothing comes to be can *sidestep* the now, whenever a things *is* at this point, it always stops its coming-to-be and then is whatever it may have come to be.'[24] The becoming within seems 'to *sidestep* the present' (*LS* 164; emphasis added). But the becoming cannot leap over this now because the internal subversion of the present can only be expressed *in* the present. The revenge of the past and future on the present can only occur *now* because there is no other time at which the past and future can subsist. Thus the present is the articulation of a crack in time, or as Deleuze puts it, 'Chronos has become a deep break' (*LS* 164). Hence the 'adventures of the present' (*LS* 164).

The Now and the Instant

We present articulates two distinct yet mutually inclusive senses: chronos presents 'the now' and aion expresses the 'instant'. The now is the present of 'incorporation'; the 'instant' is the 'present of the pure operation' (*LS* 168). The now is the time of actualisation and subversion; the instant is 'the pure perverse "moment"' (*LS* 168). The two senses of the present are mutually necessitating because aion enacts the counter-actualisation that sustains the achronological present (instant) of the measureless depths from overturning the chronological present (now) of measured extension, and keeps the latter from being confused with the former. Since that might not be very clear, let us detail the two senses of the present in Deleuze's Stoicism.

On the one hand, there is the present of chronos: the now. But in chronos Deleuze distinguishes the two opposed presents: 'good chronos' and 'bad chronos' (*LS* 164). Good chronos is 'the variable and measured present' belonging to extended bodies interacting in states of affairs, expanding out to the entire face of the universe (*LS* 168). This is the 'time of actualisation', the actual present in which individuated bodies and souls exist and are discretely measured (*LS* 168). The temporal measurement of good chronos is succession, as in Aristotle: the number of before and after. Beneath good chronos is bad chronos: the 'measureless or dislocated present' glimpsed when we infinitely divide the extension of corporeal presents to a point at which bodies and extensive measurement disappears into a corporeal cesspool (*LS* 168). Without measurably individuated bodies, succession swirls and vanishes into measureless depths. This is the 'time of depth and subversion', when the threat of the groundless shatters the worldly states of affairs into infinite shards (*LS* 168). The clear succession of good chronos descends into the chaos of bad chronos.

What Deleuze calls a 'shift of orientation' from good chronos to bad chronos implies a non-chronological time that is completely different: aion (*LS* 165). The present of aion is necessary for keeping the good chronos and bad chronos conjoined *and* disjoined, as Deleuze argues: 'there *must* be a third' sense of time 'pertaining to aion' (*LS* 168; emphasis added). Aion is necessary because it prevents the measured, actualised, extensive present from collapsing into the measureless, subverting, chaotic depths below. Put differently, the 'third' sense of the present, aion, is the surface between the chronological cosmos and the achronological chaosmos.

While it seems that aion cannot be present, since time infinitely subdivides in opposed directions, this is only because the aionic present cannot be actualised. Deleuze compares this to the distinction from Plato's *Parmenides*, more specifically, the second deduction and the subsequent appendix to the first two deductions.[25] Following Parmenides, Deleuze opposes the 'present' or 'now' of chronos to the 'the instant' of aion (LS 168). First, 'the now' (νῦν). Near the end of Parmenides' second deduction, we see 'coming-to-be' constantly threatening the being of 'the now', which eventually leads to the paradox of becoming that Deleuze uses to explain Alice's simultaneous growing and shrinking.[26] Parmenides and the young Socrates are uncomfortable with the tension between the being of the Parmenidean 'one' and coming-to-be. '[T]he now is always present to the one throughout its being ... Therefore the one always both is and comes to be older and younger than itself.'[27]

Trying to allay this tension, Parmenides opposes 'the now' to 'the instant' (ἐξαίφνης) in a curious conversation:

> Is there, then, this queer thing (τὸ ἄτοπον τοῦτο) in which it might be, just when it changes? – What queer thing? – The instant (ἐξαίφνης) ... [which] lurks between motion and rest – being in no time at all – and to it and from it the moving thing changes to resting and the resting thing changes to moving ... But in changing, it changes in an instant, and when it changes, it would be in no time at all, and just then it would be neither in motion nor at rest.[28]

The instant, Parmenides suggests, is a queer thing because it is both in time but has no temporal extension. The Greek word for 'queer' is ἄτοπον, *atopon*, which means 'out of place, strange, paradoxical, unnatural'. Its connotes homelessness, without place, dislocation. 'Plato rightly said that the instant is ἄτοπον, without a place,' notes Deleuze (*LS* 166). There is no place for temporal 'change' (μεταβάλλω) because it is no ordinary change, such as we see in locomotion, alteration or growth. Instead, the change is *instantaneous*, an infinitely subdividing second. The Greek word for 'instant' is ἐξαίφνης, an adverb meaning 'all of a sudden'. Plato uses ἐξαίφνης in *Gorgias* when talking of 'the moment of death' (ἐξαίφνης ἀποθανόντος), the instant of the infinitive 'to die', which never occurs in time.[29] It 'is the instant which perverts the present into insisting future and past' (*LS* 165). As inter-perversion is the order of aion; the instant is the present of aion. The is why, Goldschmidt claims, the 'theory of Chrysippus had attributed the same *incorporeality* (and irreality) to infinite time and to the mathematical instant, the one and the other being susceptible of division to infinity' (*SS* 194). Deleuze characterises the instant with several familiar terms – 'the paradoxical element or the aleatory point, the nonsense of the surface and the quasi-cause' – all of which describe the perversity of the incorporeal surface (*LS* 166).

A Twisted Genealogy

While Deleuze says a great deal about the chronos–aion distinction, we should not simply assume it actually is in Stoic texts, especially since Deleuze is unashamed about his penchant for 'buggery' and proclaimed, perhaps in a provoking mood, that 'it's irrelevant whether that's what [an author] actually intended'.[30] At the same time, Deleuze was rarely unfaithful in his encounters. Although Deleuze's reading might seem, to the authors themselves, 'monstrous . . . [i]t was really important to for [Deleuze's readings] to be his [the author's] own child, because the author had to actually say all I had him saying'.[31]

As we said above, Deleuze finds the chronos–aion distinction in Goldschmidt. 'Among the commentators of Stoic thought,' writes Deleuze, 'Victor Goldschmidt in particular has analyzed the coexistence of these two conceptions of time: the first, of variable presents; the second, of unlimited subdivision into past and future' (*LS* 340n.3). We should thus pose the same question to Goldschmidt. Did Stoics themselves distinguish two faces of time? And even if they did, how important was it to Stoic theory as a whole? To answer these questions, let us start with genealogies of aion and chronos.

The history of aion is complicated. The *Iliad* uses aion three times, each time referring to the force of life or vitality.[32] Heraclitus uses aion when he writes: 'A lifetime [αἰών] is a child playing, playing checkers.'[33] Here aion can be translated as 'lifetime, eternity, history, time', connoting both the time of a human life and unlimited, eternal time. Empedocles, too, uses aion in a way that suggests 'life', again referring to either an individual life or the life of the whole cosmos.[34] When Plato uses aion in his *Timaeus*, however, he means something cosmological. According to Helena Keizer, author of *Life, Time, Eternity: A Study of AIΩN in Greek Literature and Philosophy*, 'in the *Timaeus* Plato made aion mean "eternity" as opposed to "time" (*chronos*). But what Plato meant by this "eternity" is a matter of dispute.'[35] In the *Timaeus*, Keizer distinguishes ἀίδιος (37d3) and αἰῶνος (37d3), although most scholars translate both as 'eternity'.[36] Pre-Socratics, Homer and Hesiod use ἀίδιος to mean 'everlasting', often in reference to the gods. There are two uses of the adjective αἰῶνος in the *Timaeus*: 'the one applies to the model (37d3), the other to the copy (37d7)', suggesting that aion refers to both eternal forms and temporary objects.[37] The point is that Plato used aion in order to convey a concept of life that refers 'to the "eternal" continuity of the cosmos' as a model, and to material things as reflections of that model.[38] Aristotle's use of aion in *On the Parts of Animals* distinguishes between beings that are 'ungenerated and imperishable throughout all time [αἰών], but others partake in generation and perishing'.[39] In *On the Heavens*, when Aristotle speaks of the complete life of the whole universe, Keizer notices that Aristotle includes an etymology: aion is a conjunction of 'ἀεί' ('always') plus ὀν ('being') = 'always being'.[40] 'Always being' is a divine property, suggesting that aion connotes divinity and immortality. For Aristotle, aion does mean 'endless' but the 'completeness' of a fully actualised god.

The history of chronos is more straightforward. According to Hesiod's *Theogony*, Cronus is the personification of time in early mythical cosmologies, the leader of the Titans. Later in Empedocles and Anaximander, Chronos was de-personified, while the Pythagoreans saw chronos as akin to the extra-cosmic medium that the cosmos, as a living, breathing creature, inhales.[41] When cosmos inhales, the limited cosmos and the unlimited extra-cosmos interact, which is how the Pythagoreans reduce chronos to a number (ἀριθμός): the length of a cosmological breath. As we know, Plato's *Timaeus* opposes the worldly chronos to the eternal aion, such that the former is the moving image of the latter, and Aristotle's *Physics* makes chronos the number of motion with respect to before and after.

Taken together, chronos and aion form a twisted genealogy. As A. J. Festugière shows in 'Le sens philosophique du mot *Aion*', the two terms are repeatedly switched, swapped, expanded and contracted.[42] While aion used to mean the lifetime of an individual thing, it later came to mean the abstract present of an eternal life. Almost inversely, chronos went from meaning the time of a complete astronomical cycle to the extensive measurement of a corporeal change or motion.

Deleuze's Stoicism highlights one sinuous strand of this twisted genealogy, beginning with Heraclitus' 'ever-living fire' (πῦρ ἀείζωον). Heraclitus links, in a single concept, fire (πῦρ, *pyr*), life (ζωή, *zoé*) and eternity (ἀεί, *aei*).[43] A little later, the Stoics sidestep Plato and Aristotle in order to refresh the Heraclitean fire and construct their own account of the conflagration of the eternal return, thus leaning towards the sense of aion that Goldschmidt and Deleuze attribute to Stoicism. Much later, Nietzsche seizes this genealogical strand.

The Albumen A: Time

According to Philippe Mengue, aion is 'Nietzschean in inspiration and destination, but its source comes from the Greeks'.[44] In *Philosophy in the Tragic Age of the Greeks*, Nietzsche, too, digs beneath Plato and Aristotle, back to Heraclitus, in order to recover a sense of aion that is beyond the completeness, permanence, or static sense of an immortal being. 'Nietzsche's Heraclitus', writes Ned Luckacher, 'reopens the question of time's relation to Being' so that eternality applies to becoming.[45] Nietzsche initiates what we call a perversion: detaching eternality from static being and attaching it to becoming, or aion turned inside out.

Chronos and Aion in Stoicism

We can now ask: did the Stoics really distinguish between chronos and aion and was it as important for as it is for Goldschmidt and Deleuze? To be fair, reading the early Stoics' extant passages concerning time, it is hard to find 'aion' used in the Goldschmidtian and Deleuzian way. When Keizer searched through the 'Chrysippus' heading in von Arnim's *Stoicorum Veterum Fragmenta*, she only found six instances of aion, none of which seemed to function as 'an object of philosophical reflection, either as a term or a concept'.[46] Since questions of textual and conceptual infidelity thus persist, we must see if Deleuze is faithful in his buggery.

Although the early Stoics did not seem to make much of a technical distinction between two faces of time, Goldschmidt argues that the early Stoics' 'negligence of terminology' is 'repaired by Marcus Aurelius' because the *Mediations*, written centuries after Zeno, uses aion in the technical sense (*SS* 39). On Keizer's count, 'aion occurs 22 times (never in the plural)' in Marcus, and is most often linked with 'infinite' (ἀπειρία) or 'infinity' (ἄπειρος).[47] For example, 'the void of infinite time [ἀπείρου Αἰῶνος] on this side of us and on that ... For the whole earth is but a point [στιγμή], and how tiny a corner of it is this place of our sojourning.'[48] Here aion is closely associated with the unlimitedness or infinity of ἀπείρου, especially when Marcus strives to convey the infinitesimal significance of human life compared to the infinite breadth of the cosmos. Aion, in the *Meditations*, is time that overwhelms and dwarfs us: 'As a river consisting of all things that come into being, aye, a rushing torrent, is Time [αἰών]. No sooner is a thing sighted than it is carried past, and lo, another is passing, and it too will be carried away.'[49]

However, John Sellars warns, Goldschmidt is possibly unjustified in his selection of the passages he cites.⁵⁰ Both Keizer and Sellars note two passages in Marcus' *Meditations* in which 'ἄπειρος αἰών' seems interchangeable with 'ἄπειρος χρόνος', suggesting that ἄπειρος is not exclusively tied to aion. In Book II, Marcus writes: it 'must be remembered ... that all things from time everlasting have been cast in the same mold and repeated cycle after cycle, and so it makes no difference whether a man see the same things recur through a hundred years or two hundred, or through eternity [ἀπείρου χρόνῳ]'. In Book X, Marcus writes: 'For thus shall you habitually look upon human things as mere smoke and nothingness; and more than ever so, if you think to yourself what has once changed will exist no more through eternity [ἀπείρου χρόνῳ].'⁵¹ If Goldschmidt and Deleuze's claim about two different faces of time in Stoicism is based on a merely terminological distinction, the argument appears to lack of textual support.⁵²

Still, there is clearly a conceptual difference that corresponds, perhaps inexactly, to a terminological difference. Marcus usually uses chronos to speak of time as quantified extension, such as some discrete present or the span of a human life.⁵³ Aion, by contrast, 'is not used by Marcus for a human life(time) but exclusively for time on the cosmic scale'.⁵⁴ As Marcus writes: 'Fluxes and changes perpetually renew the cosmos, just as the unbroken march of time [Κρόνον] makes ever new the infinity of ages [ἄπειρον αἰῶνα].'⁵⁵ Here, chronos marks a certain extension of lived time, while aion stretches out infinitely in both directions. As Deleuze writes, 'aion is smaller than the smallest subdivision of chronos, but it is also greater than the greatest divisor of chronos, namely, the entire cycle' of the eternal return (*LS* 63–4). Marcus seems to say this, too: 'all the present of time [Κρόνον] [is] a point [Στιγμὴ] in Eternity [Αἰῶνος]'.⁵⁶

It should be clear that Stoic eternity is not an Aristotelian eternity in so far as it lacks the 'completeness' that comes from a Τέλος.⁵⁷ 'Stoic eternity', Goldschmidt notes, 'remains an inconsistent and infinite flux' (*SS* 189). It is, instead, incomplete and unlimited, the infinite speeding away in opposed directions simultaneously. To see why, consider the phrase Marcus uses when speaking of the movement of the cosmos: ἐξ αἰῶος εἰς αἰῶνα.⁵⁸ While we could translate this as 'year after year' or 'eons and eons', such translations obscure the grammatical nuances of the two Greek expressions – *ex aionos* and *eis aiona* – that describe aion as the infinite cycle of the eternal return, the endless line stretching out in both directions, and the singular point subsisting in the middle of it: the instant. From the singular point of view of the instant, time approaches *out of* (*ex*) the infinite past and stretches out *into* (*eis*) the infinite future. In short, from a point a line stretches out in two senses/directions. Borrowing a diagrammatic idea from Keizer, we get:

⟶ *ex aionos* ⟶ instant ⟶ *eis aionos* ⟶

In both directions, 'infinity' (*to apeiron*) and aion are identical. As Marcus writes: 'the yawning abyss of time [ἀιῶνος] behind you, and before you the other infinity to come [ἀπείρου]'.[59] Aion is the 'abyss' that spreads out on both sides of the instant form infinite time.

In sum, it remains slightly unclear whether or not chronos and aion functioned exactly as the technical terms that Goldschmidt and, even more so, Deleuze define them as; this is why Sellers rightfully challenges Goldschmidt's appeal to Marcus' unclear use of time in his *Meditations*. As the standard story goes, the Roman Marcus and his Stoic teachers were more invested in action and other moral matters than sorting out the technicalities of Stoic physics and logic. Marcus was mostly concerned with constructing an account of time that allowed him to live and act as a Stoic While he engaged the accounts of time given by Zeno, Chrysippus and others in order to make his case, he never mentions the Stoic masters by name. It is not clear why he passes over his Stoic predecessors in silence, although it seems, Rist points out, that the 'fundamental interrelationship of ethics and physics has eluded him'.[60]

Our claim is that, although we do not find in Marcus as clean a *terminological* distinction between chronos and aion as Goldschmidt sees, this does not necessarily mean that there was not a persistent and consistent *conceptual* distinction in the Stoic system. After all, Goldschmidt was highly celebrated by some of the most influential and venerated French scholars of the history of philosophy, such as Pierre Vidal-Naquet, for his 'overwhelming erudition, attachment to resolving problems in detail, research of subtle or exerted influences, of the courses of evolution' of a system.[61] According to Vidal-Naquet, the precision and vigilance of Goldschmidt's scholarship appears in his attention to the conceptual structuralism of a philosophical system.[62] In his *Dialogues de Platon*, for example, Goldschmidt 'strives to compare what Plato says ... of his [dialectical] method and what this dialectic is in the movement itself of the dialogues'.[63] Goldschmidt gives the highest attention to the details of a philosophical system, even when a philosopher does not directly state these details, and this is especially true of the Stoics on time. Recall the title of Goldschmidt's book: *Le Système stoïcien et l'idée de temps*. The point is that Goldschmidt (and thus Deleuze's) arguments rely more on the systematic coherence of the Stoic theory of time, less on whether or not Stoic writings explicitly referred to terms 'chronos' and 'aion'.

The Greatness of Stoic Thought

Even given the Stoic system and the idea of time, scholars disagree on how to interpret chronos and aion. Some attempt to explain away the difficulties by either affirming and rejecting one of the faces of time or blending them together; others conclude that the Stoic theory of time is hopeless, and thus ignore it completely.[64] Some, though, are more sympathetic, even if not in awe of the greatness of Stoic. John Rist, for example, argues that 'there are three stages of thought within the Stoic school on the concept of time': Zeno, Chrysippus and Marcus Aurelius.[65] Rist's point is that subsequent views of time were not meant to replace previous views but are rather 'elaborations based on an original insight'.[66] We argue that this original insight is what leads Deleuze to claim not only that there two faces of time but that they are both necessary, however irreconcilable they may initially seem.

Beyond the pre-Socratics, Platonists and Aristotelians, the Stoics develop an account of time as an incorporeal surface composed by two unequal and divergent sides, and it is this very divergence that brings them together. Pay close attention to Deleuze's words:

> time must be grasped twice, in two *complementary though mutually exclusive* fashions. First, it must be grasped entirely as the living present in bodies that act and are acted upon. Second, it must be grasped entirely as an entity infinitely divisible into past and future, and into the incorporeal effects that result from bodies, their actions and passions. Only the present exists in time and gathers together or absorbs the past and future. But only the past and future inhere in time and divide each present infinitely. These are not three successive dimensions, but two *simultaneous readings* of time. (LS 5; emphases added)

Since the three dimensions of time – past, present, future – are 'not at all three parts of a single temporality', Deleuze claims, the task is to determine how these three dimensions entail '*two readings of time*' (LS 61; emphases added). The argument rests on one claim: the two faces of time are complementary *and* mutually exclusive.

The Albumen A: Time

'The *greatness of Stoic thought*', Deleuze writes, 'is to show at once the *necessity* of these two readings *and* their reciprocal exclusion' (*LS* 61; emphases added). They can neither be torn apart nor lumped together; they converge in their divergence and diverge in their convergence. Aion and chronos are 'complete and [yet] exclude the other' in so far as they are '*necessary*', '*complementary* [and] *simultaneous*' (*LS* 61, 5; emphasis original). While these two readings are incompatible from the perspective of formal logic of corporeality, they are compatible according to a transcendental logic of incorporeals. Chronos and aion form the two faces of one incorporeal surface: *intensive aion* and *extensive chronos*. Chronos faces bodies and their cosmological states of affairs; aion faces away from the cosmos, towards the chaosmic depths.

To see how, consider Sellars's emphasis on κατα πλάτος in the Stobaeus passage cited above. Here it is again: 'no time is present exactly, but it is broadly [*kata platos*] said to be so'.[67] While Long and Sedley translated this as 'broadly', Goldschmidt translates it as: 'extension' [*l'étendue*]' (*SS* 37).[68] When we refer to the chronological present as extended and delimited because it belongs to the living present of existing bodies, time is extensive. From any state of affairs, we can extensively circumscribe a finite measure to the present. From the perspective of aion, however, wherein the present is an infinitely divisible instant, time is intensive. Part of Deleuze's insight is to demonstrate the simultaneous mutual exclusion and co-necessitation of both chronos and aion. Put differently, Deleuze is careful not to sacrifice extensity for intensity, chronos for aion, but to demonstrate their immanent yet differential relation.

Consider the difference between extensive and intensive measurements of time by recasting the same distinction from 'The Yolk A'. An example of extensive measurement of time is one minute, two hours, three days, a human lifetime and so on. If we divide one hour in half, we get two half-hours, a mere metric difference. Since there is no real change in kind between one hour, a half-hour, a quarter of an hour, an eighth of an hour and so on, different extensive measurements are equal and homogenous; they divide without changing the nature of what is being divided (*DR* 237). An intensive measurement of time, by contrast, includes heterogeneous divisions, that is, intensive time divides into singular and ordinary moments. Singular moments are singular or notable in the sense that they mark significant changes, while ordinary instants are the set of relatively unchanged moments in between singular moments. For example, the time during which a person grows increasingly angry is a set of ordinary moments, while a singular moment is the phase of transition into rage. As the intensity of anger increases, ordinary moments converge on the moment when rage explodes, and after this explosion temporal durations diverge. When the rage explodes, everything changes; there is no telling what may happen after then. The key is that intensive time is composed of heterogeneous moments, similar to the way heat is composed of ordinary degrees of hotness and singular degrees (freezing or boiling points). In sum, extensive time (chronos) organises the side of the surface facing bodies, while intensive time (aion) organises the side facing away from bodies.

It is essential to note that chronos and aion, as two complementary though mutually exclusive and simultaneous readings of time, reconfirm the Stoics' perverse materialism. As Goldschmidt writes, in so far as 'Chrysippus gave a materialist interpretation of the divisions of time ... the Stoics did not accept the mathematical inspiration of Pythagorean Platonism' (SS 41). Time, for them, is incorporeal, but it is an incorporeality that arises more from matter than from math. From corporeality, 'extended time ... takes all the reality of which it is capable without however ceasing being an incorporeal' (SS 41). Like space and λεκτα, time accompanies the world but is not a being existing in the world; it subsists as a manner of being. Further, when Chrysippus defines time as 'accompanying the world's motion', we must recall the difference in the Stoic account of eternity. Platonic and Aristotelian motion is circular and eternal, but it is an everlasting and unchanging eternality. The celestial spheres turn endlessly and perfectly. The Stoics, however, have more of a cyclical than a circular sense of the eternality of the cosmos. The cosmos does not turn endlessly and perfectly because everything burns up at the end of each cosmic period. If time accompanies the motion of matter, then it is dependent on matter moving. Stoic eternality is incorporeal yet dependent on bodies. We can, like Deleuze, borrow Nietzsche's word and call this perverse sense of the materially eternal untimely.

The Third Incorporeal

Much of Deleuze's Stoicism seeks to reveal a homologous structure amongst the three incorporeals. So far, we have argued in support of this structural homology as the product of the Deleuze's Stoicism, and we now further motivate our argument.

Deleuze's encounter with Stoicism was greatly shaped by Émile

The Albumen A: Time

Bréhier and Victor Goldschmidt, both of whom identified a homology among the incorporeals. Bréhier writes: finite 'time is in the milieu of infinite time as the [finite] place of the world is in the [infinite] void' (*TI* 55). Citing Bréhier, Goldschmidt claims that the Stoics' account of the present or limited time entails that 'the theory of time is exactly analogous to that of space' (*SS* 39). In the footnote to that claim, Goldschmidt adds that, while 'M. van Straaten formulated some reservations about the 'parallel' between time and space ... it is, according to Arius Didymus' report, already made by Chrysippus' (*SS* 232n.15). As Bréhier and Goldschmidt both see homologous structures among incorporeals, and since Bréhier and Goldschmidt significantly shaped Deleuze's encounter with Stoicism, there is more motivation for seeing this homology in Stoic theory. Recall the diagram from 'The Yolk C':

$$\text{TIME} \begin{array}{c} \text{Aion (infinite)} \\ \hline \text{Chronos (limited)} \end{array}^{69}$$

While Bréhier and Goldschmidt do not explicitly extend this homology to λεκτα, it appears in Deleuze's Stoicism. Connecting time to λεκτα is important because it connects the two faces of λεκτα to the two faces of time.[70] Recall from 'The Shell A' the distinction between infinitive verbs and their conjugated forms. Here is the corresponding diagram:

$$\Lambda\varepsilon\kappa\tau\alpha \begin{array}{c} \text{Infinitive verb (infinite)} \\ \hline \text{Conjugated verb (limited)} \end{array}$$

Aion corresponds to the infinitive verb, and chronos to its conjugations. Since the infinitive does not indicate any specific present, place, person or number, it is non-present, non-localisable, impersonal and indeterminate. Instantaneity is the temporality of infinitives, as aion is a continuous, unlimited instant that infinitely divides, never reaching a determinate extended period of time. By contrast, chronos is a repeating set of discontinuous, limited moments, of determinate nows that correspond to individuated and finite conjugations. In language from 'The Shell A', aion is the time of the static leaping of the instant, and chronos is the time of the dynamic succession of nows. Like the void, the instant or the temporality of the infinitive is infinitely divisible; it 'goes on being divided formally in the double and simultaneously direction of the past and the future' without ever individuating into a distinct conjugated form (*LS* 185). Deleuze calls aion the 'form of an *undetermined infinitive*, without person, without present, without any diversity of voice. It is poetry itself. As it expresses in language all events in one, the infinitive verb expresses the event of language' (*LS* 185; emphasis added).

As each type of incorporeal forms a surface that cloaks physical depths, the temporality of infinitives follows the transcendental logic of relations among incorporeals themselves, which Deleuze calls 'the interiority of language' and the 'communication of events among themselves' (*LS* 185). Infinitives express events, such as 'to green' or 'to cut', which are incarnated in bodies. When a tree grows leaves and turns green, it incarnates the infinitive 'to green'.[71] There is an essential relation between grammar and temporality. Bréhier puts it perfectly: 'the Stoics had made a profound remark, which, speaking of grammar, out to have more than grammatical import; it is that time is only directly applied to verbs, that is to say, to predicates that signify for them incorporeal events. Time thus has no contact with the true being of things' (*TI* 59).

Conclusion: The Instant of the Act

To conclude, let us entertain what some call an objection to the Stoic theory of time. Rist puts it thus: 'although the world begins and ends at particular points, in a sense, these points are by no means more fixed than any other points on the cosmic cycle'.[72] If the conflagration does not occur in time, if it is atemporal, then beginning and end converge on a limit, and this limit could be anywhere. To answer this objection, we connect physics to ethics via time.[73] *We* are the limit that marks the beginning and end of time. At every instant, we express the fracture in the temporal flow. We form the limit with our actions. This limit, this cut, this crack in the surface of time, is precisely the site of the act. The instant is the temporality of the act.

The instant, however, is never present, so the time for acting never arrives. The act occurs, it is real, but it never exists here and now. As Rist puts it, 'the present is *real*, even if it is not strictly speaking a momentary "now"'.[74] The instant is the reality of the present in so far as it is a subsistent, infinitely subdivisible point moving along an infinitely long line stretching across a double-sided surface. The act never shows up; it *is* never there. The act always has been or will be, and thus subsists in the past or future. At the same time, it subsists as an asymptotic threshold, except that it is located not at the far end of time but at time's heart: the instant.

Paradoxically, it is *this very impossibility of acting that calls us to action*. The Stoic imperative is thus borderline impossible (or possible only at the border): we must act now even though the decision to act is always too late or too early. The past and the future infinitely contract onto a singular point that is never fully available, and yet, despite this lack of available time, we must act, and necessarily so. The act is the ethical formulation of the event. 'Albumen B' will articulate how the act and the event are impossible yet imperative.

Notes

1. Goldschmidt does not call them 'faces', although the language is no unfaithful to the distinction he draws.
2. Interestingly, Aristotle does not give an argument as to why the investigation of time belongs to physics, although he provides arguments for why motion, infinity, place and void belong to physics.
3. Most commentators seem befuddled by considering time an ethical question. For example, Rist is unsure where to place Stoic theory of time in relation to Plato and Aristotle (J. M. Rist, *Stoic Philosophy* (Cambridge: Cambridge University Press, 1977), 273–88), while Tzamalikos argues that it is 'independent of Aristotle or Plato.' Panayiotis Tzamalikos, 'Origen and the Stoic View of Time', *Journal of the History of Ideas* 52.4 (October–December 1991): 535–61, at 537.
4. Tzamalikos, 'Origen and the Stoic View of Time', 538.
5. Aristotle, *Physics*, IV.11, 219b1.
6. Aristotle, *Physics*, IV.11, 219b7–9.
7. For fine distinctions among these translations, see Julia Annas, 'Aristotle, Number and Time', *The Philosophical Quarterly* 25.99 (April 1975): 97–113.
8. *SVF* 1.26, 11–14; emphasis added.
9. *SVF* 1.26, 14–15.
10. Philip Turetzky, *Time* (London: Routledge, 1998), 38.
11. *SVF* I.93.
12. Tzamalikos, 'Origen and the Stoic View of Time', 536. Rist, *Stoic Philosophy*, 278.
13. Aristotle, *Physics*, 223a22.
14. Plato, *Timaeus*, 37d.
15. Aristotle, *Physics*, 223b.
16. Simplicius, *Simplicius on Aristotle's Physics 6*, 934.23–30 Diels.
17. *SVF* 1.142.2–6. Also see *SVF* 1.106.11–13.

18. Turetzky, *Time*, 39.
19. Rist, *Stoic Philosophy*, 277.
20. Borges, *Collected Fictions*, trans. Andrew Hurley (New York: Penguin Books, 1999), 105.
21. SVF 2.509; emphasis added.
22. Deleuze repeats this idea throughout *Logic of Sense*, such as: 'subdivide each present, ad infinitum, however small it may be, stretching it out over their empty line' (*LS* 62).
23. Rist, *Stoic Philosophy*, 278.
24. Plato, *Parmenides*, 152c–d; emphasis added.
25. Although Deleuze actual mentions 'the second and the third hypothesis of *Parmenides*', we argue that the third deduction does not really begin until 157c. Deleuze thus overlooks the difference the section between the second and third deductions.
26. See *LS* 'First Series'.
27. Plato, *Parmenides*, 152d–e.
28. Ibid. 156d–e.
29. Plato, *Gorgias*, 523e.
30. Gilles Deleuze, *Negotiations* (1995), trans. Martin Joughin (New York: Columbia University Press, 1990), 6.
31. Ibid. 5–6.
32. Homer, *Iliad*, 16.453, 19.27, 5.585.
33. Patricia Curd (ed.), *A Presocratics Reader: Selected Fragments and Testimonia*, trans. Richard D. McKirahan (Indianapolis: Hackett Publishing Company, 2011), 52.
34. Keizer, *Life, Time, Eternity*, 60.
35. Ibid. 64.
36. Ibid. 70.
37. Ibid. 71.
38. Ibid. 80.
39. Aristotle, *On the Parts of Animals*, 644b22–4.
40. Aristotle, *On the Heavens*, 279a27; Keizer, *Life, Time, Eternity*, 89.
41. Peters, *Greek Philosophical Terms*, 31.
42. A. J. Festugière, *Études de philosophique grecque* (Paris: J. Vrin, 1972), 254–72.
43. Curd (ed.), *A Presocratics Reader*, 45.
44. Robert Sasso and Arnaud Villani, *Le Vocabulaire de Gilles Deleuze* (Paris: Librairie philosophique J. Vrin, 2003), 41.
45. Ned Lukacher, *Time-Fetishes: The Secret History of Eternal Recurrence* (Durham: Duke University Press Books, 1999), 9.
46. Helena Maria Keizer, *Life, Time, Eternity: A Study of AIΩN in Greek Literature and Philosophy, the Septuagint and Philo* (Heleen M. Keizer, 2010), 91n.123.

The Albumen A: Time

47. Keizer, *Life, Time, Eternity*, 95n.141. Sellars also points to this (*'Aiôn and Chronos*: Deleuze and the Stoic Theory of Time', *Collapse* 3 (2007): 177–205, at 17).
48. Marcus Aurelius, *Meditations*, IV.3.
49. Ibid. IV.43.
50. Sellars, *'Aiôn and Chronos'*.
51. Marcus Aurelius, *Meditations*, X.31.
52. Pierre Hadot offers a similar critique of Goldschmidt (Pierre Hadot, *The Inner Citadel: The* Meditations *of Marcus Aurelius*, trans. Michael Chase (Cambridge, MA: Harvard University Press, 2001), 131–7). John Sellars has done the gritty work of detailing all the twenty-one instances of aion and thirty-one instances of chronos in the *Meditations* (*'Aiôn and Chronos'*, 18n.43).
53. Marcus Aurelius, *Meditations*, trans. R. Haines (Cambridge, MA: Harvard University Press, 1916), II.14.
54. Keizer, *Life, Time, Eternity*, 95. Rist agrees: 'Marcus uses the word *aion* to denote infinite or boundless time, and he is willing to call each world-cycle a particular *aion*.' Rist, *Stoic Philosophy*, 284.
55. Marcus Aurelius, *Meditations*, VI.15.
56. Ibid. VI.36.
57. As we will see in 'Albumen C', Stoicsm is ateleological (providence without teleology).
58. Marcus Aurelius, *Meditations*, IX.28.
59. Ibid. IV.50; translation modified.
60. Rist, *Stoic Philosophy*, 288.
61. Pierre Vidal-Naquet, 'La mort du professeur Victor Goldschmidt de Platon à Rousseau: l'analyste opiniâtre de systèmes', *Le Monde* (10 December 1981).
62. Ibid.
63. Ibid.
64. As, for example, John Francis Callahan does. Callahan, *Four Views of Time in Ancient Philosophy* (Cambridge, MA: Harvard University Press, 1948).
65. Rist, *Stoic Philosophy*, 273.
66. Ibid.
67. *SVF* 1.105.13–18.
68. Sellars also cites the various ways other Stoic scholars have translated this phrase, including Victor Goldschmidt and Pierre Hadot. Sellars, *'Aiôn and Chronos'*, 15.
69. *SS* 39.
70. Rist also sees a close connection to verbs and time. Rist, *Stoic Philosophy*, 280–1.
71. In her incredible study of grammar in antiquity, Frédérique defends the position that attributes are expressed through infinitives, while

conjugated forms signify the determination of attribution to specific bodies. Ildefonse, *La Naissance de la grammaire*, 195, 199.
72. Rist, *Stoic Philosophy*, 281.
73. Rist differs from Goldschmidt on this point: 'For Zeno and Chrysippus time is viewed primarily as a problem in physics ... Time does not intrude upon the moral sphere. With Marcus the position is quite different. Time, the ever-changing flux, is itself a moral problem.' Rist, *Stoic Philosophy*, 287.
74. Ibid. 282.

8

The Albumen B: The Act

> At bottom, these things are simultaneously free and unfree. It is a twilight zone where necessity and humor interpenetrate ... And this consciousness grows, the nearer comes the time when it acts, when it turns to deed, when it throws off the fetters.
> Friedrich Theodore Vischer, quoted in Walter Benjamin,
> *The Arcades Project*[1]

Introduction: The Event of Death

Let us start 'Albumen B' with two acts – two deaths, in fact. First, the day Seneca died.[2] In 64 CE Seneca was caught up in the Pisonian conspiracy, which was 'a plot to kill Nero and replace him with the ringleader, C. Calpurnius Piso'.[3] Although Seneca was most likely not involved, since his nephew Lucan was, Nero thus took the opportunity to eliminate his old advisor once and for all, and so ordered Seneca to commit suicide. Rather than complain, Seneca affirmed his fate, found a blade, and cut an artery on his arm in order to bleed to death. But since he was old and frail his arteries were weak. Death would not be easy for Seneca. So he cut the arteries first on top of his legs and then behind his knees, yet even this did not kill him. Eventually, mirroring Socrates' famous death scene, Seneca asked for the hemlock, revealing yet more Stoic perversion: hemlock was insufficient for death. Perhaps finally realising that willing was insufficient, Seneca gave himself over to others: 'he was then lifted into a bath, suffocated by the vapour, and cremated without ceremony'.[4] The second death is the suicide of Gilles Deleuze. On Saturday, 5 November 1995, after years of pain and suffering, Deleuze leapt from the window of his third-floor apartment on avenue Niel in Paris's seventeenth arrondissement. The effects of a lifelong respiratory illness, a tracheotomy, and repeated attacks of suffocation, which left him 'chained like a dog' to an oxygen machine, had exhausted Deleuze.[5] In those last few months, he could barely speak, or even hold a pen. Defenestration was the evental form of his death.[6]

We begin with these two death events because of the importance of the act of dying for Deleuze and for Stoicism: for Deleuze, death is the form of the event par excellence, and for the Stoics, death is the ideal form of the act. Our task is to connect the event to the act. To make this connection, we return to the 'Stoic two methods [of interpretation] and two moral attitudes' that Deleuze found in Goldschmidt (*LS* 340n.3). Goldschmidt 'discerns two main methods of interpretations': (1) 'divination' or 'the interpretation of the cosmic scale' and (2) 'the use of representations' (SS 80, 79, 79). These two methods correspond to two moral attitudes: the cosmological perspective and the singular perspective. Both of these pairs have a double sense, that is, they move in opposite directions through which they gather together, in a single glance, a whole causal composition. Both methods and attitudes are necessary, complementary and opposed, or what Deleuze calls 'bipolarity' (*LS* 144). We now consider the 'two poles between which the Stoic ethics oscillates' in order to harness the power of this oscillation (*LS* 144). The Stoic act and the event is at the relay point of this oscillation. As we will see, the act and the event are two sides of the same object, viewed from different sides of that double-sided Stoic surface. We can formulate a table:

	Method of interpretation	Moral attitude	Ethical task
Ethics	Divination	Cosmic Perspective	Counter-Actualisation
	Usage of Representation	Singular Perspective	Actualisation

To understand what an 'act' is for the Stoics, we will consider the ideal actor: the Stoic sage. Deleuze points to the surrealist poet Joe Bousquet as the best example of the Stoic sage, especially in so far as Bousquet demonstrates the complementarity of the act and the corresponding counter-actualisation. After articulating what Deleuze might say about how to make oneself a Stoic, we conclude with a consideration of a Stoic–Nietzschean principle – love of fate, *amor fati* – in so far as it conveys an affirmative ethics that entails the doctrine of eternal recurrence, which is the topic of 'Albumen C'.

Divination

Deleuze follows Goldschmidt's account of Stoic divination, the first method of interpretation. 'The first [method]', writes Goldschmidt,

The Albumen B: The Act

'elevates, as much as humans are able, to a vision of all [*ensemble*] events such as, in all rigor, is reserved for God' (*SS* 79). Deleuze echoes Goldschmidt: it is 'a question of participating to the greatest possible extent in a divine vision' (*LS* 144). For both, divination is the art of interpreting the causal organisation of bodies, in so far as they are all part of one order of fate, so as to cultivate the cosmological perspective.

Divination is considered a method of interpretation because it is the art of reading the world as a collection of signs (*signum*, σημεῖον). This involves interpreting the deterministic chain of corporeal causes in order to reveal the co-fated organisation among incorporeal events twisting through the cosmos. Goldschmidt quotes Cicero's *De Divinatione* at length:

> since all things happen by Fate [*fato*], if there were a person whose soul could discern the links that join each cause with every other cause, then surely one would never be mistaken in any prediction one might make. For one who knows the causes of future events necessarily knows what every future event will be. But since such knowledge is possible only to a god, it is left to humans to presage the future by means of certain *signs* [*signis*] which indicate what will follow them. Things which are to be do not suddenly spring into existence, but the evolution of time is like the *unwinding of a cable* [*rudentis explicatio*]: it creates nothing new and only unfolds [*replicantis*] each event in its order. This connexion between cause and effect is obvious to . . . those who know the course of events by the *observation of signs*. They may not discern the causes themselves, yet they do *discern the signs*.[7]

Both Goldschmidt and Deleuze echo Cicero's imagery of causal chains of bodies as the 'unwinding of a cable' that 'unfolds' body to body, binding the world in a single book.[8] *Rudentis* denotes a rope, cord or chain, as in the rigging of a ship or engine of war, what sailors call a 'halyard', the line that hoists a ladder, sail or flag. The imagery is intended to convey the notion that all bodies are folded together into a singular linear story, which is what interpretation reveals. Prior to grasping this story of unified causality, it can seem so complexly knotted that it is difficult to discern how it all hangs together, and divination is a method for unfolding that complexity so that a single causal chain is legible.

This method of interpretation is possible, Cicero elsewhere states, because 'certain signs precede certain events'.[9] What are signs? Signs are not simply flayed animal entrails but the expressions that an event attributes to bodies. In short, signs are attributes or λεκτα.

Reading signs off of bodies allows the Stoics to discern the relationship among incorporeal events themselves. As Deleuze puts it, divinatory interpretation is an act of 'cutting into the thickness, of carving out surfaces, of orienting them, of increasing and multiplying them in order to follow out the tracing of lines and of incisions inscribed on them' (*LS* 143). Divination can begin *now*, with the present sign because the present contains the past and future. This is, according to Deleuze, is '[o]ne of the great strengths of Stoicism' (*DR* 76). The Stoics show

> that every sign is a sign of the present ... in which past and future are precisely only dimensions of the present itself. A scar is the sign not of a past wound but of 'the present fact of having been wounded': we can say that it is the contemplation of the wound, that it contracts all the instants that separate us from it into a living present. (*DR* 76)

To interpret the present is to *explicate* what is folded up within it. Recall some key Latin words above: *explicatio* and *replicantis*, both deriving from *plicare*, meaning 'to fold, wind together, double up'. We must be precise: divinatory explication is not simply predicting the future because divination is not limited to extensive chronological order. Instead, the interpretive move is to *read off* or to unfold the organisation of events from the arrangement of bodies, to extract aion from chronos, effects from causes. The 'event', Deleuze writes, 'is both tale and novella, never an actuality. It is in this sense that events are *signs*' (*LS* 63). Learning to divine is the apprenticeship of signs through which the world becomes a grand logical novel open for interpretation. Events express the organisation of the cosmos.

Given our corporeal constraints, we can only *infer* events from bodies. To do so, we interpret the sign as a present marker of a movement that infinitely subdivides 'into something that has just happened and something that is going to happen, always flying in both directions at once [*les deux sens à la fois*]' (*LS* 63). For example, we cannot say of Seneca that he *has* been cut and *will* soon die; we can only say that 'he *is* having been wounded (*il est ayant blessé*), and that he *is* about to die [*il est devant mourir*]' (*LS* 63; emphases original). Deleuze is reading Cicero here: 'it is not strange that diviners have a presentiment of things that exist nowhere in the material world: for all things "are", though they are removed from the standpoint of "time", they are not present'.[10] Beginning with the present, divination reads off of bodies the events spreading out into the instant, just before and just after now, and from there drifting further off into time. This is how we develop 'at least a partial vision' of the whole causal story (*SS* 81). Divination starts with the causal network immediately presented to us, connecting with the adjacent nexus of corporeal actions and passions whence it results, and spreads out therefrom. Notice the importance of propositional logic here, especially hypothetical entailment: 'If it is sunny, then it is day.'

Deleuze distinguishes 'two operations' that correspond to two sides of the same surface (*LS* 143). The first operation is 'the production of a physical surface', that is, the side of the surface facing bodies (*LS* 143). We call this surface sense 'physical' because projected on it is the map of deterministic laws of causation, as captured by the formal logic of corporeality. The second operation is the 'translation of these onto a "metaphysical surface"', that is, the side of the surface facing away from bodies (*LS* 143–4). This surface sense expresses the organisation of incorporeal events as depicted by the transcendental logic of incorporeality. These two operations 'link the event to its corporeal causes and to their physical unity' (*LS* 144). Although it begins in depths, divination is 'the art of surfaces, lines, and singular points appearing on the surface' (*LS* 143).

In so far as it is the art of discerning the cosmological organisation stretching out to the limits of the whole, 'divination', Goldschmidt writes, 'imitates as best as it can the total vision of God' (*SS* 81). From a divine perspective, there is only one cause, which comprehends them all. Put differently, there is only one body – the cosmos – that com*pli*cates all other bodies. Inversely, each individual body ex*pli*cates all other bodies. The first method of 'interpretation', writes Goldschmidt, 'is thus really a "science of the individual"' (*SS* 85). As Deleuze puts it, the 'vision of the entire causal organisation gathers in depth all the physical causes in the unity of a cosmic present, in order to elicit the vision of events which ensue' (*LS* 144). We need not encounter every single object in the world because each object is subject to the same causal unfolding, and we need not delay until we reach the proper age to begin to live as a Stoic, for the 'totality', writes Goldschmidt, 'is given at each instant' (*SS* 96). Wherever we are, whenever that may be, we can begin to discern the organisation of the world from the concrete context of our particular lives. This is the expansion from any individual to the whole cosmos.

According to Goldschmidt, the 'whole moral problem, for the Stoics, consists in *actualizing, here and now*, this law of fate' (*SS* 89). This is what is meant by the imperative to cooperate with destiny.

The art of divination is meant to make us 'agents of destiny' (*SS* 90). Discerning the causal connections that bind each present of each individual body to the entire causal chain trains us to affirm what happens at each instant. Divination distributes all events on a single surface so that we can read the book of nature, leading us closer and closer to the perspective of the whole, the cosmological perspective. This is how, Deleuze writes, '*divination* grounds ethics' (*LS* 143; emphasis original).

Cosmological Perspective

Divination grounds ethics because it trains us to affirm *everything that happens*, all events, by allowing us to interpret every event as connected through a complete causal network, all with minimal regard for our personal place in the world. Once we have glimpsed as broad a perspective as possible, we connect corporeal causes to incorporeal effects, which entails the complete causal account: from bodies to the event, from depths to surface.

Divination trains us to see the cosmological perspective, as portrayed by the opening lines of Nietzsche's 'On Truth and Lie in a Nonmoral Sense'. In the guise of a fable, Nietzsche writes:

> Once upon a time, in some out of the way corner of that universe which is dispersed into numberless twinkling solar systems, there was a star upon which clever beasts invented knowing. That was the most arrogant and mendacious minute of 'world history', but nevertheless, it was only a minute. After nature had drawn a few breaths, the star cooled and congealed, and the clever beasts had to die. One might invent such a fable, and yet he still would not have adequately illustrated how miserable, how shadowy and transient, how aimless and arbitrary the human intellect looks within nature. There were eternities during which it did not exist. And when it is all over with the human intellect, nothing will have happened ... Rather, it is human, and only its possessor and begetter takes it so solemnly-as though the world's axis turned within it.[11]

For Nietzsche, one ethical task is to overcome the all-too-human perspective and assume the non-human point of view of the cosmos.[12] Two millennia before Nietzsche, the Stoics advocated for just such a point of view.

'In so far as it is responsible for interpreting events, the first method [of interpretation] leads to the [cosmological] scale' in so far as it initiates a process of de-personalising or impersonalising (*SS* 98).[13] Depersonalisation cuts away personal desires and aversions, inclinations and disinclination, impulsions and repulsions, as when Epictetus advises us to approach everything 'without either desire or aversion' by comparing it to the experience of travelling through unfamiliar territory and happening upon a person whom we ask which of two roads leads to our destination (as when Alice happens upon the Cheshire Cat).[14] Lost in a foreign land, we do not have 'any desire to have the right-hand road lead there any more than the left-hand road; for [we do] not care to travel one particular road of the two, but merely the one leads to [our] destination'.[15] Assuming the cosmological perspective allows us to affirm both directions at once, thus forming a sort of a cosmic inclusive disjunction through which the cosmological perspective actively accepts whatever happens, whether it leads in one direction or another. While this 'tendency to strip ourselves of "the human" is constant throughout the most diverse schools', Hadot writes, it was the Stoics who initiated what Deleuze calls 'the harshest exercise in depersonalisation, by opening themselves up to the multiplicities everywhere within them, to the intensities running through them'.[16] Marcus Aurelius describes this depersonalising intensive processes through Heraclitean imagery:

> Of the life of man the duration is but a point, its substance streaming away, its perception dim, the fabric of the entire body prone to decay and the soul a vortex, and fortune incalculable, and fame uncertain. In a word all the things of the body are as a river, and the things of the soul as a dream and a vapour, and life is a warfare and a pilgrim's sojourn, and fame after death is only forgetfulness.[17]

Divination cultivates the vast perspective of the flux of the world beyond the human perspective.

Whatever it might promise, the art of divination, 'carried to its end, proves to be insufficient' because the complete cosmological perspective 'is reserved for God' (SS 79). We, humans all-too-much, are only parts of the divine whole. Although we cannot reach the full divine vision, the first method requires us to try *because* we cannot reach it. We cultivate the art of divination *because* our vision is always partial, *because* we cannot be god. If we could see from the perspective of the whole, the method would be useless, as we could already view it all. We should begin to see the humour here. 'This is why two fortune-tellers', Deleuze chuckles to himself, 'cannot regard one another without laughing, a laughter that is humorous' (LS 143–4). It is humorous to think that we could see the whole, so we just laugh, at the world and ourselves. Yet, amid our laughter, another method appears: 'the use of representations'.

Use of Representations

Although 'divination', Goldschmidt writes, 'imitates as best as it can the total vision of God', we only 'understand and act *in the manner of* God' (*SS* 81, 99; emphasis original).[18] The 'passage', as Goldschmidt puts it, from the first to the second method follows from the failure to fully assume the divine, cosmological perspective. If the first method strives to construct a vision of complete corporeal causation, beginning in physical depths and tracing out the effects appearing on the incorporeal surface, the second method moves from surface to depths. The first method traces a causal movement; the second maps the quasi-causal one. Deleuze puts it thus: in the first method 'we link the event to its corporeal causes and to their physical unity; in the other, we link it to its incorporeal quasi-cause, the kind of causality that it gathers and makes resonate in the production of its own actualisation' (*LS* 144). We use representations to reach the non-representable event.

Epictetus emphasises the use of representations throughout his *Discourses* and the *Enchiridion*, describing it in various ways, such as: the power of reasoning and discerning; the capacity to consider everything, including self-reflection; the ability to give and withhold assent; the faculty of judgement and decision; the seat of our moral character.[19] While 'usage of representations', Deleuze agrees, 'reache[s] its peak in the works of Epictetus and Marcus Aurelius', articulating details of the method raises several difficulties (*LS* 144).[20]

For Deleuze, this is the most troubling difficulty: 'the scope of the difference between representation-bodies, or imprints, and incorporeal events-effects', or the difference between representations and expressions (*LS* 145). Deleuze finds this most troubling because it connects three things that are different in nature. On the one hand are sensible representations, which concern denotations, and rational representations, which concerns significations. On the other hand, 'only incorporeal events constitute sense' (*LS* 145). This same difficulty reappears throughout *Logic of Sense*; we have depicted it as a perverse relation between depths and surface. Representation is the way of organising a sensible manifold according to the identification of an object through extensive measurements. It is the successful transaction of good and common sense (see 'The Shell B') as opposed

The Albumen B: The Act

to the perverse production of paradoxes. Deleuze sees the opposition between representation and expression as 'the opposition between the object = x . . . and the thing = x' (LS 145). The first is 'the identitarian instance of the representation in common sense'; the second is the 'nonidentitarian element of expression in the paradox' (LS 145). It is difficult to see how representations and expressions communicate because event-effects cannot be objects for good and common sense. Despite this, Deleuze's Stoicism contends that not only does the event intervene in representations, it even 'confers a very special value to the relation that it maintains with its object', that is, with the body or states of affairs in which it is actualised (*LS* 145). Although events and representations differ in nature, such that events cannot be represented, *representations envelope events.*

Returning to the deaths of Seneca and Deleuze, the denotative sentences 'Seneca died' or 'Deleuze is dead', or the concept 'mortality', have no sense if 'they do not encompass the event of dying' (*LS* 145). Sense necessitates the actualisation of the event of death in the denotation and its signification = in the concept. This is what is meant by 'encompassing or enveloping'. An event like death cannot be represented as a denotatum, manifestation or signified, but it must be 'folded' into a denotation, manifestation or signification in order to be truly 'comprehensive'. A non-comprehensive or partial representation is contingently true, which means that it is empty and abstract in so far as it fails to address the singularities composing the world.

To see the difference between comprehensive and non-comprehensive representations, think of the difference between two ways of knowing death: abstract and concrete. Abstract knowledge of death grasps the bare truth that everyone dies in so far as that truth remains external and indifferent to the singular act of *my* death. Knowing-*that* I will die does not mean confronting my finitude. By contrast, concrete knowledge of death confronts death directly and at every instance in so far as I face the possibility of dying at every moment. There is a reason why Marcus Aurelius advises us to perform every single act as if it were our last.[21] We can think of it as a kind of existential knowledge, a knowing-*how* to encounter the instantaneity death. As Blanchot might put it, concrete knowledge renders death 'a task, one which we must take up actively, one which becomes the source of our activity and mastery'.[22] 'Real knowledge', writes Bréhier, 'is much closer to an activity than to contemplation' (*TI* 63). Deleuze sees this as constructing a form of living within 'an always open problematic structure' (*LS* 145). It is one thing to know *that* death occurs; it is another thing to act as if it were always about to happen (because it is).

At the same time, there is no *who* of death. The constant haunt of death on the backside of every moment both is and is not *my* death. We see this most clearly in the case of Seneca's and Deleuze's suicides. Suicide is an event and, as such, is intimately two-faced, simultaneously the most personal and the most impersonal act.[23] Death is an impersonal instant that is never present but remains a future that never arrives or a past that has always passed.[24] For Blanchot, death is impersonal, incorporeal, pre-subjective and infinitive, contained in the verb 'to die' (*mourir*); death never happens to a person. 'Death', Deleuze writes, 'has an extreme and definite relation to me and my body and is grounded in me, but also has no relation to me at all' (*LS* 151). Here Deleuze cites Blanchot's description of 'suicide as the wish to bring about the conscience of the two faces of death' (*LS* 156).[25] Death is immanent but never present in a state of affairs, just as verbs are immanent but never exist in the nouns in which verbs conjugate. Although neither Seneca nor Deleuze died, they are dead. It is impossible to announce, 'I am dead', because there is no subject in death. Deleuze gives death a special eventual status: 'every event', he writes, 'is like death' (*LS* 152).

'Representation and its usage', writes Deleuze, 'intervene at this point' because the usage of representations turns empty abstract knowledge into existential, concrete knowledge (*LS* 147). Although he admits his appreciation for Wittgenstein's identification of meaning as use, Deleuze is careful to specify that usage or representations are not a (possible or actual) relation between a representation and a represented object.[26] Instead, it is 'the relation between representation and something extra-representative, a nonrepresented and merely expressed entity' (*LS* 146). This 'something extra-representative' is the event, and the representation's relation to it is 'envelopment'. The language of 'enveloping' (*enveloppant*) means that representation's *usage* is not a utilitarian function but a more of a topological direction. Deleuze speaks of the representation enveloping the event at its edges, stretching, bending and folding it so as to bring about a 'lining (*doublure*) or hem' (*LS* 146). As the second method of interpretation, the use of representations seeks to harness the full vibrancy of the event by enveloping it in a representation. Goldschmidt says that this involves the 'method of analysis' or infinite division, which consists in 'amplifying and deforming the appearance of a representation' so that the 'event is rigorously present' (*SS* 195).[27]

The Albumen B: The Act

Singular Perspective

While corporeals cause incorporeal effects, an incorporeal quasi-cause operates by doubling a corporeal cause. The Stoic imperative is to assume both perspectives at once: the acceptance of the present state of affairs as entailed by the causal order of the world and the rigorous willing of the actualisation of the event. The first is the cosmological perspective and the art of divination; the second is the singular perspective and the use of representations. Goldschmidt understands their mutual inclusiveness in terms of the Stoic distinction, so important to Epictetus, between 'things that are not under our control' and 'the things that are under our control'.[28] The first of Epictetus' *Discourses* begins ends with this distinction: 'I care only for what is my own, what is not subject to hindrance, what is by nature free. This, which is the true nature of the good, I have; but let everything else be as God granted, it makes no difference to me.'[29]

Stoic ethics is a double movement because it requires both methods and perspectives: the expansion of the singular into the cosmic and the condensation of the cosmos into singular things. We might think of it as the ex*pli*cation or unfolding of singular things into *all* (πᾶν) and im*pli*cation or folding-in of *all* into singular things. This double movement is an example of what Deleuze calls the infinite speed of thought because it expresses a reversible structure: 'this is not a fusion but a reversibility, an immediate, perpetual, instantaneous exchange – a lightning flash. Infinite movement is double, and there is only a fold from one to the other' (*WP* 19, 38).[30] Stoic ethics habituates thinking the whole cosmos and the singular act at the same time, in the same double-movement of thought. Cultivating a Stoic way of life demands the oscillation between these two positions, the broadest possible perspective and the narrowest possible perspective. It is the process of willing exactly what will happen at every instant, a sort of intensification of the instant wherein on strives to 'limit the actualisation of the event in a present without mixture, to make the instant all the more intense, taut, and instantaneous since it expresses an unlimited future and an unlimited past. This is the *use of representation*: the mime, and no longer the fortuneteller' (*LS* 147). Deleuze calls Stoicism an 'ethics of the mime' because it not only understands the causal order of the cosmos and the corresponding surface events, but selects what happens as exactly what is willed to happen (*LS* 147). The figure of the mime comes from Mallarmé's '*Mimique*'. Citing Mallarmé, Deleuze writes, 'the Mime side-steps the state of affairs and "whose game is limited to perpetual allusion without breaking the ice"' (*LS* 63).³¹ The mime doubles the event not in the sense of reproducing it in a state of affairs because the mime does not mimic the event. Instead, the mime extracts the infinite movement of the event in a 'pure perverse "moment"' in so far as the event is enveloped in a representation (*LS* 168).

Stoic Sage

The Stoics often depict the ideal Stoic life through the figure of the sage. While it is unclear whether or not the Stoics ever believed that there was, in history, a true sage, they point to names of figures who came close: Diogenes the Cynic, Socrates, Hercules, Cato the Younger and so on.³² Deleuze casts Hercules as embodying 'the entire Stoic thought' because his adventures lead through the depths, heights and surface (*LS* 131). While Hercules finds only emptiness and 'celestial monsters' in the sky above, and pacifies and surveys the earth below, he always 'ascends or descends to the surface' (*LS* 132). Whether it is bringing up a hellhound or pulling down a celestial serpent, Hercules as Stoic sage is not 'Dionysius down below, or Apollo up above, but Hercules of the surface' (*LS* 132). Hercules is a Stoic sage in that he engages in a 'dual battle', fighting both depths and heights, marking a 'reorientation of the entire thought and a new geography' (*LS* 132). This reorientation and new geography are a version of Stoic perversion, as Lapoujade puts it: 'Stoic ethics becomes indistinguishable from a process of perversion whose operator is the Stoic wise man (Hercules?).'³³ Deleuze also offers modern examples of the Stoic sage: 'Humpty Dumpty', 'the actor' and the 'mime' (*LS* 142, 147, 147).³⁴ Yet, most interestingly of all, Deleuze, following his teacher Ferdinand Alquié, points to a surrealist twentieth-century French poet as the true sage: 'Joe Bousquet must be called a Stoic' (*LS* 148).³⁵ Bousquet's Stoic sagacity revolves around his paralysing wound.³⁶

On 27 May 1918, when Bousquet was fighting in Vailly, France, during the First World War, he was hit by shrapnel. At just twenty-one years old, Bousquet was paralysed and thus confined to a bed for the rest of his life. Although this was not the course of events he had hoped for, Bousquet did not curse the course of nature and gnash his teeth in sorrow and disappointment. Instead, he rejected all pity, René Nelli writes, so much that 'several men in his little village forgot to *pity him*, becoming jealous of the wounded poet'.³⁷ A few lines later, Nelli calls Bousquet a Stoic. Rather than bemoan his bad fortune and sad life, he focused on the wound as fate. In his writing, the wounding was an event that demanded a response. Sometimes Bousquet calls his wound 'bizarre', 'a species of diabolical pride [*espèce d'orgueil diabolique*]'.[38]

While it might sound strange to portray a paralysed poet as the ideal Stoic sage, as it is such a contrast with the figure of a strong, hard-headed hero, Bousquet cultivated true joy in, as Nietzsche might put it, *becoming what you are*. Although he 'kept nothing of the dogmatic stance of the Stoa', Khalfa rightly notes, Bousquet practised a sort of surrealist Stoicism.[39] It was no coincidence that figures such as Max Ernst, Salvador Dalí, René Magritte, Jean Debuffet, Paul Valéry and André Breton were friends with Bousquet. Bousquet was a surreal, perhaps perverse, Stoic.

One Bousquet line, which Deleuze clearly found fascinating because he repeats it in four books and various lectures, encapsulates Deleuze's thinking on Bousquet as Stoic sage.[40] We call it the *Bousquet Proposition*:

My wound existed before me: I was born to embody it.[41]

The Bousquet Proposition marks the transition from *my* wound to *its* wound, or what Deleuze calls the shift from the 'personological' to the 'sphere of the event'.[42] The wound is a sign of an event, a crack in the cosmos that shifts a state of affairs, including the personological locale. There is not first a person to whom events occur because personhood is constituted by a set of events, such as Bousquet 'being wounded', Seneca's 'being cut' or Deleuze's 'being defenestrated'. Persons are closer to relays between events than substantial identities grounding events.

One reason why Bousquet is Deleuze's prime example of a Stoic sage is because Bousquet reduces his sense of self to the sense of the event. Bousquet does this by contemplating the acts and events organising the world without reference to himself, as Deleuze writes: 'He apprehends the wound that he bears deep within his body in its eternal truth as a pure event', prior to his personal identity (*LS* 148). Bousquet constructed an image of the world that placed his wound *before* him, an event awaiting his arrival. In this world, it is no longer necessary to say 'I'; personhood and identity vanish like morning dew in the rising sun. Acts, instead, are prior to persons; acts 'wait for us and invite us in' (*LS* 148). As Alquié writes, Bousquet 'stopped being a child of Nature in order to become a child of the Event'.[43]

Bousquet seeks 'to will and release the event, to become the offspring of [his] own events, and thereby to be reborn, to have one more birth, and to break with one's carnal birth – to become the offspring of one's events' (*LS* 149). To become the offspring of one's events means 'being worthy of the event'. As a sage birthed from the event of the wound, Bousquet becomes worthy of the event in so far as it comprehends all acts in a single act, and every event *'in a single Event'* (*LS* 153). As Lecercle writes, 'all events belong to one large metaphysical Event, another name for Fate'.[44]

The Act

The oscillation between the cosmological to the singular perspectives points the student of Stoicism towards the importance of *the act*. We define the act as the actualisation of the incorporeal event in a corporeal state of affairs, a sort of giving-body (in-carnation) to the event. More specifically, the act is the 'mobile and precise point' on the side of the surface facing the world, while the event is the corresponding paradoxical object on the other side (*LS* 153). The act and the event are thus the same paradoxical object, viewed either from one side (the act), or the other (the event).

At the end of a lecture on themes from *Anti-Oedipus*, Deleuze claims that 'it is not by chance that the Stoics are the first among the Greeks to make a theory of the event, a theory they pushed very, very far'.[45] The Stoics, he thought, formulated the first great logic of the event; later, Leibniz and Whitehead formulated, respectively, the second and third great evental logics.[46] Pushing the theory of the event 'very, very far' entails considering how the event is actualised. If 'Stoic ethics is concerned with . . . willing that which occurs in so far as it does occur', then it entails considering 'how the event could be grasped and willed without its being referred to the corporeal cause from which it results and, through this cause, to the unity of causes as *Physics*' (*LS* 142). In Stoicism, there is no non-actualised, Platonic idea of the event. Events do not lurk in a transcendent realm outside of the world. Instead, events subsist within actualised persons and states of affairs. The wound does not exist outside of Joe Bousquet, just as walking does not exist beyond bodies strolling through the Stoa. What would a wound be without a body? How could there be walking without bodies and paths? All events are like this, that is, all events are actualised in the world.

However, there is always something in an event that is irreducible to the state of affairs in which it is actualised, something that cannot be exhausted by the world. This is why we say that the act is a 'manner of being' but not a being. The act is never present *in* the world as a body is; it never exists in extended place or chronological time. In short, the act never *is*. The act attributes to bodies but does not belong to bodies. In short, it *corporealises* incorporeal effects (*SS* 107). While it is not un-actualised, it 'overflows' its actualisation, although we might call it 'indifferent' or 'neutral' to its actualisation in order to avoid Plotinian transcendence and emphasise material immanence.[47] 'The event might seem to be transcendent because it surveys the state of affairs, but it is pure immanence that gives it the capacity to survey itself by itself and on the plane' (*WP* 156). Deleuze calls it the 'splendor of the event'.[48]

In this splendour we see a double-sided structure: the act appears on the side of the surface facing states of affairs, and the event dwells on the other side, facing the chaosmic depths. The act and the event are opposed faces of the same paradoxical element operating simultaneously on both sides of the surface. We call it the event in so far as it operates as the paradoxical object facing away from the cosmos, which corresponds to the act facing the cosmos. In short, the act is the actualisation of the event, and the event is what overflows the actualisation.

Goldschmidt provides a distinction that helps us understand the relation between the act and the event. He defines 'the perfect cause' as that which 'abolishes all distance between the intention and the act, between itself and the effect' (*SS* 100). A cause is perfect if the will, act and effects completely coincide. For the Stoics, there is only one perfect cause: the cosmos or god – *deus sive natura*. Only the cosmos can, 'in a single instant, move from the intention to the act', without lag or drag (*SS* 100). There is no distance between the will of the cosmos and its action. Since there is no other world to act on, no transcendent realm beyond, the cosmos cannot act on anything other than itself. Hence the need to conceive the Stoic cosmos as both active *and* passive. Its will is its act, occurring in the same cosmological instant.

By comparison, human beings are almost inversions of the divine logic of acting. Since we are part of the cosmos and the cosmos is god, we are part of god.[49] But as *parts*, we are only partial causes. This unavoidable partiality means that we act first, and only later determine the intention behind it. Since the act is caught up in the state of affairs in the world, the act does not depend on the will.

The structure of human action moves from act to intention, thus reformulating the ethical task: to reduce the distance between act and intention. Since human action is the inverse of divine action, we must begin with the fact of the act, later seeking the intention attached to it. While the divine act proceeds from the intention to the act (although the two truly coincide in divinity), the human act moves 'backwards' from the act to the intention. Yet, despite this inverted structure, the task is the same: to make, as much as possible, the act and the intention coincide. The goal: to make what happens in the world corresponds with what is willed.

Goldschmidt's consideration of the temporality of the ethical task corroborates our argument that time is the incorporeal proper to Stoic ethics. Stoicism, he writes, seeks to cultivate 'the contemporaneity of the intention and of the act' (SS 101). This is the contemporaneity of aion, not chronos, because the successive order of chronological time always involves a distance between act and will. Aion, by contrast, gathers all events into a single time, the infinitely subdividing eternity. 'In the same way that the body occupies and carves out places in the void, similarly the act determines the present, in infinite aion, by its own extension' (SS 96). While two chronological *nows* must be distinct moments, 'it is in the same instant that our will catches up and recovers the event and that the most secret movement of our "moral person" cooperates with the course of Fate' (SS 101). Acting ethically involves cultivating, at each moment, a constant disposition that affirms the course of the cosmos, of fate. The 'originality of the Stoic theory', for Goldschmidt, is 'to interpret this eternal and immobile "being" in a temporal sense, and of conceiving as "present" during the whole duration . . . of the act that defines it' (SS 43). The eternality of aion spans the duration of an act, including the act of cutting, dying or the cause of all causes: the cosmos or god. They are singular acts at all scales. The Stoics initiate a 'temporalisation of eternity' by defining it in terms of an act (SS 43).

Counter-Actualisation

Akin with much of Stoicism, there is a second sense of the act, a movement that doubles and reverses the movement of actualisation: a counter-act or what Deleuze calls it 'counter-actualisation' (*contre-effectuation*).[50] Deleuze and Guattari describe the two sense of the act thus: 'The event is actualised or effectuated whenever it is inserted willy-nilly, into a state of affairs; but it is *counter-effectuated*

The Albumen B: The Act

whenever it is abstracted from states of affairs so as to isolate the concept' (*WP* 159; emphasis original).[51] Counter-effectuation or counter-actualisation transcends human experience without collapsing into transcendent ideas; it discovers, if not provokes, the genetic element enveloped by a state of affairs. If the act is the mobile point on the side of the surface facing the world in so far as it marks the actualisation of the event in a state of affairs, the counter-act is that mobile point on the side of the surface facing away from the world. Counter-actualisation marks the event. In Stoic ethics, the counter-act doubles the act.

We can connect the act and counter-act to the relation between physical depths and incorporeal surface. According to most scholarship of Deleuze, the process of ontological production moves in this direction: from the virtual plane of immanence (ideas, problems), through the intensive processes (spatio-temporal dynamisms, intensities), to the actual corporeal states of affairs. In *Difference and Repetition*, Deleuze calls this 'the order of reasons', an ontological model that he says is based on the figure of the egg (*DR* 251).[52] Although Deleuze uses different terms for this direction of ontogenesis, *Logic of Sense* commonly calls it 'actualisation'.[53] Much of Deleuze's writings analyses this movement. Corresponding to this, however, is the opposite movement: 'counter-actualisation'. Through counter-actualisation the Stoics consider the incorporeals in so far as they immanently contribute to the genesis of bodies. As Deleuze vividly put is, counter-actualisation allows us to consider only the 'incorporeal surface area, without stopping at the bursting within each body . . . to give us the chance to go farther than we would have believed possible', but without rising to heavenly heights or volcanic depths (*LS* 161). Counter-actualisation allows the Stoics, Deleuze, and us to encounter the immanent genetic conditions of matter from a materially bound perspective. Borrowing a term Deleuze uses in a lecture on Rousseau, this is the 'materialism of the sage'.[54]

While the act moves from surface to depths and the counter-act moves from depths to surface, they are not mere inversions of each other. The reason is that we do not encounter the same surface when moving in either direction. The act emerges from a surface that reflects the finite order of bodies, while the counter-act escapes the corporeal limits as it reaches infinite speed. Put differently, the act marks the organisation of the cosmos, while the event marks the opening onto the chaosmos. Counter-actualisation is the process of confronting that 'shadowy and secret part [enveloped by bodies] that is continually subtracted from or added to its actualisation: in contrast to the state of affairs, it neither begins nor ends but has gained or kept the infinite movement to which it gives consistency' (*WP* 156). Bodily movement begins and ends, but infinite movement neither stops nor begins; it is always in the middle, an infinitely subdividing intermezzo. In sum, actualisation slows down the infinite movement of incorporeals in order to place it in the extended present of a body, and counter-actualisation frees up infinite movement enveloped by bodies.

Freeing the movement of the event from corporeal constraints frees up a space for a minimal amount of freedom. It is only 'the free man, who grasps the event, and does not allow it to be actualised as such without enacting, the actor, its counter-actualisation' (*LS* 152). Stoic freedom is not a personal triumph or the strength to persevere, but the dissolution of the ego in the identification with the impersonal event. There has not been a true Stoic sage because it cannot be identified with any one person or name, because counter-actualisation involves shedding one's name, person and identity. Becoming a sage means no longer being Diogenes, Socrates or Bousquet, but to identify with the quasi-cause. This is what Deleuze means when he writes that the 'Stoic sage "identifies" with the quasi-cause, sets up shop at the surface, on the straight line that traverses it, or at the aleatory point that traces or travels this line' (*LS* 146). To identify with the quasi-cause means understanding the event independently of its actualisation; it means engaging the event as something that infinitely divides the instant, something that is eternally just-passed and to-come, something drifting through the void, along the line of aion. This is, simultaneously, why the sage insists on the immanence of the event in the cosmos, and wills its actualisation accordingly. The sage acts *and* counter-acts: the act '*wills the embodiment* and the actualisation of the pure incorporeal event in a state of affairs', and the counter-act '*understands the pure event*' on the surface (*LS* 146; emphasis original). To identify with the quasi-cause requires both methods of interpretation: to discern the organisation of causes and the corresponding relations among events, and to use representations in so far as they envelop something that cannot be represented. The life of the Stoic sage means, as Sean Bowden puts it, 'living in accordance with the event which never finishes coming about'.[55] No one, not even the sage, reaches the pure event drifting on the far side of the surface. Given our unavoidable corporeality, the event is a limit we are forever approaching. At the same time, we are composed of events because the surface always cloaks our bodies, because our being is determined by the organisation of events.

Suicide brings together corporeal cause and incorporeal effects in so far as it is the perfect example of a quasi-cause. When Seneca or Deleuze kill themselves, though they are the respective causes of their deaths, death is the quasi-cause of the generation of a state of affairs in which Seneca and Deleuze are dead. But the quasi-causality of death could not occur 'if the event were not already in the process of being produced by and in the depth of corporeal causes' (*LS* 147). In this sense, I cannot plan to kill myself because my death is not something I can attain, that is, death is not a goal that I can conceive of as an end-in-itself. 'It is that which never comes and toward which I do not direct myself,' Blanchot writes.[56] I can will my death only in so far as it follows from the already determined course of affairs. Suicide is the completion of a plan, the plan to complete a life, which was consciously decided and vigorously affirmed, although suicide is simultaneously the ruin of every plan and project. Death cannot be a project because it cannot be achieved, or its achievement is its necessary defeat. Death is not *my end* because it is the *end of me*. To will my death is to 'embark', Blanchot continues, 'on a kind of action that could only reach its term at infinity'.[57] Suicide is a plan without a goal, the relentless ruin of every deliberate act. Suicide perverts teleology.

Or we might call suicide a perverse teleology in so far as it constitutes neither the completion of a project nor the inversion of the orientation, but the 'turning-inside-out' of the whole structure of acting. The goal cannot be achieved, for dying is not something I do. Blanchot says it well:

> The expression 'I kill myself' suggests the doubling that is not taken into account. For 'I' is a self in the plenitude of its action and resolution, capable of acting sovereignly upon itself, always strong enough to reach itself with its blow. And yet the one who is thus struck is no longer I, but another, so that when I kill myself, perhaps it is 'I' who does the killing.[58]

Exerting the resolute will to kill oneself thus aims not at oneself but at a complete stranger. Suicide involves both 'I' and 'not-I' because, given the doctrine of eternal return that we will examine in 'Albumen C', 'I' have done this infinitely times before and yet I am still doing it now. 'I' already killed myself in the last cosmic cycle and yet I must do it now for it to occur. If I do nothing, if I fail to act, then I did not kill myself before or after. But if I do act, if I kill myself now, then

I have done this many times before and will do it again and again. Suicide, Blanchot writes, 'seem[s] to arch like a delicate and endless bridge that at the decisive moment is cut and becomes as unreal as a dream, over which nevertheless it is necessary really to pass'.[59] Death is an action that turns into passion, passion into action, again and again. Action and passion are turned-inside-out, that is, they are perverted. Death is the perversion of teleology, and it is perversion itself that is the end of the suicidal act.

A voluntary death is the perfect figure of the double-movement of act and counter-actualisation in so far as it concerns time because suicide is the will to live under the time of aion and the instant. Hence Blanchot calls it 'the apotheosis of the *instant*'.[60] He continues, 'I want to kill myself in an "absolute instant," the only one which will not pass and will not be surpassed.'[61] I cannot look forward to or back upon my suicide because it is never present. 'By committing suicide I want to kill myself at a determined moment. I link death to now: yes, now, *now*. But nothing better indicates the illusion, the madness of this "I want," for death is never present.'[62]

The instantaneity of suicide implies that to will one's own death is to will the limit between extreme activity and extreme passivity. Willing one's own death, according to Blanchot, is the attempt 'to make death an act . . . to act supremely and absolutely'.[63] In so far as suicide expresses the same paradoxical structure of absolute freedom and perfect determinism, suicide might be the most perverse example of a life lived along the arc of the eternal return. '[S]uicide retains the power of an exceptional affirmation' and negation because it succeeds only at a great loss, where one becomes 'the creator of one's own nothingness'.[64] Blanchot describes this paradoxical double-movement of the passion-action of suicide as 'lift[ing] oneself to one's full height . . . in the very midst of the fall'.[65] Neither simply ascending nor descending, the movement is both the rotation of the cosmic sphere and the horizontal drift along a straight line blazing across the surface. Suicide is the only 'absolute right . . . which is not the corollary of a duty'.[66]

How to Make Yourself a Stoic

The key to unfolding (*un*veloping) events, of reaching the surface, is through the type of 'experimentation' that Deleuze and Guattari detail in their 'Sixth' of those *Thousand Plateaus*: 'How to Make Yourself a Body Without Organs?' (*ATP* 150). Since the body

The Albumen B: The Act

without organs is what becomes of the surface in the post-*Logic of Sense* and *Capitalism and Schizophrenia* books, we can read the 'programme' detailed in the 'Sixth Plateau' as instruction for 'How to Make Yourself a Stoic Sage'. After all, it is no coincidence that references to the egg appear throughout this 'Plateau', including, the 'Dogon Egg', 'full egg', 'tantric egg' (*ATP* 149, 153, 153).

We can think of what Deleuze and Guattari consider five forms of corporeal experimentation as Stoic philosophical exercises: the hypochondriac body, the paranoid body, the schizo body, the drugged body, the masochist body (*ATP* 150). Although it is today common to conceive of the ideal Stoic as heroic indifference or coldness (arguably due to the popularity of *De Constantia*, the sixteenth-century work of Justus Lipsius), we argue that these five corporeal experiments are really Stoic experiments with forms of life.[67] Thus what Deleuze's Stoicism reveals about the figure of the Stoic philosopher is not Lipsius' cold hero but a mad sage, a surreal pervert. Recall classic Stoic sayings that straddle madness and sagacity. Seneca: 'Infinitely swift is the flight of time ... Everything slips into the same abyss ... The time which we spend in living is but a point, nay, even less than a point.'[68] Marcus Aurelius: '... fail not to note how short-lived are all mortal things, and how paltry – yesterday a little mucus, tomorrow a mummy or burnt ash'; 'the whole Ocean a drop in the Universe ... all the present a point in eternity: everything on a tiny scale, so easily changes, so quickly vanished'.[69] Epictetus: 'Never say about anything, "I have lost it," but only "I have given it back." Is your child dead? It has been given back. Is your wife dead? She has been given back.'[70] Are these words of wisdom or shrieks of madness? It is hard to say.

While Pierre Hadot depicts the importance of Stoic spiritual exercises, we push things a little further, formulating Stoic *philosophical experimentation*. More than training, Stoic experimentation seeks to cultivate madness in icy rationality, intoxication through sobriety, inebriation without drugs. Deleuze and Guattari point to several examples of perverted Stoics: William S. Burroughs's drug experiments, which seek to 'harness the power of drugs without them taking over, without turning into a dazed zombie'; or Henry Miller's attempt 'to use drugs without using drugs, to get soused on pure water'.[71] Although John Sellars rejects Thomas Africa's suggestion that Marcus' mad visions were the result of an opium addiction, we should not dismiss it outright.[72] While we are not saying that Marcus or any of the Stoics were really drug addicts, we are saying that becoming-Stoic requires a precise dose of madness and intoxication, as practised by Burroughs and Miller. To be sure, caution is necessary in striking this delicate balance because identifying with the quasi-cause requires an art of dosages. It is easy botch an experiment because, as the event is unrepresentable, we cannot know beforehand what it is like to confront the event. Deleuze and Guattari only offer one rule of experimentation: 'injections of caution' (*ATP* 150).

Conclusion: Amor Fati

For Deleuze, Stoic ethics turns on one disjunction: 'Either ethics makes no sense at all, or this is what it means and has nothing else to say: *not to be unworthy of what happens to us* [*ne pas être indigne de ce qui nous arrive*]' (*LS* 149; emphasis added). Nietzsche might put it as a choice: *amor fati* or *ressentiment*.[73] Either we will the event and seek to live in accord with the cosmos, or we despise it and complain about fate's injustice.

Out of the oscillation between the cosmological and singular perspectives, Stoic ethics cultivates an affirmation of fate. If everything happens according to fate, then there are no accidents. But if we allow accidents, we risk collapsing into the 'resentment of the event', because accidents introduce the possibility of fortune or misfortune (*LS* 149). For a Stoic sage like Bousquet, there are no accidents; everything is fated. As Nelli puts it, Bousquet's 'Stoic pride' is 'to love his fate as if he had chosen it'.[74] *Amor fati*, not resentful resignation, is the Stoic affirmation. Consider Bousquet's three characteristics of the humour-actor (*l'humour-acteur*), now deemed a Deleuze–Stoic sage:

> [1] 'to annihilate his or her tracks whenever necessary'; [2] 'to hold up among men and works *their being before bitterness*'; [3] 'to assign to plagues, tyrannies, and the most frightful wars the comic possibility of having reigned for nothing'; in short, to liberate for each thing 'its immaculate portion,' language and will, *Amor Fati*. (*LS* 151)[75]

With Guattari he echoes this later: 'There is a dignity of the event that has always been inseparable from philosophy as *amor fati*: being equal to the event, or becoming the offspring of one's own events . . . There is no other ethic than the *amor fati* of philosophy' (*WP* 159).

The affirmation of *amor fati*, encompassing the narrowest and the broadest perspectives, is the point of view of Ferlinghetti's 'fourth person singular'. Neither universal nor particular, the fourth-person singular, writes Jeff Bradley, 'rids itself of preconceptions and opens itself up to the outside, to becoming and *amor fati* . . . a decentered perspectivism'.[76] The perspective of the fourth person evacuates all other perspectives, or it explicates them all at once, in a single 'yes-saying' of the cosmological Event. Freed of the limitations of the first, second and third person, the Stoic implicates all perspectives in every perspective. The fourth person subsists as the void because it is place-less (*non-lieu*), as infinitive because unconjugated, and as aion because achronological. It loves fate because it wilfully dissolves itself to the actualisation and counter-actualisation of the surface and the depths.

Marcus Aurelius directs us on how to do this: 'You will open up a vast field for yourself, by embracing the entire universe in your thought.'[77] Bradley agrees that the fourth-person singular is Ferlinghetti's articulation of 'the Stoic ethic of willing the impersonality of the event' which 'exhorts his readers to make themselves entirely worthy of it'.[78] Assuming the perspective of the fourth person means thinking and willing that which occurs according to the necessary course of fate as necessary to my self-conception. It means relating to myself as integral to a whole cosmological unfolding. The other grammatical subject positions – I, you, he/she and so on – are replaced with 'it, *ça*, or *id*', as the division between internal and external are turned inside out. The place of the person is perverted in both directions: 'I' becomes 'it' as much as 'it' becomes 'I'. Fate is not outside of and opposed to me because I am fated. *Amor fati* entails that 'I' and 'it' are co-perverting. *I* cannot love fate; fate can only be loved by *it*. An ethics of *amor fati* thus requires the fourth-person singular. Deleuze formulates it as an imperative: 'Stop thinking of yourself as an ego [*moi*] in order to live as a flow, a set of flows in relation with other flows, outside of oneself and within oneself'.[79] To live from the perspective of this fourth-person singular, to love fate, the Stoics construct one of the most fascinating yet elusive philosophy concepts: the eternal return.

Notes

1. Walter Benjamin, *The Arcades Project*, trans. Howard Eiland and Kevin McLaughlin (Cambridge, MA: Harvard University Press, 2002), 122–3.
2. Tacitus, *The Annals*, trans. John Jackson (Cambridge, MA: Harvard University Press, 1981), LXIV.

3. Seneca, *Anger, Mercy, Revenge*, trans. Robert A. Kaster and Martha C. Nussbaum (Chicago; London: University of Chicago Press, 2012), ix.
4. Tacitus, *The Annals*, LXIV. The warm waters finally brought about the event of Seneca's death. In a late Stoic perversion, while Socrates, just prior to his death, asked that a cock be sacrificed to Asclepius, Seneca offered the liquid of the water in which he died as a libation to Jove the Liberator.
5. Deleuze wrote a delightful article on the 'exhausted' in Samuel Beckett's work. For an English translation, see Deleuze, 'The Exhausted', in *Essays Critical and Clinical*, trans. Daniel M. Smith and Michael A. Greco (London: Verso, 1998), 152–74.
6. Given this that 'Albumen B' talks a great deal about death, it might be necessary to address Badiou's comment that Stoicism and Deleuze are really philosophies of death. Since I have no idea how this claim could be true or false, we can just acknowledge it was said and leave it at that. Alain Badiou, *Deleuze: The Clamor of Being*, trans. Louise Burchill (Minneapolis: University of Minnesota Press, 1999), 12.
7. Cicero, *De Divinatione*, I.56; emphases added. Goldschmidt quotes all but the last sentence (*SS* 80).
8. Goldschmidt writes about the 'image of the unfolding of a cable', and Deleuze says that 'Cicero puts it well when he said that the passage of time is similar to the unraveling of a thread (*explicatio*)' (*SS* 80; *LS* 144).
9. Cicero, *De Divinatione*, I.118, as quoted in *SS*.
10. Ibid. I.56, as quoted in *SS*.
11. Friedrich Nietzsche, *The Nietzsche Reader*, ed. Keith Ansell-Pearson and Duncan Large (Malden, MA: Wiley-Blackwell, 2006), 114. The famous *Dream of Scipio*, as reported in Cicero's *De Re Publica*, echoes this dilation of the act. Scipio Aemiluans dreams he encounters his ancestor Scipio Africanus, which then transports him to the perspective of the stars. Such a broad perspective allows Scipio to consider the insignificance of the human perspective. For more, see Pierre Hadot, *What is Ancient Philosophy?*, trans. Michael Chase (Cambridge, MA: Belknap Press, 2004), 205–7.
12. For more on Deleuze and the non-human perspective, see Jon Roffe and Hannah Stark (eds), *Deleuze and the Non/Human* (New York: Palgrave Macmillan, 2015).
13. 'The surest way to know the cosmic end of an event', writes Goldschmidt, 'will be, while affirming it, to refrain from interpreting according to our own preferences' (*SS* 98).
14. Epictetus, *Discourses, Books I–II*, trans. W. A. Oldfather (Cambridge, MA: Harvard University Press, 1925), II.7.
15. Ibid.
16. Hadot, *What is Ancient Philosophy?*, 211; Hadot continues: 'from

Pyrrho, he remarked on how hard it is to strip ourselves of the human, to Aristotle, for whom life according to the mind is superhuman, and as far as Plotinus, who believed that in mystical experience we cease to be "human".' Gilles Deleuze, *Negotiations* (1995), trans. Martin Joughin (New York: Columbia University Press, 1990), 6.

17. Marcus Aurelius, *Meditations*, trans. R. Haines (Cambridge, MA: Harvard University Press, 1916), II.17.
18. In addition to the inability for humans to reach the divine vision, Goldschmidt also says the need for the second method is because divination merely 'proceeds by "conjecture"' (*SS* 103).
19. Epictetus, *Discourses I–II*, I.1.7, II.1.4, II.22.29; Epictetus, *Discourses, Books III–IV, The Encheiridion,* trans. W. A. Oldfather (Cambridge, MA: Harvard University Press, 1928), IV.6.34. See also A. A. Long, *Stoic Studies, From Epicurus to Epictetus: Studies in Hellenistic and Roman Philosophy* (Oxford: Clarendon Press, 2006), 275–85.
20. One difficulty, for example, is explaining how the derivation of rational representations (which are physical) from sensible representations (also physical); another is how 'that which constitutes the character of representation . . . may or may not be "comprehensible"' (*LS* 145).
21. Marcus Aurelius, *Meditations*, II.5.
22. Maurice Blanchot, *The Space of Literature*, trans. Ann Smock (Lincoln: The University of Nebraska Press, 1989), 96.
23. André Pierre Colombat draws a similar line form Stoic deaths to Deleuze's own. See André Pierre Colombat, 'November 4, 1995: Deleuze's death as an event', *Man and World* 29 (1996): 235–49, at 240.
24. 'The event is that no one ever dies, but has always just died or is always going to die' (*LS* 63).
25. To be more precise, Deleuze is pointing to the chapter titled 'The Work and Death's Space', in Blanchot, *The Space of Literature*, 85–159.
26. For more on Deleuze and Wittgenstein, see Reidar A. Due, 'At the Margins of Sense: The Function of Paradox in Deleuze and Wittgenstein', *Paragraph* 34.3 (November 2011): 358–70.
27. Goldschmidt compares this to what 'contemporary [to him] philosophy calls "structures"' (*SS* 195). Deleuze clearly agrees with Goldschmidt, without citing him (as usual), when he writes that 'Structuralism, whether consciously or not, celebrates new findings of a Stoic and Carrollian inspiration' (*LS* 71).
28. Epictetus, *Discourses I–II*, I.1.1. Surprisingly, Deleuze seems quite uninterested in this distinction, or, if he is, he casts it in a way that markedly avoids posing it in Epictetus' clear terms.
29. Epictetus, *Discourses III–IV*, IV.8.24.
30. It is tempting to identify several instances in the history of philosophy of thinking at infinite speed. For example, Deleuze sees Spinoza's

'incredible book five' of his *Ethics* as an extraordinary of thinking at infinite speeds that ends in the joyful affirmation of the world, where he also mentions Epicurus and Henri Michaux.

31. The quote within Deleuze's quote comes from Stéphane Mallarmé, *Œuvres complètes* (Paris: La Pléiade, Gallimard, 1945), 130.
32. Epictetus spoke highly of Diogenes, Socrates and Hercules throughout his *Discourses*; Seneca praises Cato and Hercules.
33. David Lapoujade, *Aberrant Movements: The Philosophy of Gilles Deleuze* (2014), trans. Joshua David Jordan (South Pasadena: Semiotext(e), 2017), 147.
34. We might also consider Melville's Bartleby, the scrivener, as a modern model of the Stoic sage. In the future, I plan to write a full essay on the figures of the Stoic sage in Deleuze's œuvre.
35. Deleuze describes the life of this 'very curious author' in a 1980 lecture, available at http://www2.univ-paris8.fr/deleuze/article.php3?id_article =215 (last accessed 8 February 2019).
36. Jack Reynolds recognises the importance of the concept of the wound in Deleuze, as he writes in the opening line to a 2007 article: 'Deleuze's œuvre is best understood as a philosophy of the wound synonymous with a philosophy of the event', as opposed to the preceedig phenomenological tradition's 'deleuzophy of the scar'. Jack Reynolds, 'Wounds and Scars: Deleuze on the Time and Ethics of the Event', *Deleuze Studies* 1.2 (December 2007): 167–94, at 52.
37. René Nelli, 'Joe Bousquet et son double', *Cahiers du sud* 303 (1950): 177–86, at 179; emphasis added.
38. Available at http://www2.univ-paris8.fr/deleuze/article.php3?id_article =215 (last accessed 8 February 2019).
39. Claude Imbert, 'Empiricism Unhinged: From the Logic of Sense to the Logic of Sensation', in *Introduction to the Philosophy of Gilles Deleuze*, ed. Jean Khalfa (London: Bloomsbury Academic, 2003), 133–48, at 139. Later Khalfa echoes this image of Bousquet, 'Deleuze seems to have seriously followed the thread of such incidents of Surrealism up to the point where Bousquet inscribes in it his Stoic paradigm, muddling up the heroic posture, erasing its grammar of the world and at once brings Surrealism to its point of philosophical identification.' Imbert, 'Empiricism Unhinged', 140.
40. In four books: *LS* 148; *WP* 159; Deleuze and Parnet, *Dialogues*, 65; *Pure Immanence: Essays on A Life* (1995), trans. Anna Boyman (New York: Zone Books, 2001), 31. Deleuze repeats this quote in several other places, such as his 1980 lectures on *Anti-Oedipus*. Available at http://www2.univ-paris8.fr/deleuze/article.php3?id_article=215 (last accessed 8 February 2019).
41. John Sellars notice a 'striking echo of Marcus Aurelius' in Bousquet's maxim: 'it was for you that it came about, and it was prescribed for you

and stands in a special relationship to you as something that was spun into your destiny from the beginning.' Sellars, 'Ethics of the Event', 161. While Sellars admits that he cannot find the Bousquet Propostion in the text Deleuze cites – Bousquet, *Les Capitales*, 103 – even though Deleuze always cites Nelli, 'Joe Bousquet et son double', 180: '*ma blessure existait avant moi: je suis né pour l'incarner*.'

42. Available at http://www2.univ-paris8.fr/deleuze/article.php3?id_article =215 (last accessed 8 February 2019).
43. Ferdinand Alquié, 'Joe Bouquet et la morale du langage', *Cahiers du sud* 303 (1950): 187–90, at 188.
44. Jean-Jacques Lecercle, *Deleuze and Language* (New York: Palgrave Macmillan, 2002), 115.
45. Available at http://www2.univ-paris8.fr/deleuze/article.php3?id_article =215 (last accessed 8 February 2019).
46. Gilles Deleuze, *The Fold: Leibniz and the Baroque* (1988), trans. Tom Conley (Minneapolis: University of Minnesota Press, 1993), 53.
47. Available at http://www2.univ-paris8.fr/deleuze/article.php3?id_article =215 (last accessed 8 February 2019).
48. Available at http://www2.univ-paris8.fr/deleuze/article.php3?id_article =215 (last accessed 8 February 2019). In the little piece called 'Lewis Carroll' in *Essays Clinical and Critical*, Deleuze uses the language of 'escape': 'Pure events *escape* from states of affairs.' Deleuze, *Essays Critical and Clinical*, 21; emphasis added.
49. Seneca, *Epistles 66–92*, trans. Richard M. Gummere (Cambridge, MA: Harvard University Press, 1920), 30.
50. Deleuze uses 'counter-actualization' in several texts. In *LS*, for example, see 150–2, 157, 161, 175–6, 178–9, 221. Lecercle suggests that 'the term [*contre-effectuation*] is probably coined on the Freudian term of anticathexis *contre-investissement* in French'. Lecercle, *Deleuze and Language*, 116.
51. Ian Buchanan claims that counter-actualisation is 'the practical basis of a transcendental empiricist ethics; it is what one does if one is ethical, if one is worth.' Ian Buchanan, *Deleuzism: A Metacommentary* (Edinburgh: Edinburgh University Press, 2000), 78.
52. '[T]he egg, in effect, provides us with a model for the order of reasons: (organic and species related) differentiation-individuation-dramatisation-differenciation' (*DR* 251).
53. 'Actualization' is all over *Logic of Sense*. In *Difference and Repetition*, the common term is 'differenciation' or, in a way, 'individuation' (*DR* 246).
54. Available at https://www.webdeleuze.com/textes/35 (last accessed 8 February 2019).
55. Sean Bowden, *The Priority of Events: Deleuze's Logic of Sense* (Edinburgh: Edinburgh University Press, 2011), 43.

56. Blanchot, *The Space of Literature*, 104.
57. Ibid. 106.
58. Ibid. 107.
59. Ibid. 105.
60. Ibid. 103; emphasis added.
61. Ibid. emphasis added.
62. Ibid. 104.
63. Ibid. 102.
64. Ibid. 103.
65. Ibid.
66. Ibid. 105.
67. Lipsius, *Justus Lipsius: On Constancy: De Constantia Translated by Sir John Stradling*, ed. John Sellars, trans. John Stradling (Liverpool: Liverpool University Press, 2006). Also see: Sellars, 'An Ethics of the Event: Deleuze's Stoicism', *Angelaki* II.3 (December 2006): 157–71, at 162–3.
68. Seneca, *Epistles 1–65*, 49.2–3.
69. Marcus Aurelius, *Meditations*, IV.48.
70. Epictetus, *Discourses III–IV*, 'Manual', 11.
71. Deleuze, *Negotiations*, 23. ATP 166.
72. Thomas Africa, 'The Opium Addiction of Marcus Aurelius', *Journal of the History of Ideas* 22 (1961): 97–102.
73. Since these terms come from Nietzsche, not from the Stoics, we are highlighting Deleuze's relationship to Stoicism as part of a longer lineage that reveals a particular kind of fidelity. According to Pierre Hadot, 'amor fati' were never used by any ancient Latin writer. Hadot, *Inner Citadel*, 143.
74. Nelli, 'Joe Bousquet et son double', 180. Nelli also calls it a 'diabolical pride'.
75. Deleuze quotes from Joë Bosquet, *Les Capitales: ou de Jean Duns Scott à Jean Paulhan* (Montolieu: Deyrolle-Verdier, 1999), 103.
76. Jeff Bradley, 'The Eyes of the Fourth Person Singular', *Deleuze Studies* 9.2 (2015): 185–207, at 186–7.
77. Marcus Aurelius, *Meditations*, IX.32.
78. Bradley, 'The Eyes of the Fourth Person Singular', 197. Bradley notices several Stoic themes in Ferlinghetti's *Her*. He cites Cherkovski's description of *Her* as 'a book of spiritual exercises', his reference to Bréhier, and his claim that 'the fourth person singular . . . is a comparison with the Stoa' (188, 191).
79. Deleuze, *Essays Critical and Clinical*, 51.

9

The Albumen C: Eternal Return

> We shall not cease from exploration.
> And the end of all our exploring.
> Will be to arrive where we started.
> And know the place for the first time.
>
> T. S. Eliot, *Little Gidding*[1]

Introduction

In 'Albumen A', we saw Deleuze draw correlations between the two faces of time – chronos and aion – and two eternal returns. Although we then looked at the two faces of time, we have not yet considered the two eternal returns. While Deleuze claims to find 'two very different eternal returns, themselves corresponding to the two times', he admits they do 'not appear (at least directly) in Stoic thought' (*LS* 340n.3). While he promises to 'return to these points', he never does (*LS* 340n.3). In order to will make good on Deleuze's unfulfilled promise, we return to the two eternal returns in 'Albumen C'.

We begin by considering the history and meaning of the Stoic doctrine of cosmic conflagration. Since this consideration evokes Nietzsche's formulation of the doctrine of eternal recurrence, we pose a question that requires the consideration of two stories of the Argentine author Jorge Luis Borges, 'Pierre Menard, Author of the *Quixote*' and 'Death and the Compass'. Borges's stories raise the paradox of action, which leads us to the Stoics' principle of ateleological providence. After this, we take up Deleuze's discussion of F. Scott Fitzgerald's mental breakdown as expressed in his essay 'The Crack-Up', and then conclude with a different kind of crack-up, the cracking up of laughter. In the final section of 'Albumen C', we survey four ancient forms of philosophical comedy, culminating in a theory of Stoic humour.

Cosmic Conflagration

The general doctrine most likely originated with the early Stoics, although they did not consistently use a single term that we could translate as 'eternal return' or 'eternal recurrence'.[2] Since the vocabulary varied with each Stoic, and Diogenes' reports likely conflate the variations, let us survey these different terms.

A Chrysippus fragment uses περίοδος χρόνου, suggesting 'the return to a starting point', as in a 'circuit ... notably in the revolution of the stars'; Jean-Baptiste Gourinat says that this term suggests a 'periodic recommencement' or 'periodic renaissance'.[3] Other modern commentators see in Marcus Aurelius, Philo and Alexander of Aphrodisias reason to use the term Παλιγγενεσία and related terms.[4] Most commonly, several authors, including Chrysippus, use the term ἐκΠύρωσις, a combination of ἐκ- ('out of, forth from') plus Πύρωσις ('firing, burning').[5] We must be precise here, as the 'usual translation of ἐκΠύρωσις as "conflagration" is misleading', Sambursky notes, 'because it suggests a sudden catastrophe'.[6] The imagery of 'out of the fire' contrasts with the watery or flood imagery of Κατακλυσμός (cataclysmos) or inundation.[7] Instead, 'ἐκΠύρωσις originally denoted that period of the cosmic cycle where the preponderance of the fiery element reaches its maximum'.[8] Conflagration is thus not cataclysmic. Fire, to the ancients, possessed the power of purification (Κάθαρσις, catharsis), more than catastrophe.[9] This means that 'conflagration' as a translation of ἐκΠύρωσις is best because it conveys that Heraclitean sense of a metaphysical fire.[10] Fire is 'the element par excellence' (*HP* 47A). After a certain period of time, the Stoic cosmos consumes itself in an incandescent blaze.[11] Combustion rather than catastrophe.

There is an order to the conflagration cycle: from the initial pure fire to the four elements, back to fire, and repeat. As Diogenes reports, the cosmos emerges

> when its substance has first been converted from fire through air into moisture and then the coarser part of the moisture has condensed as earth, while that whose particulates are fine has been turned into air, and this process of rarefaction goes on increasing till it generates fire. (DL 7.142)

Stobaeus describes the reciprocal movement that marks the return to the genetic metaphysical fire: 'from the dissolution and diffusion of earth, the first diffusion is into water, the second from water into air, the third and last into fire' (*HP* 47A).

The Albumen C: Eternal Return

Overlooking, for a moment, a few differences among the Stoics, we can map the whole cyclical order: (metaphysical) fire → air → water → earth → *all four elements* → earth → water → air → (metaphysical) fire. Speaking precisely, it is not accurate to say that, at each phase of this cycle, the whole of an element changes into another element. Instead, only *some* of the initial fire becomes air, and *some* that becomes water, until, at a later phase, all four elements intermix for the period of existence in which humans emerge. At the very beginning or end, which both coincide on the same point, is metaphysical fire.[12] With each conflagration, a cosmos emerges, in the same order and sequence, which eventually conflagrates and returns the very same cosmos. From fire to fire, each turn of the cosmos follows a 'physics of combustion'.[13] We thus agree with John Sellars's suggestion that this process is not 'an endless *series* of cycles' but 'a *single* cycle, repeated endlessly'.[14] Nemesius of Emesa puts it best:

> The Stoics say that when the planets return to the same celestial sign, in length and breadth, where each was originally when the world was first formed, at set periods of time [χρόνων περίοδος] they cause conflagration [ἐκπύρωσιν] and destruction of existing things. Once again the world returns anew to the same condition as before; and when the stars are moving again in the same way, each thing which occurred in the previous period will come to pass indiscernibly [from its previous occurrence]. For again there will be Socrates and Plato and each one of mankind with the same friends and fellow citizens; they will suffer the same things and they will encounter the same things, and put their hand to the same things, and every city and village and piece of land return in the same way. The periodic return of everything occurs not once but many times; or rather, the same things return infinitely and without end . . . there will be nothing strange in comparison with what occurred previously, but everything will be just the same and indiscernible down to the smallest details. (*HP* 52C)[15]

While Heraclitus, the Pythagoreans, and others, inspired the concept of the return, Gourinat correctly claims: 'it is indeed a Stoic doctrine'.[16] Still, not every Stoic conceived of the eternal return in the same way. Some Stoics – including Diogenes of Babylon, his student Boethius of Sidon, as well as Panaetius – refuted or rejected the doctrine in order to save the indestructibility of the world.[17] In recent scholarship, some conservative scholars have tried to explain away the logical errors in the theory, even though most of the Stoics affirmed and returned to the doctrine of the conflagration, from the first masters of the Greek Stoa – Zeno, Cleanthes, Chrysippus – to the late Roman emperor Marcus Aurelius.[18] There is something about the doctrine that grips us, that calls us back again and again. This is true of many figures in Deleuze's lineage, especially Nietzsche.

Friedrich Nietzsche, Author of Eternal Recurrence

When Nietzsche, almost two thousand years after the Stoics, first mentions the eternal return in the penultimate aphorism of *The Gay Science*, the sense of his words is incredibly similar to Nemesius' report given above. Nietzsche writes:

> What, if some day or night, a demon were to steal after you in your loneliest loneliness and say to you: 'This life as you now live it and have lived it, you will have to live once more and innumerable times more; and there will be nothing new in it, but every pain and every joy and every thought and sigh and everything unutterably small or great in your life will have to return to you, all in the same succession and sequence – even this spider and this moonlight between the tress, and even this moment and I myself. This eternal hourglass of existence is turned upside down again and again, and you with it speck of dust.'[19]

Given the strong similarity of this passage and the one from Nemesius we just examined, it is unclear why Nietzsche claims to discover, for the first time, the concept of eternal recurrence because Nietzsche was well acquainted with the concept long before he 'discovered' it in August 1881 while walking along a path in *Silvaplana*, near a pyramidal block. He was, after all, a philologist, not a philosopher, and so well aware that the Stoics formulated the concept millennia before. Deleuze, too, puzzled the question: 'Why did Nietzsche, who knew the Greeks, know that the eternal return was *his* own invention, an untimely belief or belief of the future' (*DR* 242; emphasis original). Even Jorge Luis Borges, the Argentine master who Deleuze cites in most of his books, asks the same question: 'Can Nietzsche, the Hellenist, have been ignorant of these "precursors"?'[20] Borges's short story 'Pierre Menard, Author of the *Quixote*' provides us with the means for an answer.[21]

Borges's story is an imagined review of a fake French writer, the eccentric Pierre Menard, who sought to a write a new and improved version of Cervantes's *Don Quixote*, one that includes the historical events that followed its 1615 publication. 'Pierre Menard did not want to compose *another* Quixote,' Borges writes, 'he wanted to compose *the* Quixote.'[22] More than mere copying, Menard aimed to

The Albumen C: Eternal Return

write that Spanish classic *again for the first time*. 'His ambition was to produce a number of pages which coincided – word for word and line for line – with those of Miguel de Cervantes.'[23] To ensure this rewriting was a first writing, Menard wrote endless drafts, spanning thousands of pages, all of which were burned without anyone else seeing them. In the end, while both texts were identical, Menard's was 'almost infinitely richer'.[24]

As Pierre Menard used 'the technique of deliberate anachronism and fallacious attribution', we use this same new technique to understand the eternal return and Nietzsche's claims of originality.[25] First, swap out the names: 'Pierre Menard' becomes 'Friedrich Nietzsche' (although it might be just as well to insert 'Zarathustra', 'Dionysius' or 'The Antichrist'). Second, replace the title: *Don Quixote* becomes *The Eternal Return*. While Pierre Menard used the same words as Cervantes, although his were infinitely richer, Nietzsche will use the same conceptual structure, but is infinitely richer. Moreover, Menard's and Nietzsche's re-writings were '[m]ore ambiguous ... but ambiguous is richness'.[26] We see how Nietzsche's eternal return is infinitely richer and more ambiguous than the Stoics' if we compare the ancient formulation:

> The periodic return of everything occurs not once but many times; or rather, the same things return infinitely and without end ... there will be nothing strange in comparison with what occurred previously, but everything will be just the same and indiscernible down to the smallest details. (*HP* 52C)

with the nineteenth-century version:

> This life as you now live it and have lived it, you will have to live once more and innumerable times more; and there will be nothing new in it ... and everything unutterably small or great in your life will have to return to you, all in the same succession and sequence.[27]

While not verbally identical word for word, the two formulations are conceptually identical part for part.

While Hadot is right to notice that an 'abyss appears between' Nietzsche's and the Stoics' use of the eternal return, he is wrong to think that this abyss makes them incompatible.[28] The latter is infinitely richer in so far as Nietzsche immobilizes the Stoic doctrine so that the ancient concept and the Nietzschean concept recur *in* each other; the earlier version returns in the latter. In our language, 'Nietzsche was able to rediscover depth only after conquering the surfaces' (*LS* 129). The depths are the ideas of the early Greek pre-Socratics into which Nietzsche dove into and swam through in his early works (*The Birth of Tragedy*, *Philosophy in the Tragic Age of the Greeks*, 'Homer's Contest') and Schopenhauerian pessimism ('Schopenhauer as Educator', 'The Relation between a Schopenhauerian Philosophy and a German Culture'). By diving into the depths, like a nineteenth-century German Empedocles diving into the volcano, Nietzsche gives the eternal return a *double existence*. Not only does Nietzsche return, via the concept of infinite recurrence, to Stoicism, but the Stoics recur in Nietzsche, via the same concept. On the first go around, the course curves along the arc of a circle; on the second, the line flattens out into a straight line – the same concept but a difference in priority. The Stoic doctrine appears to prioritise the circle, while Nietzsche finds a straight line. In a moment, we will align these with the two faces of Stoic time: the circle with chronos and the straight line with aion. To get there, we need to first turn to another Borges story.

'Death and the Compass'

In Borges's 'Death and the Compass', Erik Lönnrot, a famous detective in an unnamed city (possibly Buenos Aires), pursues a series of murders that seem to follow a Kabbalistic pattern. Three murders happen on the third days of December, January and February, respectively. At the scene of the first murder, a message left in the typewriter of a slain rabbi says: 'the first letter of the name has been uttered'.[29] Lönnrot connects this to the Tetragrammaton, the unsayable four-letter name of God – YHWH – and his arch nemesis, Red Scharlach. At the second and third murder scenes, similar messages were found: 'The second letter of the name has been uttered' and 'The last letter of the name has been uttered'.[30] Convinced that the killing was not finished, since the Tetragrammaton has four letters, and aware that the Jewish calendar designates the beginning of a new day at sunset (the murders happened at night), Lönnrot divines that the murders actually occurred on the fourth, not the third, of the respective months. 'Symmetry in time', Lönnrot noticed, and 'symmetry in space'.[31] A final murder, he further divines, would thus occur on 4 March. Eventually, the detective's office plots the locations of the murders on a map, which, taken together, form the west, north and east cardinal points of a compass rose. The south part of the city was still unaffected, and thus should be the site of the fourth murder.

Lönnrot travels to Triste-le-Roy, the site at the south point of

The Albumen C: Eternal Return

the compass, in order to catch the murderers unaware. But when he arrives, two imposing men seize Lönnrot. As Scharlach steps out of the shadows, Lönnrot realises that he is caught in a maze of revenge. Scharlach explains that, although he had sworn himself to avenge the death of his brother, who Lönnrot personally sent to die in prison, the Kabbalistic pattern of the murders was unintended. Scharlach never intended to kill that rabbi, the first murder victim, and it was the rabbi, not Scharlach, whose cryptic writing was left in his typewriter, which Lönnrot interpreted as the first letter of the Tetragrammaton. While the emergent pattern was accidental, Scharlach embraced the event in order to exploit Lönnrot's 'rigorously strange' 'perspicacity' and lure him to the final murder site.[32] At the instant of their face-to-face encounter, their positions are reversible. Lönnrot, once the hunter, is now the hunted, and the reverse for Scharlach. Then, as 'an impersonal, almost anonymous sadness' comes upon him, Lönnrot consoles himself by affirming the doctrine of the eternal return. Scharlach had made the labyrinth overly complicated, Lönnrot explained, for 'I know of a Greek labyrinth which is a single straight line'[33]:

> Along this line so many philosophers have lost themselves that a mere detective might well do so too. Scharlach, when, in some other incarnation you hunt me, feign to commit (or do commit) a crime at A, then a second crime at B, eight kilometers from A, then a third crime at C, four kilometers from A and B, halfway en route between the two. Wait for me later at D, two kilometers from A and C, halfway, once again, between both. Kill me at D, as you are now going to kill me at Triste-le-Roy.[34]

Lönnrot is describing Zeno's paradox of infinite divisibility, which structures the line of aion. At his last moment, before the impossible event of death, Lönnrot straightens out the rounded compass so that it forms a labyrinthine straight line. Scharlach accepts this shift in the labyrinth. 'The next time I kill you', he responds, 'I promise you the labyrinth made of the single straight line which is invisible and everlasting.'[35] The criminal then steps back and shoots Lönnrot.

Both detective and criminal double each other in so far as they form the two movements leading out from the same event: the 'to shoot' (*tirer* or *tuer*) enveloped by the final murder scene in which Scharlach shoots Lönnrot. Not only does Scharlach kill Lönnrot with the detective's own pistol, even their names are doubles of each other.[36] The two would meet again until the next recurrence, and the event waits for them to reach the end of their inverted paths through the same labyrinth. Scharlach and Lönnrot are thus Borgesian embodiments of what Deleuze calls the 'living formulation of philosophy':

> philosophers are beings who have passed through a death, who are born from it, and go towards another death, perhaps the same one ... they themselves believe that they are dead, that they have passed through death; and they also believe that, although dead, they continue to live, but in a shivering way, with tiredness and prudence ... the philosopher is someone who believes he has returned from the dead, rightly or wrongly, and who returns to the dead in full consciousness. (*DR* 11)

'Death and the Compass' fascinated Deleuze, as he quotes that fabulous line – a 'labyrinth that is a single straight line' – several times. Usually, the line appears when he is thinking about time, such as, Kant's 'reversal of the movement–time relationship' or the third synthesis of time in *Difference and Repetition*.[37] These two figures of the labyrinth – the circular compass and the infinitely divisible straight line – correspond to two senses of time: the compass refers to circular labyrinth of chronos, while the line refers to aionic straight line.[38] Further, these two senses of time correspond to two eternal returns. There is, Deleuze explains, in 'aion a labyrinth very different from that of chronos – a labyrinth more terrible still, which commands *another* eternal return' (*LS* 62; emphasis original). One return is cyclical, another a straight line.

On the cyclical return, the present is everything because the past and future determine subsistent dimensions of an extended temporal whole. Every chronological present is extensively determined, whether it is the smallest body or the entire cosmos; there is no change in kind between this or that present. As Marcus Aurelius notes, 'the longest comes to the same thing as the shortest' (*HP* 52H). This is why 'the present time', Marcus continues, 'is of equal duration for all'.[39] On the return of the straight line, however, the present is nothing, a mere mathematical point or instant, because the aionic present constantly decomposes 'into elongated pasts and futures' (*LS* 62). Past, present and future are simultaneous and subsistent, rather than successive and existent.

There are thus two returns corresponding to two times and two labyrinths: the first is always limited and definite, the second eternally unlimited and infinitive. The first is 'the physical and cyclical Chronos of the variable living present', and the second is the forking 'path [*l'allée*] stretching far ahead and far behind' (*LS* 61; translation mine). 'One is cyclical,' Deleuze claims, 'the other is a pure straight line at the surface' (*LS* 61). It is a straight line because it never turns back on itself, but reaches out as 'a pure straight line the two extremities of which endlessly distance themselves [*s'éloigner*] from each other and become deferred into the past and the future' (*LS* 61).

Paradox of Action

The two eternal returns express the paradox of action. One half of the paradox involves the circular, chronological eternal return; the other, the straight line of the aionic eternal return,

In the circular return, the event is enveloped in a present state of affairs. Stoic ethics is concerned with willing the event, that is, affirming its actualisation in a state of affairs. It is because the event is actualised, Goldschmidt writes, that 'the doctrine of the eternal return and the determinism that it envelops concludes not with the laziness argument but by a call to freedom' (*SS* 190). To will the event is to act in accord with nature, and every act occurs in the present. We must, and can, act *now*. There is no other time to act, for the past is already done and the future always to come. Even though the moments before and beyond encircle the present, they remain forever out of reach. Just as we drown in water whether we are twenty thousand leagues down or an inch from the surface, we are as cut off from the yesterday or tomorrow as we are from the time of Zeno or the next conflagration. Bound to the present by the limits of the past and the future, we have only now, the extended chronological present. Moreover, since this life as we now live it has already come round infinitely many number of times before, every act is already finished. Like Bousquet's wound, the act exists before us, awaiting our will, and we have no choice but to affirm what had and will always happen. Whatever deed is done, it was done before because it is the course of the cosmos.

And yet, *and yet* – we must act. Yes, we already acted; yes, every deed was destined prior to our supposed choice to do so. Yet act we must. We have no say in the matter because it already happened, but we cannot *not* act. Hence one side of the double bind of time: action is *impossible yet necessary* because every 'forward' turn round the circle is simultaneously a turn backwards, in so far as the passage of chronological time requires what happens at each moment to pass away into the past. To see this, imagine walking along the arc of a fixed circle. As we move 'forwards' in time, what we encounter ahead of us also moves 'backwards in time' so that both movements

– forwards and backwards – happen simultaneously. Even more, as we ourselves move towards the future, we are simultaneously moving towards the past. The chronological eternal return follows that same double-sensed logic.

The other half of the paradox of action follows the straight line of the aionic eternal return. Here is a second double bind of time, now coming from the straight line rather than the circle: we simultaneously *must yet cannot* act at every instant because the 'now' never exists in aion. Even if we stop pining for a nostalgic past or yearning for better future in order to focus on the present, we find not a robust present but what Goldschmidt calls an 'evanescent virtuality' (*SS* 194). Trying to act *now* never happens because the 'present itself dissipates in an infinitesimal instant' (*SS* 196).[40] Since the present is inexistent in aion, endlessly dividing beneath our feet, we seem unable to act. The time to act never arrives, or every act is always too late or too soon. And yet, *and yet* – now is when we *must* act. This is the temporality of the aionic eternal return, the labyrinth of the straight line. We never act because that line subdivides infinitely at every point. We never get around to acting yet we cannot *not* act at every instant.

On both returns, we are compelled to act even though we cannot, or perhaps it is better to say that we are must act *because* we cannot. Referencing Cicero's *De Fato*, Deleuze puts it thus: 'The Stoic paradox is to affirm destiny and to deny necessity' (*LS* 169). The doctrine of eternal recurrence entails this double, paradoxical affirmation, which corresponds to Deleuze's 'affirmative synthetic disjunction', that is,

> the erection of a paradoxical instance, an aleatory point with two uneven faces which traverses the divergent series as divergent and causes them to resonate through their distance and in their distance. Thus the ideational center of convergence is by nature perpetually decentered ... This is why it seemed that an esoteric, ex-centric path was opened to us, a path altogether different from the ordinary one. (*LS* 174)

The paradox of action compels a perverse imperative, especially when compared to Kant's imperative (which is even more perverse when we consider how greatly Stoicism shapes deontology). While the categorical imperative commands the universalisation of every intention, the 'eternal return says', for Deleuze, 'whatever you will, will it in such a manner that you also will its eternal return' (*DR* 7). Calling it 'Zarathustra's moral test', although it is also Zeno's or Chrysippus' test, Deleuze sees a 'formalism' that perverts or 'overturns Kant on his own ground' (*DR* 7). Such willing contracts the whole of time into an instant. The straight line folds up every point in time, as the rotational force is full at every point where a tangent touches the circle. Instead of relating the will to an abstract formal law or implementing a test for evaluating an intention, the eternal return makes 'repetition itself the only form of a law beyond morality' (*DR* 7). The dual forms of the circle and the straight line together enact a 'brutal form [*forme brutale*]' in so far as they bring together universal and the particular in a single inclusive disjunction: a singular act assumes and entails a universal determination (*DR* 7).[41] A singular act is like Bousquet's wound, a pre-individual singularly that exists prior to his wounding. The dual form of the eternal return 'dethrones every general law, dissolves the mediations and annihilates the particulars subjected to the law' (*DR* 7). 'Today's task', which we might call the Stoic's task, 'is to make the empty square circulate and to make pre-individual and non-personal singularities speak' (*LS* 73). The dual eternal returns form a double figure that perverts the categorisation that emerges like a mist from the formal logic of affirmative and negative, universal and particular, categorical and hypothetical, assertoric and apodictic. It is like taking the third terms in Kant's Table of Judgements – infinite, singular, disjunctive, problematic – and pushing them along the arc of the circular eternal return. The Stoic doctrine exceeds the general–particular dualism through the perverse imperative of the Stoic act, leading to the singular.

Providence without Teleology

One reason why Chrysippus included the discussion of 'the world's renewal ... after certain periods of time' in his book *On Providence* is because the doctrine of the eternal return bears on the providential organisation of the Stoic cosmos. To understand Stoic providence, we must remember that it is ateleological. As much as the Stoics affirm providence, they reject final causes.

The commentators concur on the Stoics' principle of ateleological providence. Michael Frede, for example, writes: 'the Stoics rejected ... Aristotelian final cause as causes, properly speaking'.[42] Frederique Ildefonse writes that 'Stoic cosmology is not a finalist representation of nature' but 'a materialism of the power of bodies'.[43] Here Ildefonse notices resonances with Spinoza's 'rational philosophy – *more geometrico*, founded on a fully actual reality, a unique substance which is God or nature, free of finality'.[44] According to

Bréhier, 'the Stoic theory of causality explicitly contests the primacy that Plato and Aristotle had accorded to the end [*à la fin*] and to form [*à la forme*]' (*SS* 91). 'Unlike Aristotle', notes Boeri, 'who had used τέλος [end] and σκοπός [target, goal] interchangeable to make reference to end, the Stoics distinguished two kinds of finality' – target and end – that respectively align with the corporeal and incorporeal distinction.[45] 'While a σκοπός (expressed by a noun: "happiness") is a body,' Boeri writes, 'a τέλος (expressed by a verb or, in the Stoic jargon, by a predicate: "being happy") is an incorporeal.'[46] 'If it is true', writes Deleuze, 'that passions and evil intentions are bodies, it is true that good will, virtuous actions, true representations, and just consents are also bodies' (*LS* 143). Thus the target is happiness in so far as it is set up before us as something at which we aim our actions, intentions and desires because the *target is a body*. The end, however, either is or is not attributed to the state of affairs in which we exist. So, if the ethical end of Stoicism is 'living in accord with nature', then the end is an incorporeal attribute. The end is not a bodily thing but the acquisition of the attribute 'being happy'. If providence concerns ends, and teleology concerns targets, then providence concerns incorporeal surface effects and teleology concerns corporeal causal depths. 'Providence', Bréhier agrees, 'is estimated only by its effects, not its divine essence' (*CAS* 204).

We can see this principle of 'providence without teleology' in the characterisation of the sage as archer or bowman. Deleuze cautions about this image: 'the archer should not be understood as a moral metaphor for intention' because Stoics reject teleology (*LS* 146). Aiming the bow is not like forming an intention to actualise an indeterminate possibility but more like aligning oneself with, and affirming one's place in, the course of the cosmos. The sage acts not in order to realise a potential target beyond nature but 'in order *to have done* all that which depended on one in order to attain the end [*le but*]' (*LS* 146; emphasis added). This conjugated form – 'to have done' – marks the temporality of the sage's act. The sage does not aim to act contrary to fate but to take on what is 'up to her' or 'subject to her will' in order *to have lived* in accord with nature. The sage seeks to reach the point at which the incorporeal end is not a corporeal target but the archer's act. Perched on the limit marking the beginning and end point of a cosmic cycle, the sage-archer aims at this instant, not an unrealised τέλος. The instantaneous limit is both a part of (because corporeal) and apart from (because incorporeal) the cosmos because it is the coincidence of the first and final movements

The Albumen C: Eternal Return

of the cosmic cycle. The target at which the archer aims transforms from the circle into the straight line as the arrow's movement infinitely subdivides at every instant, as in Zeno's paradox or Lönnrot's labyrinth. This is 'where the arrow flies over its straight line while creating its own target; where the surface of the target is also the line and the point' (*LS* 146). This point marks the erasure of the distance between intention and action. The bowman becomes the surface (or limit where the chronological eternal return begins and ends) *and* the shooting of the arrow is the straight line (of the aionic eternal return) *and* the point that is shot at (or the infinitesimal point in the chaosmic depths). The eternal returns carry a 'vertiginous movement endowed with a force . . . one which selects, one which expels as well as creates' (*DR* 11). If the sage has an intention, it is to have done with intending and *to have acted* in accord with the cosmos.

Put differently, Stoic sagacity is the point at which the archer, the shooting of the arrow, and the target contract into a singular act. The sage does not strain for an end but waits for the arrival of the event because she '*understands the pure event* in its eternal truth, independently of its spatio-temporal actualisation, as something eternally yet-to-come and always already passed according to the line of the aion' (*LS* 146; emphasis original). The sage knows the event cannot be fully actualised in the physical depths due to its incorporeality, but at the same time, she '*wills the embodiment* and the actualisation of the pure incorporeal event in a state of affairs and in her own body and flesh' (*LS* 146; emphasis added). This is the double-sensed logic of simultaneous actualisation and counter-actualisation, which Deleuze calls the 'Stoic will as προαίρεσις', Epictetus' word for 'choice, will, selection' (*LS* 146).[47] 'Stoic ethics', in short, 'consists in willing the event as such' (*LS* 142). When the sage acts, when the archer shoots, she becomes the 'quasi-cause of the incorporeal event' (*LS* 147). The sage does not create the event like a bodily cause, but instead 'operates and wills only what comes to pass' as a quasi-cause 'doubling the physical causality' (*LS* 147). The sage's act is the actualisation of the event in 'the most limited possible present . . . the pure instant at which it divides itself into future and past' (*LS* 147). What happens is meant *to have-happened*, in the past perfect. The Stoic sage wills the past perfect of the present.

This sense of προαίρεσις expresses ateleological providence. In so far as we occupy the instant, providence is eternally here and now. This suggests that Mansfield is wrong to claim that the conflagration at the beginning/end of the world is synonymous with providence and that the state of the conflagration is the best possible world because this would make the very act of world-creation non-providential.[48] If the conflagration were the best state, Mansfield argues, then it would be counter-providential to create an inferior cosmos. In response, we argue that every point on the circle, not just the originary metaphysical fire, is the beginning-end, just as every point on an infinite line is the exact middle.[49] Hence another inclusive disjunction: either there is no beginning or end or every point is both beginning and end. Either way, we are always at the limit of the eternal return, the edge of the cosmos. This is precisely how the sage sees the cosmos, which Spinoza might call *sub specie aeternitatis*.[50] Seneca describes this sense of finding oneself alone at the edge of the cosmos: 'It will be like the life of Jupiter, at the time when the world is dissolved and the gods have been blended together into one, when nature comes to a stop for a while.'[51] Providence is not only that final/first blaze of metaphysical fire, but subsists at every instant. We are always perched at the limit separating and connecting the beginning and the end of the cosmic cycle. Providence is eternally *right now*, this very instant.

Fitzgerald's Crack-Up

This sense of ateleological providence, and the archer-sage's *proairetic* willing of the event, is captured by what Deleuze considers one of the most devastating and masterful propositions:

> '*Of course all life is a process of breaking down . . .*'[52]

This is the first sentence of F. Scott Fitzgerald's three-part essay 'The Crack-Up' (French translation: 'La Fêlure'), from the February 1936 issue of *Esquire* magazine.[53] For Deleuze, this essay is the unfolding of that masterful proposition, as it is depicted in Fitzgerald's explanation of an alcohol-induced 'disintegration of one's own personality'.[54]

The most important part of Fitzgerald's proposition is the first two words: 'of course'. According to the *Oxford English Dictionary*, 'of course' is a condensation of a group of phrases reaching back to the 1540s, including, 'of the ordinary course' and 'as a matter of course'.[55] 'Of course' is the affirmation *of* the *course of* the *cosmos*, or what the Stoics call *fatum*. The course of nature is a series of events that mark the points at which the surface of bodies splits open, but without revealing something deeper or higher. Nothing is deeper than the surface cut, of course.

The Albumen C: Eternal Return

In Fitzgerald's essay, a wealthy, handsome couple – likely F. Scott and his wife Zelda (who herself experienced crack-ups throughout her life, eventually dying in her own conflagration) – has everything they need and want. Life was grand for the young people in the *Tales of the Jazz Age*. At the same time, just as everything seemed to be going marvellously well on this side of paradise, there were 'microcracks, as in a dish', creeping along the other side (*ATP* 198). The reason was that the course of Fitzgerald's life was not in accord with the course of nature. Swept up by the extravagances of the age, they did not even notice what was happening until it was too late, for 'the big sudden blows that . . . don't show their effect all at once' slowly but forcefully appear.[56] Yet happen they did, and by nature's decree. Their lives were double-sided, full of the beautiful and the damned. Fitzgerald turned to a philosophy 'of a first-rate intelligence' in any attempt to bring into accord the course of his life and the course of nature.

The mark of that philosophy is 'the ability to hold two opposed ideas in the mind at the same time, and still retain the ability to function'.[57] Recalling the paradoxical double-sided surface, we hear Stoic resonances: to move in opposed directions (*sens*) at the same time (*à la fois*). Later in the essay a conversation with an unknowing Spinozist taught Fitzgerald a lesson in this philosophy, just as he sensed the cracks forming: 'Listen,' she said. 'Suppose this wasn't a crack in you – suppose it was a crack in the Grand Canyon . . . if I ever cracked, I'd try to make the world crack with me. Listen! . . . it's much better to say that it's not you that's cracked – it's the Grand Canyon.'[58] The lesson was that the crack-up was not *his* but the *world's*. It did not just happen to Fitzgerald, the person, as it was a cosmological event, like the cleft of the Grand Canyon. *It*, not 'I', cracks up, the 'it' of Ferlinghetti's 'fourth person singular'. Soon, Fitzgerald realised that 'there was not an "I" anymore'.[59] The crack-up was a 'self-immolation', a literary conflagration.[60] 'I must continue to be a writer', he came to will, 'because that was my only way of life, but I would cease any attempts to be a person.'[61] This harsh exercise in depersonalisation made him feel 'like a little boy left alone in a big house, who knew that now he could do anything he wanted to do, but found that there was nothing that he wanted to do'.[62] Fitzgerald was striving to align himself with fate, to will the 'of course'.

By willing his crack-up as the same as the Grand Canyon, Fitzgerald perched himself along the border between inside and outside, self and world. As Deleuze writes, a 'crack is neither internal nor external, but is rather at the frontier' (*LS* 155). The crack is actualised deep within the cosmos; it subsists as a silent 'imperceptible, incorporeal' break in the surface of bodies. As Fitzgerald abused his body, caught in alcohol-fuelled passion of love and hate for the Lost Generation, the crack was actualised; yet as the crack grew, it remained incorporeal. When Fitzgerald wrote of the crack's depersonalised truth, he wrote in the name of the personal breakdown that he bears deep within his own body, from 'all the gallons of alcohol they have drunk which have actualized the crack in the body' (*LS* 157). It is only then, downtrodden and drowning in booze, his sense of self nearly demolished, that Fitzgerald could have asked the deepest question: 'Whatever could *have happened* for things to have come to this?' (*ATP* 194; emphasis added).

Conclusion: A Laughing Stoicism

To be clear, Deleuze is not advocating for alcoholism or self-harm. He is merely trying to articulate what it would mean to will the event, to affirm fate in all its glory and gory. The cyclical eternal return brings back every event, no matter how great or small. As Nemesius said above, 'everything will be just the same and indiscernible down to the smallest details' (*HP* 52C). From the soaring heights of *The Great Gatsby* to the devastating doldrums of bankruptcy and his wife's madness, all must return in the exact same order and sequence ad infinitum. Stoicism is about living, meaning that any abstract affirmation of the conflagration would be false; only its concrete confirmation and seal is true. Deleuze thus asks the troubling question: '[S]hould we go a short way further to see for ourselves, be a little alcoholic, a little crazy, a little suicidal, a little of a guerilla – just enough to extend the crack, but not enough to deepen it irremediably?' (*LS* 157–8). In abstraction, Stoicism seems wholesome and sensible, but in its concrete details, Stoicism is a little alcoholic, a little crazy, a little suicidal, a little guerrilla.

Like Stoicism, alcoholism is not the search for pleasure but for a distinct effect: the 'extraordinary hardening [*induration*] of the present' (*LS* 158). Notice the French word *induration*. It comes from the Latin *induratus* and includes the verb *durare*, meaning 'to harden'. The sense of hardness has a temporal valence. Something en*dure*s if it lasts over time; it is in*dur*ate if it spans a *dur*ation. The effect of alcoholism is a hardening in the sense of an extended duration where

The Albumen C: Eternal Return

a past subsists in a present. This is the indurate present, the hardness of which derives from the determinism of the providential cosmos. Cosmological determinacy hardens the present. What happens now has already happened infinitely many times before, and will happen infinitely many times after. I have done each and every thing I will ever do, which Deleuze calls 'the hardness of the present auxiliary: I have-loved, I have-done, I have-seen' (*LS* 158). This is the hard determinism of the circular eternal return, fixing the present on two sides, the past and the future.

At the same time, the hard, determined present surrounds a soft centre of a second moment like a volcano 'formed about a soft core of lava' (*LS* 158). This second moment 'exists in an entirely different and profoundly modified way' in so far as it is soft and 'ready to burst' (*LS* 158). This signifies the impossible freedom that comes with the imperative to act: we *both* must *and* cannot act at every instant. This is not the hardened circle but the infinitely divisible line that succumbs to every touch like 'liquid or viscous glass' (*LS* 158). The present is determined, 'hardened and tetanised', but the imperative to act freely, to will the event of the present, is contained within these rigid boundaries. Sinking into the infinitely dividing soft instant makes the rigid edges of the present fade away, which pushes both near and distance pasts and futures equally far away. If time is a number line, where numbers one and two mark the corners of the hard present, as we continuously subdivide the spaces in between, the edges of one and two soften away. Or perhaps it is wrong to speak of an act, because all acts, drawn together, become like numbers on a line, and perhaps it is better to speak of the *entr'acte*, the tender quasi-act between two acts, surrounded by the indurate past and future.

Since the past and the future are hardened, 'the alcoholic does not live at all in the imperfect or the future' but instead in the '*past perfect (passé composé)* – albeit a very special one' (*LS* 158; emphasis original). The past is perfect in the sense that it is over and done with, completed upon arrival. The future is as determined as the past, for the future of the cyclical eternal return is also the past, which Fitzgerald realises: whatever I do now, I *have done* infinitely many times before. The course of fate carries the imperative to act, even if that act is determined. And yet, this very imperative to act entails the soft freedom to act at this instant. We must act *now*, even while the 'now' infinitely divides into an 'infinitesimal interval'.[63] This perverse necessity yet impossibility of acting brings a sort of 'manic omnipotence [*tout-puissance maniaque*]' wherein the alcoholic feels caught between the lightest freedom and heaviest bondage at the same time (*à la fois*). The effect is a 'strange, almost unbearable tension' between the hardened circle of the deterministic eternal return and the soft line of the indeterminate eternal return, which takes the past perfect form of a 'I have-drunk (*j'ai bu*)' (*LS* 158, 159). The hardening of the present 'I have' is the effect of the past determining the present, that is, the effect is the present long since hardened by the past, the result of the determination of corporeal causes. Yet there is also 'the effect of the effect [*l'effet de l'effet*]' (*LS* 159). This is when the present auxiliary verb – 'I have' – does not contain past bouts of drinking but instead expresses the 'infinite distance' of the participle 'drunk'. 'Everything culminates in a "*has been*"' (*LS* 159).[64] This has been done before; everything happens according to a matter of course. The present is hardened by the eternal return of the natural cycle. At the same time (*à la fois*), however, cracks form at every instant, as the perspective of a singular life encounters not the promise of a circle but a straight line that demands yet prevents continuous action. The course of life does not wait for me to decide, but continues ad infinitum. Thus, now is the time, at every instant, for me to act, even though this *has been* done before infinitely times. Fitzgerald called it a 'laughing Stoicism'.[65]

Notes

1. T. S. Eliot, *Four Quartets* (Orlando: Harcourt Books, 1971), 59.
2. John Sellars, *Stoicism* (Berkeley: University of California Press, 2006), 97.
3. Jean-Baptiste Gourinat, 'Éternel retour: temps périodique dans la philosophie stoïcienne', *Revue philosophique de la France de l'étranger* 127 (2002): 216.
4. Ibid. 215.
5. Plutarch, *Moralia, Volume XIII: Part II, Stoic Essays*, trans. Harold Cerniss (Cambridge, MA: Loeb Classical Library, 1976), 1053b. Philo and Alexander also report uses of ἐκπύρωσις (*HP* 52A, 52F).
6. Samuel Sambursky, *Physics of the Stoics* (Princeton: Princeton University Press, 2014), 105n.82.
7. Thomas G. Rosenmeyer, *Senecan Drama and Stoic Cosmology* (Berkeley: University of California Press, 1989), 149.
8. Sambursky, *Physics of the Stoics*, 105n.82.
9. Michael Lapidge, 'Stoic Cosmology', in *The Stoics*, ed. R. M. Rist (Berkeley: University of California Press, 1978), 161–86, at 180.

The Albumen C: Eternal Return

10. Still, we should also appreciate that the Stoics turned 'fire into a principle which is closer to elementary thermodynamics than to anything resembling a fire that burns' (A. A. Long, 'The Stoics on World-Conflagration and Everlasting Recurrence', *The Southern Journal of Philosophy* XXIII, Supplement [1985]: 13–37, at 15). Stoic fire evokes biological heat that conserves as it consumes.
11. Long, 'The Stoics on World-Conflagration and Everlasting Recurrence', 21.
12. While metaphysical fire gets everything started, the empirical fire that we experience, the flaming hot light that burns, is also produced. In fact, different Stoics distinguish different kinds of fire. As Mansfield puts it, Cleanthes distinguishes between 'burning and destructive fire on the one hand, benevolent, sustaining, and vital fire on the other', while Zeno Stobaeus distinguishes between generative (or 'designing fire') and non-generative types of fire. Jaap Mansfield, 'Providence and the Destruction of the Universe in Early Stoic Thought. With Some Remarks on the "Mysteries of Philosophy"', in *Studies in Hellenistic Religions* (Leiden: E. J. Brill, 1979), 151–5. We can think of generative, metaphysical fire as resembling the unstable, fully dynamic state of the cosmos at the beginning of the universe, a sort of pure energy or galactic combustion. See John Sellars, *Stoicism* (Berkeley: University of California Press, 2006), 98–9 and Long, 'The Stoics on World-Conflagration and Everlasting Recurrence', 21.
13. Long, 'The Stoics on World-Conflagration and Everlasting Recurrence', 21.
14. Sellars, *Stoicism*, 99.
15. Origin reports that there was at least one, rather minor, Stoic who posited some slight variation in the cycles, so that each conflagration sparked a slightly different cosmos. See Michael J. White, 'Stoic Natural Philosophy (Physics and Cosmos)', in *The Cambridge Companion to the Stoics*, ed. Brad Inwood (Cambridge: Cambridge University Press, 2003), 143; Jacques Brunschwig, *Les Stoïciens et leur logique* (Paris: J. Vrin, 2006); and Jonathan Barnes, 'La doctrine du retour éternel', *Revue philosophique de la France et de l'étranger* 127.2 (2002): 421–40, at 421.
16. Gourinat, 'Éternel retour: temps périodique dans la philosophie stoïcienne', 213. Apart from Plato and Aristotle, who rejected the postulation of the destruction of the cosmos, most Stoic predecessors posited some version of a cyclical theory of destruction, including, among others, Hesiod, Heraclitus and Empedocles. See David Furley, 'Cosmology', in *The Cambridge History of Hellenistic Philosophy*, ed. Keimpe Algra et al. (Cambridge: Cambridge University Press, 2005), 412–49, at 439.
17. Mansfield, 'Providence and the Destruction of the Universe in Early

Stoic Thought', 186–7. Long, 'The Stoics on World-Conflagration and Everlasting Recurrence', 13.
18. See Long, 'The Stoics on World-Conflagration and Everlasting Recurrence', 13–14.
19. Friedrich Nietzsche, *The Gay Science* (1882), trans. Josefine Nauckhoff, ed. Bernard Williams (Cambridge: Cambridge University Press, 2001), 273.
20. Jorge Louis Borges, 'The Doctrine of Cycles', *Collected Fictions*, trans. Andrew Hurley (New York: Penguin Books, 1999), 119. Since there has not yet been a good study of the relationship between Deleuze and Borges, I plan to soon write one.
21. At the beginning of *Difference and Repetition*, Deleuze cites 'Pierre Menard' as a model for writing a commentary, similar to what we are writing now. 'In the history of Philosophy,' writes Deleuze, 'a commentary should act as a veritable double and bear the maximal modification appropriate to a double' (*DR* xxi). This is, in essence, the structure of what we call an 'encounter'. What we do in this book is neither simply Stoic nor Deleuzian, but a sort of double that is formed at the conjunction of both, and which bears the maximal modification that is appropriate to the double. Our book enacts 'a kind of slow motion, a congelation or immobilization of the text' (*DR* xxii). This immobilisation happens to both the Stoic and Deleuze texts that we are reading and into which we are inserting our reading. We are not simply repeating, without change, what they both wrote in their respective texts. Instead, we are repeating them both, at the same time and in two directions – into the past and into the future – and thereby creating a 'double existence' of both sets of texts (*DR* xxii). The eternal return is the temporal figure of this doubling.
22. Borges, 'Pierre Menard', in *Collected Fictions*, 91.
23. Ibid. 91.
24. Ibid. 94.
25. Ibid. 95.
26. Ibid. 94. Also, remember, from 'The Shell B', that ambiguity is the primary structure of Stoic paradoxes.
27. Nietzsche, *The Gay Science*, 273.
28. Pierre Hadot, *The Inner Citadel: The Meditations of Marcus Aurelius*, trans. Michael Chase (Cambridge, MA: Harvard University Press, 2001), 145.
29. Borges, 'Death and the Compass', in *Collected Fictions*, 149. John Irwin claims that this 'tale [is] meat to double "The Purloined Letter" of Edgar Allen Poe'. Irwin, *The Mystery to a Solution*, 437. This might suggest a difference between Freud, Lacan and Derrida, each of whom points to Poe's story, while Deleuze seems to incline towards Borges's writing.

The Albumen C: Eternal Return

30. Borges, 'Death and the Compass', 150, 151.
31. Ibid. 152.
32. Ibid. 147.
33. Deleuze quotes this at *LS* 62.
34. Borges, 'Death and the Compass', 141.
35. Ibid.
36. Irwin cleverly shows this doubling occurs even in the names 'Lönnrot' and 'Red Scharlach'. *Rot* means 'red' in German, and Red Scharlach can mean 'Red Scarlet' also in German. 'Elsewhere Borges tells us that *Lönnrot* is Swedish, but neglects to add that in Swedish the word *lönn* is a prefix meaning 'secret', 'hidden' or 'illicit'. Thus Lönnrot, the secret or hidden red, pursues and is pursued by his double Red Scharlach (Red Scarlet), the 'double red' or 'twice red'. John T. Irwin, *The Mystery to a Solution: Poe, Borges, and the Analytic Detective Story* (Baltimore: The Johns Hopkins University Press, 1996), 30. See also John T. Dyson, 'On Naming in Borges's "La Muerte y La Brujala"', *Comparative Literature* 37.2 (Spring 1985): 140–68, at 142–3.
37. Gilles Deleuze, *Kant's Critical Philosophy: The Doctrine of the Faculties* (1963), trans. Hugh Tomlinson and Barbara Habberjam (Minneapolis: University of Minnesota Press, 1984), vii; *DR* 111.
38. We should not that Michael White is uncertain about 'whether any Stoics entertained the distinction between a "conception of time as *circular* (with just one world cycle "joined" at beginning and end by the *ekpurosis*) and a conception of time as linear"'. White, 'Stoic Natural Philosophy', 142–3. The strange quotation punctuation is because White is citing himself from a different book: Michael J. White, *Agency and Integrality: Philosophical Themes in the Ancient Discussions of Determinism and Responsibility* (Dordrecht: Springer, 2011), 174.
39. Marcus Aurelius, *Meditations*, II.14.
40. Also see Ibid. VIII.3, 36.
41. While Deleuze is not here explicitly talking about the two eternal returns, but instead collapses them into one, the claims can be extended to both.
42. Michael Frede, 'The Original Notion of Cause', in *Essays in Ancient Philosophy* (Minneapolis: University of Minnesota Press, 1987), 125–51, at 130.
43. Frédérique Ildefonse, *Les Stoïciens I: Zénon, Cléanthe, Chrysippe* (Paris: Les Belles Lettres, 2000), 40–1. They retain, Ildefonse notes, only 'the efficient cause, moving or producing', which takes the form of acting and being acted upon. Ibid. 40.
44. Ildefonse, *Les Stoïciens I*, 40.
45. Aristotle, *Politics*, 7.13.1331b30–4; Boeri, 'The Stoics on Bodies and Incorporeals', *The Review of Metaphysics* 54.4 (2001): 723–52, 746. We should note that, while the Greek for 'end' is τέλος, it is a τέλος

without teleology, a non-teleological telos. While this sounds confusing, this is a concept that most of the Hellenic materialists, including the Epicureans and Sceptics, sought to develop. See Ryan J. Johnson, *The Deleuze–Lucretius Encounter* (Edinburgh: Edinburgh University Press, 2017), 237; Pierre-Marie Morel, *Épicure* (Paris: Vrin, 2010), 188–9.
46. Boeri, 'The Stoics on Bodies and Incorporeals', 746. Boeri cites Stobaeus, *Excerpts*, 2.78, 7–11; 2.86, 5–7, 2.97, 15–96, and 6.
47. The Greek προαίρεςις is the name for decision-making part of the ruling faculty (ἡγεμονικόν). It comes from αἵρεςις, meaning 'to take with or by the hand, grasp, seize' or 'to take, get into one's power'.
48. Mansfield, 'Providence and the Destruction of the Universe in Early Stoic Thought', 159–63.
49. Long seems inclined to agree with us: 'Probably the early Stoics supposed that whatever state of affairs obtains at any given moment is the best state as viewed from a divine perspective.' Long, 'The Stoics on World-Conflagration and Everlasting Recurrence', 25.
50. Baruch Spinoza, *Spinoza: Complete Works, Ethics*, ed. Michael L. Morgan, trans. Samuel Shirley (Indianapolis: Hackett Publishing Company, 2002), V.22, Scholium. Long associates this perspective with the conflagration, but we see it as possible at every instant. Long, 'The Stoics on World-Conflagration and Everlasting Recurrence', 24.
51. Seneca, *Epistles 1–65*, trans. Richard M. Gummere (Cambridge, MA: Harvard University Press, 1917), 9.16.
52. Deleuze's translation: '*Toute vie est bien entendu un processus de demolition*' (*LS* 180).
53. F. Scott Fitzgerald, 'The Crack-Up', *Esquire* (February 1936), 69. While Fitzgerald's contemporaries panned the essay, Deleuze praised it: 'few texts possess this finally character of a masterpiece, or are able to impose silence or force such terrified acquiescence as Fitzgerald's *The Crack Up*.' It was followed up in the next two issues: 'Pasting it Together' appeared in March 1936 and 'Handle with Care' in April 1936.
54. Fitzgerald, 'The Crack-Up', 76.
55. In the original French of *Logique du sens*, Deleuze translates 'of course' as *bien entendu*. Although *bien entendu* relates to the sense of 'hearing, understanding' (from the verb *entendre* or 'to hear, understand, listen, mean, agree', coming from the Latin *intendere*, meaning 'to hold out, stretch, strain; turn attention to; focus') and not the Latin *currere*, both express the sense of agreeing or aligning with natural course of things.
56. Fitzgerald, 'The Crack-Up', 69.
57. Ibid. 69.
58. Ibid. 74. Although Fitzgerald recognises Spinoza's influence in his interlocutor, she responds: 'I don't know anything about Spinoza.'

The Albumen C: Eternal Return

59. Ibid. 59.
60. Ibid. 78.
61. Ibid. 82.
62. Ibid. 79.
63. I am using Goldschmidt's translation of Marcus' Greek (*SS* 196). Marcus Aurelius, *Meditations*, IV, 48, 50, V.24.
64. Deleuze used the English 'has been': '*Tout culmine en un* has been' (*LS* 186).
65. Fitzgerald, 'The Crack-Up', 84.

Conclusion: Cracking the Egg

Five Forms of Ancient Philosophical Comedy

As we began our book with the Four Ancient Philosophical Orientations, we now conclude with Five Forms of Ancient Philosophical Comedy. We add a fifth form because we speak of comedy, and we cannot speak of ancient comedy without including Diogenes the Cynic. Echoing the end of 'Albumen C', this marks a different kind of crack-up, the cracking up of laughter. Comedy reveals a unique dimension of Stoicism.

Recall the four philosophical orientations from the 'Introduction': pre-Socratic depth, Platonic height, Aristotelian inwardness and Stoic surface. Each of these aligns with a form of comedy: pre-Socratics slapstick, Socratic irony, Aristotelian wit and Stoic humour. Compared to the first three ancient comedic forms, Stoicism is perverse. To see how Stoic comedy turns the depths and heights inside out through a double-sided paradoxical surface humor, let us work through each one by one. This table helps keep us focused:[1]

School	Orientation	Operation	Comedy
Pre-Socratics	Depth	Subversion	Slapstick
Plato/Socrates	Height	Conversion	Irony
Diogenes the Cynic	Rawness	Reversion	Sarcasm
Aristotle	Interiority	Inversion	Wit
Stoics	Surface	Perversion	Humor

Pre-Socratic Slapstick

Slapstick, a kind of lowbrow humour, is characterised by excessively physical and exaggerated routines, such as cartoonish violence and surprise props. The term 'slapstick' (in Italian: *batacchio*) refers to a prop popularised in the sixteenth-century Italian *commedia dell'arte*.[2] It is a percussion instrument made of two small slats of wood, bound

Conclusion: Cracking the Egg

at one end, which creates a loud *crack* sound when slapped together. Actors hit each other with the slapstick in order to create the loud sound effect associated with pain but without actually hurting. Chase scenes and beatings – as in Shakespeare's *Comedy of Errors*, Buster Keaton gags or Marx Brothers routines – exemplify slapstick. The pre-Socratics can be said to use an early form of slapstick because their metaphysical explanations caricature matter through excessively 'physical language' and corporeal concepts (*LS* 134). They are 'physical' in so far as they are denotative, that is, in so far as they brusquely point to brute matter. 'Every denotation', Deleuze writes, 'is prolonged in consumption, pulverization, and destruction' (*LS* 135). Consider the examples of Democritus, Thales and Empedocles.

DEMOCRITUS AND HIS ATOMS

To explain the natural world, Democritus takes a body and pulverises it into tiny particles falling through the void. As the atomists shatter the world into infinite tiny bodies, knowledge too is destroyed in the deep. Atomism descends into matter. 'In reality we know nothing,' Diogenes reports, 'for truth is in the depths' (DL 9.72). Ancient atomism is a kind of philosophical slapstick in so far as it, in response to a simple query about the nature of things, shatters worlds and words into infinite crumbs. Democritus was known as the laughing philosopher, after all.

'EMPEDOCLES AND HIS VOLCANO'[3]

Having placed thought deep inside the caverns, Empedocles too philosophised through destruction. He 'philosophized with a hammer, the hammer of the geologist and the speleologist' (*LS* 128). With this, Empedocles pulverised the world into the four classical material 'roots' or 'rhizomata (ῥιζώματα)' (which Aristotle later calls 'elements', στοιχεῖον) – earth, air, fire, water – as well as the forces of Love and Strife that mix and separate them. The exaggerated nature of these roots and opposing forces smack of slapstick. Yet it is his death, Diogenes reports, that was the clearest example of pre-Socratic slapstick. One morning, when Empedocles 'got up, he set out on his way to [Mount] Etna; then, when he reached it, he plunged [himself] into the fiery craters and disappeared, his intention being to confirm the report that he had become a god' (DL 8.69). Afterwards, however, the truth came out because one of his bronze slippers, which he famously wore, was thrown back up by the flickering flames deep within the volcano. It could have been a scene in a Chaplin film.

Thales and his Water

Thales claimed that 'water is the universal primary substance' (DL 1.27).[4] An astute mathematician who abandoned mythical explanations, Thales saw into 'the depths of nature without the help of fantastical fable'.[5] Yet even with a purely empirical perspective, when Thales articulated his central philosophical proposition, he ends up with pie on his face. As Nietzsche says: 'Thales had seen the unity of all that is, but when he went to communicate it, he found himself talking about water!'[6] One Thales anecdote perfectly captures the slapstick character of the aquatic metaphysician: 'once, when he was taken out of doors by an old woman in order that he might observe the stares, he fell into a ditch' (DL 1.34).[7] Falling into a ditch while contemplating the heavens is philosophical slapstick par excellence.

Socratic Irony

The *Oxford English Dictionary* defines 'irony' as the 'expression of one's meaning by using language that normally signifies the opposite, typically for humorous or emphatic effect'. It is more of a style of highbrow humour, as to lowbrow slapstick. In Greek Old Comedy, *eiron* (εἴρων) was one of the three stock comedic characters, which Aristotle defines as understatement, 'mock modesty', or self-deprecator, and appears in many of Aristophanes' plays, such as the god Dionysius in *The Frogs*.[8] *Eiron* is the regular opponent of *alazon* (ἀλαζών), the imposter or braggart.[9] *Eiron* cuts down the exaggerations of *alazon* by depreciating his own abilities. These are, P. M. Gooch writes, the 'two vices at the opposite poles of truthfulness: *alzoneia*, playing up the truth, and *eironeia*, playing down the truth'.[10] In his discussion of *eironeia*, Aristotle explicitly names Socrates.[11] Hence originates 'Socratic irony'.[12] Without much strain, we can see these character types in many Platonic dialogues, with Socrates as the *eiron* and his interlocutor as the *alazon*.

As opposed to the physical language of pre-Socratic slapstick, Socratic irony relies on what Deleuze calls an 'idealistic language' in so far as it refers only to higher ideal forms (*LS* 134). Although Socrates sounds like he designates things, he actually signifies ideals.

Conclusion: Cracking the Egg

When he asks the 'What is *x*?' question and his interlocutor points to a particular body, thinking it is a matter of designation, Plato scoffs and gestures upwards, to the immaterial first principles above. 'Plato laughed', Deleuze writes, 'at those who were satisfied with giving examples, pointing or designating, rather than attaining Essences' (*LS* 135). An ironist, for Deleuze, is always 'seeking a first principle, a principle which comes even before the one that was thought to be first, he finds a course that is even more primary than the others. He constantly goes up and down.'[13] Socrates is not asking *who looks* beautiful or *which* body *seems* beautiful, but *what is* beauty-in-itself. When he speaks of beauty, Socrates means the opposite of what he says, the beauty beyond all beauty, which both must and cannot be beautiful (due to the threat of the self-predication of the forms of the third man argument). Socratic irony is that, even though Socrates does not claim to know or have access to the forms, many of his interlocutors believed he was guilty of mock-modesty or fake ignorance.

Cynic Sarcasm

The backside of Socratic irony is the Cynic sarcasm of Diogenes of Sinope. Cynic humour uses irony without abstraction. Diogenes was reportedly called 'Socrates gone mad' or what Frédéric Neyrat calls *'the madness of Socrates incarnated'* (DL 6.54).[14] Rather than ironic, Cynic sarcasm carried sharper, pricklier, cutting retorts and taunts, perhaps even leading to what Deleuze calls a 'curious system of provocations' (*LS* 129–30). Once, to take one of many such anecdotes, when Plato was giving a lecture in which 'Plato defined Man as an animal, biped, and featherless', Diogenes left, found, perhaps killed, and 'plucked a fowl and brought it into the lecture-room with the words, "Here is Plato's man"' (DL 6.40). Another time, after Diogenes was sold as a slave, the 'auctioneer asked in what was he proficient, he replied, "In ruling men"' (DL 6.74). Rather than disdaining the dullard who responded to Socrates' ironic questions by pointed at matter, cynic sarcasm mocked the whole division – particular versus universal, physical versus ideal, depth versus height – in order to affirm the brute rawness of nature beyond human conceit. Perhaps suffocating from such conceit, Diogenes may have 'died voluntarily by holding his breath' (DL 7.76). A sarcastic death, if there ever was one. As the Stoics viewed Diogenes as one of the only examples of a true sage, we should hear echoes of Cynic sarcasm in Stoic humour. If the Stoic operation is perversion, then the Cynic operation is reversion, a return to the pre-human rawness and the laughter of animals.

Aristotelian Wit

In his *Nicomachean Ethics*, Aristotle defines 'wit' (εὐτράπελος) as the mean concerning 'leisure and amusement'. The excess is buffoonery (βωμολοχία), as he writes: those 'who carry humor to excess are thought to be vulgar buffoons, striving after humor at all costs, and aiming rather at raising a laugh then at saying what is becoming'.[15] The buffoon is the man of unseemly jesting, a ludicrous, foul-mouthed person who is 'slave of his sense of humor, and spares neither himself nor others if he can raise a laugh'.[16] The deficiency is boorishness (βωμολόχος), as he writes: those 'who can neither make a joke themselves nor be put up with those who do are thought to be boorish and unpolished'.[17] The boor is an unfeeling, bawdy person, who 'contributes nothing [to social intercourse] and finds fault with everything'.[18] The Greek term βωμολόχος refers to a crude person who lurks around sacrificial altars in order to steal the meat of the sacrificed animal.[19]

In between the buffoon and the boor is the ready-witted person who 'joke[s] in a tasteful way . . . which implies a sort of readiness to turn this way and that'.[20] Wit belongs to charm or tact, as 'it is the mark of a tactful person to say and listen to such things as befit a good and well-bred person'.[21] The Greek is εὐτράπελος, meaning 'versatile, easily turning, nimble', and refers to a 'supple, pliant character, who can adapt readily their manners and language to times, persons, and circumstances'.[22] Witty persons conduct themselves with grace and ease; their practiced dexterity allows them to flawlessly adapt to any situation. The condition for wit is a balanced yet feeling soul, which is acquired by an aristocratic upbringing, deliberative practice and refinement of habits. Hence in the *Rhetoric* Aristotle defines wit as 'well-bred insolence'.[23] Such a fine soul allows him to discern, at every occasion, what is the most suitable witticism or jest for a conversation. Wit exemplifies the hylomorphic sense of the 'inwardness' because it is the soul, the form of the person, that permits him to adroitly navigate a situation.

Conclusion: Cracking the Egg

Stoic Humour

While Diogenes and the 'Cynics', writes Deleuze, 'already made humor a philosophical weapon against Socratic irony', the Stoics made humour into a 'dialectical principle' (*LS* 9). We see here a difference in dialectics between the Cynics and Stoics. While the Cynical dialectic operates only by mocking principle of negation, the Stoics turn their philosophical interlocutor inside out, which is a flattening rather than a negating.[24] Initially, humour is the perversion of the ironic desire for first principles, but for the Stoics 'principles count for little, everything is taken literally'.[25] Rather than referring to a causal principle located above or below, '[h]umor is the art of consequences or effects'.[26] Humour is not transmitted through highbrow plays on words or lowbrow gags because it sits right on the surface of things, like a tick awaiting a passer-by. 'Humor is the art of the surface, which is opposed to the old irony, the art of depths and heights' (*LS* 9).

Stoic humour perverts an impasse between the pre-Socratics' physical language and Plato's idealistic language. Before the Stoics, the choice was either 'to eat one's words' by turning concepts into matter (like Democritus, Empedocles and Thales), or 'to say nothing', as Socrates numbs the tongues of his interlocutors like the sting of a torpedo fish.[27] Rather than eating one's words or silencing one's tongue, the Stoics construct a paradoxical surface that separates things and words yet affirms both. Rather than choosing between bodies or ideals, things or words, the Stoics affirm that paradoxical double-sided surface that joins them together. Hence a perversion of their predecessors. Thus Stoic humour is neither slapstick nor irony. Both corporeal depths *and* an immanent incorporeal surface are needed for the sage to laugh because it is only then that the perverse relation between then appears.

'Humor is the art', Deleuze writes, 'of the always displaced aleatory point', rather than the lost origin (ἀρχή) or inevitable conclusion (τέλος); 'the savoir-faire of the pure event' rather than the abstract knowledge of transcendent beings; 'the "fourth person singular"' rather than the 'we' of slapstick, the 'I' of irony and the 'us' of wit (*LS* 141). Humour hinges on the aleatory point in so far as it marks the paradoxical passage from one side of the surface to the other. The key is that the passage through the surface is seamless; there is no impossible jump to the 'subtranscendence of chaos (the Volcano [of Empedocles]) and the super transcendence of a god' (*WP* 43).

Instead, we move along the same smooth plane but, paradoxically, end up on the other side, like ants travelling along both faces of M. C. Escher's *Möbius Strip II*. Consider, for example, Epictetus' humorous response to the spreading of disparaging rumours about him. 'If you learn that someone is speaking ill of you', writes Epictetus, 'don't try to defend yourself against the rumors; respond instead with, "Yes, and he doesn't know the half of it, because he could have said more."'[28] Rather than fighting back or stepping above, Epictetus' humour speeds it up, and thus 'makes something shoot off' in a different, unexpected direction.[29]

The paradoxical double-sided surface configures the logic of Stoic humour. As Deleuze notes, 'humor is the art of the surfaces and of the doubles' (*LS* 141). While we might say that all comedy is a kind of doubling, the difference is in *how* this doubling occurs. Pre-Socratic slapstick doubles by distorting, expanding and overemphasising what is doubled; it doubles the weight of the original, making it fall into infernal depths. Slapstick, in short, subverts. Socratic irony doubles by negating. Irony converts the original into its opposite, usually through a ruthless dialogue that ends with everyone feeling numb and dumb. Only another world can save us. Aristotelian wit doubles by internalising the order of priority. What was previously the first, the material composite, becomes secondary to the form within. In response to all three, Epictetus says: 'If I were a slave to one of these philosophers I would taunt him constantly, even if I got a beating every day in consequence. If he said, "Put some oil in the bath, boy," I'd go grab the fish sauce and pour it over his head.'[30] Stoic doubling is perverse. This is why Stoic humour is different from wit. To the refined Aristotelian, the sage can sound both buffoonish or boorish.

Lapoujade describes 'the pervert's sense of humor: object with so much zeal that in the end the law is turned on its head and ends up permitting what it was supposed to prohibit'.[31] Speaking of Zarathustra's 'black humor [*humour noirs*]', Deleuze points to 'a within-the-law and a beyond-the-law united in the eternal return' (*DR* 7). We might think of Lacan's relationship with Kant and the Marquis de Sade. While Lacan suggests that Sadism is the ideal inversion of Kantian deontological ethics, it is better to say that Sadism is the material perversion of Kant. Sade is not Kant turned upside down but inside out. We find a parallel in John Stuart Mill's utilitarian ethics and Leopold von Sacher-Masoch. Masoch is the perversion of Mill; utilitarianism turned inside out.[32] Here we finally tie humour to ethics. 'If perversion holds so much importance in *The Logic of*

Conclusion: Cracking the Egg

Sense,' writes Lapoujade, 'it is also and above all because of its *ethical* dimension.'[33] Lapoujade is very clear about the doubling operation in perverted ethics: 'doubling is the quintessential ethical act; it is the meaning behind Stoic ethics as *The Logic of Sense* presents it'.[34]

Stoic ethics and humour pervert previous philosophies in the same way: physical yet surreal, deep yet superficial. That is, they double corporeal depths with the incorporeal surface. Deleuze associates such doubling with the mime, a figure of perversity if there ever was one. The 'mime directs and doubles the actualization, measures the [corporeal] mixtures with the aid of an [incorporeal] instant without [corporeal] mixture, and prevents them from overflowing' into transcendence (*LS* 147). We call it the 'counter-effectuation', or extraction of the event from states of affairs[35] Stoic humour extracts the event from a corporeal context and simultaneously incarnates a λεκτα in a body. Humour thus sparks an incorporeal transformation, like any speech act. Put differently, humour quasi-causes a change in a state of affairs. The world is cracked open, just for a split second, so that the infinite possibilities for meaning slip through. For example, recall how Epictetus consoles a man who lost his wife and child. 'Did a child of yours die? No, it was returned. Your wife died? No, *she* was returned. "My land confiscated." No, it too was returned.'[36] According to the doctrine of the eternal return, wherein everything great and small, whether it is a broken jug or a loving spouse, must return. As the saying goes, kill your darlings again and again.[37] Epictetus advises us to love fate by willing everything and anything that happens *both* as if it had happened infinitely many times before *and* as if it were to happen infinitely many times again.

Finally, compare Stoic humour to a typical joke telling. A joke usually works by creating a tension that is later released with punch line. The audience recognises the site of the punch line and laughs in response. In Stoic humour, however, a punch line never arrives; there is no insight into hidden ironic meaning, no witty smugness from aristocratic upbringing. Instead, tension is created but not released; the tension is always there, just as existence in the Stoic cosmos is the tension created by the constant corporeal intermixing. In Stoic humour, a state of affairs intensifies, but the event never appears. Eventually, without our willing, we crack up laughing.

The comic Steve Martin's description of his stand-up comedy is an instance of contemporary Stoic humour.[38] 'What if I created a tension and never released it?' he asked himself long ago.[39]

What would the audience do with all that tension? Theoretically, it would have to come out somewhere. But if I kept denying them the formality of a punch line, the audience would eventually pick their own place to laugh, essentially out of desperation. This type of laugh seemed stronger to me, as they would be laughing at something *they chose*.[40]

Similarly, Stoic humour provokes laughter 'without jokes'.[41] Like the eternal return, wherein we know that each event happened before, even though we have no knowledge of prior passings, we have the sense that Stoicism is funny, although we may not know why. We cannot say in advance how to act or why it is funny. As Martin explains, 'you had to be there'.[42] Just as we cannot locate a punch line that would relieve a pent-up tension, the event is non-localisable; it always just has or is about to happen. All we can do is laugh and say, 'Yes, one more time, please, and infinitely more after that.'

On 12 September 1980, Deleuze concluded a lecture by attributing to Spinoza 'a species of very kind laughter, the laughter of a man who speaks freedom and power'.[43] Given Spinoza's Stoic affiliations, this is unsurprisingly a very Stoic species of laughter. In Stoicism, freedom and power come from the doctrine of the eternal return. Given the two senses of the eternal return – as circle and infinitely divisible straight line – we are simultaneously subject to the impossibility of acting other than how we have been determined to act, but also subject to the imperative to act at this instant. The Stoic response to this paradox of action is to laugh and to will exactly what happens. The joke never lands, or it has already landed and we just missed it. Stoicism need not be so serious, for *amor fati* is a very funny affair. The ethics of Stoic humour is to laugh at what happens as the natural course of affairs, rather than to gnash teeth, complain and conjure up another, better world, beyond the one and only cosmos we must love and live. Stoic humour helps us become worthy of the event by affirming fate and cracking up with laughter. Every morning, the egg cracks open, the yolk and the albumen spill out into the void, and everything burns up in the conflagration. Soon after that, the world begins again and again, cracking up with laughter each and every time.

Notes

1. While we do not go into it here, we could add another column to the table, one about the kind of writing most associated with the respective

schools and kinds of comedy: pre-Socratics wrote *Treatises*, Plato wrote *Dialogues*, Aristotle wrote *Lectures* and the Stoics wrote *Anecdotes*.
2. Judith Chaffee and Oliver Crick, *The Routledge Companion to Commedia dell'Arte* (New York: Routledge, 2015), 185–92.
3. Gilles Deleuze, *Nietzsche and Philosophy* (1962), trans. Hugh Tomlinson (New York: Columbia University Press, 1983), 110; emphasis added.
4. Aristotle, *Metaphysics*, 1.3 983b.
5. Friedrich Nietzsche, *Philosophy in the Tragic Age of the Greeks*, trans. Marianne Cowan (Washington, DC: Regnery Publishing, Inc., 1998), 42. Or in Deleuze and Guattari's words: 'When Thales thought leaps out, it comes back as water' (*WP* 38).
6. Nietzsche, *Philosophy in the Tragic Age of the Greeks*, 45.
7. Also see Plato, *Theaetetus*, 174a.
8. Aristotle, *Nicomachean Ethics*, 1108a15.
9. Marvin Carlson, *Theories of the Theatre: A Historical and Critical Survey, from the Greeks to the Present* (Ithaca: Cornell University Press, 1993), 23.
10. Gooch, 'Socratic Irony and Aristotle's "Eiron": Some Puzzles', *Pheonix* 41.2 (Summer 1987): 95–104, at 95.
11. Aristotle, *Nicomachean Ethics*, 1127b25.
12. Gooch, 'Socratic Irony and Aristotle's "Eiron": Some Puzzles', 95.
13. Gilles Deleuze and Claire Parnet, *Dialogues* (1977), trans. Hugh Tomlinson and Barbara Habberjam (New York: Columbia University Press, 1977), 68.
14. Frédéric Neyrat, *Atopias: Manifesto for a Radical Existentialism*, trans. Walt Hunter and Lindsay Turner (New York: Fordham University Press, 2018), 26.
15. Aristotle, *Nicomachean Ethics*, 1127b33–1128a17.
16. Ibid. 1128a35–36.
17. Ibid. 1127b33–1128a17.
18. Ibid. 1128b1–2.
19. James Donnegan, *A New Greek and English Lexicon: The Words Alphabetically Arranged* (Donnegan, 1842), 369.
20. Aristotle, *Nicomachean Ethics*, 1128a12–15.
21. Ibid. 1128a18–19.
22. Donnegan, *A New Greek and English Lexicon*, 713.
23. Aristotle, *Rhetoric*, 1389b12.
24. In *Human, All Too Human*, Nietzsche notices the prioritization of negation in the Cynics: 'the Cynic merely continues to negate,' while the Stoics turn dialectics into an art of perversion. Friedrich Nietzsche, *Human, All Too Human I* (Stanford: Stanford University Press, 1995), 275.
25. Deleuze and Parnet, *Dialogues*, 68.

26. Ibid.
27. Plato, *Meno*, 80a–b2. We see here a difference between Deleuze's Stoicism and Badiou's Platonism in that Badiou really admires Socrates' 'reducing the sophist to silence,' as he describes Socrates' silencing of Thrasymachus in his hyper-translation of Plato's *Republic*. Alain Badiou, *Plato's Republic: A Dialogue in Sixteen Chapters*, trans. Susan Spitzer (New York: Columbia University Press, 2013), 14–44.
28. Epictetus, *Discourses*, 'Fragments', 33.9.
29. Deleuze and Parnet, *Dialogues*, 68.
30. Epictetus, *Discourses Books I–II*, II.20.
31. Lapoujade, *Aberrant Movements*, 144; emphasis original.
32. In a future essay I will flesh out the Mill–Masoch encounter, which parallels the Kant–Sade encounter.
33. David Lapoujade, *Aberrant Movements: The Philosophy of Gilles Deleuze* (2014), trans. Joshua David Jordan (South Pasadena: Semiotext(e), 2017), 147; emphasis original.
34. Ibid. 147.
35. Deleuze and Parnet, *Dialogues*, 49.
36. Epictetus, *Discourses*, 'Fragments', 11.
37. This is attributed to many greats but first appearing in the last of Sir Arthur Quiller-Couch's 1913–14 lectures delivered at Cambridge entitled *On the Art of Writing*: 'Whenever you feel an impulse to perpetrate a piece of exceptionally fine writing, obey it – whole-heartedly – and delete it before sending your manuscript to press. *Murder your darlings.*' Quiller-Couch, 'On Style', in *On the Art of Writing* (Mineola, NY: Dover Publications, 2006), 203; emphasis original.
38. As further motivation of this connection, Steve Martin drew inspiration from Lewis Carroll: 'Appearing to be silly nonsense, on examination they were *absolutely logical* – yet were still funny. The comedy doors opened wide open, and Lewis Carroll's clever fancies from the nineteenth century expanded my notion of what comedy could be.' Martin, *Born Standing Up: A Comic's Life* (New York: Scribner, 2008), 74–5; emphasis original.
39. Ibid. 111.
40. Ibid.
41. Ibid. 112.
42. Ibid. 113.
43. Gilles Deleuze, *Cours Vincennes: la puissance, le droit naturel classique*, 9/12/1980, https://www.webdeleuze.com/textes/9 (last accessed 8 February 2019).

Bibliography

Africa, Thomas, 'The Opium Addiction of Marcus Aurelius', *Journal of the History of Ideas* 22 (1961): 97–102.

Algra, Keimpe, *Concepts of Space in Greek Thought* (Leiden: E. J. Brill, 1995).

Algra, Keimpe, Jonathan Barnes, Jaap Mansfeld and Malcolm Schofield (eds), *The Cambridge History of Hellenistic Philosophy* (Cambridge: Cambridge University Press, 2005).

Allen and Greenough's New Latin Grammar (Newburyport, MA: Focus Publishing, 2001).

Alquié, Ferdinand, 'Joe Bouquet et la morale du langage', *Cahiers du sud* 303 (1950): 187–90.

Angelova, Emilia, 'Quasi-Cause in Deleuze: Inverting the Body Without Organs', *Symposium: Canadian Journal of Continental Philosophy* 10.1 (2006): 117–33.

Annas, Julia, *Hellenistic Philosophy of Mind* (Berkeley and Los Angeles: University of California Press, 1992).

Ansell Pearson, Keith and Duncan Large (eds), *The Nietzsche Reader* (Oxford: Wiley-Blackwell, 2006).

Anttila, Raimo, *Greek and Indo-European Etymology in Action: Proto-Indo-European *ag?-* (Amsterdam: John Benjamins Publishing, 2000).

Apostolos Pierris (ed.), *The Empedoclean Κόσμος: Structure, Process, and the Question of Cyclicity Papers* (Patras: Institute for Philosophical Research, 2005).

Aristophanes, *Birds*, ed. and trans. Jeffrey Henderson (Cambridge, MA: Harvard University Press, 1995).

Aristotle, *The Complete Works, Volumes 1 and 2*, ed. Jonathan Barnes (Princeton: Princeton University Press, 1995).

Atherton, Catherine, *The Stoics on Ambiguity* (Cambridge: Cambridge University Press, 1993).

Badiou, Alain, *Deleuze: The Clamor of Being*, trans. Louise Burchill (Minneapolis: University of Minnesota Press, 1999).

Badiou, Alain, *Plato's Republic: A Dialogue in Sixteen Chapters*, trans. Susan Spitzer (New York: Columbia University Press, 2013).

Baker, J. A., *The Peregrine* (New York: New York Review of Books, 1967).

Baratin, Marc, *La Naissance de la syntaxe à Rome* (Paris: Éditions du Minuit, 1989).

Barnes, Jonathan, 'La doctrine du retour éternel', *Revue philosophique de la France et de l'étranger* 127.2 (2002): 421–40.

Beaulieu, Alain, 'Deleuze et les Stoïciens', in *Gilles Deleuze: héritage philosophique*, ed. Alain Beaulieu and Manola Antonioli (Paris: Presses universitaires de France, 2005), 45–72.

Bell, Jeffrey A., 'The World is an Egg: Realism, Mathematics, and the Thresholds of Difference', *Speculations* IV (2013): 65–70.

Bénatouïl, Thomas, 'Le système stoïcien', in *Philosophie antique*, ed. Jean-François Pradeau (Paris: Presses universitaires de France, 2010), 131–49.

Benjamin, Walter, *The Arcades Project*, trans. Howard Eiland and Kevin McLaughlin (Cambridge, MA: Harvard University Press, 2002).

Bennett, Michael James, 'Cicero's *De Fato* in Deleuze's *Logic of Sense*', *Deleuze Studies* 9.1 (2015): 25–58.

Bennett, Michael James, *Deleuze and Ancient Greek Physics* (London: Bloomsbury Academic, 2017).

Bennett, Michael James, 'Deleuze's Concept of "Quasi-Causality" and its Greek Sources', an invited talk at the Classics Department Lecture Series, Dalhousie University, Halifax, Canada, 30 November 2014.

Bergson, Henri, *Time and Free Will*, trans. F. L. Pogson (New York: Macmillan, 1910).

Bering, Jesse, *Perv: The Sexual Deviant in All of Us* (New York: Scientific American/Farrar, Straus and Giroux, 2013).

Blanchot, Maurice, *The Space of Literature*, trans. Ann Smock (Lincoln: The University of Nebraska Press, 1989).

Boeri, Marcelo D., 'The Stoics on Bodies and Incorporeals', *The Review of Metaphysics* 54.4 (2001): 723–52.

Borges, Jorge Luis, *Collected Fictions*, trans. Andrew Hurley (New York: Penguin Books, 1999).

Borges, Jorge Luis, *Ficciones*, trans and ed. Anthony Kerrigan (New York: Grove Press, 1994).

Bousquet, Joë, *Les Capitales: ou de Jean Duns Scott à Jean Paulhan* (Montolieu: Deyrolle-Verdier, 1999).

Bowden, Sean, *The Priority of Events: Deleuze's Logic of Sense* (Edinburgh: Edinburgh University Press, 2011).

Bradley, Jeff, 'The Eyes of the Fourth Person Singular', *Deleuze Studies* 9.2 (2015): 185–207.

Brunschwig, Jacques, *Papers in Hellenistic Philosophy* (Cambridge: Cambridge University Press, 1994).

Brunschwig, Jacques, *Les Stoïciens et leur logique* (Paris: J. Vrin, 2006).

Buchanan, Ian, *Deleuzism: A Metacommentary* (Edinburgh: Edinburgh University Press, 2000).

Bibliography

Calcidius, *On Plato's Timaeus*, ed. and trans. John Magee (Cambridge, MA: Harvard University Press, 2016).
Callahan, John Francis, *Four Views of Time in Ancient Philosophy* (Cambridge, MA: Harvard University Press, 1948).
Carlson, Marvin, *Theories of the Theatre: A Historical and Critical Survey, from the Greeks to the Present* (Ithaca: Cornell University Press, 1993).
Carroll, Lewis, *Alice Through the Looking-Glass* (New York: Bloomsbury, 2001).
Carroll, Lewis, *The Annotated Hunting of the Snark* (New York: W. W. Norton & Co., 2006).
Caruso, Francisco, *Sources for the History of Space Concepts in Physics: From 1845–1995* (Rio de Janeiro: Centro Brasileiro de Pesquisas Físicas, 1996).
Cassin, Barbara, 'The Muses and Philosophy: Elements for a History of the *Pseudos*', in *Contemporary Encounters with Ancient Metaphysics*, ed. Abraham Jacob Greenstine and Ryan J. Johnson (Edinburgh: Edinburgh University Press, 2017).
Caston, Victor, 'Something and Nothing: The Stoics in Concepts and Universals', *Oxford Studies in Ancient Philosophy* 17 (1999): 145–213.
Chaffee, Judith and Oliver Crick, *The Routledge Companion to Commedia dell'Arte* (New York: Routledge, 2015).
Charle, Christophe, 'Bréhier (Émile, François, Désiré)', *Bibliothèque de l'Éducation* (1986), 40–2.
Christensen, Johnny, *An Essay on the Unity of Stoic Philosophy* (Scandinavian University Books, 1962).
Cicero, *De Natura Deorum*, trans. H. Rackham (Cambridge, MA: Harvard University Press, 1933).
Cicero, *On Academic Scepticism*, trans. Charles Brittain (Indianapolis: Hackett Publishing Company, Inc., 2006).
Cicero, *On Old Age, On Friendship, On Divination*, trans. W. A. Falconer (Cambridge, MA: Harvard University Press, 1923).
Cicero, *On the Orator: Book 3. On Fate. Stoic Paradoxes. On the Divisions of Oratory: A. Rhetorical Treatises*, trans. H. Rackham (Cambridge, MA: Harvard University Press, 1942).
Clement of Alexandria, *The Writings of Clement of Alexandria, Vol. II: Miscellanies*, trans. The Rev. William Wilson (Edinburgh: T. & T. Clark, 1867).
Colombat, André-Pierre, 'November 4, 1995: Deleuze's death as an event', *Man and World* 29 (1996): 235–49.
Curd, Patricia (ed.), *A Presocratics Reader: Selected Fragments and Testimonia*, trans. Richard D. McKirahan (Indianapolis: Hackett Publishing Company, 2011).
DeLanda, Manuel, *Intensive Science and Virtual Philosophy* (London: Continuum, 2002).

DeLanda, Manuel, 'Space: Extensive and Intensive, Actual and Virtual', in *Deleuze and Space*, ed. Ian Buchanan and Gregg Lambert (Edinburgh: Edinburgh University Press, 2005).

Deleuze, Gilles, *Bergsonism* (1966), trans. Hugh Tomlinson and Barbara Habberjam (New York: Zone Books, 1988).

Deleuze, Gilles, *Cinema 1: The Movement Image* (1983), trans. Hugh Tomlinson and Barbara Habberjam (Minneapolis: The Athlone Press, 1986).

Deleuze, Gilles, *Cinema 2: The Time Image* (1985), trans. Hugh Tomlinson and Robert Galeta (Minneapolis: University of Minnesota Press, 2001).

Deleuze, Gilles, *Cours Vincennes*, transcripts, https://www.webdeleuze.com/sommaire (last accessed 8 February 2019).

Deleuze, Gilles, *Desert Islands and Other Texts, 1953–1974* (2002), trans. Michael Taorima, ed. David Lapoujade (Los Angeles: Semiotext(e), 2004).

Deleuze, Gilles, *Empiricism and Subjectivity: An Essay on Hume's Theory of Human Nature* (1953), trans. Constantin V. Boundas (New York: Columbia University Press, 1991).

Deleuze, Gilles, *Essays Critical and Clinical* (1993), trans. Daniel W. Smith and Michael A. Greco (Minneapolis: University of Minnesota Press, 1997).

Deleuze, Gilles, *Expressionism in Philosophy: Spinoza* (1968), trans. Martin Joughin (New York: Zone Books, 1990).

Deleuze, Gilles, *The Fold: Leibniz and the Baroque* (1988), trans. Tom Conley (Minneapolis: University of Minnesota Press, 1993).

Deleuze, Gilles, *Foucault* (1986), trans. Sean Hand (Minneapolis: University of Minnesota Press, 1988).

Deleuze, Gilles, *Kant's Critical Philosophy: The Doctrine of the Faculties* (1963), trans. Hugh Tomlinson and Barbara Habberjam (Minneapolis: University of Minnesota Press, 1984).

Deleuze, Gilles, 'Lettre-préface' to Jean-Clet Martin, *Variations: La Philosophie de Gilles Deleuze* (Paris: Payot, 1993).

Deleuze, Gilles, 'Lucrèce et le naturalisme', *Les Études philosophiques* n.s., 1 (1961), 19–29.

Deleuze, Gilles, *Masochism: Coldness and Cruelty* (1971), trans. Jean McNeil (New York: Zone Books, 1989).

Deleuze, Gilles, *Negotiations* (1995), trans. Martin Joughin (New York: Columbia University Press, 1990).

Deleuze, Gilles, *Nietzsche and Philosophy* (1962), trans. Hugh Tomlinson (New York: Columbia University Press, 1983).

Deleuze, Gilles, *Proust and Signs* (1964), trans. Richard Howard (Minneapolis: The Athlone Press, 2000).

Deleuze, Gilles, *Pure Immanence: Essays on A Life* (1995), trans. Anna Boyman (New York: Zone Books, 2001).

Bibliography

Deleuze, Gilles, *Spinoza: Practical Philosophy* (1981), trans. Robert Hurley (San Francisco: City Lights, 1988).

Deleuze, Gilles, *Two Regimes of Madness: Texts and Interviews, 1975–1995*, ed. David Lapoujade, trans. Ames Hodges and Mike Taormina (New York: Semiotexte, 2006).

Deleuze, Gilles, *La Voix de Gilles Deleuze en ligne*, http://www2.univ-paris8.fr/deleuze/article.php3?id_article=1 (last accessed 8 February 2019).

Deleuze, Gilles and Félix Guattari, *Anti-Oedipus: Capitalism and Schizophrenia I* (1972), trans. Robert Hurley, Mark Seem and Helen R. Lane (New York: Viking Press, 1977).

Deleuze, Gilles and Claire Parnet, *Dialogues* (1977), trans. Hugh Tomlinson and Barbara Habberjam (New York: Columbia University Press, 1977).

Descartes, René, *The Philosophical Writings of Descartes, Vol. II*, trans. John Cottingham, Robert Stoothoff and Dugald Murdoch (Cambridge: Cambridge University Press, 1984).

Donnegan, James, *A New Greek and English Lexicon: The Words Alphabetically Arranged* (Donnegan, 1842).

Dosse, François, *Gilles Deleuze and Félix Guattari: Intersecting Lives*, trans. Deborah Glassman (New York: Columbia University Press, 2011).

Drozdek, Adam, '*Lekton*: Stoic Logic and Ontology', *Acta antiqua Academiae Scientiarum Hungaricae* 42.104 (2002): 93–104.

Due, Reidar A., 'At the Margins of Sense: The Function of Paradox in Deleuze and Wittgenstein', *Paragraph* 34.3 (November 2011): 358–70.

Durie, 'Immanence and Difference: Toward a Relational Ontology', *Southern Journal of Philosophy* 40.2 (2002): 161–89.

Dyson, John T., 'On Naming in Borges's "La Muerte y La Brujala"', *Comparative Literature* 37.2 (Spring 1985): 140–68.

Eliot, T. S., *Four Quartets* (Orlando: Harcourt Books, 1971).

Encyclopædia Britannica, vol. 21, ed. Hugh Chisholm (Cambridge: Cambridge University Press, 1911).

Epictetus, *Discourses and Selected Writings*, trans. Robert Dobbins (London: Penguin Classics, 2009).

Epictetus, *Discourses, Books I–II*, trans. W. A. Oldfather (Cambridge, MA: Harvard University Press, 1925).

Epictetus, *Discourses, Books III–IV, The Encheiridion*, trans. W. A. Oldfather (Cambridge, MA: Harvard University Press, 1928).

Epicurus, 'Letter to Herodotus', in *Epicurus: The Extant Remains*, ed. and trans. Cyril Bailey (Oxford: Clarendon Press, 1926).

Euripides, *Hippolytus*, in *Euripides: Children of Heracles, Hippolytus, Andromache, Hecuba*, ed. and trans. David Kovacs (Cambridge, MA: Harvard University Press, 1995).

Faulkner, Keith W., *Deleuze and the Three Syntheses of Time* (New York: Peter Lang Inc., International Academic Publishers, 2005).

Ferguson, John, *Clement of Alexandria* (New York: Twayne Publishers, 1974).
Ferlinghetti, Lawrence, *Her* (New York: New Directions, 1960).
Ferlinghetti, Lawrence, *San Francisco Poems* (San Francisco: City Lights Books, 2003).
Festugière, A. J., *Études de philosophique grecque* (Paris: J. Vrin, 1972).
Fischer, Gustav, *Latin Grammar: Etymology and an Introduction of Syntax* (Schermerhorn, 1879).
Fitzgerald, F. Scott, 'The Crack-Up', *Esquire* (February 1936).
Frede, Michael, *Essays in Ancient Philosophy* (Minneapolis: University of Minnesota Press, 1987), 304.
Frede, Michael, 'Fatalism and Future Truth', *Proceedings of the Boston Area Colloquium in Ancient Philosophy* VI (1990): 195–239.
Frede, Michael, 'The Original Notion of Cause', in *Essays in Ancient Philosophy* (Minneapolis: University of Minnesota Press, 1987), 125–51.
Frede, Michael, 'The Stoic Notion of a *Lekton*', in Stephen Everson (ed.), *Companions to Ancient Thought: 3 Language* (Cambridge: Cambridge University Press, 1994).
Galen, *Three Treatises on the Nature of Science*, trans. Michael Frede (Indianapolis: Hackett Publishing Company, 1985).
Gaskin, Richard, *The Sea Battle and the Master Argument, Aristotle and Diodorus Cronus on the Metaphysics of the Future* (Berlin: De Gruyter, 2011).
Gildersleeve, Basil L. and Gonzalez Lodge, *Gildersleeve's Latin Grammar* (1895) (Wauconda: Bolchazy-Carducci Publishers, 2003).
Goldschmidt, Victor, 'Remarques sur la méthode structurale en histoire de la philosophie', in *Metaphysique et histoire de le philosophie. Recueil d'études offert à Fernand Brunner* (Neuchâtel: Éditions de la Baconnière, 1981).
Goldschmidt, Victor, '*Stoic Logic* par Benson Mates', *Revue de métaphysique et de morale* 59.2 (April–June 1954): 213–14.
Gooch, P. W., 'Socratic Irony and Aristotle's "Eiron": Some Puzzles', *Pheonix* 41.2 (Summer 1987): 95–104.
Gopnick, Adam, 'Introduction to *The Annotated Hunting of the Snark*', in Lewis Carroll, *The Annotated Hunting of the Snark* (New York: W. W. Norton & Co., 2006).
Gourinat, Jean-Baptiste, 'Éternel retour temps périodique dans la philosophie stoïcienne', *Revue philosophique de la France de l'étranger* 127 (2002): 213–27.
Gourinat, Jean-Baptiste, 'Matter and Prime Matter', in Ricardo Salles (ed.), *God and Cosmos in Stoicism* (Oxford: Oxford, 2009).
Gourinat, Jean-Baptiste, *Premières leçons sur le Manuel d'Epictète: comprenant le texte intégral du Manuel dans une traduction nouvelle par Jean-Baptiste Gourinat* (Paris: Presses universitaires de France, 1998).

Bibliography

Gourinat, Jean-Baptiste, *Le Stoïcisme* (Paris: Presses universitaires de France, 2014).

Gourinat, Jean-Baptiste, 'The Stoics on Matter and Prime Matter: "Corporealism" and the Imprint of Plato's *Timaeus*', in Ricardo Salles (ed.), *God and Cosmos in Stoicism* (Oxford: Oxford University Press, 2009).

Graeser, Andreas, *Zenon von Kition: Positionem und Probleme* (Berlin: de Gruyter, 1975).

Guattari, Félix, *The Guattari Reader*, ed. Gary Genesko (Oxford: Blackwell, 1996).

Hadot, Pierre, *The Inner Citadel: The Meditations of Marcus Aurelius*, trans. Michael Chase (Cambridge, MA: Harvard University Press, 2001).

Hadot, Pierre, *Philosophy as a Way of Life: Spiritual Exercises from Socrates to Foucault*, ed. Arnold Davidson (Malden: Wiley-Blackwell, 1995).

Hadot, Pierre, *What is Ancient Philosophy?*, trans. Michael Chase (Cambridge, MA: Belknap Press, 2004).

Hahm, David E., *The Origins of Stoic Cosmology* (Columbus: Ohio State University Press, 1977).

Halsey, Charles Storrs, *An Etymology of Latin and Greek* (Boston, MA: Gunn, Heath, & Co., 1882).

Harman, Graham, *Object-Oriented Ontology: A New Theory of Everything* (London: Pelican Books, 2018).

Harman, Graham, *The Quadruple Object* (Zero Books, 2011).

Harven, Vanessa de, 'How Nothing Can be Something: The Stoic Theory of Void', *Ancient Philosophy* 35.2 (2015): 405–29.

Havdra, Matyas, *The So-Called Eighth* Stromateus *by Clement of Alexandria* (Leiden: Brill, 2017).

Hegel, G. W. F., *Phenomenology of Spirit*, trans. A. V. Miller (Oxford: Oxford University Press, 1977).

Heidegger, Martin, *Early Greek Thinking*, trans. David Farrell Krell and Frank A. Capuzzi (New York: Harper & Row, 1975).

Homer, *The Iliad: Volume II, Books 13–24*, trans. A. T. Murray and William Wyatt (Cambridge, MA: Harvard University Press, 1925).

Homer, *The Odyssey*, trans. Robert Fagles (London: Penguin Classics, 1999).

Homer, *The Odyssey: Books 13–24*, ed. George E. Dimock, trans. A. T. Murray (Cambridge, MA: Harvard University Press, 1919).

Hughes, Joe, *Deleuze and the Genesis of Representation* (New York: Continuum, 2008).

Husserl, Edmund, *Ideas Pertaining to a Pure Phenomenology and to a Phenomenological Philosophy, First Book*, trans. F. Kersten (The Hague: Martinus, 1982).

Hussey, Edward, *Physics Books III and IV* (Oxford: Clarendon Press, 1983).

Ildefonse, Frédérique, *La Naissance de la grammaire dans l'antiquité classique* (Paris: J. Vrin, 1997).
Ildefonse, Frédérique, *Les Stoïciens I: Zénon, Cléanthe, Chrysippe* (Paris: Les Belles Lettres, 2000).
Imbert, Charles, *Pour une histoire de la logique. Un heritage platonicien* (Paris: Presses universitaires de France, 1999).
Inwood, Brad (ed.), *The Cambridge Companion to the Stoics* (Cambridge: Cambridge University Press, 2003).
Inwood, Brad, 'Chrysippus on Extension and the Void', *Revue internationale de philosophie* 45.178 (1991): 245–66.
Inwood, Brad, 'The Origin of Epicurus' Concept of Void', *Classical Philology* 76 (1981): 273–85
Irigaray, Luce, 'Du fantasme et du verbe', *L'Arc* 34 (1968).
Irwin, John T., *The Mystery to a Solution: Poe, Borges, and the Analytic Detective Story* (Baltimore: The Johns Hopkins University Press, 1996).
Isnardi-Parente, Margherita, 'La notion de'incorporel chez les stoïciens', in *Les stoïciens*, ed. Gilbert Romeyer Dherbey and Jean-Baptiste Gourinat (Paris: J. Vrin, 2005)
Johnson, Ryan J, *The Deleuze–Lucretius Encounter* (Edinburgh: Edinburgh University Press, 2017).
Johnson, Ryan J., 'Homesickness and Nomadism: Traveling with Kant and Maimon', *Polish Journal of Philosophy* 10.2 (Fall 2017): 45–69.
Kant, Immanuel, *Critique of the Power of Judgment*, trans. Paul Guyer and Eric Matthews (Cambridge: Cambridge University Press, 2001).
Kant, Immanuel, *Critique of Pure Reason*, trans. Paul Guyer and Allen W. Wood (Cambridge: Cambridge University Press, 1999).
Kant, Immanuel, *Groundwork of the Metaphysics of Morals*, trans. Mary Gregor and Jens Timmermann (Cambridge: Cambridge University Press, 2012).
Kant, Immanuel, *Lectures on Logic*, trans. J. Michael Young (Cambridge: Cambridge University Press, 2004).
Kant, Immanuel, *Metaphysical Foundations of Natural Science*, trans. Michael Freidman (Cambridge: Cambridge University Press, 2004).
Kant, Immanuel, *The Metaphysics of Morals*, trans. Mary Gregor (Cambridge: Cambridge University Press, 1991).
Karatani, Kojin, *Isonomia and the Origins of Philosophy*, trans. Joseph A. Murphy (Durham, NC: Duke University Press, 2017).
Kaye, John, *Some Account of the Writings and Opinions of Clement of Alexandria* (London: J. G. & F. Rivington, 1835).
Keizer, Helena Maria, *Life, Time, Entirety: A Study of AIΩN in Greek Literature and Philosophy, the Septuagint and Philo* (Heleen M. Keizer, 2010).
Khalfa, Jean (ed.), *Introduction to the Philosophy of Gilles Deleuze* (London: Bloomsbury Academic, 2003).

Bibliography

Kingsley, Peter, *Ancient Philosophy, Mystery, and Magic: Empedocles and Pythagorean Tradition* (Oxford: Clarendon Press, 1997)
Kneale, William and Martha Kneale, *The Development of Logic* (Oxford: The Clarendon Press, 1962).
Kroon, Caroline, 'Causal Connectors in Latin: The Discourse Function of Nam, Enim, Igitur and Ergo', *Cahiers de l'Institut de linguistique* 15.1–4 (1989): 231–43.
Lampert, Jay, *Deleuze and Guattari's Philosophy of History* (London: Continuum, 2006).
Lapidge, Michael, 'Stoic Cosmology', in *The Stoics*, ed. R. M. Rist (Berkeley: University of California Press, 1978), 161–86.
Lapoujade, David, *Aberrant Movements: The Philosophy of Gilles Deleuze* (2014), trans. Joshua David Jordan (South Pasadena: Semiotext(e), 2017).
Lecercle, Jean-Jacques, *Badiou and Deleuze Read Literature* (Edinburgh: Edinburgh University Press, 2010).
Lecercle, Jean-Jacques, *Deleuze and Language* (New York: Palgrave Macmillan, 2002).
Lee, Kyoo, *Reading Descartes Otherwise: Blind, Mad, Dreamy, and Bad* (New York: Fordham University Press, 2012).
Liddell-Scott-Jones Greek–English Lexicon: http://stephanus.tlg.uci.edu/lsj/#eid=1&context=lsj (last accessed 8 February 2019).
Lipsius, Justus, *Justus Lipsius: On Constancy: De Constantia Translated by Sir John Stradling*, ed. John Sellars, trans. John Stradling (Liverpool: Liverpool University Press, 2006).
Long, A. A., *From Epicurus to Epictetus: Studies in Hellenistic and Roman Philosophy* (Oxford: Clarendon Press, 2006).
Long, A. A., 'The Stoics on World-Conflagration and Everlasting Recurrence', *The Southern Journal of Philosophy* XXIII, Supplement (1985): 13–37.
Long, A. A., *Stoic Studies* (Berkeley: University of California Press, 2001).
Lovejoy, Arthur O., 'Kant's Classification of the Forms of Judgment', *The Philosophical Review* 16.6 (November 1907): 588–603.
Lucretius, Titus Carus, *De Rerum Natura*, ed. and trans. Cyril Bailey (Oxford: Clarendon Press 1947).
Lukacher, Ned, *Time-Fetishes: The Secret History of Eternal Recurrence* (Durham, NC: Duke University Press Books, 1999).
Mallarmé, Stéphane, *Oeuvres complètes* (Paris: La Pléiade, Gallimard, 1945).
Manning, Gideon, 'The History of Hylomorphism', *Journal of the History of Ideas* 74.2 (April 2013): 173–87.
Mansfeld, Jaap, *Prolegomena: Questions to be Settled before the Study of an Author, or a Text* (Leiden: Brill, 1994).
Mansfield, Jaap, 'Providence and the Destruction of the Universe in Early

Stoic Thought. With Some Remarks on the "Mysteries of Philosophy"', in *Studies in Hellenistic Religions* (Leiden: E. J. Brill, 1979).

Marcus Aurelius, *Meditations*, trans. R. Haines (Cambridge, MA: Harvard University Press, 1916).

Martin, Steve, *Born Standing Up: A Comic's Life* (New York: Scribner, 2008).

Mates, Benson, *Stoic Logic* (Berkeley: University of California Press, 1961).

Meinong, Alexius, *Über Möglichkeit und Wahrscheinlichkeit. Beiträge zur Gegenstandstheorie und Erkenntnistheorie* [On Possibility and Probability. Contributions to Object Theory and Epistemology] (Leipzig: J. A. Barth). Reprinted in *Meinong 1968–78, Vol. VI: XIII–XXII*, 1–728.

Mignucci, Mario, 'The Stoic Analysis of the Sorites', *Proceedings of the Aristotelian Society* n.s., 93 (1993): 231–45.

Morel, Pierre-Marie, *Épicure* (Paris: J. Vrin, 2010).

Nail, Thomas, *Lucretius I: An Ontology of Motion* (Edinburgh: Edinburgh University Press, 2018).

Nelli, René, 'Joe Bousquet et Son Double', *Cahiers du sud* 303 (1950): 177–86.

Neyrat, Frédéric, *Atopias: Manifesto for a Radical Existentialism*, trans. Walt Hunter and Lindsay Turner (New York: Fordham University Press, 2018).

Nietzsche, Friedrich, *Daybreak: Thoughts on the Prejudices of Morality* (1881), trans. Maudemarie Clark and Brian Leiter (Cambridge: Cambridge University Press, 1997).

Nietzsche, Friedrich, *The Gay Science* (1882), trans. Josefine Nauckhoff, ed. Bernard Williams (Cambridge: Cambridge University Press, 2001).

Nietzsche, Friedrich, *Human, All Too Human I, The Complete Works of Friedrich Nietzsche, Volume 3*, trans. Gary Handwerk (Stanford: Stanford University Press, 1995).

Nietzsche, Friedrich, *Philosophy in the Tragic Age of the Greeks*, trans. Marianne Cowan (Washington, DC: Regnery Publishing, Inc., 1998).

Nietzsche, Friedrich, *Untimely Meditations* (1876), trans. R. J. Hollingdale, ed. Daniel Breazeale (Cambridge: Cambridge University Press, 1997).

Nietzsche, Friedrich, *The Nietzsche Reader*, ed. Keith Ansell-Pearson and Duncan Large (Malden, MA: Wiley-Blackwell, 2006).

Oreglia, Giacomo and Evert Sprinchorn, *The Commedia dell'Arte*, trans. Lovett F. Edwards (New York: Hill & Wang Pub, 1968).

Osborn, Eric, *Clement of Alexandria* (Cambridge: Cambridge University Press, 2008).

Outler, Albert C., 'The "Platonism" of Clement of Alexandria', *The Journal of Religion* 20.3 (July 1940): 217–40.

Palmer, Helen, *Deleuze & Futurism: A Manifesto for Nonsense* (London: Bloomsbury Academic, 2014).

Bibliography

Palmer, John, *Parmenides and Presocratic Philosophy* (Oxford: Oxford University Press, 2013).

Pasquino, Pasquale, 'Le statut ontologique des incorporels dans l'ancien stoicisme', *Les Stoiciens et leur logique. Actes du Colloque de Chantilly, 18–22 séptembre 1976*, ed. J. Brunschwig (J. Vrin, 1978), pp. 333–46.

Paul, 'Epistle to Titus', in *Holy Bible*, King James Version, Reference edn, Thru the Bible Radio, 1976.

Peters, Francis E., *Greek Philosophical Terms: A Historical Lexicon* (New York: New York University Press, 1967).

Pini, Giorgio, *Categories and Logic in Duns Scotus* (Leiden: Brill, 2002).

Plato, *Complete Works*, ed. John M. Cooper and D. S. Hutchinson (Indianapolis: Hackett Publishing Company, 1997).

Plotinus, *Ennead II*, trans. A. H. Armstrong (Cambridge, MA: Harvard University Press, 1966).

Plotinus, *Ennead VI*, trans. A. H. Armstrong (Cambridge, MA: Harvard University Press, 1988).

Plutarch, *Moralia, Volume XIII, Part II. Stoic Essays*, trans. Harold Cherniss (Cambridge, MA: Harvard University Press, 1976).

Plutarch, *Moralia, Volume XIII: Part II, On Stoic Self-Contradictions*, trans. Harold Cerniss (Cambridge, MA: Harvard University Press, 1976).

Plutarch, *Parallel Lives, Volume VII: Demosthenes and Cicero, Alexander and Caesar*, trans. Bernadotte Perrin (Cambridge, MA: Harvard University Press, 1919).

Powers, Nathan M., 'Void and Space in Stoic Ontology', *Journal of the History of Philosophy* 52.3 (July 2014): 411–32.

Prantl, Carl, *Geschichte der Logik im Abendlande* (Leipzig: S. Hirzel, 1855).

Price, Daniel M. and Ryan J. Johnson (eds), *The Movement of Nothingness: Trust in the Emptiness of Time* (Aurora, CO: The Davies Group Publishers, 2012).

Press, Gerald A., *Development of the Idea of History in Antiquity* (Montreal: McGill-Queen's Press, 2003).

Quiller-Couch, Sir Arthur, *On the Art of Writing* (Mineola, NY: Dover Publications, 2006).

Quintilian, *Institutio Oratoria: Books I–III*, trans. H. E. Butler (Cambridge, MA: Harvard University Press, 1980).

Reynolds, Jack, 'Wounds and Scars: Deleuze on the Time and Ethics of the Event', *Deleuze Studies* 1.2 (December 2007): 167–94.

Ricœur, Paul, *Husserl: An Analysis of his Phenomenology*, trans. Edward G. Ballard and Lester E. Embree (Evanston: Northwestern University Press, 1967).

Rist, J. M., 'Categories and Their Uses', in *Problems in Stoicism*, ed. A. A. Long (London: The Athlone Press, 1971).

Rist, J. M. (ed.), *Stoic Philosophy* (Cambridge: Cambridge University Press, 1977).

Rist, J. M., *The Stoics* (Berkeley: University of California Press, 1978).
Roffe, Jon and Hannah Stark (eds), *Deleuze and the Non/Human* (New York: Palgrave Macmillan, 2015).
Roffe, Jon, 'Deleuze's Concept of Quasi-Cause', *Deleuze Studies* 11.2 (2017): 278–94.
Rosenmeyer, Thomas G., *Senecan Drama and Stoic Cosmology* (Berkeley: University of California Press, 1989).
Salankis, 'Mathematics, Metaphysics, and Philosophy', in Simon Duffy and Paul Patton (eds), *Virtual Mathematics: The Logic of Difference* (Manchester: Clinamen Press, 2006).
Salin, Édouard, 'Notice sur la vie et les travaux de M. Louis Bréhier, membre de l'Academie', *Comptes rendus des séances de l'Académie des inscriptions et belles-lettres* 98.2 (1954): 172–85.
Sambursky, Samuel, *Physics of the Stoics* (Princeton: Princeton University Press, 2014).
Sandbach, F. H., *The Stoics* (Indianapolis: Hackett Publishing Company, 1994).
Sasso, Robert and Arnaud Villani, *Le Vocabulaire de Gilles Deleuze* (Paris: J. Vrin, 2003).
Schopenhauer, Arthur, *The World as Will and Representation, Vol. 1*, trans. E. F. J. Payne (New York: Dover Publications, 1966).
Schrift, Alan D., *Twentieth-Century French Philosophy: Key Themes and Thinkers* (Malden, MA: Wiley-Blackwell, 2005).
Sedley, David, 'Epicurean Physics', in *The Cambridge History of Hellenistic Philosophy*, ed. Keimpe Algra, Jonathan Barnes, Jaap Mansfeld and Malcolm Schofield (Cambridge: Cambridge University Press, 1999), 362–81.
Sedley, David, 'Two Conceptions of Vacuum', *Phronesis* 17.1: 175–93.
Selcer, Daniel, *Philosophy and the Book: Early Modern Figures of Material Inscription* (London: Continuum, 2010).
Sellars, John, 'An Ethics of the Event: Deleuze's Stoicism', *Angelaki* II.3 (December 2006): 157–71.
Sellars, John, '*Aiôn* and *Chronos*: Deleuze and the Stoic Theory of Time', *Collapse* 3 (2007), 177–205.
Sellars, John, *The Art of Living: The Stoics on the Nature and Function of Philosophy* (London: Bristol Classical Press, 2009).
Sellars, John, *Stoicism* (Berkeley: University of California Press, 2006).
Seneca, *Anger, Mercy, Revenge*, trans. Robert A. Kaster and Martha C. Nussbaum (Chicago and London: University of Chicago Press, 2012).
Seneca, *Epistles 1–65*, trans. Richard M. Gummere (Cambridge, MA: Harvard University Press, 1917).
Seneca, *Epistles 66–92*, trans. Richard M. Gummere (Cambridge, MA: Harvard University Press, 1920).

Bibliography

Seneca, *Epistles 93–124*, trans. Richard M. Gummere (Cambridge, MA: Harvard University Press, 1925).
Sextus Empiricus, *Against the Logicians*, trans. Richard Bett (Cambridge: Cambridge University Press, 2006).
Sextus Empiricus, *Against the Physicists*, trans. Richard Bett (Cambridge: Cambridge University Press, 2012).
Sextus Empiricus, *Outlines of Pyrrhonism*, trans. R. G. Bury (Cambridge, MA: Harvard University Press, 1933).
Shusterman, Richard, *L'Infini* (Bordeaux: Presses universitaires Bordeaux, 2002).
Simplicius, *Simplicius on Aristotle's Physics 6*, ed. David Konstan (Ithaca: Cornell University Press, 1989).
Smith, Daniel W., *Essays on Deleuze* (Edinburgh: Edinburgh University Press, 2012).
Smith, Daniel W., 'From the Surface to the Depths: On the Transition from *Logic of Sense* to *Anti-Oedipus*', *Symposium: Canadian Journal of Continental Philosophy* 10.1 (2006): 135–53.
Somers-Hall, Henry, *Deleuze's Difference and Repetition* (Edinburgh: Edinburgh University Press, 2013).
Soni, Jimmy and Rob Goodman, *A Mind at Play: How Claude Shannon Invented the Information Age* (New York: Simon & Schuster, 2017).
Sorabji, Richard, *Matter, Space and Motion* (Ithaca: Cornell University Press, 1988).
Spinoza, Baruch, *Spinoza: Complete Works*, ed. Michael L. Morgan, trans. Samuel Shirley (Indianapolis: Hackett Publishing Company, 2002).
Stoicorum Veterum Fragmenta, Volumen I–IV, Joannes Ab Arnim (col.) (Stuttgart: *Bibliotheca Scriptorum Graecorum et Romanorum Teubneriana*, 1903–1905).
Suetonius, '*Lives of the Caesars Volume I*', trans. J. C. Rolfe (Cambridge, MA: Harvard University Press, 1914).
Surya, Michel, *Georges Bataille: An Intellectual Biography*, trans. Krzysztof Fijalkowski and Michael Richardson (London: Verso, 2010).
Tacitus, *The Annals*, trans. John Jackson (Cambridge, MA: Harvard University Press, 1981).
Taylor, C. C. W. (ed. and trans.), *The Atomists, Leucippus and Democritus* (Toronto: University of Toronto Press, 2010).
Thucydides, *History of the Peloponnesian War*, ed. M. I. Finley, trans. Rex Warner (Harmondsworth: Penguin Classics, 1972).
Todd, Robert B., 'Cleomedes and the Stoics Concept of the Void', *Apeiron: A Journal for Ancient Philosophy and Science* 16.2 (December 1982): 129–36.
Todd, Robert B., 'Monism and Immanence: The Foundations of Stoic Physics', in John Rist (ed.), *The Stoics* (Berkeley: University of California Press, 1978), 137–60.

Trois milliards de pervers: Le Grande Encyclopédie des homosexualités (March 1973).

Turetzky, Philip, *Time* (London: Routledge, 1998).

Tzamalikos, Panayiotis, 'Origen and the Stoic View of Time', *Journal of the History of Ideas* 52.4 (October–December 1991): 535–61.

Valpy, Francis and Edward Jackson, *A Manual of Latin Etymology, as Ultimately Derived, with but Few Exceptions, from the Greek Language* (London: Longman & Co., 1852).

Van der Ben, N., 'The Strasbourg Papyrus of Empedocles: Some Preliminary Remarks', *Mnemosyne* 52.5 (1999): 525–44.

Vernant, Jean-Pierre, *Origins of Greek Thought* (1962) (Ithaca: Cornell University Press, 1984).

Vidal-Naquet, Pierre, 'La mort du professeur Victor Goldschmidt de Platon à Rousseau: l'analyste opiniâtre de systèmes', *Le Monde* (10 December 1981).

Watson, Gerard, *The Stoic Theory of Knowledge* (Belfast: Queen's University, 1966).

White, Michael J., *Agency and Integrality: Philosophical Themes in the Ancient Discussions of Determinism and Responsibility* (Dordrecht: Springer, 2011).

White, Michael J., 'Stoic Natural Philosophy (Physics and Cosmos)', in Brad Inwood (ed.), *The Cambridge Companion to the Stoics* (Cambridge: Cambridge University Press, 2003).

Williams, James, *Gilles Deleuze's Logic of Sense: A Critical Introduction and Guide* (Edinburgh: Edinburgh University Press, 2008).

Woodard, Roger D. and David A. Scott, *The Textualisation of the Greek Alphabet* (Cambridge: Cambridge University Press, 2014).

Index

λεκτα/, λεκτόν, 79–83, 98–9, 107–20, 127, 131–4

absurdity, 13
  and denotation, 154–5
  and manifestation, 155–6
  and signification, 156–7
act
  disjunctive, 176, 189–92
  infinite, 176, 182–5
  problematic, 176, 192–5
  singular, 176, 185–9
affirmative, 59, 65–71, 149, 184
aion, 12–16, 98–9, 203–23, 242–6
Algra, Kiempe, 82, 91–3
ambiguity, 153, 162–3
amor fati, 114, 228, 248–9
Anaximenes, 3, 19, 72
apodictic, 60, 65–71
Aristophanes, 3, 108, 280
Aristotle
  and ἀριθμὸς, 205–6
  and the elements, 4, 29–30
  and interiority, 4–7, 14, 36–41, 70, 278
  and inversion, 6, 41
  and logic, 149–59
  and place, 82, 85–93
  and the Sea Battle, 160
  and time, 204–9
  and wit, 14, 278, 282–4
assertoric, 60, 65, 68–71, 194
atoms, 84, 129
attribute, 50–2, 112–14
Aurelius, Marcus, 215–18

Bennett, Michael James, 56, 72, 108, 195
Blanchot, Maurice, 235–6, 245–6
body
  and causality, 49–53, 67–8, 232
  and corporeality, 112–17, 209–10
  and cosmos, 232–6, 241–3
  and divisibility, 84–91

Bousquet, Joë, 14, 228, 238–40, 248, 264–5
  the Bousquet Proposition, 239–40
Bréhier, Emile, 15–16, 27–8
  and Aristotle, 34–6, 205
  and attribute, 112–13
  and incorporeals, 79–81
  and place, 85–8
  and the scalpel, 50–2
  and time, 220–2
  and void, 89–90, 95
Brunschwig, Jacques
  and incorporeals, 79–81, 90
  and something, 25–8

canonical incorporeals, 72–91
Carroll, Lewis, 9–11, 59, 120–4, 133, 191
causal
  network, 53, 63, 231–2
  series, 67–71, 189
causes
  corporeal, 45, 54–70, 120–2, 229–40
  efficient, 7
  formal, 4–7, 30
  infinite, 68–71
  material, 4, 29–30
  quasi, 11, 54–73, 244–8
  transitive, 67–71
chronos, 13–16, 98–9, 203–4, 208–22, 262
Chrysippus, 149–50, 153
  and λεκτόν, 110–11
  and bodies, 83–7
  and disjunction, 189–91
  and eternal return, 256–8, 264–5
  and time, 205–9, 217–21
  and void, 91, 94–6
Cicero, 29, 60, 188, 229–33
Cleanthes, 110
Clement of Alexandria, 48–9, 55–7, 110
Cleomedes, 90, 94–5
connective synthesis, 70, 121–6; *see also* synthesis

303

cosmic conflagration, 157, 256–8, 267–70
counter-actualisation, 180, 228, 242–7
Crack-up, 255, 268–9
cyclical infinity, 207

Death and the Compass, 260–2
Democritus, 84, 279
denotation, 98–9, 117–19, 128–31, 154–8, 192, 234–5
dialectic, 148–51, 177–9, 195, 283
Diogenes the Cynic, 278–9, 281–3
divination, 228–34
double causality, 62–4, 109–10

Empedocles, 3, 6, 279–80
Epictetus, 160, 176, 233–7
  and humor, 284–5
Epicurean
  atoms, 79–84, 88–9, 129
  void, 79–84, 88–9, 129
Ergo, 143, 164–6
eternal return, 71, 204, 258–72
  cycle, 216, 262–4
  straight line, 264–5
extension, 85–95, 155, 208–12, 219
  and Galen, 91–2, 159

Ferlinghetti, Lawrence, 130, 248–9, 269
Fitzgerald, F. Scott, 14, 255, 268–71
Frede, Michael, 54, 109, 114, 132

genesis
  dynamic, 10–11, 119–21, 126–7
  static, 59–65, 70–1, 119–21, 126–7
the Giants, 26–31
Goldschmidt, Victor, 15–16, 33
  and λεκτα, 108, 149
  and divination, 228–42
  and incorporeals, 81, 90, 98–9
  and time, 203–5, 212–22, 263–4
  see also aion
Guattari, Pierre-Félix, 37, 69–70, 179–81, 246–8

Hadot, Pierre, 179, 247
Handbook of Paradoxes, 175–82, 195–7
Heraclitus, 72, 213–15
Homer, 109, 192, 213
humor, 233, 278–84
hypothetical, 65–71

igitur, 164–8
Ildefonse, Frédérique
  and bodies, 29–30, 33, 50, 53

and grammar, 82, 265
and integration, 38
immanent, 32–4, 38, 68–9
incorporeal
  compatibility, 35, 64–71
  and the Heap, 159–60, 182–6
  impassive, 31–3, 48, 90, 109, 117
  and the Liar, 160, 176, 186–9
  and the Master, 160, 177–82, 189–91
  and the Nobody, 161, 176, 192–4
  surface, 11–13, 34–40, 48–53, 60–72, 114–35, 158–63
  transformation, 181, 285
independent terms, 67–71
integration, 38–40, 60–1, 121–2, 133–4
  derivative, 39
  integral, 38–9
intensity, 95, 130, 219
Inwood, Brad, 80, 96

Kant, Immanuel
  and infinite proposition, 184–8
  and modality, 294
  and relation, 53
  Table of Judgements, 59, 63–71, 164
  and transcendental logic, 63–71

Laërtius, Diogenes, 1–3, 7–8, 85–7, 159–62
language, 57, 82, 92–8, 107–34, 145–68, 186, 195–6
  esoteric, 10, 123–6
  ironic, 279–83
Lapoujade, David, 5–7, 72, 125
Lecercle, Jean-Jacques, 30, 121, 125, 240
logic
  and disjunction, 69–70, 189–91, 264–5
  propositional, 143, 149, 151–3, 164–6
logical compatibility, 54, 64–5
logique du sens, 55, 182
Long, A. A., 81–3
Lucretius, 84–5, 88–9

manifestation, 117–19, 131, 154–8, 191–2
materialism, 10, 17, 26–7, 40–1, 53–5, 96–7; *see also* perversion
modality, 65, 70–1, 190–4
motion, 86–90, 205–7, 212–14

necessity, 66–71, 189–91
Nietzsche, Friedrich, 258–9

Index

order, 107, 115–21, 126–7, 131–4; *see also* genesis

paradox, 178–88
  of action, 14–15, 255, 263–4
  and common sense, 143–8
  and disjunction, 189–91
Parmenides, 88–9, 210–12
perspective
  cosmological, 228–34
  singular, 228, 236–9
perversion, 5–6, 25, 187, 196, 205–6, 278, 283–4
Plato
  and conversion, 5–6, 41, 278
  and eternity, 132
  and the Forms, 27–9
  and height, 4, 14, 38, 278
  and the instant, 212–15
  and irony, 278–84
  and time, 205–9
Plutarch, 80–7
pseudos, 58
Pythagoreans, 16, 214, 220, 257

representation, 155, 234–8, 265–6
Rist, J. M., 31, 207–8, 217–18, 222

Sellars, John, 177, 215–19, 247, 257
Seneca
  and corporeality, 25–6, 49, 112–14
  and his death, 227–9, 235–6, 245–7 *see also* suicide
signification, 117–19, 131, 156–8, 191–2, 234–5
Snark, 123–4, 191
Socrates, 49, 179, 227, 238, 280–3
soul, 27–8, 33, 206, 211, 282
space, 40, 89–98
Spinoza, Baruch, 15
  and being, 28, 32, 53
  and laughter, 286
  and universals, 152, 161, 177–8
subsistence, 11, 30–2, 40, 94–5
subversion, 3–6, 210–11
suicide, 227, 245–6
synthesis
  conjunctive, 121–7
  connective, 121–2, 125–7
  disjunctive, 121, 124–7
  effects of, 123–6, 163–5
  phases of, 122–6, 218–19

Table of Judgements, 59, 64–7
  formal logic, 67–8
  transcendental logic, 68–71, 184, 188–9, 265
Thales, 3, 19, 280, 283

verbs, 12, 33, 98–100, 129–33, 221–2
voice, 110–12, 116–19

Zeno, 109–10, 143, 159, 205–6

EU representative:
Easy Access System Europe
Mustamäe tee 50, 10621 Tallinn, Estonia
Gpsr.requests@easproject.com

www.ingramcontent.com/pod-product-compliance
Lightning Source LLC
Chambersburg PA
CBHW050203240426
43671CB00013B/2237